Being a Safe Place for the Dangerous Kind

Being a Safe Place for the Dangerous Kind

Michael Bradley

Good Son Books
1854 W. Chateau Ave.
Anaheim, CA 92804
For submission guidelines please contact:
Roy Robbins at royrobbins@sbcglobal.net

ISBN-13: 9780692414125 (Custom Universal)
ISBN-10: 0692414126

Library of Congress Control Number: 2015904842
Mike Bradley, Gilbert, AZ

The Dangerous Kind used with permission from Graeme Sellers, *The Dangerous Kind* (Graeme Sellers, 2012).

TABLE OF CONTENTS

RECOMMENDATIONS

"The church today is not always a safe place for people who feel weak, dysfunctional, ashamed, addicted, or broken. Our culture expects us to be models of perfection—and then the church is too quick to remind us of our faults and defects. Yet that is not the way it is supposed to be. God's people, of all people, should provide a place of healing. My friend Mike Bradley is the man to write this message. He has been through the valley. He has experienced pain that no parent should have to endure. Yet he has emerged from the valley with a clear revelation of God's power to restore. You will find healing in these pages."

J. Lee Grady
Former Editor, Charisma Magazine and Director, The Mordecai Project

"Theology, for the rigor in our thinking and excellence in scholarship it demands, is easy. It's living that's hard. And not just living, but living as though our hearts are on fire because the Eternal One's breath stirs the embers of our existence. When this is our experience we find ourselves living paradoxically: on the dangerous edge of his power and in the safe refuge of his love and grace. This paradox deserves to be studied. But it cannot be merely studied; it must move from idea to practice, from phraseology to reality, as Dietrich Bonhoeffer wrote. In Mike Bradley's interesting and readable work *A Safe Place for the Dangerous Kind,* we find a compelling call to living as safe havens wherein people can taste and see for themselves that God is good.

'Non-Christians need a safe place,' contends Mike in the opening chapter, 'Christians who are wounded or weary need a safe place. Christians who want to make a significant difference in the lives of others need a safe place. We all need a safe place.' Drawing upon his extensive experience as a pastor, seminary president, and director of the Alliance of Renewal Churches, Mike offers a wide-ranging and engaging discussion of what it means to be and to offer to others a safe place to receive and grow in God's love. This is a long overdue book. I enthusiastically commend it."

Graeme Sellers, National Leadership Team
Alliance of Renewal Churches

"There are times when Christians present themselves as having it all together, when in fact the opposite may be the truth. That facade keeps others at a distance and limits not only the nature of our relationships with each other, but also with God. Even more, does that façade hurt ourselves as we live with pain, struggles, hurts, and issues that go unspoken, unresolved, unhealed, and unforgiven. In *Being a Safe Place for the Dangerous Kind* Michael describes with clarity and power the heart of Jesus, and the call to create a time and place where we can be who we are—sinners in need of a Savior, and find healing in Jesus' name. In doing so, we can begin to offer that gift to others within the family of God, but more importantly, to those who do not yet know of God's mercy and grace."

Mark Vander Tuig, Service Coordinator
Lutheran Congregations in Mission for Christ

"More than a vision, *Being a Safe Place for the Dangerous Kind* must become the reality of congregational life. There is really only one safe place, life in Christ. In Christ we experience the life-transforming power of His love. Those disciples who had followed Jesus for three years engaged in creating a safe place for those who came to faith at Pentecost. They immediately passed on to others what they first received. Life in Christ is safe but it's also challenging. When one encounters The Way, The Truth, and The Life, everything begins to change. It is impossible to maintain the status quo. Michael not only describes the attributes of a safe place, but he helps his readers look critically at our own words and actions that can easily cause others to experience our congregations as an oppressive and unwelcoming place. Above all, Michael provides the reader with encouragement and direction, creating action plans to transform the atmosphere in every congregation to become a truly safe place in Christ Jesus."

Rev. John F. Bradosky, Bishop, North American Lutheran Church

"*Being a Safe Place for the Dangerous Kind* is more than a book—it is a life message. Mike has carried this word in his heart long before it went to print. It's time now to read the full message. Your turn. It is not peripheral; it is central to the Gospel. Think Pharisee, merit system, performance, pretending. We've all done it. We need a safe place to live the truth in order to declare the right Gospel. Mike helps us with this essential and sometimes tricky process."

Paul Anderson, Founder and Director Harvest Communities, St. Paul, MN

"Having served as a pastor and church leader for the better part of thirty years, I've seen my share of trends and 'fads' come and go when it comes to ministry and how to do church. During this time I've encountered a few books and authors whose message transcends these debates because they focus on a guiding philosophy of ministry that is rooted in the person and ministry of Jesus. In this approach to ministry, who we are and what we are becoming is just as important, if not more so, than what we do and how we do it. *Being a Safe Place for The Dangerous Kind* by Mike Bradley is just such a book.

Mike demonstrates from scripture how Jesus was a safe place for everyone He encountered, and makes the point that the same should be true of us as His followers. Mike asks the question, 'What do people encounter when they encounter you and me?' Good question. Do they encounter nice people with good morals, or do they encounter the safe place that Jesus was for others?

I appreciate the emphasis Mike places on our need to experience Jesus as a safe place for our own lives. The truth is that we are all broken and in need of Christ's healing presence. This is a book I will be recommending to pastors, leaders, and anyone who wants to learn how to be a safe place for people to find healing and wholeness in Christ."

Jack Moraine, Senior Pastor
Vineyard Community Church, Gilbert, AZ
Southwest Regional Leader, Vineyard USA

ABOUT THE COVER ART

THE PORTRAIT THAT adorns the cover of this book is an original painting by gifted artist Marni Selmanson-Davidson who lives in Los Angeles. Marni was a member of a young adult group called *Prodigal* that my wife, Debi, and I led in Rapid City, South Dakota years ago. Marni's husband-to-be, Brian Davidson, was also a member of the group at that time. In fact, that's where they met, fell in love, and eventually married. I was privileged to be the presiding pastor at their wedding. Their daughters, Ayla and Tallis, are like nieces to Debi and me. We have remained close to Marni, Brian, and the girls over the years. Because of this close, personal relationship with her, it is more meaningful to me than words can say that Marni would agree to create and put to canvas her interpretation of the safe-place vision.

As I worked on the book I found myself thinking about the cover. I wanted something unique that by its very nature would provoke and stir people to think; because that is want I want this book to do. It's not my purpose to write something that will make us feel all warm and fuzzy inside, but rather stir us to be intentional in reflecting on how we can be transformed to think, speak, and act more like Jesus—because that is what the Safe-Place Dangerous Kind metaphor is all about.

When I unpacked the portrait in my home in Gilbert, Arizona, my attention was immediately drawn to the three crosses most visible on it. The number three spoke to me of the Trinity—Father, Son, and Holy Spirit—who are involved in transforming and empowering us to live as a safe place for the dangerous kind.

The crosses spoke to me of the cross upon which Christ was crucified. On that cross the work of Jesus was finished, enabling us to receive his gifts of forgiveness of sin and healing for shame. It was on that cross that true love was made incarnate and made real. In this sense, the cross of Christ is a safe place. Furthermore, in being willing to go to the cross Jesus modeled for us a life sacrificially given so that others might live free, a life that to the religious and to God's enemy, the devil, was dangerous. When we in turn pick up the crosses that God calls us to in our own lives, we, like Jesus, live as the dangerous kind.

I have placed Marni's painting on the mantle piece over our fireplace. As I sit and meditate on it, I find myself thinking on how much I love the colors, the creativity, and the openness to interpretation that this work of art offers. Being a safe place for the dangerous kind is like that. A person being transformed by the Lord is a beautiful expression of his creativity and will manifest a wide variety of safe-place, dangerous kind characteristics. Each of us may reflect different attributes of the same reality, each person offering a different shade of interpretation than another, but all originating from the same source, the same master artist.

I imagine Marni at home in her studio looking at a blank canvas and beginning to dream with one ear attuned to the Lord and another to what I wrote about what it can means to live as someone who is a safe place. As she listened she began to put brush to canvas, first one stroke and then another. I imagine her beginning to picture in her mind's eye what this portrait would look like when completed. With each caress of the brush along the canvas surface the potential of what the portrait would look like when finished became clearer. In the same way, God, the Master Artist, sees us not just for who we are, but also for who we can be, and he sets to work on the canvas of our lives. He transforms us one brush stroke at a time, each one bringing into greater clarity the masterpiece he wants to make us.

Such is one of the great gifts that creative artists give us, whatever their medium. Marni's is painting. We are the Lord's. I'm still meditating on this portrait. Debi and I are honored to display it prominently in our home. It reminds us of a friend who is dear to us, and it reminds us of the God whom together we love, worship, and serve. The Master Artist. The one who modeled for us on the cross in a very real and tangible way what it means to live as a safe place for the dangerous kind.

ACKNOWLEDGMENTS

THE ONLY REASON I can begin putting thoughts to paper for this book is because I have been blessed with so many people in my life who have been a safe place for me. Foremost has been my family, especially my bride, Debi Asper-Bradley. Debi, you've never given up on me, you've always believed in me, you've always been there for me, and always loved me with God's unconditional, unshakable, and extravagant love. You above all people have brought the Lord's healing combination of grace and truth to bear on my life and because you have, I've been transformed and set free to become the man I am today. I love you and am so thankful to God for you!

Andrew Michael, Joseph Ross, Rachel Christine, Stephen Daniel, and Benjamin John, a father could not have better children than you. You too have always loved me and never given up on me, even when there were times I was ready to give up on myself. You have been God's revelatory mirror for me, helping me see things about myself that God wanted to transform and good things he wanted to affirm. From each one of you I have learned so much about the Lord and about being a person who is safe, just by being your dad.

To my mom and my mother-in-law—thank you. Mom, this all started with you. It all began when you, as a little Iowa farm girl, would walk by yourself for miles to attend a small country church outside of Glenwood. Something in you back then was drawn toward a relationship with God. And that desire was reproduced in me, and is the genesis for all that has transpired in my life. I love you, Mom. And Myrtle, a guy could not have a better mother-in-law than you. You have been a friend, encourager, counselor, and prayer warrior for me all the years I've known you. I love you.

There have been friends and fellow pastors along my journey like Al Asper (my father-in-law), Danny Mullins, Joe Johnson, Robert Walter, Eric Bluhm, Bob Mabry, Tom Brashears, Brendon Fairley, Leroy Flagstad, and Charles Miller. Each of you has been my friend, colleague, and a safe place in my life. I have learned so much from you and have seen my life transformed by knowing you. In addition to these brothers there have been many other pastor-friends whom God has used to speak into my life. You know who you are. Thanks to you all.

Graeme Sellers, you have been the one who helped connect the safe-place message with the call to be the dangerous kind. You incarnate for me what it means to be both a safe place and a follower of Jesus who is dangerous for the kingdom of God and to the dominion and purposes of the devil. Thanks, Graeme. A man could not have a better friend than you. Who else would spend an entire day with his friend trying to master the Nintendo Wii Frisbee golf game while his toddler son covers himself in white flour?

Thank you to the staff and students at The Master's Institute (MI), a seminary and Christian leadership school in St. Paul, Minnesota, where I was blessed to serve as president for ten years. You allowed the safe-place vision to take root there and together we've seen so many seminary and school of ministry students experience authentic transformation in the context of a safe place atmosphere. Thank you Kevin, Sharon, Kendra, Wanda, Heidi, Marissa, and Kim. And much thanks goes to Curt Rosen, my friend and long-time chairperson for the MI Board of Directors, along with the men and women who served so faithfully on that board over the years.

Thanks to my editor, Kim Engel-Pearson. Kim, you taught me so much about writing that I did not know previous to this project, and I am so thankful to you for the countless hours you spent reading through it word by word. But in addition to that, you shared how pieces of this project were personally impacting your life and that encouraged me to believe this was a project worth doing and worth completing.

There is one more specific group I cannot forget to thank. Debi and I owe you a debt of gratitude we can never repay. You were there with us in that most traumatic moment and painful season of our lives—the death of our son, Andy. The presence of God in and through you ministered to Debi and me more than you will ever know. You were a safe place in our lives before that moment even occurred and you were our safe place while we were going through it. Thank you Gwen and Arlen Pequette, Patti and Dave Rempel, Sherry and Tom Casey, Robbie and Lee Ahrlin.

Finally, thank you to the One who has always been my safe place and continues to be that for me to this very day—*my granite strength and safe harbor God.* Thank you, Father, Son, and Holy Spirit. I love you and it is for your glory that I attempt to capture on the following pages some of the thoughts and reflections you've given me over the years concerning what it means to be a safe place for the dangerous kind. May this book be used to bring glory to you, and to further transform us all so we are empowered to think, speak, and act more like Jesus who is *the* safe place for the dangerous kind.

PREFACE:
THE CHURCH AT HER BEST

THE CHRISTIAN CHURCH at her best operates in the mystery of hiddenness. In an era of celebrity, self-promotion, and social media, when even some Christian individuals and churches are getting caught up in the deluge, this is often overlooked. When non-Christians speak of the church it is often to criticize select examples from our history that we are rightly not proud of, or to shine a spotlight on the arrogant and angry, judgmental and condemning few that give Christianity a black eye. I do not deny our historical missteps and I do not try to rationalize and justify away those walking negative advertisements of the Christian faith.

But there is so much more to Christianity and being a follower of Jesus than most people realize, because the church at her best operates in the mystery of hiddenness. Followers of Jesus have operated this way throughout history. Without press release and acclaim we have built hospitals and provided medical care where there was none; sometimes in lands far away, sometimes in lands close to home, in lands at peace, and especially in the midst of genocide and war. We have intentionally searched for those places that need clean water and nutritious food and then sought to supply both, while also training indigenous peoples how to provide for themselves. Other ministries offer life skills training to help those in the developing world make a living for their families, giving them a sense of pride and dignity as they do.

Quietly, the church has sought to provide care for the forgotten in every culture and country around the globe. We have been there to care for the orphans and widows, the old and infirm, and those who are suffering from diseases that have altered history, whether it is the plague or the pox, cholera or malaria, polio or tuberculosis, leprosy or HIV/AIDS. Where you can find any of these you will find the church faithfully and unselfishly at work. When the disenfranchised and marginalized have been in need of protection, shelter, and sanctuary the church has been there. All of this in addition to the willing and generous provision of billions upon billions of dollars to do the work of the church and to care for the needs of the world, a provision that has not come merely from Christians who are wealthy, but from followers of Jesus who themselves are among the world's poor and middle class. Wherever there has been suffering and hardship, catastrophe and injustice, the Christian church can be found operating at her best in the mystery of hiddenness.

Such was the case as an author sat in a New York City restaurant following what we now know as 9/11. As he sat there, he recorded what he observed:

> The Red Cross was handing out work gloves and breathing masks, fresh socks and clean boots. Restaurants were setting up barbecue grills on sidewalks and cooking free food for rescue workers. Soft drink manufacturers donated beverages. Humanitarian groups and corporations set up trust funds with hundreds of millions of dollars for the families of victims.[1]

This was the response of Christians and non-Christians alike in those initial days and weeks in the aftermath of one of the most horrific days in American history. Fire and police personnel along with other first responders literally gave their lives in an attempt to rescue those caught in the towers or buried in the rubble. Medical personnel and other citizens of New York City selflessly gave of themselves and their resources. For all these actions and more, Americans should be grateful and proud. I certainly am.

The work of restoring the city continued for days on end following that first week. Those days themselves turned into weeks, those weeks became months, and those months have now become years. The physical restoration

---

1 Bill Hybels, *Courageous Leadership* (Grand Rapids, MI: Zondervan, 2002), 16.

of the city continues and the perseverance of the American spirit is evident. However, there has been another restoration not as visible but just as critically important taking place. It is the restoration of broken hearts and wounded souls. It is this kind of restoration Christianity is uniquely fit for. It is a hidden work, but again, that's where we can be at our best. We don't need notoriety, we don't ask to be given credit, and we don't need to be followed by the press or to have what we do recorded on social media. The opportunity to serve and to make a difference is all that followers of Christ want and need. In the wake of 9/11, we were there, and that's what author-pastor Bill Hybels wrote of in his book *Courageous Leadership:*

> Work of a deeper kind was happening behind the scenes in downtown Manhattan during these days. While many pastors and church volunteers joined with charitable agencies in helping to meet physical and material needs, they also went beyond that—far beyond it. Ordinary Christ-followers like you and me sat in restaurants, office buildings, and temporary shelters, addressing with courage and sensitivity the deep concerns of the soul. Meeting one-on-one and in small groups, they cried with people. They prayed with people. They listened. They embraced. They soothed.
>
> It happened twenty-four hours a day for days on end. It was the untold media story, the clip that never made it to the network news. While many fine organizations met the external needs of people, the church was there to do what it is uniquely equipped to do: to offer healing to deeply wounded souls.[2]

What Hybels witnessed those days was the church at her best. No matter what form it takes—house church, cell church, steeple church, mega church, or small church—Christians at their best are present with people in the most traumatic moments of their lives, and present to celebrate the most joyous. In this most horrific moment of American history, the church was there with the

---

2   Ibid..

love of Jesus Christ, a love "that conquers sin and wipes out shame and heals wounds and reconciles enemies and patches broken dreams and ultimately changes the world, one life at a time."[3]

This was not featured on CNN, Fox News, or Facebook. We did not ask it to be and we did not need it to be. That's not why the church does what it does. We don't show up to give care and aid to those in need for the notoriety and acclaim. We do it because God has loved us with a love that is unshakable, unconditional, and extravagant, and in gratitude to him we want to share that same love and care for others. The church shows up simply to love, and to set people free from every sort of bondage and captivity that would keep them from living lives of significance and meaning.

Christians are at their best when they are selflessly helping people in need, bringing hope and healing in every sense in a community that is safe. Followers of Christ are at their best when they are committed to not merely presenting Christ, but being like Jesus with the ones he would have been with. We are at our best when we operate and serve in the mystery of hidden-ness and refuse the spotlight of celebrity, notoriety, and acclaim. When we go wherever in the world the Lord sends us to impact people with his power and love, that's the church being who God longs for us to be. Christians who live like this are more than merely nice and moral people. Christians who live like this are a safe place for the dangerous kind. And that is what this book is about.

My intent is that this not be another in an unfortunately-long line of books published over the past two decades that spend most of their time telling Christians in general, and leaders in particular, how they've been doing it all wrong. The bride of Christ has been assailed over the past twenty years. That is not the intent of this author or this book.

I love the church. She is beautiful and wonderful. Yes, there are times when we are like a magnificent work of art that is damaged and broken. However, when this happens to a priceless work of art, we don't throw it away. We tenderly and lovingly try everything we can to restore it. That is my heart for the church. Have we been unsafe people, unsafe churches at times?

---

3 Ibid., 21.

Yes, we have. But I don't want to bash the church. I want to see her beautified. I want to see her restored.

God loves the church. He is not blind to our faults, or our sins. Yet, he loves us still. This book's intent is to paint a picture of who we can be at our best, and to encourage and exhort us to position ourselves before the Lord so he can tenderly and lovingly restore us. The church at her best is beautiful and loved by God. At our best we think, speak, and act like Jesus. The church tenderly and lovingly restored will be a safe place for the dangerous kind.

PART ONE

INTRODUCING THE
SAFE-PLACE VISION

1

In the Fire and in the Chaos

*My help and glory are in God—granite-strength and safe-harbor
God—so trust him absolutely, people, pour out your hearts to him,
for God is our refuge!*

— Psalm 62:7–8, The Message and NIV

G OD IS GOOD in the fire and he's good with chaos. Just ask Shadrach, Meshach, and Abednego about the former, and check out Genesis, chapter one, regarding the latter. I'm grateful he's good in both because it was in the fire and in the chaos of the two most painful events of my life that the Lord began to teach me the critical importance of being a safe place.

The first event was waking up on the morning of our oldest child's eighteenth birthday, only to discover he had suddenly and mysteriously died in the early morning hours. Andy died on the same day he was born—December 19. Red hair, electric smile, and Dick Van Dyke-like gifts in song, dance, and physical comedy; this was our firstborn, our son. What a joy he was to everyone who knew him. Andrew Michael Bradley lived a life that impacted us all. He lived a life that ended far too soon.

A parent should never have to bury his or her own child. They should never have to plan the funeral service. But my wife and I did. Having been the pastor for a church with a large number of senior citizens I had planned and participated in numerous funerals each year. Each one was a holy moment, a sacred experience. But this was different; this was my own son's service. Words fail when trying to recount the horror and trauma we experienced as a family that first day and in the days to follow. However, in the wake of Andy's death our granite-strength and safe-harbor God truly was our refuge. He really did protect and sustain us with his presence, goodness, and power.

I did not always *feel* his presence, nor did my wife and children. But following Andy's death the Lord truly was Emmanuel, God *with* us; and he continues to be so to this day. It has been this presence and strength that have enabled us to do more than merely survive. He has made it possible for us to once again find the love, joy, and peace we wondered if we would ever be able to recover. It has been his ability to redeem even the worst life has to offer that has given Debi and me a restored sense of purpose and meaning, one that may be stronger now than before.

God is our refuge and redeemer. That is no trite cliché or powerless theological title. It is a very real work that he does. The living God whom Christians love and serve is able to be our refuge while we are going through the worst and most horrific moments of our lives. He enables us to endure that which we do not think is endurable with a strength that is not our own; it's his. Our God is able to redeem the most painful of experiences and bring something good and transformational out of them. He has certainly done this for us.

In the wake of Andy's death, God has been my safe place. There is a powerful and well-known picture of storm-driven waves crashing in on a lighthouse with a man standing in the doorway. It's a photograph of the La Jument lighthouse off the shores of France that was taken by Jean Guichard in 1989. That storm was my life, that man was me, and that lighthouse was and is my God. He has been my refuge and my redeemer in the fire and in the chaos.

And it was in this most terrible of moments he began teaching me the critical importance of what it means to be a safe place. Since then the Lord has not only been teaching me, he has been at work transforming me into the very thing he is showing me. Yes, God is good in the fire and he's good with chaos.

The second painful event was watching helplessly as a large vibrant church was reduced to a shell of itself over the course of just a few years. It was my church, my community, where I served on the pastoral team. We had witnessed over a decade of growth and prosperity in every sense of the word. The decay of this congregation began at a time of transition, when misguided leadership and poor decisions laid the foundation of an unsafe environment. The church's leadership became fragmented. Some leaders were adhering to toxic beliefs and practices that stemmed from their own inner woundedness and lack of wholeness. And to be sure, I was not without fault in this tangled web. Over time, our sense of unity was lost and unhealthy teachings ultimately hurt church members and set them against one another. Even the high-ranking, denominational officials, who were supposed to protect a congregation in such tumultuous times as this, refused to intervene.

Yet, even here in the fire and chaos of a wounded and hemorrhaging congregation, God, the one who can redeem all things, was at work teaching me the importance of creating an emotional, relational, and spiritual atmosphere that is safe. It was in the midst of an unsafe place that the Lord was at work shaping and forming many of us to be that which he was teaching us.

It was out of these two events that God birthed in me a passion and set me on a journey to discover what it means to be a safe place. Along the way I've become convinced this is an essential key for increasing our effectiveness in developing healthy leaders and disciples in the church, and living lives of witness in the world. I've watched as Christians have caught the vision and began to grow in what it means to be a safe place. They've become more than merely nice and moral people, living nice and moral lives. They've become followers of Christ who are potent for the purposes of God and a real threat to the dominion and purposes of the devil.[4]

---

4   See Graeme Sellers, *The Dangerous Kind* (Graeme Sellers, 2012), Kindle ed.

THE PRINTED PAGE

Over the years I've been asked to commit this God-given life message to the printed page. Until now I have resisted. I've resisted because I know God still has more to teach me. I am certain that as soon as I write it down there will be more I learn.

But it's time to get started. I can't wait any longer. It's time to capture in words what God has shown me to date. It's time to write it the best I can so my family and friends will have some insight into who I am and why I do what I do. And it's time to record for others what I believe is critically important for healthy Christian living, a message that is for everyone who wants to make an eternal, transformational difference in peoples' lives. As I begin, finally, to write, I take great encouragement from the words of author Anne Lamott:

> Almost all good writing begins with terrible first efforts. You need to start somewhere, so start by getting something—anything—down on paper. One friend says the first draft is the down draft—you get it down. The second draft is the up draft—you fix it up. You try to say what you have to say more accurately. And the third draft is the dental draft, where you check every truth to see if it's loose or cramped or decayed or even, God help us, healthy.[5]

I am compelled to start writing by the words of Thomas Merton: "God utters me like a word containing a partial thought of himself. But if I am true to the concept that God utters in me, if I am true to the thought in him I was meant to embody, I shall be full of his actuality and find him everywhere in myself."[6] Helping Christians grow in what it means to be a safe place is, for me, that "partial thought of himself" and the "concept that God utters in me." It is that truth of God that "I was meant to embody."

Each time I am tempted to leave this teaching and develop it no further, I am haunted, in the best sense one can be haunted, by a prophetic word shared

---

5 Anne Lamott, in Dan Allender, *To Be Told: Know Your Story, Shape Your Future* (Colorado Springs, CO: Waterbrook Press, 2005), Kindle ed.

6 Thomas Merton, *Seeds of Contemplation* (New York: Panthea Books, 1956), 56.

through a sister-in-Christ whom I do not even know. It is a word given to the body of Christ at-large some years back. A portion of the word "jumped off" the written page at me when first I read it. I knew this was a word from God to me, and I've written it in my Bible as a reminder. She was sharing about spiritual warfare and in that context she wrote, "Another level in this warfare will be in the form of intimidation, which will try to back you from the positions I have called you to hold . . . the message on which they are to focus for the body of Christ." Being a safe place is a position God has called me to hold.

So here I go. My prayer is that this book will make some helpful contribution to the relational and missional task God has given the body of Christ, and that the Holy Spirit will make this teaching revelation to those who read and study it, resulting in transformation, not merely a download of information. And it's my hope that reading this book will result in an increasing number of Christians who refuse to settle for being merely nice and moral people, but instead choose to live as followers of Jesus who are potent for the purposes of God.

Non-Christians need a safe place. Christians who are wounded or weary need a safe place. Christians who want to make a significant difference in the lives of others need a safe place. We all need a safe place. That is what this book is about. May it be used to further transform us all so that, as my friend Graeme Sellers says, we live the rest of our lives kicking at the darkness until it bleeds daylight!

2

WE ALL NEED A SAFE PLACE

*"I will now rise up," says the Lord. "I will put the one
who longs for it in a safe place"*

— PSALM 12:5B (HCSB)

WE ALL NEED a safe place. We all need a place where the hunger to be loved in the deep places of our hearts can be satisfied with a love that is unconditional, unshakable, and extravagant; a place where God's love is the gold standard through which every issue we face and every relationship we develop is viewed. We all yearn for a community of relationships where we can just be ourselves and feel we really belong, a place where we don't have to wear masks of some sort in order to be genuinely accepted and wanted. Christians and non-Christians alike desire relationships with people who truly welcome the real questions and doubts we struggle with and take the time to engage us in authentic dialogue. And we all need a place where things hidden in the dark recesses of our lives can finally be brought into the light with no fear of judgment or condemnation, no fear of being shamed or discarded. Christians and non-Christians alike need a safe place.

Picture a place where you have friends who are for you and against anything that would harm you, friends who refuse to let you settle for anything less than all God has for you. Imagine a community where the truth of God's Word is not watered down but where the grace of God influences where, when, and how it's shared. Just think of the blessing it would be to have God's healing combination of grace and truth being brought to bear upon the emotional, relational, and spiritual wounds from your past that still have been influencing your present in unhelpful ways. All of this can be found in a person and community that are safe.

Imagine the joy of being set free from old ways of thinking and behaving that have not been helpful and have held you captive for years. Envision a place where God's forgiveness of sin and healing for shame are being brought to bear upon broken relationships and broken hearts. Picture a place where it is safe to fail, and to learn and grow from your failures, a place where there are people who believe in you before you even believe in yourself. Everyone needs a place like this—a place that is safe.

CHRISTIANS CAN BE UNSAFE

Jesus is that safe place for us, and he desires to empower and transform us to be that for others. Unfortunately, followers of Christ are not always known for being a safe-place people. Too often we are experienced as being unsafe. For instance, consider the following:

One seventeen-year-old churchgoer described her experience bringing a gay friend to church: "The youth pastor knew I was going to bring him, and even though his talk really had nothing to do with homosexuality, he still found a way to insert 'God created Adam and Eve, not Adam and Steve' into his comments. I was sitting there, just dying. This happened more than once. My friend was at a point where he was interested in seeing what Jesus might offer, and the door was just slammed shut."[7]

Why do this? Why, when there is an opportunity to share the good news of God's extravagant love for us, and who Jesus is and what he can do in our lives, would you sabotage someone from receiving it? When you have the opportunity to establish a relationship with someone who needs to know Jesus, why would you drive that person further away from him?

Do we really need to take these kinds of verbal jabs at people? Does it make us more effective in our mission? Does it serve the purpose of drawing a non-Christian nearer to knowing the love of God and his gift of salvation? Does it glorify God, or please our Heavenly Father? In an instance like this, I wonder whom Father God is more upset with: the person others perceive as struggling with sin, or with the Christian who ridicules and shames them?

Unfortunately, this kind of experience with Christians who are unsafe is repeated far too often. And each time it happens, it strengthens the stereotype that Christians are not safe-place people. Consider the example of a young adult who told me her story of an encounter with unsafe Christians, an encounter that influenced her to satisfy her spiritual thirst in places other than Christianity. As a young teen she had three best friends, all of whom claimed to be Christians. One night they told her they loved God and loved her. What soon followed, however, did not feel like love. In angry, judgmental tones they told her that if she did not repent of her sins she not only was going to hell but deserved to go there as well.

These three young girls may have thought they were sharing truth with their friend, but in the end it was a graceless truth that served the purposes of the enemy more than the purposes of God. That night these Christian friends were unsafe rather than safe-place people. Because they were not safe, they missed a great opportunity. They missed the chance to help their friend experience God's extravagant love and receive his incredible gift of salvation.

---

7   David Kinnaman and Gabe Lyons, unChristian: What a New Generation Thinks about Christianity . . . and Why It Matters (Grand Rapids, MI: Baker Books, 2008), 42.

Rather than draw their friend closer to God, they drove a wedge between her and the Lord that exists to this day.

It is not only non-Christians who experience followers of Christ as being unsafe; Christians experience one another in that way too. Consider the experience of a young choir director's wife. She and her husband had recently moved across country to accept a position at a church. Both of them were hungry for more of whatever God had for them. Whenever someone taught, exhorted, or challenged them, all they wanted to know was—is this in line with the Word of God? If it was, they wanted it. The first week after moving, they attended a Sunday evening worship service at the church where the choir director would be serving. Following worship they walked out of the building with a group that included one of the elders and his wife.

"I have a question," said the choir director's wife. "What's that?" responded the elder. "I loved the beauty of the singing in the spirit (singing in tongues) tonight, but I'm wondering if it is in keeping with what scripture says about the gift of tongues needing to be interpreted?" Rather than recognize and seize a teachable moment, the elder became red-faced and angry. "No wonder we're not getting anywhere as a church with leaders like you who ask questions full of doubt instead of faith!" The young wife shrank back and decided then and there she would no longer ask this man and the group he represented any faith questions.

The choir director took the elder aside and told him in no uncertain terms that he owed his wife an apology and if it were not forthcoming they would meet on this matter with the senior pastor the next day. The elder did apologize, but it was evident that it was forced and not genuine. The damage had been done. This Christian leader was unsafe and had missed a golden opportunity to help a sister-in-Christ grow in her relationship with the Lord.

ESPECIALLY IMPORTANT IN A POSTMODERN CULTURE

Growing in what it means to be a safe place is especially important for increasing our effectiveness in developing healthy disciples and leaders in the church, and living lives of witness in a postmodern culture. The cultural context we live in today is different than the one I was born in just six short decades ago. Things have changed in extremely significant ways during my lifetime, ways that necessitate the body of Christ rediscovering what it means to be a safe place. If we do not, we will miss opportunities to transform our world with the love and power of God.

One significant change in my lifetime is that in the postmodern context Christianity is often viewed through a lens of skepticism, cynicism, and distrust. That was not the case when I was a boy. In the 1950s, society generally viewed Christianity with great trust and respect. This was true of persons and institutions of authority in general. The advent of postmodern thinking, combined with trust-breaking events such as the Vietnam War, Watergate, and a seemingly endless string of very public moral failings by priests and pastors, have eroded society's trust in, and respect for, authority in general and Christianity in particular.

The influence of postmodern thinking has been significant. Among the convictions that have impacted us since the 1960s is the belief that truth is relative and tolerance is a value to be adhered to above all others. Truth as relative or subjective, rather than absolute and objective, makes the individual rather than some outside source (such as the Bible) the arbiter of what is and is not true. The idea that truth is absolute and objective has fallen by the wayside, giving even greater permission to the centuries-old propensity of human beings to want to do what is right in their own eyes even when it may place someone else in harm's way.

Tolerance has become the essential value in western culture. There is, of course, some agreement that there are things we should still be intolerant of, such as murder, rape, and child and spousal abuse. Other than a few examples however, the call to be tolerant is so loud and unquestioned in our current cultural context that people who do dare to wonder aloud whether it is a value to be accepted and applied without discernment often find themselves being accused of being "haters" and shamed into silence. Author and Alliance of Renewal Churches (ARC) pastor, Dave Drum writes,

It turns out a request for tolerance is often simply a hidden appeal to adopt society's points of views. It really isn't about tolerating and being civil toward those with differing opinions at all; it's an attempt to silence disagreement, especially if that disagreement is rooted in a transcendent source like the Bible.[8]

The removal of any belief in an authoritative source for absolute truth, a growing distrust of persons and institutions of authority, and the experience by too many with Christians who are unsafe, has put followers of Christ who want to transform the world with the love and power of God in an extremely challenging situation. Thus, growing in what it means to be a safe place is a pivotal issue for the body of Christ in postmodern culture. It is essential because it will impact absolutely every relationship we have and absolutely everything we do. It will impact who we are as individuals. It will impact how we parent and the health of our marriages. It will impact the tenor of our relationships with others at work, school, and in the neighborhoods in which we live. It will impact how we love and care for others, and how we live lives of witness. It will impact how we preach, teach, and pray, and how we use the gifts of the Holy Spirit to minister God's love and power to others. Most of all, it will impact our relationship with the Lord.

A METAPHOR FOR TRANSFORMATION

Jesus often used metaphor as a way to communicate God's goodness and his invitation to enter into a way of living that is full of love, adoption, joy, peace, rest, worth, and significance (see John 10:10; Matthew 11:28–30; John 1:12; John 6:37). Being a safe place is a metaphor for transformation. It is designed to help us be intentional in seeking to be transformed so that we think, speak, and act more like Jesus, nothing more, nothing less, and nothing else.

However, growing in what it means to be a safe place is never meant to be an end in itself, because growing to be more like Jesus will not only make

---

8 Dave Drum, *Jesus' Surprising Strategy: A Mandate and a Means for City Transformation* (Tucson, AZ: Adam Colwell's WriteWorks Publishing), Kindle ed.

us a safe-place people, it will also produce a metamorphosis in our lives that will make us potent for the purposes of God and a real threat to the purposes and dominion of our enemy, the devil. Author and pastor Graeme Sellers calls Christians who live like this *the dangerous kind,* because they live as more than merely nice and moral people. They live as Christians whose lives are dangerous for the kingdom of God and to the dominion and purposes of the enemy.[9]

The world needs us to be more than merely good people. Christians who settle for being merely good have little of substance or value to offer a world where even non-Christians can be good people, sometimes even more so than some Christians. Those who settle for only being nice, moral churchgoers, are no real threat to the dominion and purposes of the devil because it is possible to live that kind of life, be liked by others, but have no real transformative effect on those around you.

Believers who settle for living like this may be liked, they may even be admired to some extent, but they will be easily ignored. People will ignore them because the way they live may not fully present and challenge others with the alternative way of living that the kingdom of God offers us. That way of living is at the same time inviting and comforting, challenging and unsettling.

Those whose lives are potent for God's purposes will not be so easily ignored or explained away. Why? Because they are Christians who yearn for God to break in on them with the fullness of that alternative reality the kingdom of God offers. They are followers of Christ who yearn deep within their beings for the Lord to do whatever he needs to do in them so he can do whatever he wants to do through them. This way of living, this kind of transformation, is the fruit a safe place is designed by its very nature to produce.

If our lives are to bring glory to God and serve as real threats to the purposes of the enemy, we must grow in what it means to be a safe-place people so we can be transformed and empowered to live like Jesus did—as one who is at the same time a safe place and the dangerous kind. Jesus was not one or the other; he was both. And the truth is that growing in what it means to be the former will always produce the fruit of the latter.

---

9 See Sellers, *The Dangerous Kind.*

WE ALL NEED A SAFE PLACE

We all need a safe place and that's what this book is about. Part One introduces the safe place vision and briefly addresses the concept of living as the dangerous kind. The rest of the book will identify and examine aspects and characteristics that can help make an individual, a group, and a church a safe place. The chapters of this book will include narrative designed to cast a vision for the importance of being a safe place, and examine the major characteristics that can make us just such a people. Exercises for reflection and response will be included in some chapters because my hope is we will all actually be transformed to think, speak, and act more like Jesus, because Christians and non-Christians alike need a safe place.

3

An Essential Key

*Even if we dare be obedient to the Lord and go wherever
he sends us to live lives of witness and to develop healthy
disciples and leaders, who do people encounter when they encounter
you and me?*

B EING A SAFE place is an essential key for developing healthy disciples and
leaders in the church and living lives of witness in the world. It is essential
for us because it was essential in the life and ministry of Jesus. Consider the
following stories.

THE WOMAN AT THE WELL

The weight of the water jar was light in the woman's hands as she made
her daily pilgrimage to the well. That would not be the case on the return
trip home. She would need to shift the weight of the jar, now filled with
water, from one arm to the other. The trip would be taxing and arduous.

However, the weight of water was nothing compared to the weight of sin and shame she carried everywhere, every minute, every day. But this day would be different. This would be the day God's improbable provision of forgiveness of sin and freedom from shame broke through in her life. On this day the sin and shame that so heavily weighed her down would be lifted. All because of an encounter she was about to have with a man, an encounter that would change her life forever, one that by all rights should never have occurred.

He was male, she female. He was a Jew, she a Samaritan. According to cultural norms they should never have been talking, let alone having a conversation that became so personal, so intimate, so quickly. He engaged her simply and innocently enough. "I'm tired and thirsty," he told her. That was it. Though a holy man, a rabbi, he did not address the sin and shame that marked her life and drove her to the well alone each day. He simply engaged her in conversation, one person to another. She may have initially questioned his intent and felt uncomfortable, but there was something different about this man that kept her there and kept the conversation going.

As they talked it became apparent there was, in fact, something extraordinary about this seemingly ordinary man. His very persona and presence was inviting and accepting. He was a man who wanted nothing from her. This was a first. Men always wanted something. The woman and the man spent time together. They talked. He listened. He cared.

In the end, her very ordinary, daily appointment became a divine appointment, an encounter that left her so transformed she ran back to the people who had ostracized her and told them they had to come and see this man. At first glance he appeared ordinary, but something about him was different, extraordinary. He had told her everything she had ever done. She had found someone who fully knew who she was and still accepted her, someone who was not scared away by her past and who seemed genuinely interested in her, someone who related to her with a combination of grace and truth that was healing to her soul. For the first time in her life she had encountered a man who was safe. And it absolutely transformed her life.

A Pharisee under the Cover of Darkness

While the woman arrived at her encounter in the heat of day, the Pharisee came under the cover of darkness. Nicodemus had questions, lots of important questions. He had heard this same man's teaching and it had challenged his thinking and shaken beliefs and assumptions he and other Pharisees had taken for granted. But he was afraid and embarrassed to ask Jesus on the spot, so he went to him later when none of his fellow Pharisees were around. The man didn't care. He was willing to welcome those who came to him at any time, under any circumstances. Nicodemus sensed this and asked the questions, the real questions, he'd wanted to ask but had been afraid to. And the man answered.

We don't learn in Scripture but church history tells us Nicodemus the Pharisee becomes a follower of Jesus Christ. What Scripture does tell us is that Nicodemus stepped out publicly to help bury Jesus after his very public death, risking his own reputation in the process. In that encounter under the cover of darkness, Nicodemus's life was forever changed, all because he met a man who was safe. He'd finally met a man who was safe enough to ask the questions of life that really mattered. He'd found a man whom he could question without fear of being shamed and rejected. Nicodemus had found someone who was safe, and his life was forever transformed.

A Disciple with Doubts

"I will not believe it until I see the nail marks in his hands and put my finger where the nails were and put my hand into his side," said Thomas. Thomas was a disciple of the man, the rabbi. He had been one of those who followed him, traveled with him, ate with him, and talked with him. To hear the rabbi they loved had actually risen from the dead was too good to be true. He wanted it so badly to be true, but something this extraordinary, well, he'd have to see it for himself. The word of his friends was just not enough for something this important. Who could blame him? Christians for centuries have. We've labeled him "Doubting" Thomas when the reality is, wouldn't we have done the same? It is so easy for us to believe the rabbi was raised from the dead with the historical records at our disposal. But on that day, in that moment, wouldn't we have said a loud amen to Thomas's declaration?

A week later Thomas and other followers were together when the risen rabbi walked into the middle of their gathering, somehow appearing in their midst even though the doors had been locked. The rabbi looked at Thomas and said, "Put your finger here, and look at my hands. Put your hand here in my side. Stop being an unbeliever and believe." For so long we have read this text as a rebuke. We've assumed an attitude and tone in Jesus' voice that the scripture itself does not give us. Rather than rebuke, could it have been an understanding response? Rather than a reprimand for faithlessness, could it have been an answer to an authentic question? This rabbi met people where they were and helped them move from doubt to belief, from faithlessness to faith. So he meets Thomas right where he is, and Thomas was authentically transformed. "My Lord, and my God!" he exclaimed.

Church history tells us this doubting Thomas goes on to be the apostle of the gospel in far away India. Thomas was so transformed he became willing to risk his life to travel to a distant land to share with others the good news that had changed his. All because he'd had an encounter with a man who was safe, safe enough to express his doubts to, safe enough to ask what he really wanted to ask.

AN ESSENTIAL KEY FOR JESUS

The woman at the well, Nicodemus, and Thomas—all encountered the same man. All three had their lives radically transformed. And the essential key in each encounter was that they met someone who was safe. Jesus was a safe place for the lost and searching, the wounded and weary. He was safe for the religious and those who had no religion. And because he was safe, souls were saved, disciples were made, and lives were forever changed.

Being a safe place was an essential element in the life and ministry of Jesus. It was a key for the development of healthy disciples and leaders, and for enabling people to live lives of bold and effective witness. If this was such an important part of how Jesus carried out his mission, how much more must it be for us?

Creating an emotional, relational, and spiritual atmosphere that's safe is critical in helping ordinary people be transformed into extraordinary followers of Jesus. When people experience this kind of conversion they increasingly think, speak, and act more like Jesus in the power of the same Holy Spirit who empowered Christ. As a result, they experience an increase in their effectiveness for living lives of witness, and become the kind of healthy Christian disciples and leaders God can use to impact individuals, communities, and nations for his purposes because, like Jesus, they are safe. Thus, it bears repeating—being a safe place was an essential key in the life and ministry of Jesus. It is for us as well.

A GROWING STEREOTYPE

Unfortunately, rather than being known as safe-place people, Christians are too often perceived and experienced as being unsafe. A stereotype that is spreading rapidly across our country is that Christians are arrogant and angry, judgmental and condemning people. Note that this stereotype focuses primarily on who we *are*, not on what we *do*. We can do good things but if who we are in the process is perceived and experienced as unsafe by others, we will be hindered in the very thing we long for, to connect people with God's love and power.

This negative stereotype of Christianity needs to be changed. However, that will require men and women who genuinely desire something more than simply accumulating more information and building big bible brains. Instead, it will require people who really want to be transformed, men and women who really want to be empowered to think, speak, and act more like Jesus. And that kind of authentic change in a person's life has the best chance of happening in an atmosphere full of God's love and power, acceptance and forgiveness, and his healing combination of grace and truth; in short, in the context of an atmosphere that is safe.

RELATIONSHIP IS THE TASK

Examining what it means to be a safe place will not only help us focus on who we are as persons, but also on the tenor of our relationships with others. This is important because scripturally for the Christian, who we are and what we do are organically connected. Some believers would disagree with me on this. They may not say it with words, but you can see it in how they live and in the priorities they set in life.

There are some who are so passionate about accomplishing great things for the kingdom of God that they would say we need to focus more on what we've been called to do, rather than be concerned about who we are and the tenor of our relationships. There's too much important work to be done, they'd say. We shouldn't have to be so touchy-feely, or spend so much time and effort worrying about hurting someone's feelings.

As followers of Christ, however, we must pay attention to the relational atmosphere we are creating as well as the task we are carrying out, because God has given us both a great commission (the task) and a great commandment (the relational atmosphere). The great commission speaks to the task: go into all the world to make disciples (see Matthew 28:18–20). It's a God-given call to live a life of witness in the world and to make disciples. The great commandment on the other hand speaks to the relational atmosphere in which that task is to be carried out—loving God, self, and others (see Matthew 22:37–39).

Being a safe place will provide a healthier emotional, relational, and spiritual atmosphere in which biblical truth can be communicated and experienced. This in turn can increase our effectiveness in accomplishing the task God has set before us. Relationship and task are organically connected and both are impacted by the presence or absence of an atmosphere that's safe.

THIS STILL BEGS THE QUESTION

Developing God's people as disciples and leaders who are living missional lives in a postmodern world. This is the task, the call to arms that Christian leaders around the world are being challenged to take up today. In actuality, there's little that's new about this. Equipping God's people as disciples, leaders, and witnesses is as old as our Christian faith itself.

What is new are the unique characteristics of the postmodern era we live in and the deluge of information regarding each aspect of the call—discipleship, leadership development, missional living, and postmodernity. Never before in all of history have Christian leaders had so much information available to them and, in many ways, thrust upon them, as they do today. Each focus has its own plethora of books, CDs, and conferences to offer, not to mention all the articles on each topic that are just a few keystrokes away on the Internet. However, in the midst of all that information and activity, an important question is often overlooked—even if we dare be obedient to the Lord and go wherever he sends us to live lives of witness, and to develop healthy disciples and leaders, who do people encounter when they encounter you and me?

The concepts of postmodernity, leadership development, missional living,[10] and discipleship are among the most recent in a series of waves that have washed over the body of Christ during the past few decades. In the 1980s and '90s, a tidal wave of books and conferences on the condition of postmodernity crashed in on Christian leaders throughout the United Sates. Authors and conference speakers told us we had moved into a new era with a new set of assumptions and questions. Life as we knew it had changed, they said. The ways we practiced being leaders and doing church would have to undergo an extreme makeover.

For instance, how we communicate truth would have to undergo a radical transformation, because in the postmodern world truth was now relative rather than absolute, more relational than propositional, and the individual, not an outside authoritative source, determines what is true and not true. We were told that because we're now living in a postmodern era things needed to change, particularly the way we do church. To be fair, the postmodern discussion can ask some very good and important questions. If we are willing to wrestle with them from a position of humility, and not react defensively out

---

10 The phrase "missional living" is another way to describe living lives of witness in the world.

of our own insecurity, the discussion can enable us to become more effective in sharing our faith, serving as leaders, and being the church.

However, even if we agree we're living in a postmodern era, this still begs a question: Who do postmoderns encounter when they encounter you and me? Do they encounter Christians who, like Jesus, are a safe place, or people who are unsafe? Are they encountering followers of Christ who are full of God's extravagant love and forgiveness, and his healing combination of grace and truth? Or, do they encounter Christians who are arrogant and angry, judgmental and condemning?

Friends who surf tell me waves come in sets. Sure enough, no sooner had the postmodernity wave washed over the body of Christ that a wave of leadership development came crashing in. Youth ministers, children's ministers, music ministers, associate pastors, and senior pastors all flocked to leadership conferences around our country, listening to the keynote speakers and buying and reading their books. Suddenly we needed to be training all church staff members to be leaders who could envision and develop strategic plans, not merely serve as shepherds and ministers faithfully caring for the sheep.

There was much good information and practice shared in these books and conferences, to be sure. However, an important focus was often lacking in most of them: a focus on the emotional, relational, and spiritual health of leaders. Most of the books, conferences, and websites focused on a leader's competencies. They said little about a leader's relationship with Christ, any involvement in a healthy community, or their growth in godly character and wholeness. And in this wave of information we often lost sight of a key factor for developing healthy leaders: information in books, classes, and conferences doesn't build leaders, leaders build leaders. Even as healthy disciples (which we were to discover in one of the next waves) are most effectively developed in relationships, so are healthy leaders. Still, we paid our money, attended the conferences, and actually did grow in our effectiveness as leaders in many ways.

However, even if a person agrees with the need for developing pastors and other staff members as leaders, this still begs a question: Who will people encounter when they encounter those pastors and staff members as leaders?

Will they encounter a pastor-leader (or children's minister, youth pastor, or worship leader) who, like Jesus, is a safe place for them because he or she is growing more emotionally, relationally, and spiritually whole? Or, will they encounter someone who is unhealthy in those areas and, as a result, is unsafe?

The body of Christ was still awash in the waves of postmodernity and leadership development when the next big wave hit us—the missional living wave. Missional living is a phrase used by some to speak about living lives of witness in the world. The missional living wave told us that being seeker-sensitive, attractional Christians who focused primarily on getting people inside the four walls of a church with the hopes they'd have a great experience was no longer acceptable. This wave reminded us that it has never been God's will to for us to spend most of our time inside our churches, inviting and waiting for the lost and searching to come to us. We are called to go wherever in the world God sends us to impact them with his love and power. The missional living wave encouraged and exhorted us to leave our church buildings, go to where the lost are, and be like Jesus with the people Jesus would have been with.

I am thankful for the focus of this wave but it is important to remember that this it is not something new. Christians have been living missional lives ever since Jesus rose from the dead and sent the Holy Spirit to dwell in us. Does this focus get lost in many of our lives from time to time? Yes, it does. It's easy to fall into a comfortable and complacent, nice and moral way of living a Christian life, easier than most of us would care to admit. But if the missional living message is presented as new revelation we do a disservice to Christians throughout the ages who have lived lives of witness in the world while being active members of churches.

For example, Celtic Christians were very intentional in living lives of witness in the world around them. It is an over-generalization if the missional message consciously or subconsciously infers that the only thing followers of Christ have been practicing until now is a fortress mentality. Every decade throughout history has had its share of Christians living intentional lives of witness in the world while working at the same time to build strong congregations.

This critique of Christians living only out of a fortress mentality may not be the message that writers of books and speakers at conferences and in various organizations mean to communicate, but it can easily be the message interpreted and heard. The unintended result can be the creation of an unsafe atmosphere in which one group of Christians criticizes and condemns another while rationalizing the criticism as an inspirational challenge. Unless we are careful to examine what we are communicating and the way in which we're communicating it, this message, which at its best is meant to inspire Christians to leave their churches and go out into the world to love and serve others, can often have the effect of heaping more shame on church members. It can leave them feeling more inadequate rather than more empowered. And it can even pit them one against the other.

Hasn't Christian living always really been a combination of both building strong congregations and living lives of witness in the world? Can't strong, corporate Christian bodies be important for developing whole, healthy, and empowered disciples for missional living? It seems one of the most helpful points of this wave has been to remind us to be more intentional about giving time and attention to both; and for that, I give its advocates thanks.

However, even if we agree we're to be more intentional in leaving our churches and going out to live lives of witness in the world around us, this still begs a question: Who are those we are seeking to be in relationship with and witness to encountering when they encounter you and me? Are they encountering Christians who are safe or unsafe? Christians whose lives woo and draw others toward Jesus, or lives that repel them from him?

Now, even as we stand knee-deep in the waves of being a missional people in a postmodern era with a commitment to leadership development in the church and living lives of witness in the world, the next wave has broken in over us, the wave of life-on-life discipleship. The life-on-life discipleship wave advocates that disciples are best made in committed relationship with another Christian, not merely by sitting in a classroom or bible study. This wave has deposited its own collection of conferences and books, organizations and websites, all calling us to go make disciples in the context of these life-on-life relationships.

Discipleship in these intentional and accountable relationships is needed, we're told, because it is possible to sit in church services, bible studies, and small groups simply transmitting information rather than experiencing transformation. This certainly can be true to some degree, but let's not underestimate the human ability to deceive ourselves, and others, even in the context of intentional, accountable relationships. Such relationships are not a fail-safe. At their best they can position us for further Christ-like transformation. These relationships are not designed in theory to only be conduits for informational dumps, but to create an atmosphere for authentic transformational experience. However, what their first-generation proponents design them for is not automatically what is lived out by generations 2.0, 3.0, and so on.

Even if we dare be obedient to the Lord and go wherever he sends us in this postmodern world to live lives of witness, and develop healthy leaders and disciples, a question still remains: Who do people encounter when they encounter you and me? Someone who is safe or unsafe? This is a question of critical importance to consider lest we get stuck focusing on only what we do for the Lord and forget to consider who we are as persons and who we are in our relationships with others. This question is of critical importance because it is possible to become so focused on carrying out the Great Commission and presenting Christ that we forget to be like Christ with those we are interacting with.

DO BE DO BE DO

ARC leader and teacher Robert Walter once reminded some of us in his excellent seminar, Building Healthy Leaders, that Frank Sinatra used to sing a little ditty that went like this: "Do be do be do." Many Christians, Robert said, don't sing that lyric. Instead we sing, "Do do do do do." We're so focused on doing that we've lost that sense of the importance of being. Christians who are more concerned with only doing and ignore the importance of their being can push people away from Jesus rather than draw them closer. They can, in a word, be unsafe.

Michael Frost shares a story that illustrates this point in his book *Exiles: Living Missionally in a Post-Christian Culture*. Frost writes of inviting a former missionary to Jordan to share about his experiences with a group of high school students in a public school in Australia. Initially the students were interested, but, as can often happen, as the presentation wore on the teens began to lose interest and their attention waned. They weren't misbehaving badly but they were restless and began talking amongst themselves. The missionary stopped his presentation and reprimanded the kids for not being attentive. He demanded they settle down. This only exacerbated the situation. A few teens actually whistled and jeered. This irritated the missionary even more and he raised his voice to demand they be quiet because he was a guest in their school and should not be treated in this manner. This only encouraged the students to act out more. Then the missionary really got angry and told them the Bible claims a fool says in his heart there is no God. "If you don't believe, then you are fools," he shouted at the students.

Frost had had enough and finally walked up front to settle the group down. He gently told the students their behavior was inappropriate but that he did not think they were fools. "You're pretty decent teenagers who are capable of thinking through the important issues of faith and religion," he said. Then he dismissed them early. As the students filed out, the missionary now directed his anger at Frost. "How dare you humiliate me like that!" he screamed. "I am a guest in this school. I shouldn't be treated this way by those children!" Frost picks up the story from here:

> At that, I turned to him and said sternly, "Right now, you're not a guest in this school. You're not a missionary from Jordan. Right now in this setting, before these students, you are Christ. You are the closest thing these kids will ever get to seeing what Jesus looks like. They don't go to church or attend Sunday Schools. The only chance they will ever get to see what Christ is like is when they walk in here to take these religious education sessions. So, when you call them fools and berate them for their lack of faith, you show them that that's how Jesus sees them. And as far as I can tell, in the gospels, the only time Jesus ever abuses people for their lack of piety, he's speaking to

the religious leaders!" The missionary was too concerned with presenting Christ rather than being Christ.[11]

Was this Christian missionary always this way? Who knows? Maybe he was just having a bad day. Maybe this was a momentary lapse. Whether it was a momentary lapse or not, however, who he was as a person left more of a mark on these kids than sharing about what he did as a missionary. His being, more than his doing, impacted those kids that day.

Did that one Christian missionary truly represent all Christians that morning? Was he typical of what it means to truly be a Christian? Of course not. For every one Christian who may seem miserable, there are a hundred who are joyfully helping to send shipments of food and medical supplies to areas of the world that cannot afford them. For every one Christian who seems hateful, there are a hundred living and ministering with the poor and homeless. For every one Christian who is condemning, there are a hundred who are onsite helping those in need in the wake of a tsunami, hurricane, earthquake, or some other natural disaster. For every one Christian who is hypocritical there are one hundred who are helping to dig wells for clean water where there are none, and fighting diseases most people don't want to get near.

Do the negative stereotypes of Christians truly represent what it means to live life as a follower of Jesus? No, they don't. Unfortunately, we live in a culture where the bad news gets more attention than the good; and it is often the bad news about who we are, not just what we do that gets the attention. This is why understanding and growing in what it means to be a safe place is essential. God has not called us to do, he has called us to be; and it is often our being that impacts others for the kingdom of God, not merely our doing. Consider the testimony of Penny:

"Nadine and I would sit for hours in her room," Penny began. "Mostly we would talk about boys or school, but always by the end of it, we talked about God. The thing I loved about Nadine was that I never

---

11 Michael Frost, *Exiles: Living Missionally in a Post-Christian Culture* (Peabody, MA: Hendrickson Publishers, 2006), 14.

felt like she was selling anything. She would talk about God as if she knew Him, as if she had talked to Him on the phone that day. She was never ashamed, which is the thing with some Christians I had encountered. They felt like they had to sell God and it's like they really weren't listening to me; they didn't care, they just wanted me to buy their product. It had been so easy just to dismiss Christians as nuts, but here was Nadine. I didn't have a category for her."[12]

Being like Christ, not merely presenting Christ or Christian claims, will increase our effectiveness in doing the tasks God has given us to do in the world. Doing Christian ministry, whether leadership development, discipleship, or living lives of witness, will not be as effective if we are not being the people God has called us to be and can transform us to be. It is not only our doing that will be a witness to the world that we are Christ's followers, but our being people who love one another and our neighbors as ourselves (see John 13:34–35 and Matthew 22:37–39). It is who we are that may give people the courage to be vulnerable and transparent with us, which is an essential element for any authentic transformation to take place. Who we are as persons can provide people the freedom to give voice to the questions they really want to ask, or to speak out the doubts they're really wrestling with, because they've found a place where they are not afraid they'll be shamed or discarded.

We all still need to be encountered by someone who, like Jesus, is a safe place. Jesus was a safe place for the lost and searching, the marginalized and disenfranchised. He was a safe place for his disciples, for the woman at the well, for the woman caught in adultery, for the Pharisee Nicodemus who came to him under the cover of darkness, for Zacchaeus, and for the man who was so full of demons his name had become Legion. For all these people and more, Jesus was a safe place, and because he was safe, they experienced an authentic transformation in their lives. Because Jesus was a safe place for them, they were drawn toward and connected with God rather than being driven away from him. Because of the safe place they discovered

12 Donald Miller, *Blue Like Jazz: Nonreligious Thoughts on Christian Spirituality* (Nashville, TN: Thomas Nelson Publishers, 2003), 46–47.

in Christ, they were transformed and empowered to live the rest of their lives as followers who are the dangerous kind, people empowered by the Holy Spirit to be dangerous for the kingdom of God and to the dominion and purposes of the enemy.

Being a safe place will increase our effectiveness as missional Christians who are launching out into a postmodern world to draw others to faith in Jesus, and develop them as healthy leaders and disciples in the context of life-on-life relationships. It was an essential key for Jesus and it remains an essential key for us today.

4

WHAT'S IN THE AIR MAKES A DIFFERENCE

In the same way the atmosphere can impact us physically in helpful or harmful ways, what we breathe in emotionally, relationally, and spiritually can impact us too. There is an atmosphere that can help us thrive and flourish as followers of Christ. But there is also an environment that can weaken and eventually quench our passion, our faith, and even our relationship with the Lord.

"YOU REALIZE YOU just changed the atmosphere in this place, don't you?" That's the question a worker at the Gospel Rescue Mission in Los Angeles just had to ask Dirk Duhlstine. Dirk and his teenage son, Josiah, were part of a group helping out around the mission that morning. Ladies had been filing in as they did every day, expecting nothing more than a place to rest and something to eat; just another ordinary day at the mission. However, this day had turned out to be anything but ordinary for those who walked through the doors. Dirk, a gifted guitarist and worship leader, and Josiah, a gifted cellist, had greeted the ladies with a sweet combination of classical music followed by a smooth transition into some foot-stomping, hand-clapping, shout-for-joy inspirational worship music.

As the ladies entered they became emotionally engaged in a way that was rarely seen around the mission. So when Dirk and Josiah were finished, one of the workers had to make sure they knew what they'd done—"You realize you just changed the atmosphere in this place, don't you?" Something had shifted in the air that morning. The woman worked there every day so she noticed it. The music Dirk and Josiah had been playing, along with the spirit in which they played it, had shifted something in the atmosphere, something so significant that it had a visible affect on the women who gathered in the mission that day. What's in the air makes a difference.

WHAT'S IN THE AIR MAKES A DIFFERENCE

Changing the emotional, relational, and spiritual atmosphere is one of the essential effects that growing in what it means to be a safe place can have in the life of an individual, a small group, or an entire congregation. It's an effect that can increase our ability to develop healthy leaders and disciples in the church, and empower God's people to live lives of witness in the world. Leaders and disciples are not developed in a vacuum, nor do we live as witnesses in a vacuum. We attempt to do all of these in a culture, environment, or atmosphere—whatever word you choose to use—that can have a direct impact upon our effectiveness, or the lack thereof.

It's been said, if we do not affect what's in the world, what's in the world will affect us. In the same way, it could be said, if we don't affect what's in the air, what's in the air will affect us. The Lord first began to speak to me about this in July 2010 when I went backpacking in the Big Horn Mountains of northern Wyoming. I was invited to go along with my sons, Joe and Ben; daughter, Rachel; son-in-law, Bert; Jack (Joe's chocolate Labrador), and Tojo (Rachel and Bert's Japanese Akita). One of my favorite times of the day on that trip was stepping out of the tent each morning, taking a deep breath of refreshing mountain air, and making a pot of campfire coffee (there most certainly will be good coffee in heaven!). Have you ever had that experience of taking in a deep breath of fresh, clean air in a pristine wilderness area? Have you ever felt refreshing, crisp air filling your lungs and making your whole body come alive? I did that morning.

On the other hand, have you ever taken a deep breath of air filled with the pollution of toxic fumes? As I stood there, inhaling that crisp mountain air, I immediately flashed back to an early morning's deep breath in the slums of Mumbai some years ago. What was in the air that day did not make my body come alive. Rather, the stench that filled the atmosphere attacked my nostrils and lungs. My eyes watered, my nose burned, and I began to cough. The mountain air was refreshing and life-giving. The air in the slums of Mumbai was toxic and death dealing.

How about this? Have you ever been in a room when someone walks in and you sense a tangible change in the atmosphere for the better, a change that happened for no other reason than this person was present in the room? We had a student like this at The Master's Institute Seminary where I served as president. Her name was Melody Ortenblad, but no one called her Melody. We all called her Joy because whenever she walked into the classroom, joy walked in with her, and it changed the atmosphere for the good.

Then there's Joe Johnson. Joe is my mentor and my friend. He's made an impact on literally thousands of people around the world. But few, if any, of us call him Joe. We call him Sweet Papa Joe because when he walks in the room the love and heart of Father God walk in with him. It fills the air. It changes the atmosphere just because Joe walked in the room.

Or, how about the opposite? Have you ever been in a room where the atmosphere just absolutely deflates or becomes heavy, depressed, or oppressed just because a certain person walks in? The presence of the former is refreshing and life giving, helping to create an atmosphere in the room that's safe. The presence of the latter makes the room's emotional, relational, and spiritual atmosphere toxic and unsafe.

In the same way the atmosphere can impact us physically in helpful or harmful ways, what we breathe in emotionally, relationally, and spiritually can impact us too. There is an atmosphere that can help us thrive and flourish as followers of Christ. But there is also an environment that can weaken and eventually quench our passion, our faith, and even our relationship with the Lord.

We can help create an atmosphere that is crisp and clean and has a refreshing scent that draws people toward Jesus. Or, we can create and sustain an environment that is foul and toxic, producing a stench that can drive Christians and non-Christians away from the Lord and all he has for them. There is an atmosphere that is safe and there is one that is unsafe. Either can be experienced in the life of an individual Christian, or in a Christian church, para-church ministry, or family. What's in the air makes a difference.

THE SANCTUARY IN COLORADO

Graeme Sellers and I experienced the reality of an atmosphere that can help faith thrive and flourish in June 2011 as we listened to the story of the building of a retreat center called The Sanctuary. The Sanctuary is located near Buena Vista, Colorado, with the Collegiate Peaks of the Rocky Mountains as its "backyard." Owners Kevin and Julie Ortenblad built a beautiful lodge for pastors and Christian workers to get away to be with the Lord and to be refreshed and restored. Graeme and I had gone there so he could spend some time working on his now-published book *The Dangerous Kind,* and I wanted to spend some time in prayer for The Master's Institute Seminary.

As you set foot on the grounds of The Sanctuary you tangibly sense the peace and presence of God. Something good is in the air. And this is no mere coincidence because that's the atmosphere Kevin and Julie have intentionally asked the Lord to create and sustain there. Their commitment to participate with the Lord through their abandoned obedience, intercessory prayer, and spiritual warfare are essential elements in this atmospheric shift.

As Graeme and I sat with Kevin at breakfast one morning, we asked him to tell us the story of The Sanctuary. We listened with our hearts to the faith-building stories of how he and Julie heard God direct each detail of the building of this beautiful center. Kevin shared multiple stories of how God supplied all that was needed, many times in improbable ways. One example was the Lord's provision for the stone masonry that was to go in the lodge. Kevin and Julie bathed every step of the building in prayer, and in that context they traveled all over Colorado looking for just the right masonry. They finally had settled on a rock to use, and went to a place called Glorious Stone. The owner had three hundred tons of the rock that they used in their building project. Normally the rock should have cost $25.00 per square foot. Out of nowhere the owner asked the Ortenblads to give her much less than she had invested in it. In the end, they paid only $4 per square foot. Kevin told us a number of similar stories. The atmosphere in that kitchen and throughout the grounds of The Sanctuary was full of faith and trust in God, and perhaps most of all, a willing abandonment to his purposes for their lives.

What made it all the more powerful for me, however, was also how willing and transparent Kevin was in sharing some of the struggles he had during the process. He didn't just tell some phony, full-of-faith kind of story. What Kevin shared was an authentic journey in following the Lord that also included moments of wondering what he was doing, moments of doubt and questioning. For instance, there was December 6, 2007, when the Ortenblads had sold their family farm and Kevin wondered, "Really? Now what? Are we really going to go ahead with this dream? How will that work?" Then there was May 31, 2008, when they actually drove off from their farm after having completed the sale of the land, the house, and the machinery. "Now what, God?" Kevin asked. "I don't have the skill for what you're calling us to do." Kevin shared that at that moment he heard God say, "You sound just like Moses. I guess you'll have to rely on me like he did."

God was good though, and provided everything they needed. Today The Sanctuary is welcoming pastors and Christian workers from around the country into an atmosphere that is rich with a tangible sense of God's presence and peace. Kevin wrote me recently and said, "I found out that to slay giants and to dream God-sized dreams, you need a big God. He taught me that if you never dream the impossible, you'll never see the supernatural. I would not change one day of this journey now. Many days I borrowed Julie's faith, and that got me through. God may give you someone with more faith to journey with. Borrow theirs when you need it, and give them yours when they need it. The journey may be hard, but Jesus walked one of those too."

As Kevin told us stories of The Sanctuary, Graeme and I sat there thinking, "We want what Kevin's got!" We were breathing in what was in the atmosphere of that place and of Kevin's life. We were breathing in faith, trust, and a willingness to live a life of abandonment to God's purposes for our lives. As we breathed in what was in the air, we wanted to take a Holy-Spirit led risk just like Kevin and Julie had. The more Kevin spoke, the more God was at work effecting an atmospheric shift within Graeme and me. We left The Sanctuary a few days later, different than when we had arrived because we had been breathing in what was in the atmosphere of The Sanctuary in Buena Vista, Colorado. What's in the air makes a difference.

WHAT IS ATMOSPHERE?

What do I mean when I use the term air or atmosphere? Air, atmosphere, culture, and environment are all words used to describe the beliefs, values, behaviors, practices, and traditions, that influence who people are, and how living and working together is experienced. To use one of these terms is to speak of the state of health, or lack thereof, in the life of an individual or organization. Furthermore, it distinguishes one group from another. I will use each of those terms interchangeably in this chapter, but for the most part I use the word atmosphere in the rest of the book because that is the term we use in the church network for which I serve as director—the Alliance of Renewal Churches (ARC).

We are often consciously unaware of the culture we live or work in, or of the profound influence it has on our lives. One way to understand it is that often the unspoken message is "this is the way we do things here," and that "way" influences the beliefs, behaviors, and practices of those in that particular culture. For instance, as I work on this chapter the New England Patriots are getting ready to play the Seattle Seahawks in the 2015 Super Bowl. As they prepare, they are being accused of illegally deflating footballs in a playoff game the week before so that their players could more easily grip and throw the ball.

While reporting on this story, respected sports journalist Michael Wilbon said that the Patriots have cultivated a culture of cheating in their organization. He pointed out past instances where the team clearly did cheat as well as noting that there were other instances of accusation and suspicion of cheating over the years. Thus Wilbon's contention that they had created a culture in which cheating was deemed acceptable behavior, and that this culture had influenced someone in the organization to engage in the practice of deflating footballs. If the accusations are proven to be true (as I write this, the investigation by the NFL is ongoing), it will illustrate the power and influence a culture can have on a person's thinking and behavior. This can be true whether it's on a sports team, in business or education, or in a family and organization of faith. What's in the air can make a difference.

Every Christian lives, works, and ministers in a culture. The environment of our families, small groups, or churches affects the ways that we relate to one another and conduct our ministries. The atmosphere in any group can either prevent it from more fully realizing its potential in Christ, or create an atmosphere that is so emotionally, relationally, and spiritually healthy that it creates a fertile soil, as it were, where seeds of faith and transformation can bear fruit and flourish.

A corporate entity that is intentionally seeking to create a healthy culture has an advantage over those that are not. This is not only true in the realm of faith, but in areas such as the business world. Patrick Lencioni writes in *The Advantage*, "The single greatest advantage any company can achieve is organizational health. Yet it is ignored by most leaders even though it is simple, free, and available to anyone who wants it."[13] While I agree with Lencioni that organizational health is available to all, I disagree that it is simple or free. There is a cost to be counted when an individual, family, or church body makes a commitment to becoming healthier. It will take time, effort, and the hard and painful work of breaking off attitudes such as pride, rebellion, stubbornness, and complacency.

The most helpful starting point in changing the atmosphere in a family, small group, or congregation is not to talk or focus on changing culture in the larger entity as much as it is to focus on our own lives by inviting God

---

13   Patrick Lencioni, *The Advantage: Why Organizational Health Trumps Everything Else in Business* (San Francisco, CA: Jossey Bass, 2012), 1.

to help us identify and embrace the kingdom values he wants us to embrace. That's what I'm doing, and that's what I'm inviting the leaders and churches in our network to do. We believe God has given us a list of kingdom values to integrate into our lives and we are asking him to use those values to change us first, and then through us to change our families and churches. This may seem like a small thing to do, but that's often God's kingdom way of doing things. In his kingdom economy it is the faithful sowing of small seeds in fertile ground that grow to be the largest shrub around (see Matthew 13:6, 22, 31–32).

It is important that we are aware of the fact that the atmosphere of an individual's life or that of a small group or church is not automatically positive just because it is Christian. There are Christians and churches whose atmosphere is healthy and those that are toxic. And wherever the air is toxic, God calls us to follow the example of Jesus to affect what's in the air before what's in the air affects us.

JESUS WAS AN ATMOSPHERIC CHANGE AGENT

Everywhere Jesus set foot he effected a shift in the atmosphere. Graeme Sellers writes of this in *The Dangerous Kind*:

> It seems all he had to do was make an appearance and entire towns turned upside down. His presence was an atmospheric event, producing shifts in people's experience, perceptions, and understanding. So close and true his friendship with the Father, so saturated with heaven's own fragrance was Jesus that the kingdom invaded through him. The ministry of Jesus *unleashed an atmospheric shift* flowing from his intimacy with the Father. The crowds pressing him on every side loved it; they may not have known what, exactly, they were responding to, but they were irresistibly drawn to him and the things he did and the way he made them feel. Wherever he showed up, whenever he spoke, whatever he did—he was constantly setting off seismic sensors in the unseen realms. When he preached, demons cried out

in defiance. When he healed, devils scrambled for cover. When he re-leased those trapped in bondage to dark powers, evil spirits recoiled in dismay [emphasis mine].[14]

"Producing shifts in people's experience, perceptions, and understanding." Wherever Jesus set foot, this was the effect of his presence. Wherever he was present the atmosphere was changed, and because it was changed, people's lives were forever transformed. For instance, wherever Jesus was present, faith was released into the air and people breathed it in. This was true for the woman who had suffered with the issue of bleeding for twelve years (Mark 5:25–29). Jesus' presence affected an atmospheric shift. The air was filled with faith. The woman breathed it in. As a result she came to him with an expectant heart and was healed. She was not only healed physically, but emo-tionally, relationally, and spiritually as well. She was set free from the shame that accompanied her disease and was restored in relationship with family and friends, and most of all, with God. Because of what was in the air, the wom-an's experience, perception, and understanding all underwent a monumental shift that day, a shift that changed the direction and trajectory of her life.

Wherever Jesus was present, the authority and power of heaven were released into the atmosphere and effected change. We read of this in the story of the centurion in Luke 7:1–10. His beloved servant was about to die. But Jesus had set foot in the region. The centurion recognized this and breathed in deeply the authority and power of Jesus that was in the air. As a result he was so filled with trust in what the Lord had authority to do and could do, that his servant was healed without Jesus even needing to enter the centurion's home.

Wherever Jesus was present, a sense of expectancy stirred in peoples' hearts, so much so that it compelled them to spring into action. Such was the case for the friends of a paralyzed man in Luke 5:18–25. Jesus was teaching and ministering in the area, and one of the effects of his presence was a pal-pable sense of expectancy in the air. Those four friends took a deep breath and when they did, they were not to be denied. They knew that if they could just get their friend into the presence of Jesus, good things would happen for him.

---

14 Sellers, *The Dangerous Kind*, 37–38.

Their expectant hearts drove them the proverbial extra mile. Jesus was teaching in a house nearby but it was so crowded that they couldn't get through the doorway. No problem. They just climbed up on the roof instead. Then they lifted their friend up. Have you ever tried to life a person up the side of a house? It's hard work. But they were breathing in expectancy and faith, not hopelessness and doubt, and that gave them strength for the job at hand.

Next, they created a hole in the roof tiles and lowered their friend into the presence of the Lord. What happened then was more than even the four men had dared hope for. Their friend was not only healed, his sins were forgiven. Not only did Jesus deal with the man's physical paralysis, but with his emotional and spiritual paralysis as well. As so often seems to happen in the gospels, Jesus would not let the man and his friends settle for less than all he had in store for them. On that day all five experienced a shift in their experience, perception, and understanding. All because Jesus was present, all because of what was in the air.

Wherever Jesus was present, the enemy cowered in fear and had to leave. The first time Jesus preached (Mark 1:21–28) we're told that an evil spirit began shouting, "Why are you interfering with us, Jesus of Nazareth? Have you come to destroy us? I know who you are—the Holy One sent from God!" Jesus cut him short. He quieted the unclean spirit with a simple word, and it was silent. Even the unclean spirits sense what's in the atmosphere and they know, better than we, that what's in the air truly does make a difference.

Wherever Jesus walked he affected the atmosphere rather than allowing what was in the air to affect him. He was an agent for atmospheric change. Now, God has called us to join him in his work of creating an atmosphere beneficial for his kingdom work to continue today through the power of the Holy Spirit. He has called us to help create and sustain an environment that is emotionally, relationally, and spiritually safe so:

- Souls might be saved
- Broken and wounded bodies, emotions, and relationships might be healed
- Those oppressed and demonized might be set free

- Forgotten ones might not be forgotten but instead be welcomed and cared for in the family of God
- Disciples might be made who are being transformed to think, speak, and act more like Jesus
- Whole and healthy leaders who are first and foremost followers of Jesus might be developed
- That God's people might all be filled with the power of the Holy Spirit and empowered to live fully into his purposes for their lives

We are called by Jesus to live lives that are dangerous for the kingdom of God and to the purposes and dominion of our enemy. Living a life like that requires an atmosphere that's safe, one in which we can authentically be who we in order to be transformed and empowered to live more like Jesus. So, how do we affect and change what's in the air? That is the focus of our next chapter.

5

AFFECTING WHAT'S IN THE AIR

*We can affect what's in the air because the same Holy Spirit who
was in Jesus, and empowered him to affect the atmosphere through
all he said and did, now dwells in you and in me.*

WHAT'S IN THE atmosphere we're seeking to create and sustain in our
own lives, our families, our workplaces, our play places, and in our
churches? What do others breathe in when we walk into the room or when
they walk into our church? What do people sense when they're present
with us in the sacred space that is the fifteen-foot circle around wherever
in the world it is that we happen to be standing? Do they sense an emotional, relational, and spiritual atmosphere that is refreshing, invigorating,
and life-giving? Or, is it a stench that is toxic, one that harms relationships
and quenches faith? Some questions we can ask to help discern whether
we're creating an atmosphere that is safe versus one that is unsafe include
the following.

Is the atmosphere you're in safe for you and others, emotionally, relationally, and spiritually? Is it a place where you can truly be yourself, a place

where you don't have to pretend to be someone you're not in order to be loved and accepted? Or, is it an unsafe place where you live in fear that if others really knew you, you would be judged, shamed, and discarded?

Are your spiritual lungs having a hard time catching their breath because they're being filled with legalism and toxic shame? Or, is the air clean and crisp because you're breathing in the refreshing, life-giving combination of God's grace and truth?

Is the air you're breathing one in which the Bible in its entirety is still believed to be the Word of God, or is the air polluted with a belief that not everything in God's Word is in fact, God's Word? Is reading and studying the Bible viewed as a place you love to come to meet and be with the Lord, or is it viewed as a duty and expectation, as something to check off your list of things to do as followers of Christ?

Is the atmosphere in which you live and serve filled with the gospel, the announcement of what God, in Christ, has done for us that we can never do for ourselves? Or, is it an atmosphere that asks you to do one more thing after another in order to be accepted by God and to earn his approval and favor?

Are you breathing in air that renews a practice of persistent, shameless, and expectant prayer that intentionally contends for the purposes of God? Or, is the air stale because prayer is something you rush through from time to time, or turn to as an afterthought when nothing else seems to be working? Is prayer a central part of your faith family or is it only given lip service? Is it eagerly entered into with the belief and expectancy that God does hear and respond to our prayers? Or is it taught and preached, but rarely practiced in an intentional manner?

Is the air you're breathing one in which the presence, power, and gifts of the Holy Spirit are celebrated, not merely tolerated? Are they practiced in a responsible or irresponsible manner? Does the atmosphere fill you with a conviction that, while not denying reality, there is a superior reality God would have you experience and trust him for? Is it air that fills your lungs with a healthy disregard for the impossible, or is it more like the stifling air in Nazareth where Jesus could "do no mighty works" (see Mark 6:1–6), an air that fills us with the complacency of settling for less?

Are you and I moving and living in an atmosphere where a sense of God's manifest presence is welcome and normal while not being manipulated? Are we living and ministering in an environment of expectancy because a belief in the real presence of Jesus means it's normal to believe God still speaks today, and we can experience him acting and breaking through in our lives? Or, are we breathing air that speaks of the presence of God but does not expect nor even desire to experience that presence today, air that is filled with the fear that expecting experience of any sort automatically leads to manipulation and an unhealthy emphasis on emotion?

What are other things you would like to see filling the atmosphere of your own life or the life of your church that would make it a safe place for others? Take some time to think on this and record your ideas in the space below. As you do, remember this: What's in the air does make a difference.

WE CAN AFFECT THE ATMOSPHERE

Wherever we go we can affect what's in the air for the Kingdom of God. We can be atmospheric change agents just like Jesus was. In fact, isn't this what Jesus calls us to be when he teaches us to pray, "Thy Kingdom come, Thy will be done, on earth as it is in heaven"? Jesus teaches us to pray heaven's realities down onto the earth here and now. When and where that happens, there *will be* a shift in the atmosphere. Where you find the kingdom rule of God increasing in the lives of people, you will find a place and people being increasingly transformed into a safe place.

We can affect what's in the air others breathe when they're with us in our homes, our work places, our play places, and in our churches because the same Holy Spirit who was in Jesus, and empowered him to affect the atmosphere through all he said and did, now dwells in you and in me. As the apostle Paul reminds us in 1 Corinthians 3:16, "Don't you realize that all of you together are the temple of God and that the Spirit of God lives in you?"

It was the Holy Spirit's presence and power that enabled Jesus to affect the atmosphere for good. In Acts 10:38 Peter tells Cornelius and those gathered in his home, "And you know that God anointed Jesus of Nazareth with the Holy Spirit and with power. *Then* Jesus went around doing good and healing all who were oppressed by the devil, for God was with him" (NLT).

Did we hear how the apostle Peter described Jesus? He did not say Jesus the Christ or Jesus the Messiah. He said Jesus of Nazareth. It was Jesus, the Son of God now fully human, who was anointed with the Holy Spirit and *then* went around doing good and healing all who were oppressed by the devil. This is good news because it gives us hope that we too as human beings can be filled with the same Holy Spirit that filled the Lord, and live and minister in God's power even as he did. It is this same Holy Spirit whom Jesus was anointed with that God calls us to continue being filled with. "Don't be drunk with wine, because that will ruin your life. Instead, keep on being filled with the Holy Spirit, singing psalms and hymns and spiritual songs among yourselves, and making music to the Lord in your hearts. And give thanks for everything to God the Father in the name of our Lord Jesus Christ" (Ephesians 5:18–20, NLT).

As we humble ourselves before the Lord and intentionally welcome the work of his Holy Spirit in our lives, we can be healed where we are broken, be set free from anything holding us captive, and grow more mature and whole in who we are. As we continue to be intentional about being filled with the Spirit, we are empowered to affect the atmosphere:

- Through the power of prayer; through asking and declaring, loosing and binding
- Through the power of God's Word proclaimed, taught, and lived out
- Through the power of practicing holy habits
- Through the power of witness and testimony
- Through the power of our own transformed lives, transformed by the Lord so that we think, speak, and act more like Jesus
- Through the power of loving, forgiving, and serving others
- Through the power of humbly tending and mending broken relationships
- Through the power of God at work in and through the Sacraments

- Through exercising the authority and power of the Lord that he has given us to proclaim the gospel, heal the sick, set free the captives, and release the ones living in darkness

As we are filled with the power of the Holy Spirit, we can affect a shift in the atmosphere wherever we go and wherever we set foot. The presence of the Spirit can enable us to fill the air with that which is beneficial for kingdom relationships, transformation, and mission to take place. And as we do, more souls will be saved, and healthy disciples and leaders will be developed.

BEWARE: WE CAN POLLUTE THE AIR TOO

How can we partner with the Lord in creating and sustaining the atmosphere he longs for us to live and minister in? We can begin by acknowledging that while it is most certainly true that we can affect a shift in the air for kingdom realities and purposes, it is also true that we can pollute the air, making it unsafe.

We pollute the air all the time. With our factories, our vehicles, and in so many other ways, we physically pollute the very atmosphere in which we live and move. In the same way we can pollute the atmosphere physically, we can pollute it emotionally, relationally, and spiritually. And when we pollute the air, we create an atmosphere that is unsafe.

So the question to ask is this—how am I polluting the air? If we are to be agents for atmospheric change, we start with the atmosphere of our own lives. We must have the courage of King David to pray with integrity and say to God, "Search me, O God, and know my heart. Try me and know my thoughts. And see if there be *any* grievous way in me, and lead me in the way everlasting" (Psalm 139:23–24, emphasis mine). As we pray, let's keep in mind that the combination of our insecurities, emotional wounds (some of which we are aware, some of which we've buried in a hidden place), and sin makes our capacity for self-deception enormous. Not only do we deceive ourselves, we even rationalize and justify our unwillingness to acknowledge where God needs to transform us by using spiritual language, at times even misinterpreting and misapplying Scripture itself.

This is why we need a safe place. We need brothers and sisters who have helped create an atmosphere in which being ruthlessly honest with ourselves is viewed as a strength, a place where authentic transparency and vulnerability is celebrated, not condemned. With that said, stop for a moment before reading on and write down in the space below some ways human beings pollute the atmosphere emotionally, relationally, and spiritually.

We pollute the air when we:

Just a few of the ways we pollute the air, making the atmosphere unsafe for Christians and non-Christians alike are when:

- We gossip
- We speak a word of judgment over a non-Christian, a brother or sister in Christ, or another church
- We hold onto unforgiveness and bitterness toward someone, and invite others to join us in that
- We choose unbelief, skepticism, and cynicism rather than faith
- We use fear, anger, and toxic shame as motivators
- We choose to settle for less than all God has for us and create an atmosphere where it's acceptable to do so
- We allow jealousy of another brother or sister or another church influence us to think and speak ill of them

It is of particular importance that we realize leaders can pollute the air too, and that when they do, those they've been called to lead and serve breathe in foul air. Whatever leaders don't let God transform, they will transmit, impacting the lives of others in unhealthy and unhelpful ways. Some of the ways leaders pollute the air include the following:

- When leaders seek to advance an agenda, theology, or practice that is theirs but not God's, and seek to rationalize and justify it by using spiritual words or the influence of their title, position, and prestige
- When leaders seek to reinterpret the Word of God and make it mean something it does not mean so they can live the way they want to live, rather than repent and live according to God's ways
- When leaders allow their own need to be needed and their own need to be seen as someone significant influence them to seek out position, prestige, and celebrity
- When leaders forget they can accomplish more as team—locally, regionally, nationally, and internationally—than as any gifted individual person or congregation, and do not work as a team
- When leaders of small churches allow their own insecurities to cause them to criticize, judge, and condemn larger churches and large church pastors
- When leaders of large churches allow their abundance of resources, along with their own insecurities and proud hearts, to cause them to criticize, judge, and distance themselves from their need for smaller churches and small church pastors

Oh how we must grieve our Heavenly Father when we pollute the atmosphere. It must grieve him when he sees not only how it affects us, but also how it creates an unhealthy atmosphere for Christians and non-Christians to breathe in.

OPPORTUNITY TO RESPOND

How have you been polluting the air? Why don't you take time right now to ask Father God to speak to you and show you if there is any way you have been polluting the air and grieving him. Pray the prayer David prayed: "Search me, O God, and know my heart. Try me and know my thoughts. And see if there be any grievous way in me, and lead me in the way everlasting." Then, be silent and listen. Record what you hear in the space below:

Now confess how you have been polluting the air to God and tell him you want to repent of this. Ask for his forgiveness and then thank him and acknowledge that you receive it. Next, ask the Lord to fill you afresh with the presence and power of the Holy Spirit. Ask him to expel anything unholy as he fills you with he who is holy. Finally, my friends, hear and receive the good news of God's grace, mercy, and forgiveness: "If we confess our sins, he is faithful and just to forgive us our sins and to cleanse us from all unrighteousness" (1 John 1:9, ESV). As a called and ordained minister of the church of Jesus Christ, I declare to you the forgiveness of all your sins in the name of the Father, the Son, and the Holy Spirit. Amen. Beloved, your sins are forgiven. The ways you've been polluting the air have been forgiven. You are free.

One thing to note before moving on is to consider if there is anyone you have wounded in the process of polluting the air. If there is, consider going to them to confess this and ask for their forgiveness, especially if you are a leader who has been polluting the air from your pulpit or in other ways from your leadership position. Do not do this too quickly out of some false sense of shame. Take time to ask the Lord about this and as he reveals to you whom you need to speak to and what you need to do, then be obedient to go to them and ask their forgiveness. This act alone may go a long way toward clearing the air and move you further along in helping to create and sustain an atmosphere beneficial for safe-place living.

BREATHING FRESH AIR INTO THE ATMOSPHERE

So, rather than polluting the air, how can we begin to be more intentional about releasing fresh air into the atmosphere? The answers to this question will be addressed more thoroughly throughout the balance of this book.

However, before we begin to explore those answers, it is important to note that building a safe-place atmosphere happens one heart at a time and begins with each one of us.

We cannot control who others are or what they do. We can, however, position ourselves before God to receive his work of transformation. He can change us from being air polluters into men and women through whom the elements of heaven's atmosphere are released into the air here on earth, elements that will enable people who are choking on stale and foul air to breathe in the fresh air of hope and life.

6

What Does a Safe
Place Look Like?

*Being a safe place is nothing more, nothing less, and nothing else
than wanting to think, speak, and act more like Jesus.*

WHAT DOES BEING a safe place look like? It looks like Jesus! Remember, being a safe place is nothing more, nothing less, and nothing else than being transformed to live like Jesus; and why not? His life is *the* living definition of what it means to be a human being at its best. Being a safe place is a metaphor designed to help us be more intentional about positioning ourselves before the Lord so he can do his work of transforming us to think, speak, and act more like him. With that said, why don't we look at one of the many encounters Jesus had with individuals in Scripture and consider whether he was a safe place for this person, and if so, what it was that made him safe.

JESUS AND THE WOMAN AT THE WELL

The encounter I'm thinking of is the meeting between Jesus and the woman at the well found in John 4:1–42. Before reading on, I'd like you to do the following exercise. Begin by taking time to pray and ask God to speak to you through this passage of Scripture. Then, grab a Bible and read those verses. Read them from more than one version if you have access to others. Now, take some time to be quiet before the Lord and ask him, "Jesus, were you a safe place for this woman? If so, how? What did you say or do that made you safe for her?" Then, write what comes to your mind in the space below:

Following are some of the insights that I share in classes that I teach on being a safe place. One of my first observations is that Jesus was a boundary breaker. He was willing to cross cultural and religious boundaries that others would not. For instance, he crossed a gender boundary when he, a male, was willing to stop and speak with a female. He crossed an ethnic and religious boundary as a Jew when he readily engaged a Samaritan in conversation. Jesus broke yet another boundary when he was willing to be seen conversing with a sinner in public, something most religious leaders of his day would not dare to do.

Jesus broke multiple boundaries in order to minister to someone others avoided. His love and concern for this woman would have appeared scandalous to some, but then that's one of the most important marks of being a safe-place person—loving scandalously as Jesus did. He didn't just cross boundaries. Jesus broke whatever boundary he had to in order to let people know he genuinely loved and cared for them. This willingness made him a person who was safe for others.

Another insight from this passage of scripture is that Jesus appeared to be more concerned with the need behind the woman's behavior than with the behavior itself. She is a sinner, that's certain. But the Lord doesn't make her sin the first thing he talks with her about. One of the refreshing things about

Jesus is that he doesn't seem to feel any great need to make people aware of their sinfulness as the first order of business when he encounters them. Rather, it seems that his first priority is to connect and care.

Just being with people is a priority for Jesus. He spends time with them in public. He visits with them in their homes. He hangs out with them, eats with them, and asks them questions. And he listens really well. Sometimes Jesus asks a question in order to meet a need in a person's life. Other times, as he does with this woman, he asks a question in order to allow them to meet a need in his life. In this case all he asks for is a drink of water, and in doing so he begins to establish a connection with the woman. It's a connection that will enable him to let her know that he truly cares for her and cares deeply about the need in her life that is manifested in the behavior everyone else is so focused on.

It's not that the woman's behavior is unimportant to Jesus, because it is. But for him, the greater concern is the need behind the behavior; it's that unmet need that has compelled her to engage in the behavior that has estranged her from the people in her village and from the Lord. Jesus cares for this woman and is concerned with the real need in her life. She's thirsty—emotionally, relationally, and spiritually thirsty. And he has water unlike any other that can quench her thirst. The need is what he chooses to primarily focus on with her, not the behavior. This makes him safe.

For some reason, we on the other hand feel compelled to make sure people know we're aware of their sin as the first order of business in our relationships with them. We are unsafe when we do this. We come off as being a "holier than thou" kind of people and this attitude of superiority is what most people are allergic to. They're not so much allergic to truth, even biblical truth. What they are allergic to is truth shared arrogantly.

The last thing an arrogant presentation of truth communicates is that we genuinely care about people. There is an old youth ministry adage that I think is especially true in this postmodern culture in which one of the primary characteristics for so many is broken trust and fractured relationships: People will not care what you know until they know you care. When we seek to let people know we truly care as our first order of priority in our relationships with them, when we are more concerned with the need behind their behaviors than the behaviors themselves, we will be well on our way to being a safe place for them.

Yet another jewel that can be discovered in this encounter with the woman is that Jesus speaks truth to her but with no apparent hint of condemnation. This is not surprising when we remember that John 1:14 tells us Jesus is full of both grace and truth. When combined, grace and truth are God's healing combination. A safe-place people will not water down the truth just to make people feel all warm and fuzzy, because they know that withholding truth that can set people free is an unloving thing to do. On the other hand, they allow God's grace to influence where, when, and how they share that truth. When we do this, we are being like Jesus—we are being a safe place.

Yet another insight from this story is that Jesus does not simply see this woman as a sinner in need of salvation. He sees her as he does so many other people in Scripture—as hurting, wounded, and lost people who are trying to meet the needs that control them in unhelpful ways. He does not require her to "clean up her act" or "get right with God" before he is willing to relate to her. She is worth loving and being with simply because she has been made in the image of God. This is how someone who is a safe-place person will view people.

Yet another safe-place characteristic of Jesus in this encounter with the woman is that he does not expect her to act any differently than she does. She does not yet have the Holy Spirit of God living within her to influence and empower her to live any differently than she does. As a result, Jesus isn't shocked or abhorred at the sin she has engaged in. And this is his position toward everyone who does not yet experientially know him as Savior and Lord. Jesus hates sin because of how it separates us from God, but he does not distance himself from us because of it. He is not surprised or shocked by sin. There is nothing about people that scares him away from them. When we don't expect others to act any differently than they have the power to, and are not scared away by their sin, we are being a safe place.

Perhaps one of the most important takeaways to be noted from this encounter of Jesus with the woman at the well is that he not only forgives her sin but also heals her shame. She probably came to the well alone each day because of the cloud of shame that hovered over her life. And as was the case for this woman, it is not only forgiveness of sin that so many people need today, but healing for their shame as well. Jesus provides both. When we provide both, we are being a safe place for others just as Jesus was for this solitary woman he met at the well in the heat of the day.

Before moving on, let's consider the impact that being encountered by someone who is safe had on the woman's life. We see it recorded in John 4:39–42. She is so affected by this encounter that she cannot keep the news to herself. She has to tell someone. She's so compelled by who and what she has experienced that she runs back to the village and tells the people who shamed and ostracized her about this amazing man and what he had done for her life. She exhorts them to find out for themselves who he is and what he has to offer.

They do. They spend a few days with Jesus and come to the same conclusion the woman had—this is the Messiah, the Christ. This is the one who forgives us of sin and heals our shame. All of this is made possible because this very ordinary woman has a very extraordinary encounter with someone who is a safe place for her.

A SAFE-PLACE EXERCISE

Following is an exercise that can help you begin to identify characteristics that will make us a safe place for others. Take some time to ask and answer the following questions in the space provided:

- Who has been a safe-place person in your life?
- What are the characteristics that made that person safe for you?
- How has knowing this person impacted your life? Are you a different person as a result of knowing him or her? If so, how?

Now, ask and answer these questions:

- Have you experienced a person, particularly a Christian, who has been unsafe for you?
- What characteristics made this person unsafe?
- How did your experience of that person impact you?

This can be a good exercise to do with a small group of people—or with your spouse if you are married—and begin to collect a list of safe-place characteristics. It can also be a good exercise to do as a church staff and then reflect on how this list of characteristics matches up with who you are as a staff or church. Depending on what you note, it can affirm where and how you are already being a safe place, or where and how God wants to transform you so you can grow in being more like Jesus in this regard.

What did you come up with on your lists? Whatever the content, it is a start toward beginning to define what a safe place looks like. I encourage you to wrestle with and think through your own way of defining what it means. I don't believe there is going to be one right definition. Each of us might catch different aspects of what it means to be a safe place, and by writing down our own definitions and sharing them with one another we can develop a fuller picture of what it means to be a person or church that is a safe place.

UNSAFE CHARACTERISTICS

Another way to reflect on this is to consider characteristics that make us unsafe. You began to do this in the second part of the exercise on the previous page. Henry Townsend and John Cloud list the following characteristics of unsafe people in their book *Safe People*. Unsafe people:

- Think they have "it all together" instead of admitting their weaknesses
- Are religious instead of spiritual (religious = more concerned with rules and appearance than inner authenticity)
- Are defensive instead of open to feedback
- Are self-righteous instead of humble
- Only apologize instead of changing their behavior
- Avoid working on their problems instead of dealing with them
- Demand trust, instead of earning it
- Believe they are perfect instead of admitting their faults
- Blame others instead of taking responsibility
- Lie instead of telling the truth
- Are stagnant instead of growing
- Avoid closeness instead of connecting
- Are only concerned about "I" instead of "we"
- Resist freedom instead of encouraging it
- Flatter us instead of confronting us
- Condemn us instead of forgiving us
- Stay in parent/child roles instead of relating as equals
- Are unstable over time instead of being consistent
- Are a negative influence on us, rather than a positive one
- Gossip instead of keep secrets[15]

A GROWING LIST OF SAFE-PLACE CHARACTERISTICS

Following is a list of safe-place characteristics. This list is a compilation of my own study and the feedback given by people who have participated in doing the safe-place exercises you've just done. This is not meant to be an exhaustive list, so add the characteristics you thought of to this list.

Please note that I've written this inventory in alphabetical order. That is intentional. I wanted to avoid suggesting an order of priority or value

---

15 Henry Townsend and John Cloud, *Safe People* (Grand Rapids, MI: Zondervan, 1995), 27ff.

regarding these characteristics. They are all important. They are all part of what makes an individual or group a safe place.

- **Accepting.** Safe-place people accept others and are able to differentiate between acceptance and approval. They are able to unconditionally accept others while not necessarily approving of their beliefs, behaviors, or choices.
- **Allow God to bump their agenda aside.** Safe-place people are not so focused on their own agenda that they are not willing to yield when God wants to bump their agenda aside
- **Are able to enjoy life.** Safe-place people are passionate about serving the Lord while at the same time knowing how to enjoy life. They do not take themselves so seriously that they do not take time or know how to play and laugh with others.
- **Are concerned with being like Christ rather than merely presenting Christ.** Safe-place people are aware it is possible to be so busy presenting Christ to others that we can forget to be like him. Their priority is to be like Jesus with those Jesus would have been with.
- **Are willing to cross boundaries.** Safe-place people are willing to cross religious, cultural, ethnic, gender, and age boundaries, and don't allow concern about their own reputation to hinder them from crossing those boundaries.
- **Available and willing to be inconvenienced.** Safe-place people make themselves available to be with people, and are willing to be inconvenienced.
- **Avoid giving glib and easy answers, ready-made clichés.** Safe-place people seek to avoid giving people glib and easy answers, ready-made clichés, or canned speeches.
- **Avoid misinterpreting and misapplying Scriptures.** Safe-place people seek to grow in a correct understanding and application of Scripture, seeking to practice healthy exegetical practices in a context of community that can help them grow in their understandings, insights, and applications of Scripture.

- **Believe in others before others believe in themselves.** Safe-place people believe in others before others believe in themselves. They seek to call out what they see in others and create opportunities for people to grow into the best version of who they can be.
- **Compassionate.** Safe-place people exhibit the same compassion Jesus Christ had for all peoples no matter what their worldviews, religion, or lifestyle choices may be.
- **Differentiate between legalism and God's truth.** Safe-place people seek to differentiate between legalism and the truth of God's Word. They differentiate between cultural preferences and practices, and biblical exhortations and commands.
- **Discerning and wise.** Safe-place people ask God to help them grow in wisdom and discernment. They will be people who do not overreact to situations or people on the one hand, and are not naïve on the other, but will listen to what is shared with them by people and then seek God's wisdom and discernment (see Daniel 2:14).
- **Don't force God's truth on others.** Safe-place people will not shy away from sharing God's truth with others but will seek to do it in a way that does not force his truth on others.
- **Don't use spiritual language to rationalize or justify wrong belief, behavior, and practice.** Safe-place people refuse to use spiritual sounding language, even Scripture, to rationalize or justify their wrong belief, behavior, and practice.
- **Experience God's healing in their lives.** Safe-place people have experienced healing for the memories or wounds in their past that still influenced their present in unhelpful ways, and are willing to continue experiencing his healing touch in their lives as needed.
- **Experientially rooted in God's grace.** Safe-place people realize there is a difference between knowing God's grace theologically and intellectually as opposed to actually experiencing it in their own lives. God's grace is manifest in their lives in a multitude of ways.

- **Experientially rooted in God's truth.** Safe-place people seek to be experientially rooted in God's truth and do not settle for knowing it only in an academic, intellectual way. They believe that if there is a difference between God's truth and their life experiences, it is their lives, not God's Word that needs to be changed.
- **Faithful in the fundamentals.** Safe-place people seek to be faithful in practicing the fundamentals of the Christian faith.
- **Forgiveness of sin and healing for shame.** Safe-place people believe we need both forgiveness of sin and healing for shame, and that Jesus died to provide both.
- **Forgiving.** Safe-place people have experienced the power of God's forgiveness in their own lives and seek to forgive others. They do not force a premature process of forgiveness on themselves or others just for the sake of saying they have forgiven some one. On the other hand they refuse to stay stuck in the moment of unforgiveness and seek whatever help they need to experience and then share with others God's gift of forgiveness.
- **Free from toxic shame.** Safe-place people realize there is a shame that is toxic to healthy living and have been set free from this shame by God's love, power, grace, and joy in their lives. They refuse to be shamed, and they do not shame others.
- **Full of both grace and truth.** Safe-place people seek to bring God's healing combination of grace and truth to bear on people's lives.
- **Good listener.** Safe-place people are engaged and attentive when listening, not thinking of how they want to respond, nor do they interrupt. They listen, ask more questions, and then listen some more.
- **Grateful.** Safe-place people seek to practice living with a grateful heart toward God and others (see Luke 17:11–19).
- **Growing in wholeness.** Safe-place people intentionally seek to grow in emotional, relational, and spiritual wholeness.
- **Honor.** Safe-place people seek to create an atmosphere of honoring others, particularly the spiritual mothers and fathers of their faith, and the servant-leaders in their communities.

- **Humble.** Safe-place people seek to walk and live in humility (see Luke 17:7–10; Proverbs 11:2)). They refuse to live in a self-righteous, holier-than-thou, or self-promoting manner. They resist any temptation to be prideful in a sinful manner, or think themselves to be better than others.
- **Joy-filled.** Safe-place people are characterized by joy. They are the antithesis of the negative, sourpuss Christian stereotype.
- **Know God delights in them.** Safe-place people know God delights in them, not just that he loves them. They know they are the twinkle in his eyes.
- **Know God works through them even when they don't deserve it.** Safe-place people know God works through them even when they don't deserve him to. They know they are not only saved by grace, but that they serve and minister by God's grace as well.
- **Know how to celebrate and party.** Safe-place people know how to celebrate and party. Many of the festivals and holy days in the Old Testaments were opportunities for God's people to celebrate. God actually built celebration and parties into Israel's calendar. The story of the prodigal son concludes with a celebration, a party (Luke 15:31, NLT). Safe-place people know how to party in healthy ways.
- **Know how to laugh.** Safe-place people know how to laugh and have fun. They don't take themselves so seriously that they are unable to laugh at themselves; and they know how to laugh with but not at other people. They can even imagine Jesus laughing at certain situations in life, at himself, and even with, but not at them.
- **Know how to rest and relax.** Safe-place people know how to rest and relax. They work out of a place of rest rather than working hard to rest. They are intentional to build in various times and places for rest into their schedules, and encourage and help others to do the same.
- **Live authentic emotional lives.** Safe-place people seek to be emotionally authentic while not using that as an excuse to misbehave. They seek to be healed emotionally when and where God shows them they need growth and healing.

- **Love and value people.** Safe-place people love and value others, no matter what some of their lifestyle choices, worldviews, or belief systems are, simply because they have been made in the image of God. They love and value people whether or not they ever become Christians.
- **Make it a safe place to risk failing.** Safe-place people make it a safe place to risk failing. They help people celebrate when they take Holy Spirit-led risks, even though they may fail. They help others process and learn from failures, reminding them that they themselves are not failures.
- **Make people feel included and like they belong.** Safe-place people seek to create an atmosphere where people are included and feel like they belong even before they believe.
- **Make room for disappointment with God.** Safe-place people make room for disappointment with God in people's lives, and give people the freedom to give voice to that disappointment in any way they feel the need to (see Psalm 44:23–26).
- **Make room for uncertainty and doubt.** Safe-place people recognize that having the freedom to express uncertainty and doubt is important in our relationships with others who no longer automatically view traditional figures and sources of authority as valid. They recognize that in a culture characterized by so much skepticism and cynicism, making room for an authentic expression of uncertainty and doubt is an essential part of making Christian individuals and congregations a safe place.
- **Make room for differing opinions on theology.** Safe-place people seek to create a safe place for authentic dialogue regarding differing opinions on theology.
- **Minister to the needs behind people's behaviors.** Safe-place people minister to the needs behind and beneath people's behaviors. While acknowledging that those behaviors are not unimportant, they will seek to identify and minister to needs that influence and drive those behaviors.
- **Model appropriate transparency and vulnerability.** Safe-place people model both transparency and vulnerability but seek to be wise about when and with whom they do this.

- **Not judgmental and condemning.** Safe-place people are not judgmental or condemning. They refuse to get their own sense of worth or significance by judging and condemning others.
- **Practice authentic caring.** Safe-place people seek to authentically care for people, whether or not they ever come to believe in Jesus as Savior and Lord. They refuse to be viewed or experienced as spiritual sales people or spiritual headhunters.
- **Refuse gossip.** Safe-place people refuse to spread gossip about other people or organizations (see Proverbs 11:13).
- **Refuse to spread bad reports.** Safe-place people refuse to mis-diagnose situations or give into fear and then spread bad reports that will deprive people of the wisdom and courage needed to make decisions and follow the Lord's leading.
- **Refuse indiscriminate tolerance and relative truth.** Safe-place people do not agree with the practice of indiscriminate toler-ance and belief in relative truth. While understanding postmodern culture places a high value on both tolerance and relative truth, safe-place people believe there is a time and a place to be intolerant and that there is truth that is absolute.
- **Resist offering grace-less, shame-filled truth.** Safe-place peo-ple are aware you can offer truth in a grace-less, shame-filled man-ner, and resist doing that.
- **Refuse to settle for being religious.** Safe-place people refuse to settle for being religious. They choose to be more concerned with true, inner authenticity than be influenced and concerned with keep-ing rules and outward appearances.
- **Seek to create a safe place for authentic dialogue.** Safe-place people seek to talk with others, not at them. They create a space where people are free to discuss, question, doubt, and explore faith at their own pace.
- **Seek to recognize the true enemy.** Safe-place people refuse to identify or treat other people as they enemy. They recognize that all of humankind shares one true enemy, the devil.

- **Settled sense of identity.** Safe-place people are comfortable in their own skin because they live out of a settled sense of identity rather than working hard and striving to have a sense of being loved and affirmed, of being a person of worth and significance. They do not need the prestige of positions or titles, nor do they need to self-promote in order to meet those needs.
- **Speak truth from a shared position of brokenness and healing.** Safe-place people refuse to share truth in a holier than thou attitude. They share truth from their own position of brokenness and healing
- **Tear down strongholds.** Safe-place people are intentional about tearing down strongholds in their own lives and in the lives of others. They refuse to continue believing lies to be truth, and refuse to run to those lies in order to medicate their pain or feel a sense of security.
- **Trust God and refuse the urge to fix others.** Safe-place people trust that God cares more for people than they do, that he is active in their lives (sometimes behind the scenes), and they refuse believing it is their responsibility to fix others.
- **Unconditional love.** Safe-place people seek to love others unconditionally and extravagantly just as they have been loved.
- **Understand and respect confidentiality.** Safe-place people are able to be trusted with matters of the heart and behavior. They will keep whatever is shared with them confidential except in matters that involve someone doing harm to themselves or others (see Proverbs 11:13).
- **Value intellect, study, and learning.** Safe-place people do not ask others, or themselves, to check their brains at the door. They value intellect as a gift given by God, and make the effort to be good stewards of that gift through study and learning, learning in the classroom, in life, and in their relationships with others.
- **Welcome and receive truth-tellers.** Safe-place people welcome and receive truth-tellers in their lives, even when it stings. They welcome feedback and refuse to be defensive.

- **Willing to stand and fight.** Safe-place people are willing to stand and fight when necessary, believing there are things worth fighting for. They especially stand and fight in prayer, contending for the purposes of God in their own lives and in the lives of others.

DEVELOPING A SAFE-PLACE ACTION PLAN

Before reading further, take a few moments to identify two safe-place characteristics that you would like to grow in this year. List those characteristics below:

1.
2.

Now select the one you would most like to grow in. Then, use the following template to develop an action plan that can help you be intentional to follow through in your desire to become more like Jesus.

- If I had to pick one of these to grow in more this year it would be

  _____.

- Actions I can take to position myself before God so he can help me grow in my desire to be a safe place for others include:

  1. Seek God's guidance in prayer

  2.

  3.

  4.

  5.

Some examples of action steps you can take include:

- Reading a book on the characteristic you would like to grow in
- Sharing your action plan with a mentor or spouse and ask them to pray for you and check on your progress from time to time
- Listen to teaching CDs about this characteristic
- Get to know someone who manifests this characteristic, interview them, and spend time with them
- Seek counseling, inner healing prayer, or spiritual direction

These are only a few examples of action steps you can take. You can think of more on your own, or ask a trusted, mature Christian to help you brainstorm other steps for your plan.

In prayer, ask God to provide everything and everyone needed to help effect those changes in your life this year.

WORKING TOWARD A DEFINITION OF BEING A SAFE PLACE

As I have spent time in God's Word and in prayer reflecting on what it means to be a safe place, I've developed some working definitions that have been helpful for me. They are:

- Being a safe place is learning from the life of Jesus, how to most effectively relate to people so they will have the opportunity to be impacted by the love and power of God
- Being a safe place is about being like Jesus with those Jesus would have been with
- Being a safe place is a relationship, or community of relationships, that intentionally creates an emotional, relational, and spiritual atmosphere of freedom for the purpose of transformation, a transformation more and more into the image of Jesus Christ so we increasingly think, speak, and act more like Jesus

- Being a safe place is learning when and how to protect others from my strengths

What do you think of these definitions? What aspects of them do you like and agree with? What aspects raise questions for you? Share them with your spouse or those you've invited into your safe-place journey. Discuss them. Pray about them. See what the Lord may say to you through them. Then, take a stab at writing your own definition of what it means to be a safe place in the space below:

Following are some quotes that could also serve as definitions for what it means to be a safe place:

Oh the comfort, the inexpressible comfort of feeling safe with a person; having neither to weigh thoughts nor measure words, but to pour them all out, just as they are, chaff and grain together, knowing that a faithful hand will take and sift them, keep what is worth keeping, and then, with the breath of kindness, blow the rest away.[16]

A friend is a person with whom you dare to be yourself; your soul can be naked with him. He seems to ask you to put on nothing, only to be what you are. He doesn't want you to be better or worse. When you are with him you feel as a prisoner feels when he is declared innocent. You do not have to be on your guard. You can say what you think, so long as it's genuinely you. He understands those contradictions in your nature that lead others to midjudge you. With him you breathe freely. You can avow your little vanities and indecent hates, your meanness and absurdities and in opening them up to him they are lost, dissolved in the white ocean of his loyalty. He understands.

---

16 Dinah Craik, *A Life for a Life* (Goucestershire, United Kingdom: Dodo Press, 2008), 184.

You do not have to be careful . . . He likes you. He is like fire that purges to the bone. He understands.[17]

Before we go on to explore more of what it means to be a safe place for the dangerous kind, it is important to clarify what the word "safe" means. That will be the focus of the next chapter. Then in the chapters that follow that we will identify two more reasons that make growing in being a safe place an essential key for Christians who want to increase their effectiveness in living lives of witness in the world, and developing healthy disciples and leaders in the church. Those reasons are:

1. Being a safe place will make us more effective by incarnationally tearing down the negative stereotypes people possess of followers of Christ, stereotypes that hinder people receiving the good news God offers them.
2. Being a safe place will make us more effective by helping us create an atmosphere that is a safe place for growth and transformation.

---

17 C. Raymond Brean in Bruce Larson, *The Preacher's Commentary, Volume 26: Luke* (Nashville, TN: Thomas Nelson Publishers, 1983), Kindle ed.

7

CLARIFYING WHAT "SAFE" MEANS

"Is he—quite safe?" "Safe?" says Mr. Beaver. "Course he isn't safe.
But he's good."

— C. S. LEWIS
The Lion, The Witch, and The Wardrobe

GOD IS GOOD, but he's not safe. This is Mr. Beaver's reply when Lucy asks if Aslan the Lion is safe in the C. S. Lewis classic *The Lion, The Witch, and the Wardrobe*. Many people agree with his assertion. I disagree. I believe God is both. He is most certainly good and he is also most certainly safe.

Lucy's question is one that continues to reverberate in the hearts and minds of people throughout the world today. And it's not just God's nature that is being doubted. The character of his followers and their churches are being questioned too. Are Christians safe people? Can a church be a safe place? The answer for many is obvious: "Of course God isn't safe, and neither are those who claim to follow him nor the places where they gather to worship."

Is God safe? Can individual Christians be safe people? Can a church be a safe place? How we answer these questions will determine to a great extent whether people will be drawn to God and the claims of Christianity, or driven further away. And the key in responding to these doubts will depend upon our definition and application of the word safe.

UNDERSTANDING OUR DEFINITION IS KEY

The way we understand and use a particular word can dramatically alter how others hear it and experience it. "Did you ever wear thongs," asked one of my sixty-something golf partners. The four of us had been working our way around the golf course, talking of life in the 1960s between shots. We reminisced about hairstyles, clothes we wore, music we listened to (and still listen to), political turmoil, coming of age, and girls. As we hit one errant golf shot after another, we carried each other back to life as teenagers. "Did you ever wear thongs?" asked one of the guys again. We were dumbstruck. All the air went out of our conversation. Finally, another guy in our group muttered, "Thongs? At our age why would any of us even think of wearing a thong?" "Not *a* thong," said our friend, "Thongs. You know, like sandals. Remember when we called sandals thongs?"

The way someone defines and uses a particular word often determines whether or not you can agree with them. For instance, Mark Buchanan has written an excellent book entitled *Your Church Is Too Safe: Why Following Christ Turns the World Upside Down.* He asserts that Christians and churches can be *too* safe. You might think that I would categorically disagree with Buchanan. But I don't because I understand how he's using the word safe—and I agree with his definition and application. In his introduction he writes,

> There's an enormous gap between the life Jesus offered and the life we're living. We feel it. We see it. We sense that whatever else Jesus came preaching, *this* can't be what he had in mind: a roomful of people nodding to old platitudes, nodding off to old lullabies, perking up to Jonah-like rants, jumping up to split hairs or break company at

the smallest provocation. When did we start making it our priority to be safe instead of dangerous, nice instead of holy, cautious instead of bold, self-absorbed instead of counting everything loss in order to be found in Christ?[18]

I could not agree with Mark Buchanan more. His writing challenges a way of living that is in fact *too* safe because people are playing it safe. His use of this word is not at odds with how I am using it in this book. Being a safe place does not mean playing it safe. They are two completely different things. There is a significant distinction between what Buchanan and I are writing about, and that distinction is rooted in our definitions and applications of our key word—safe.

ANOTHER WAY TO DEFINE AND UNDERSTAND SAFE

There is a way to define and understand the word *safe* that is essential in the discussion about being transformed and empowered to live as Christ-followers who do in fact turn the world upside down. *Merriam-Webster's Dictionary* defines safe as: 1) secure from liability to harm, injury, danger, or risk; 2) free from hurt, injury, danger, or risk; 3) involving little or no risk of mishap, error; 4) careful to avoid danger or controversy; or 5) dependable or trustworthy.[19] The last of Merriam-Webster's definitions is the only one that can be applied to God when we say that he is our safe place. Therefore, it is the definition I am using in this book.

If we understand the word safe to mean "dependable or trustworthy," then the answer to Lucy is that God is most certainly good *and* he is most certainly safe because we can always depend upon and trust him:

- To unconditionally love and accept us

---

18   Mark Buchanan, *Your Church Is Too Safe: Why Following Christ Turns the World Upside Down* (Grand Rapids, MI: Zondervan, 2012), Kindle ed.

19   www.merriam-webster.com/dictionary/safe.

- To tell us the truth and upset our lives when necessary
- To convict us, but not condemn us, when we need it
- To set healthy boundaries for our lives
- To believe in us before we believe in ourselves
- To forgive us when other people are struggling to forgive us
- To hang in there with us when everyone else has turned and walked away
- To transform and use people we never would (thus, Saul becomes Paul)
- To guide and empower us in taking Holy Spirit-led risks
- To be a safe place for us when we fail

BEING AND FEELING ARE NOT THE SAME THING

God is good and he is safe. However, that does not mean he will always *feel* safe to all people at all times. It's important we realize that a person or place that is safe will not always *feel* safe. This injects a dialectical tension into our discussion. Dialectical tension is a literary tool that does not exclude or water down what seem to be contradictory statements in order to reach a shallow agreement. It allows, even forces, people to struggle and think through seemingly contrary beliefs in order to grasp and understand a fuller expression of truth. Examples of this tool rooted in Scripture are discussions regarding the nature of the Trinity and what it means to be in the world but not of it. In our case dialectical tension causes us to wrestle with a very important reality—a safe-place people will not always feel safe, even though they really are.

We see this paradox illustrated in an episode of the television show M.A.S.H. when Dr. Hawkeye Pierce encounters a wounded North Korean solider. Pierce, a doctor whose heart is full of compassion for all people and who is opposed to the war, has only one thing in mind as he encounters the soldier—to provide medical care. When Pierce draws near, the soldier—who cannot speak English, while Pierce cannot speak Korean—points his rifle at the doctor. The man is afraid. He does not feel safe. He thinks Pierce wants to hurt him.

Why did Hawkeye not feel safe to the wounded North Korean? Because there was no context of relationship to help the soldier understand Pierce's true intent. The lack of a relational context, along with other factors, can cause a safe-place person or community to feel unsafe to the very people they are actually being a safe place for.

WHY A SAFE-PLACE PEOPLE DON'T ALWAYS FEEL SAFE

There are many reasons a safe-place people may not always feel that way to others. To begin with, they will not feel safe for those who believe love always feels warm and fuzzy. It doesn't. Love sets healthy boundaries and that does not always feel compassionate even though it is in fact an expression of compassion. For example, my wife and I set boundaries for our children when they were younger because we loved them. We wanted to protect them from harm. So we told them things like, "Don't touch the top of a hot stove" and "Don't run out into the street" and "Don't bite your brother." These were expressions of love and concern on our part, but our kids didn't always understand that. When we set boundaries for them, even in the most loving of ways, we didn't always feel safe to them.

A safe place will not feel that way for those who only want to play it safe. Being a safe-place person or congregation does not mean we avoid taking risks. In fact, it involves doing that very thing. It is always a risk to love someone, especially those who are challenging to love. It is always a risk to leave someplace where you're comfortable out of obedience to God and move on to a place that's an unknown to you. It can be a risk to continue having faith that God will answer a prayer and keep his promise after experiencing one year after another of no fulfillment. And it is a risk for some people to finally allow God to touch and heal that place of pain and woundedness they've held on to for so long. Being a safe place is not about playing it safe. It does in fact involve taking Holy Spirit-led risks.

A safe place will not feel safe to those who only want to maintain the status quo. This is an issue many people in every generation wrestle with. At one time they were the ones willing to count the cost and take the risks required to usher in needed change. Then, as the years go by they're tempted to give in and become the part of the group that is willing to settle for protecting the status quo. They may even begin to view younger generations as being restless and unwise, as immature and impatient—the same way they were viewed by the generations who preceded them. People who have slipped into protecting the status quo, even when Holy Spirit-led change is being called for, will not view or feel those calling for that change to be a safe place.

A safe-place people may not feel safe to those who are unwilling to deal with spiritual- and character-formation issues in their lives. We won't always feel safe to someone as we try to help them understand that there may be pain in their past that is influencing their present in unhelpful and even unhealthy ways. Even when truth is brought in the most grace-filled ways it can still sting, and when it does, the bearers of that grace-filled truth will not feel safe.

A safe-place people will not feel safe to those who want to protect position, prestige, and power. We see this in Luke 11:38–48 when Jesus tells the Pharisees, "You love to sit in the seats of honor in the synagogues and receive respectful greetings as you walk in the marketplaces." Jesus had come to save, not condemn, the world, but the Pharisees were more interested in protecting their positions, prestige, and power than acknowledging the Messiah had finally come. To them, Jesus, who was full of grace and truth (John 1:14), did not feel safe.

And most especially, a safe-place people will not feel safe to those who live in bondage to fear or shame. When Jesus meets the woman at the well in John 4, it is very likely he did not initially feel safe to her, even though he was safe. It would have been understandable if she initially felt some fear when this Jewish man (not culturally acceptable on both counts) takes time to sit and initiate a conversation with her, a Samaritan woman (see John 4:1–9). It would have been understandable if Jesus initially feels unsafe for her when he mentions her sexual history and current living situation (see John 4:15–18). This conversation may have immediately hooked on a toxic sense of shame within her. Even though Jesus' intent was to bring his healing combination of grace and truth to bear on her life, it is likely he didn't feel safe when they first met.

PEOPLE MAY STILL GET HURT

It is important we be aware of the fact that even though our heart's intent is to become more safe for others, people may still get hurt. They will get hurt because in the process of growing in what it means to be a safe place we will fail. We will still have moments when we're unsafe toward one another. We are works in progress. The good news is that even in these instances God can work for good in our lives. If we humble ourselves before the Lord and one another, confess our sin and ask for forgiveness, our moments of failure can become times of transformation. Those moments can become places where God teaches us more about being a safe place.

I more than anyone am aware of how miserably I have failed at being a safe place so many times for my family, my teammates in ministry, and in relationships with people in the world. My continuing journey is reflected in author Leonard Sweet's reflections. He writes,

> In my attempt to live a life of superlatives, not merely positives, I blow it more often that I make it. All my life I will struggle with unworthy, unsanctified thoughts, unholy behavior, and a splintery self. Without mentors and masked angels who routinely apply swift kicks to my soul's backside, [those who know me] would have been still more disappointed.[20]

---

20 Leonard Sweet, *Soul Salsa: 17 Surprising Steps for Godly Living in the 21st Century* (Grand Rapids, MI: Zondervan Publishing, 2000), 13.

Being a safe-place people will never be a completed work this side of heaven. It is a process, journey, and adventure that will continue until we go home to heaven. It is a maturing heart's intent.

NOT ALL-INCLUSIVE

The safe place-dangerous kind metaphor is not meant to be an all-inclusive description of who God is, or of what he wants the bride of Christ to be. No one metaphor alone can describe either. The majesty and awesomeness of the Living God is too large to be summed up in one word or phrase. The beauty of the bride of Christ is too multifaceted to be captured in a single word picture. It is my hope and prayer that God can use this metaphor to arrest our attention and transform our lives so that we increasingly think, speak, and act more like Jesus.

Being a safe place for the dangerous kind is not meant to be something we only study or write about. It is not something to be theologized about and discussed over a good cup of coffee or tea. It is a reality to be lived. As Brian McLaren writes,

> In the . . . church on the other side, our words will not stand alone. Our message will be a life: words plus deeds. Words of faith without works of love will not survive; no one will listen . . . Was it St. Francis who reputedly said to his young trainees, "Everywhere you go, preach the gospel, and when it is absolutely necessary use words?" . . . Words of truth will not be less important, but they will seek to be servants of mystery, not removers of it as they were in the old world.[21]

He goes on to say, "Believers telling their neighbors the good news will still use words, and with great care. But they will know that their words must be

---

21 Brian McLaren, *The Church on the Other Side* (Grand Rapids, MI: Zondervan, 2000), 88–90.

the tip of the iceberg, buoyed by a life lived well with laughter, love, compassion, and generosity."[22] I agree.

There are two more reasons that make rediscovering what it means to be a safe place essential for Christians living in a postmodern and post-Christian context. We will address them in the following chapters: Tearing down negative stereotypes and creating a safe place for growth and transformation.

---

22 Ibid., 90.

8

TEARING DOWN THE
NEGATIVE STEREOTYPE

*The negative stereotype of Christians will not be torn down through
debate or reason alone, if at all. It will only be torn down one
relationship, one heart at a time through encounters with followers
of Christ are who are safe.*

A N INCREASING NUMBER of people are embracing the stereotype that
Christians are arrogant and angry, judgmental and condemning people.
Consider the following quotes:

> Most people I meet assume that "Christian" means very conserva-
> tive, entrenched in their thinking, antigay, anti-choice, angry, vio-
> lent, illogical, empire builders; they want to convert everyone, and
> they generally cannot live peacefully with anyone who doesn't believe
> what they believe.[23]

---

23 Kinnaman and Lyons, *unChristian*, 26.

I'd listen to a Christian if I thought they *really* cared, I mean really cared about me as a person, not just some other notch on their Christian belt or something. Whenever I've talked to Christians I feel like the only thing they're concerned with is telling me what they know, just talking at me, not to me, or letting me talk to them [emphasis mine].[24]

A Chicago prostitute was unable to buy food for her two-year-old daughter. When her friend asked if she had ever thought of going to a church for help, she cried, "Church! Why would I ever go there? I was already feeling terrible about myself. They'd just make me feel worse![25]

While these quotes sting, we cannot deny their reality, nor can we deny the power they have in influencing what people believe it means to be a Christian. The negative stereotype of Christians will not be torn down through debate or reason alone, if at all. It will only be torn down one relationship, one heart at a time through encounters with followers of Christ are who are safe.

WHAT ARE PEOPLE STUMBLING OVER?

When someone holds a negative stereotype of Christianity, that stereotype, rather than the claims of the gospel, is often what they have difficulty with. 1 Peter 2:5–8 says,

And you are living stones that God is building into his spiritual temple. What's more, you are his holy priests. Through the mediation of Jesus Christ, you offer spiritual sacrifices that please God. As the Scriptures say, "I am placing a cornerstone in Jerusalem, chosen for great honor, and anyone who trusts in him will never be disgraced."

---

24 Philip Yancey, *What's So Amazing About Grace?* (Grand Rapids, MI: Zondervan, 1997), Kindle ed.

25 Ibid.

Yes, you who trust him recognize the honor God has given him. But for those who reject him, "The stone that the builders rejected has now become the cornerstone." And, "He is *the stone that makes people stumble*, the rock that makes them fall." They stumble because they do not obey God's word, and so they meet the fate that was planned for them [emphasis mine, NLT].

In a postmodern culture, it's to be expected that people will stumble over any claim of truth based upon a holy book, even if that holy book is the Bible. Postmodernity embraces the philosophy that truth is relative and subjective. It no longer accepts modernity's view of truth as being absolute and objective.[26] Furthermore, it recognizes the individual's right to determine what is or is not true rather than demanding trust in an outside source of authority. Thus, it is no surprise when people stumble over a presentation of truth based upon the Bible.

Stumbling over the truth claims of Christianity is understandable. However, it is completely unacceptable when that which people stumble over is who we are as persons. As followers of Christ we cannot control the former, but we can do something about the latter. We can call all Christians around the world to embrace the safe-place vision and join together in being transformed to think, speak, and act more like Jesus. Where we embrace that vision and are intentional in seeing it actualized in our lives we will then be able to begin tearing down the negative Christian stereotype one relationship at a time.

TURNING TOWARD OTHER SOURCES OF SPIRITUALITY

Experiences with Christians behaving badly influence people to turn to other sources of spirituality to satisfy their hunger for something real and transcendent. And make no mistake about it, more people are spiritually hungry

---

26 The modern era encompassed the years from the Enlightenment through the mid-1960s.

and thirsty than we think. They're just not viewing Christianity as the place where those longings can be satisfied. Consider the following:

> Many people want to talk about God, but not just anybody is safe to talk to. I remember in high school, a new Christian myself, hearing that Monica had become a Christian over Easter vacation. This surprised me, as Monica was a beautiful and popular cheerleader with a reputation of hanging out with a pretty wild crowd. But rumor had it that she had visited relatives over Easter and had "gotten saved." I sought her out and cautiously asked her if the rumors were true. They were, she assured me, and told me "everyone" knew I was a Christian and so she was looking forward to getting to know me and having me introduce her to some other Christians. Then she told me something that I didn't expect to hear. "You know, the whole crowd I hang out with, all of them are thinking about God. A lot of times even when we're drinking or getting high, we talk all night about God and our beliefs and our doubts and stuff."
>
> Now years later, I wonder why none of them felt safe coming to me, since "everyone" knew I was a Christian. I think they sensed and they were probably right back then—that if they approached me, I would push too hard and not give them space. I wouldn't have been a spiritual friend, but rather a spiritual salesman.[27]

Is it fair to base one's understanding of what it means to be a Christian on a single person who comes off as more of a spiritual salesman than a spiritual friend? Of course not, but it's precisely what happens far too often. This is how stereotypes are born and grow in strength. People often don't take the time or effort to discern between the bad examples of a small sample group within a much larger group. They simply look at that small sample and conclude that this is what the entire people group is like.

---

27   Brian D. McLaren, *More Ready Than You Realize: Evangelism as Dance in the Postmodern Matrix* (Grand Rapids, MI: Zondervan, 2002), 38–39.

Does a single encounter with an individual or small group of misbehaving Christians accurately represent the Christian faith? No. For every arrogant Christian there are a hundred who are joyfully and humbly helping to send shipments of food and medical supplies to areas of the world unable to afford them. For every Christian who seems angry, there are a hundred loving and serving the poor and homeless. For every small group of Christians who are judgmental there are one hundred onsite helping to dig clean water wells, and build and staff schools and hospitals where there are none, whether or not the people in need are Christian. For every supposed follower of Christ who is condemning there are one hundred onsite helping those in need in the wake of a tsunami, hurricane, earthquake, or some other natural disaster with no hint of condemnation in their attitudes, only unconditional love and compassion.

The growing negative stereotype of what it means to be a Christian does not truly represent what it means to live life as a follower of Christ. Unfortunately, we live in a culture where the bad news gets more attention than the good. It is the few Christians behaving in a manner that is unsafe who continue to give life to the negative perception of what it means to be a follower of Jesus.

Unfortunately, we all can have moments in which we manifest one or more unsafe characteristics. I know I have. But even those moments can be turned into something positive if we will humble ourselves, confess our failure and sin, and ask for forgiveness from those we have offended and hurt. When we adopt this posture, moments that seemed to be failures become places of maturation as we learn more about ourselves, and experience God's transforming work in our lives.

CHRISTIANS EMBRACE THE STEREOTYPE TOO

It is not only non-Christians who hold a negative stereotype of what it means to be a follower of Christ. A growing number of Christians do too and, at times, understandably so. It is a sad and unfortunate reality that there are times when Christians are unsafe for one another, which in turn feeds the negative stereotype. I remember just such a moment when an entire room full of Christian teenagers were left with a bad taste in their metaphorical mouths about what it means to be a Christ-follower, not because of the claims of our faith, but because of the unsafe behavior of a person in authority.

As a young youth pastor I was invited to speak at the chapel service for a Christian high school in our community. I was not only a youth pastor at a local church, but had just begun serving as the assistant basketball coach for the girls and boys basketball teams at this school. In that capacity I had begun developing positive relationships with many of the teens in the school, including some who had no involvement in sports whatsoever. My position as basketball coach was a gateway into the lives of these kids, and I counted it a great privilege and responsibility.

Then came the day when I was asked to speak at the school's weekly chapel service. I prayed and prepared for weeks. There I was, finally sitting beside the stage, waiting to share a message I believed God had given me specifically for these senior high teens. I was excited and nervous at the same time. As I sought to calm my emotions I was taken aback as the principal suddenly began rebuking and shaming the students for not having brought their Bibles with them. He'd asked them to lift up their Bibles and when only a handful did, he verbally assaulted the entire group. As he criticized and condemned the teens, shoulders began to sag and heads drooped. The emotional and spiritual wind was knocked out of these kids before my eyes.

"What am I going to do?" I thought to myself. "How am I going to get these kids to re-engage after that?" The principal introduced me and I walked up on stage. As I moved behind the podium, all I could think of was *Wayne's World*, a recently released movie at the time, featuring Mike Meyers, a cast member of Saturday Night Live. It was a comedy spoof of two zany friends who hosted a local cable television show. Standing behind the podium I looked out over the crowd of disheartened students. My gaze moved toward the back wall of the gymnasium where the chapel service was held. There stood the principal and the teachers, all with arms crossed. "I'm sorry, Mr. Thomas" (the school principle, but not his real name), I said. "I didn't know we were supposed to bring our Bibles today [mine was hiding on a shelf built into the podium]. I just thought we'd take time to reflect on the theological ramifications of *Wayne's World*."

The students broke into laughter. Heads came up. Shoulders straightened. Mr. Thomas and the teachers, however, did not laugh. Noting their angry countenances, I wisely chose to move on. "Well, you know what," I told the crowd, "I did remember to bring my Bible after all. Here it is." Reaching down, I grabbed it off the shelf, held it in the air, and said, "Let me read from Luke chapter four." I went on with the teaching I'd prepared for the day, the students hanging on my every word—or so I remember.

Looking back, that day actually deepened my relationships with many of those kids, and those relationships went on to bear much fruit for God's purposes in their lives. Over the next few years a number of the teens, athletes and non-athletes alike, would seek me out to talk. Many of them confided and trusted in me. We were often able to pray together and watch God work in their lives. Without consciously realizing it (me or them), they had already begun to identify me as a safe place.

The principal and teachers were not bad people. In fact, they were good people in many ways, and some good things happened at the school over the years. But how much more could have happened for good had a cloud of toxic shame not enveloped the school? How many students left the school wounded by caustic comments and uncaring attitudes? How many of them left weighed down by the long list of rules they had to keep in order to be "okay with God"? How many of them missed out on what the Lord could have done in their lives had the school's atmosphere been more safe rather than unsafe?

THE POWER OF DISCOVERING A SAFE PLACE

In March 2005, I was in Finland, staying with my hosts and friends, Pastor Timo and Dr. Maarit Aro-Henila. They shared a story with me about a woman impacted by God in an evening worship service because she sensed something different about Timo and Maarit. This woman, unbeknownst to them, had come that night with the perception that Christians were unsafe and not to be trusted. At the end of the evening she and her husband of just a few months approached Timo and Maarit. The couple wanted them to pray a blessing on their marriage. As the woman cautiously presented her request, Maarit sensed there was something else she was longing to share but was afraid to do so. She took a risk and asked the woman if there was anything more she wanted to tell her.

The woman began to cry. This is was her second marriage, she shared, and she was concerned that her sin from the first marriage would keep she and her new husband from being blessed by God. She told Timo and Maarit this had been weighing heavily on her heart and she hadn't dared share it with any other Christian because she was afraid they would simply judge, scold, and lecture her about her divorce in the previous marriage. But during the worship service she had sensed Timo and Maarit were different. There was something about them that drew her forward and gave her the courage to risk sharing the fear that had been holding her heart captive. There was something about them that influenced the woman to risk trusting again.

What the woman encountered in Timo and Maarit that evening was neither judgment nor condemnation. They did not judge, scold, or lecture her. Instead, they listened with the compassion of Christ. They grieved with the woman over how she had been treated by other Christians, including her first husband. In the end, Timo and Maarit were able to lead her in prayers of repentance and forgiveness for the sin she had confessed and for a fresh filling of the Holy Spirit. The cloud of toxic shame on her life was burned away and she was set free to receive more of what her Heavenly Father had for her. Then Timo and Maarit had the joy of declaring a blessing over this couple and their marriage in Jesus' powerful name.

This Christian woman's negative stereotype of who other Christians are and how they would respond toward her was torn down that night through this incarnational, life-on-life encounter with two safe-place Christians. There was something she sensed in the atmosphere that night. There was something in the air that gave her hope and courage to step out, be vulnerable, and experience God's healing and transforming work. This is the power and effect of being a safe place at work: people are healed, set free, and their capacity to receive more of what God has for them is increased.

BAD NEWS GETS THE PRESS

It's unfortunate that a year rarely goes by when some public event reinforces this negative stereotype of what it means to be Christian. A few years ago, *USA Today* carried a headline in which it quoted a well-known Christian celebrity calling for the assassination of a South American leader. Following 9/11, another influential Christian leader publicly declared that this had happened because there were homosexuals in the World Trade Towers. A few notable Christians publicly proclaimed the reason Hurricane Katrina hit New Orleans was because it was decadent and filled with sinners. Year after year names are added to the litany of fallen Christian leaders, both Catholic priests and Protestant pastors. On a regular basis they seem to make the headlines, often caught in some behavior they themselves had publicly preached against as sin. These kinds of things simply confirm for many people that Christians truly are arrogant and angry, judgmental and condemning.

Some years ago this negative stereotype was publicly reinforced through a heartbreaking event in Wyoming. I remember it because it happened on my birthday. Debi and I and our five children lived in Rapid City, South Dakota, at the time. We were sitting in our family room one evening watching a local news show. The city's news stations had all dispatched crews to cover the event. Including the nearby air force base, Rapid City was at that time a community of some 70,000 people. While not large in comparison to other cities, this made it the center of that geographical area. This meant if any newsworthy event happened anywhere in that region, television crews from Rapid City would cover it.

So there I sat in our family room, watching the news. I was horrified as I heard the breaking story—a young man had been murdered in Wyoming. The reason? Reportedly, it was because he was gay. I could not believe it. The life of a human being had been savagely beaten out of him simply because he was homosexual. How could one human being do that to another?

That wasn't the end of the story, however. A few days later I was sickened in my heart as I watched the coverage of the young man's funeral. By now all the national news outlets had arrived to cover the story. Cameras focused on the sidewalk leading into the church where the funeral service would be held. People packed both sides of the walkway. Many were yelling and holding up signs. Signs like, "God hates fags," "Turn or burn," and "He got what he deserved." My heart broke for this young man's family and friends who had to walk through all of this on their way to the funeral service for their son, relative, and friend.

And my heart broke for the body of Christ. Yet again we were being publicly painted as arrogant and angry, judgmental and condemning people. Who knows if those holding the signs and spewing hateful words at the processional were really Christians? They may have just been religious. Being religious and being Christian are two different things. Whether they were or weren't Christians, however, was unimportant. What was important to me was that in the minds of men and women who were watching the national news coverage, those who held the disgusting signs were Christians. The negative stereotype was once again given life and reinforced.

IT'S TIME TO TAKE CHRISTIANITY BACK

Even as I'm working on this book another example of Christians behaving badly has come to my attention. My friend, Greg Boyd, asked if I would read the manuscript for a new book he's writing. In the book, he recounts an infamous interview between radio host Alan Colmes and a former vice president of the Southern Baptist Convention. What Boyd writes of this interview grieves my heart:

> At one point in this interview, Drake admitted that he regularly prayed for the death of President Obama, whom he referred to as "the usurper that is in the White House." Shocked by this admission, Colmes several times asked Drake to clarify himself. Each time Drake emphatically reiterated that he regularly asked God to smite Obama down. When the incredulous Colmes inquired how a Christian pastor could pray such a hateful thing, Wiley proudly responded that it

is because he "believes the whole Bible," including its imprecatory prayers.[28]

Is it any wonder this negative stereotype of what it means to be a Christian is so often accepted as fact? God's people who were called to be known for their unconditional and extravagant love, for their compassion and generosity, are now too often known for anything but that. How sad that called to be known as the world's greatest lovers, we are now just as likely to be known as the world's greatest haters. When did we lose the reputation as people who love with a love that is unconditional, unshakable, and extravagant? Why do we love so poorly, not only non-Christians, but often one another as well?

It's time to take Christianity back! When Christians, not the true Christian faith itself, is the stumbling block people are tripping over, its time to take back the public perception of what it means to be a follower of Christ. Its time to tear down the negative stereotype and replace it with the truth, the truth that Christians can be known first and foremost for the unconditional, unshakable, and extravagant love of God we have for one another and the world.

May we never forget the command our Lord Jesus gave us, "A new commandment I give to you, that you love one another: Just as I have loved you, you also are to love one another. By this all people will know that you are my disciples, if you have love for one another" (John 13:34–35, ESV). The Lord, the ruler of our lives, tells us, I have a command for you. A command is not optional; it's mandatory. A command is not merely advice or an opinion; it's a marching order to be obeyed. God forgive us for our disobedience. Cause this command of yours to cut us to the heart to the point that we repent and begin to live out what you modeled for us through the empowering presence of your Holy Spirit.

It will not be reason, or persuasion, or any propositional presentation of truth that will tear down the monstrous stereotype of Christianity in our culture today. This negative characterization will primarily be torn down when

---

28 Gregory A. Boyd, *The Crucifixion of the Warrior God: Re-Interpreting Old Testament Violence in Light of the Cross* (Downers Grove, IL: InterVarsity Press, 2015), 27.

non-Christians and wounded Christians encounter followers of Jesus who are growing in what it means to be a safe place; Christians who are being transformed to increasingly think, speak, and act more like Jesus. This makes being a safe place one of the crucial missional issues of our day.

9

A SAFE PLACE FOR GROWTH AND TRANSFORMATION: GROWING IN EMOTIONAL, RELATIONAL, AND SPIRITUAL WHOLENESS

Now may the God of peace himself sanctify you completely, and may your whole spirit and soul and body be kept blameless at the coming of our Lord Jesus Christ.

— 1 THESSALONIANS 5:23, ESV

CREATING AN ATMOSPHERE that encourages becoming more emotionally, relationally, and spiritually whole as persons is the most significant reason there is for growing in what it means to be a safe place. Growing in wholeness

will have a positive impact on every facet of our lives as individuals and congregations. It is also a key component in answering a question we asked in
an earlier chapter—Who do people encounter when they encounter you and
me? Do they encounter Christians who are safe or unsafe?

A MAJOR HINDRANCE

Not growing more whole and mature as persons is a major hindrance to becoming a safe place. Some Christians are unaware that this is God's will for
them; others are simply unwilling to believe they need it. This is unfortunate
because believers who refuse to become more emotionally, relationally, and
spiritually healthy will experience a decrease in effectiveness as they seek to
carry out God's purposes.

It is also unfortunate because our lack of wholeness and our immaturity
work together as an ugly perfect storm that creates and gives life to the negative Christian stereotype we spoke of in the previous chapter. Growing in
wholeness is essential for tearing that stereotype down and for making us
more effective in developing healthy leaders and disciples in the church, and
living lives of witness in the world.

TRANSFORMATION AND
WHOLENESS IS GOD'S WILL

The atmosphere of an individual's life, or that of a small group or church,
cannot be assumed to be safe merely because it is Christian. The two are not
automatically synonymous. Some environments within Christendom are actually toxic. Just listen to the following testimony.

> I grew up in a legalistic church environment. Spiritual growth was
> measured by external measures, such as, certain clothing restric-
> tions, avoidance of particular behaviors, church attendance, and
> the approval of others. A wholeness that encompassed one's physi-
> cal, emotional, and spiritual life was never taught. Overweight, poor

eating habits, ungodly attitudes, gossip, and double standards were accepted as normal. Because of the unpublished "do's and don'ts list" and the judgment that followed any failure to abide by them, I was left with a sense of shame, and a lack of understanding of God's grace. I also failed to see the larger picture of what wholeness meant to God. Consequently, I lived many years feeling distant from God and was emotionally starved and immature. Somehow I didn't realize the overall connection between my emotional, spiritual, and physical health.[29]

It is God's will to transform us. He knows that as we become more whole as individuals, the environments of our families and congregations will increasingly become a safe place. The Lord not only wants to save our souls, he wants to transform who we are and how we live here and now.

And we know that for those who love God all things work together for good, for those who are called according to his purpose. For those whom he foreknew he also predestined to be conformed to the image of his Son, in order that he might be the firstborn among many brothers (Romans 8:28–29, ESV).

So all of us who have had that veil removed can see and reflect the glory of the Lord. And the Lord—who is the Spirit—makes us more and more like him as we are changed into his glorious image (2 Corinthians 3:18, NLT).

God longs not only to give us new life, but to also help us grow in all that new life has for us so that things from our past do not continue to influence our present in unhelpful ways. Peter Scazzero reminds us, "Yes, it is true that when we come to Christ, our sins are wiped away and we are given a new

---

29 Gwen Ebner, *Wholeness for Spiritual Leaders: Physical, Spiritual, and Emotional Health Care* (Create Space, 2009), 17–18.

name, a new identity, a new future, a truly new life."[30] However, he goes on to say, "We need to understand this does not mean that what our past lives were, won't continue to influence us in different and sometimes unhelpful ways."[31]

As followers of Christ, we are not only called to receive a new life eternally, we are called to experience a new way of living here and now. Perhaps a helpful word picture of God's desire for us to experience freedom and transformation after having received the gift of new life would be the encounter between Jesus and Lazarus in John 11:38–44 (NLT):

> And again Jesus was deeply troubled. Then they came to the grave. It was a cave with a stone rolled across its entrance. "Roll the stone aside," Jesus told them. But Martha, the dead man's sister, said, "Lord, by now the smell will be terrible because he has been dead for four days." Jesus responded, "Didn't I tell you that you will see God's glory if you believe?" So they rolled the stone aside. Then Jesus looked up to heaven and said, "Father, thank you for hearing me. You always hear me, but I said it out loud for the sake of all these people standing here, so they will believe you sent me." Then Jesus shouted, "Lazarus, come out!" And Lazarus came out, bound in grave clothes, his face wrapped in a head cloth. Jesus told them, "Unwrap him and let him go!"

There was still more work to be done in Lazarus even though he'd been given new life. Life anew was not enough. There were old, stinking grave clothes that needed to come off. What would it have been like for Jesus to give life back to Lazarus and then leave him in bondage, all wrapped up in those stinking grave clothes? That's not what someone who loves you would do, is it? Jesus loved Lazarus, and because he loved him, the Lord not only wanted Lazarus alive, he wanted him freed! This is just as true of us as it was of Lazarus. The God who loves us so unconditionally and extravagantly is not

---

30 Peter Scazzero, *Emotionally Healthy Spirituality* (Nashville, TN: Thomas Nelson, 2006), 29.
31 Ibid., 29.

afraid of our stinking grave clothes. He does not turn away from us. He longs for us to not only be alive, but to be transformed and to be free. If we do not surrender to and welcome this work of God in our lives we will experience one or more of the following:

1. We will repeat the example of Israel and continue falling back into old ways of thinking and behaving.
2. We will be more susceptible to temptation and sin.
3. What we do not allow God to transform we will transmit.

FALLING BACK

If we're not authentically transformed to be more like Jesus we will repeat Israel's experience of falling back into old ways of thinking and behaving. This pattern is seen in Scripture passages such as the following:

- The Israelites did evil in the Lord's sight. They forgot about the Lord their God, and they served the images of Baal and the Asherah poles (Judges 3:7, NLT).
- After Ehud's death, the Israelites *again* did evil in the Lord's sight (Judges 4:1, NLT).
- The Israelites did evil in the Lord's sight. So the Lord handed them over to the Midianites for seven years (Judges 6:1, NLT).
- As soon as Gideon died, the Israelites prostituted themselves by worshiping the images of Baal, making Baal-berith their god. They forgot the Lord their God, who had rescued them from all their enemies surrounding them (Judges 8:3–34, NLT).
- *Again* the Israelites did evil in the Lord's sight. They served the images of Baal and Ashtoreth, and the gods of Aram, Sidon, Moab, Ammon, and Philistia. They abandoned the Lord and no longer served him at all (Judges 10:6, NLT).

If we settle for only receiving God's gift of forgiveness of sin, but do not embrace his work of transformation and growth in wholeness, we will repeat Israel's pattern; and we do repeat it. We fall back into old unhelpful ways of believing and behaving time and time again. Who among us has not cried out as the apostle Paul did in Romans chapter seven, saying or thinking something like, "Why am I doing the thing I don't want to do? Why am I not doing the good thing I want to do? Why can't I change? I really want to change!" If we do not acknowledge our need for God's transforming work and power in our lives we will fall back into old ways of responding to life situations and other people that are not helpful for us, or them.

Let me share an example from my own life. In 2007 I was helping lead a team of Christian leaders on a trip to the state of Orissa in eastern India. We were there to assist with leadership development for pastors, men who really were primarily farmers in small, remote villages. They had no formal training but had been appointed as pastors in their villages because the Christians there needed shepherds.

We had been asked to host a first-ever leadership conference for these farmer-pastors. It was an amazing time. We experienced God using us to encourage and strengthen those who were discouraged. We witnessed the Lord equipping these men to be more effective ministers in their mountain villages. And we saw God heal many of them, both physically and emotionally.

The morning after the conference ended, our team was evaluating how it had gone. As part of this processing I received affirmation after affirmation from the team for messages I had shared, and for the effectiveness of prayer ministry that flowed out of those teachings. I thanked them and then asked for input concerning anything I could do differently or improve on in the future. Silence. Finally, one team member made a suggestion. She said that she noticed I tended to focus primarily on the right side of the room when I spoke. She suggested it might be good for me to make sure I also turned to give the left side of the room eye contact so they would not feel left out.

I thanked her for the helpful feedback, but inside I was hurt. I was frustrated and angry that such a seemingly small detail would be brought up in the scope of all the more important things that had happened during the conference. I let it stew in me and for the rest of the trip avoided her as much as possible. On the surface no one really noticed anything, not even that team member; but I noticed. I noticed that I was using more time and emotional energy than I needed to in thinking about this. And I saw how I allowed it to drive a wedge in the relationship between my teammate and me. Now I was angry with myself.

I kept thinking about this experience after we returned home from India. Her response to my invitation for feedback would help me be a better communicator, and she had shared it in a very loving way. So why was I so upset over this? Why did it bother me? Why was I giving so much time and energy to replaying the conversation over and over again in my head?

I began to ask God about it in prayer. One day as I was processing it with him, I heard myself say out loud, "Lord, I'm so frustrated. There were so many more good and important things happening at that conference. There was no need for her to pick out such a trivial point. I'm tired of trying so hard to be a good leader. But no matter how hard I try it's like I can never do it good enough." There it was. There was the root that gave life to my frustration and anger. There was the root whose impact upset me and drove a wedge in my relationship with my teammate. I can never do it good enough.

As I reflected on this further, I realized this wasn't something new. This was a thought and a feeling that I had been struggling with my entire life. Somewhere along the line I had picked up this message that no matter how hard I try, it's never going to be good enough. And it was as if that message had created a hole inside of me that I had spent my entire life trying to fill by working really hard and performing really well. But no matter how hard I worked and how well I performed, I wasn't able to fill that hole and heal that emotional wound it had created.

Over time I'd fallen into an ongoing pattern. I'd work really hard, perform really well, but then someone would make a comment like my India teammate had made and it would send me spiraling downward to a place of frustration and hopelessness. Out of that painful place I would then react in ways that either hurt the other person or me, or in some cases both of us. As in India, I would smile on the surface, thank them for their advice but then distance myself from them. Other times I'd respond with an outburst of frustration and anger that would surprise and hurt someone who had just been trying to be help me.

I really wanted to change. I was tired of this repetitive pattern, but I kept falling back into it. This time, however, I finally reached out for help. Counseling aided me in recognizing and processing this repetitive pattern and its harmful effects on me. It also helped me identify the old message as a lie, equipped me to catch the lie more quickly, and taught me how to tell myself the truth. Inner healing prayer helped connect me to God's power of forgiveness and healing. God revealed where this lie had begun to take root in my past, enabled me to forgive those who had planted it, and set me free from its influence. Counseling and inner healing prayer didn't do away with the events of the past, but through them God was able to set me free from its influence and hold on me in the present. As a result, I was empowered to begin responding in new, more constructive ways when receiving helpful critique from others.

The power of God to heal and transform us so that we don't fall back into old, unhelpful ways of believing and behaving is real. What's your pattern that you want to be set free from? What are the old ways you don't want to fall back into? Find someone mature and whom you trust, then share those things with them. Ask them to pray with you and to help you discern how to pursue growth in wholeness so that falling back into these old patterns becomes something more and more rare in your life.

SUSCEPTIBLE TO TEMPTATION AND SIN

If we are not being authentically transformed by God we make ourselves more susceptible to temptation and sin, sometimes in very public settings. It seems all we need to do is watch the Internet or cable news for the next story of a Christian who has succumbed to greed, lust, or pride. I don't even need to mention the names of the more famous Christians you've read or heard about over the past couple of decades who have had moral failings; you know the litany of who they are and their transgressions.

Some succumb to emotional or sexual affairs. Others end up destroying vibrant ministries or congregations as they give in to sinful attitudes of pride, arrogance, and a subconscious desire to build their own kingdom rather than God's. Each time it happens it not only has a traumatic effect on those individuals and their families, but on their churches and ministries, and on the witness of Christianity in the public eye.

A common thread in almost every one of these stories is that those involved did not have people in their lives that were a safe place for them. Some of the leaders who fell did not feel they had someone safe to turn to, someone whom they could be truly vulnerable and transparent with. They did not have someone whom they believed would stand by them and be for them if they dared to reveal what was really going on behind the scenes in their lives. Others did not have someone who was willing to risk confronting them with the truth, even if it meant losing their relationship with the leader or, perhaps, losing a job.

On the surface we see the temptation and sin that leads to someone's fall. However, below the surface often lie legitimate, God-given needs that have not been met in healthy, appropriate ways. As a result, those who succumb to temptation and sin are often seeking to medicate their pain or fill the emotional holes in their lives in unhealthy, illegitimate ways.

We all need a safe place we can run to when the pain is too great or when we're unable to meet, in healthy ways, the needs God has built into us. If we don't have that place, we'll try our best, we'll work hard to change, but ultimately, like Israel, we'll fall back into our old patterns and be more susceptible to temptation and sin than we otherwise would have been.

WHAT WE DO NOT ALLOW GOD TO TRANSFORM WE WILL TRANSMIT

Another reason we need a safe place for growth and transformation is that whatever we don't allow God to transform we will transmit. If we are not growing in wholeness we will pass on our woundedness, and our struggles with temptation and sin, to others. Let me illustrate this point with another example from my own life.

For generations the men on my father's side of the family struggled with unrighteous anger, and I was not free from that battle. I really started to wrestle with this issue after getting married because I did not want to be a man who took his anger out in ways that hurt others, especially his wife or children— but I did. I never hurt them physically, but when I got angry there were times I hurt them emotionally and verbally. Each time it happened, I was ashamed and I repented, vowing it would never happen again, but it did. I was a Christian and a leader, yet I was doing the very thing I didn't want to do. And no one knew because it happened in private, never in public.

I knew that if I was not transformed and set free from this bondage of unrighteous anger, I would continue this unhealthy and harmful pattern, and I would transmit it to my sons and my daughter—perhaps even to subsequent generations. The last thing I wanted was for them to be hurt by my struggle only to have it eventually become their own. But God was good. He reached out to me in grace and encountered me in a variety of ways through a number of safe-place people and began a process of healing, freedom, and transformation in my life.

One of the absolutely essential keys was the presence of people who were a safe place for me, especially my wife, Debi. I had people (and continue to have people) who loved me unconditionally and still believed in me even when I did not deserve it. I had people who did not give up on me and fought in prayer for God's purposes in my life. I had people who were willing to tell me truth and set healthy boundaries for me even though they knew I might choose to cut off relationship with them.

Most of all, Jesus was a safe place for me. Whether in my own life, or as I read of Jesus' relationships with people like Peter and others in Scripture, I am amazed and thankful for his ability and willingness to see us for who he knows we can be, not just for who we are. And I am so deeply grateful for how he does not give up on us, and is always at the ready to bring his healing and freedom to bear on our lives.

Having people in our lives that are a safe place can give us the courage to bring the things we've kept hidden in the darkness into the light. People who are a safe place will affirm you when you're honest, vulnerable, and transparent. They will be *for* you and *against* anything that will harm you. They will not reject you, shame you, or abandon you. They will speak God's truth to you in love and grace, and when necessary, set healthy boundaries for you. And they will do all they can to assist you in finding and connecting with the help you need.

10

WHAT IS GROWING IN WHOLENESS?

S O, JUST WHAT is growing in wholeness? It is experiencing healing from God in any place where we are injured, broken, damaged, or in bondage, and as a result are being hindered from living into the full potential of our relationship with God and others. This work of God will impact our entire beings; it will have a transformational effect on us emotionally, relationally, and spiritually. Becoming more whole as persons is critically important because without such growth, wounds from our past can continue to influence our present in unhelpful ways.

Wounds, traumas, and memories from the past that are not healed can cause us to respond to people and situations in ways less helpful and effective than we might otherwise respond. Don't do what I did for too many years— avoid the good works of God in your life, his works of healing and freedom, transformation and maturation. If I have any one primary regret looking back on my life it's this—that I did not consciously and intentionally seek to grow in more emotional, relational, and spiritual wholeness sooner. I certainly needed it. We all need it. We live in a broken, fallen world. And under even the best of circumstances, we get beat up in some way, shape, or form by the world, the flesh, the devil, or a combination of all three.

We are all kind of like the old refrigerator you move after letting it sit there for ten to twenty years and you finally get a new one. You move the old one out to bring the new one in and discover the accumulation of all kinds of gunk. We all have accumulated gunk back there that needs to be cleaned up. Wholeness issues are like that. We all have something that needs to be cleaned up in our lives. We all at some point have a need for healing in our broken lives. And as Christians, we all have a need for the life of Jesus to be more fully formed in us so we can be transformed and set free from:

- Old ways of thinking that are not helpful for us; lies we've been believing as truth
- Old habits that are not helpful for us, even though for some of us at times those old habits may have helped us survive a challenging season of life
- Old, sinful motives and attitudes
- Old ways of responding to challenge and stress that are not helpful or healthy for us
- Old emotional wounds of the past that are still impacting our present in unhelpful and unhealthy ways
- Old, unhelpful ways of dealing with our hidden insecurities and unmet needs for love and affirmation, worth and significance

Of this I am certain: Growth in wholeness, or the lack thereof, will impact our effectiveness as leaders, disciples, and witnesses. I cannot encourage you strongly enough—allow God to bring his work of healing, freedom, and transformation to bear on your lives. Don't wait as long as I did; don't waste any more time. Invite God to transform and set you free so you can grow more emotionally, relationally, and spiritually whole.

GROWING US IN WHOLENESS IS GOD'S WORK

It is critically important that we recognize growing in wholeness and experiencing God's healing in our lives *is God's work,* not ours. It is the work of God, not the work of human beings that brings authentic transformation to bear on our lives. How God brings his power to heal and set us free can involve different means for different people. Among the various means God seems to use consistently are the following:

- Sovereign God encounters
- Life-on-life relationships with people who are safe
- Intentional awareness and examination of our responses to people and situations
- Counseling to raise awareness and facilitate renewing of the mind
- Inner healing prayer for healing of wounds and memories from the past that are still influencing our present in unhelpful ways
- Spiritual direction for the purpose of intentional soul care
- Freedom prayer for freedom from spiritual harassment, oppression, and bondage to unclean spirits

Sovereign God encounters. For some, the Lord's work of healing and freedom may involve a sovereign God encounter such as the one I call my Chicago healing experience. In the late 1980s I attended a leadership conference in Chicago, Illinois. I thought I was there to learn about leadership, but God had a different agenda for me—to heal a father-wound that I was not consciously aware that I had, and to set me free from the negative impact in had had on my life for decades.

As one of the keynote speakers brought his message to a close, he asked us to move into small groups to pray with one another. I don't remember who the speaker was or even what he was talking about. I can't remember why we were put in small groups after his teaching. What I do remember is that as we went around our group, each man began to cry as he was prayed for.

I was the last one who would be prayed for and by the time they came to me I had made up my mind that I was not going to succumb to what I believed to be blatant emotional manipulation. So when the men asked how they could pray for me I said, "Well, life and ministry are going really fine for me these days, so maybe you could ask the Lord to continue blessing me, my family, and my ministry." They said they'd be happy to do that. They surrounded me, laid their hands on my shoulders, and began blessing me in Jesus' name.

Then, there it was—a small pooling of water in the corner of one of my eyes, the kind of pooling that sometimes happens when you yawn. I began to fight it as soon as I felt it. I *was not* going to make a fool of myself. But the pool got larger and larger until it had no choice but to begin trickling down my cheek. And then from a place deep within me came an audible sob. One sob, then another, and yet another, and then the proverbial damn burst. I have only cried this deeply one other time in my life—on the morning of December 19, 1997, as I held the body of my oldest son who had died sometime during the night.

As I cried one of the men asked, "What is it, Mike?" Through the sobs I heard myself finally answering, "I don't know, I don't know, I don't know. I just wish he had held me." Then the sobs not only continued, they intensified. "Who, Mike? Who do you wish had just held you," the brother-in-Christ asked me. "I don't know!" I responded, irritated at being pushed and prodded with questions when I was obviously upset. Didn't this person know any better than to bother me at a time like this? "Who, Mike? Who do you wish had just held you," he gently asked again. "I don't know! I don't know! I don't know!" I responded sharply. Then, there it was. The words came forth from within and just hung out there in the air for everyone to hear, "I just wish my dad had held me!" And the sobs and cries continued.

The men kept praying over me. What they prayed I have no idea. I do know that eventually the sobs subsided, we all went back to our rooms in the Catholic monastery where we were lodged, and I fell asleep. The next morning I woke up and went to the African Chapel on the third floor of the monastery (each of the four floors had a chapel that was decorated in a particular country's or continent's décor). I sat in the rear with my back against the wall, took out my Bible and began to read. As I did I heard a voice. Whether it was truly audible, or simply audible in my own my mind I cannot say, but this I know—I heard a voice. The voice said, "Stop, put your Bible down for a moment." As I did, I began to see a picture on the inside of my forehead as if there was a movie screen there. In the picture was a body sitting on a throne. There was a light shining so brightly that I could not see the face or head, only the torso and legs. A young boy was standing before the throne. Then I heard the voice again, "Crawl up on my lap and let's read my Word together." On the movie screen inside my head the little boy climbed up onto the lap, two large arms gently embraced him, and together they began to read the Word of God. Then I picked up my own Bible and began to read the Word of God.

A few months after returning from Chicago to Rapid City where we lived, Debi came to me and asked, "What's happened to you?" I wasn't sure what she meant, so I asked, "What do you mean?" "Well, something has happened to you. Ever since you returned from Chicago you aren't as driven as you used to be, and you haven't gotten angry at all. What's happened?" I couldn't give her an answer, but I was encouraged to know that she was seeing some change in a pattern of living that I had been battling for as long as I could remember. That pattern included putting in the hours at work that were not only required of me but even more, whatever it took to get the job done and get it done well. And the pattern included occasional outbursts of rage over the smallest of issues in life, a rage that would include saying hurtful, mean-spirited things to Debi.

I was viewed publicly as being among the most loving, patient men many had ever met. None of them would have imagined that I had a problem with anger and took it out on the person I loved most in the world. Oh, occasionally they'd see me "hit the wall" and get "a little short" with one of them, but it was always chalked up to how hard I worked, how I went the extra mile, making it easy to overlook and forgive. I was known for having one of the best work ethics they'd ever seen, known for being a man who would go the extra mile and then some, known for being a leader who had the heart of a servant. I was given a lot of strokes of affirmation for these characteristics they perceived as positive and desirable in a leader.

What none of them knew, what I myself was not conscious of, was that underneath this great work ethic, underneath this willingness to go the extra mile and then some, underneath this willingness to serve, *was a drivenness to prove that I was worth loving.* Somewhere along the path of my life this drivenness had taken root in the absence of the physical and emotional connection I had needed from my dad but had not received.

I thought about Debi's question and observations for days. Finally, I realized I had experienced a sovereign encounter with God in Chicago. And in that encounter he had done a healing work in a place of my life that I did not even consciously know was wounded, a wound that was driving me to medicate the pain and fill the hole by outworking everyone I knew in order to prove I was worth loving. In the process, I was wearing myself out to the point that I could too easily explode over small, insignificant details, or not be as patient as I otherwise would have been because I was just so emotionally fatigued.

What I know now is that even though I had a good father who was present with me, there had still been something in me that had quite naturally wanted to be held, to be affirmed, and to be validated by my dad; and he had not done that. He had not been able to do that because it had never been done for him. But I didn't realize that. All I knew was that I was angry about not being loved in the way I longed to be loved. As a result, I had been living my life trying to earn the love I wanted, and trying to ignore or bury the anger I was feeling within, only to see it eventually "come out sideways," coming out and sliming those who didn't deserve to be slimed.

I had an emotional wound and my Father God came to me and sovereignly placed his healing hand on it. His power to heal set me free from the drivenness to perform and the sin of rage that I had manifested for so many years.

This sovereign encounter with the love and power of God was a crossroads moment for me. I had already had a measure of success in life, in business, and in ministry, but I had not been able to move more fully into the destiny God had for me. My lack of wholeness had been causing me to settle for less than all the Lord had in store for me. Sovereign God encounters like the one I was blessed with will be one means through which the Lord helps some people become more whole and mature.

Relationships with people who are safe. While some people may experience a sovereign healing from God, others will experience his work of healing and freedom as he brings them into relationship with men and women who are safe-place people. Being a person who is safe is a key element in being someone through whom God can impart healing and freedom to others.

Joe Johnson and Larry Crabb describe such relationships in the following ways:

> Jesus' presence with us enables us to risk facing the truth. To be safe we do not protect others from facing the truth because truth sets us free. Safety does not mean denying the truth. God protects us from harm by revealing the truth about our brokenness or sin, which is wounding us.[32]

> What do we believe about each other, not only when we're on our best behavior, but when we're irritating and demanding? As I uncover what's bad within me, a spiritual friend stays relaxed. He sees something else. I know of little else so powerful as confessing wretched failure and having a friend look on you with great delight. The more I see my sin in the presence of a spiritual community [that is safe], the more I see Christ and celebrate Him and long to know him and be like him. The safety necessary to own my badness comes when someone believes that I am in Christ and that he is in me. Then anything can be faced without fear of being discarded.[33]

The delight we have in one another in such times is not a delight that overlooks our sin or woundedness. Our delight is in a brother or sister in Christ who has the courage to risk being real because they want nothing to hinder them from becoming more like Jesus. A person who is a safe place is a person who will bring the healing combination of God's grace and truth to bear on our lives.

When Christians are unsafe, we will keep hidden things that hinder the formation of the life of Jesus within us. We dare not reveal the things we struggle with if we fear we are going to be lectured, judged, shamed, or even discarded. If followers of Jesus are to experience more of his life being

---

32   Joe Johnson, from a sermon at Trinity Lutheran Church, Rapid City, South Dakota.
33   Larry Crabb, *The Safest Place on Earth* (Nashville, TN: Word Publishing, 1999), 98.

formed in them on deeper levels, they need safe-place relationships. They need relationships where they are given freedom to express their pain, and to express their doubts and questions, their struggles with temptation and sin, all without fear of being shamed, condemned, or rejected. They need a place where they can experience the unconditional love and acceptance of God, along with his healing combination of grace and truth.

Counseling. Another means of God's healing touch in our lives is through counseling with trusted, mature counselors and therapists who can help us discover and grow in our awareness of some of the things involved in our woundedness. Gifted, trustworthy counselors can help us uncover and discover those things that are hindering our growth in wholeness, and can guide us in renewing of our minds (Romans 12:1–2). This renewing of our minds can help us identify lies we've believed as if they were truth, and then begin to help bring our lives more in line with the truth of God's Word. The effect of the renewing of our minds will be a move toward becoming more whole emotionally, relationally, and spiritually.

Inner healing prayer. Still another means of God's healing touch is inner healing prayer ministry through schools of prayer ministry such as Immanuel Healing Prayer, Sozo Healing Prayer, and Elijah House prayer ministry, to name only a few. In this kind of prayer God brings his healing power to bear on those places and memories where we are wounded and broken, on places that have left emotional holes within us that we try to fill in illegitimate, unhelpful ways. God's power at work through inner healing prayer has had a powerful, transformative impact on my life; it can upon yours too. Many churches throughout the United States today have prayer ministers in their congregations, or know those they can connect you with.

Spiritual direction for the purpose of intentional soul care. Spiritual direction is a historic practice of the Christian church. A commitment to meeting and working with a spiritual director is one means of intentionally caring for our souls in the context of a culture inundated with an obsession on body types and physical fitness. While we focus on exercise and diet for the body, who is caring for the soul?

Spiritual direction simply refers to the goal of time spent together with a spiritual director. It is a bit of a misnomer because the spiritual director is not directing the person they are working with. They are there to help guide a process in which the person can become aware of God's promptings and voice in their life. It is actually the Holy Spirit who is directing the time spent together between a spiritual director and a directee. Morris Dirks defines Christian spiritual direction as, "help given by one Christian to another which enables that person to pay attention to God's personal communication to him or her, to respond to this personally communicating God, to grow in intimacy with this God, and to live out the consequences of the relationship."[34]

Caring for our souls in an intentional manner is critical for growth in emotional, relational, and spiritual wholeness. The fruit of spiritual direction can be an experience of healing from things within us that have been hindering us from more fully experiencing the abundant life God longs for us to live, and freedom from things in our past we did not know we were in bondage to.

Freedom prayer. Finally, another means of God's healing touch are freedom appointments that can help set us free from unclean spirits that have attached themselves to us and to our woundedness. Unclean spirits can come through the doors of our lives that we open to them through overt sin, or through sinful and unhelpful reactions (such as unforgiveness, bitterness, hate) to those times when we've been truly hurt and abused.

In all this talk of inner woundedness and the harmful impacts it can have on our lives, there is good news! The good news is this: the fact that we have been traumatized and wounded *does not have to be the final word* in our story— if we do not want it to be! Part of the great news about being Christians is that we believe in a God who is so great, and who is so present and active in our lives, he can take our worst trauma and deepest wounds and somehow turn them around and use them to make our lives, lives of victory, not victimization.

As someone once said, stuff happens; stuff happens in this world that is fallen and broken. However, what we do with the stuff, what we do with our

---

34 Morris Dirks, *Forming the Leader's Soul: An Invitation to Spiritual Direction* (Soul Formation, 2013), Kindle ed.

trauma and emotional woundedness is up to us. The question now for us is this: Will we run from God, or toward him? Run toward him with your stuff. He knows how to use it for good by bringing his power to heal and set free to bear on it, thus transforming us and helping us grow more emotionally, relationally, and spiritually whole.

A CLOSING QUESTION AND PRAYER

As we close this chapter, let me leave you with an important question you might ask yourself and a helpful prayer you might pray. The question: What is the hard truth that I am running from, have been running from, or have buried deep beneath the surface of my life? As we seek to grow in health and wholeness, a powerful and wonderful prayer we can pray is this prayer from the Great Welsh Revival: *Lord, do whatever You need to do in me, so that you can do whatever you want to do through me.*

Praying this prayer and experiencing God's answer to our prayer will enable us to become more whole and grow in being someone who is a safe place for others. Growing in what it means to be a safe place is not, however, meant to be an end in itself. It is designed to create the emotional, relational, and spiritual atmosphere in which we can experience a transformation and empowerment from God that enables us to think, speak, and act more like Jesus. This transformation and empowerment will enable us to live as more than merely nice and moral people. It will enable us to live as Christians who are making significant differences in the lives of others, to live as Graeme Sellers articulates it, as followers of Christ who are dangerous for the kingdom of God and to the dominion and purposes of the enemy.

11

THE DANGEROUS KIND

The dangerous kind are followers of Christ who refuse to settle for anything less than all God has for them. They long for the Lord to do whatever he needs to do in them so he can do whatever he wants to do through them so that the works and words of Jesus might continue in the world today.

B EING A SAFE place is never meant to be an end in itself. It has a purpose. That purpose is to create an atmosphere in which people can be transformed and empowered to think, speak, and act more like Jesus. The effect of this transformation will enable Christians to live as more than merely nice and moral people. It will empower them to live as followers of Christ who are a real threat to the purposes and dominion of the devil in the world today.

Don't get me wrong. There is nothing wrong with being nice, unless that's all we are. Jesus did not die just to make us nice. Jesus died so we would live like he did, as someone who is making a significant, eternal difference in people's lives through the power of the Holy Spirit. That's the life Jesus lived, and because he lived that way, religious leaders, civic leaders, and the enemy of God—the devil—all considered him to be someone who was dangerous. And that's the kind of life the Lord longs for us to experience—not one that settles for being merely nice and moral, but one that longs to be dangerous for the kingdom of God and a real threat to the dominion and purposes of the devil.

1 John 3:8 tells us Jesus came to destroy the works of the devil, and this is still his intent and work through the lives of Christians today. The dangerous kind are followers of Christ who are "courageously proactive in implementing strategies that penetrate and weaken the influence of evil in the world today."[35] I agree wholeheartedly with Graeme Sellers who writes,

> Too long we have settled for religious compliance and inoffensive comportment. Now is the moment to raise our danger quotient! Jesus didn't suffer torture and execution to make anyone nice; he died to make us dangerous—dangerous for and dangerous to; dangerous for the kingdom of God and dangerous to the dominion of the enemy. All who call on the name of Jesus are thrust into the heart of a cosmic conflict in which the stakes are ultimate: life and death.[36]

We are living in perilous times. A cursory glance around the world substantiates that fact. Because we live in a perilous time, the world needs followers of Christ who are intent on raising their danger quotient; it needs Christians who are committed to living as the dangerous kind.

THE SAFE PLACE-DANGEROUS KIND PARADOX

Being a safe place for the dangerous kind sounds paradoxical. Is it possible to be safe and dangerous at the same time? In reality you cannot be one without at the same time being the other. This was wonderfully illustrated in an email

---

35 Thomas B. White, *The Believer's Guide to Spiritual Warfare* (Ventura, CA: Regal Books, 2011), Kindle ed.

36 Sellers, *The Dangerous Kind*, Kindle ed.

I received from a friend who is a member of our national leadership team for the ARC.

In his email he spoke of how his wife and a woman who lived in their neighborhood had developed a friendship while walking dogs. Over time their friendship grew. One day this woman asked his wife if she could share something she'd never told anyone. She was having, as she put it, "poltergeist" problems in her house and in an old barn that was on her property. Since they were Christians, wondered the woman, could they come and deal with this problem. My friend and his wife agreed. However, before going to this woman's property, they asked if she wanted to make certain her own heart was Christ's home. She eagerly said yes, and they shared the gospel with her. The woman was only too glad to accept Jesus as Savior and Lord right on the spot, repenting of some past occult involvement in the process.

With that settled, my friends set a time to meet with her at her house. When the day came they walked through both the house and the barn, and around the perimeter of the property with the woman, exercising the authority and power Christians have in the name of the Lord Jesus Christ. Problem solved. In the email, my friend and his wife shared what happened next:

> Our friend is excited that God has opened her eyes and saved her. She says, "I didn't realize how lost I was!" She's already started to tell some of her friends what God has done and is telling them that their involvement in the occult is wrong. She is coming to church on Sunday and has already invited a friend to come with her (she's never been herself!). The friend has another non-churched person experimenting with some occult stuff and is another of my wife's dog loving friends. This is amazing to me. I feel like we are tapping into a whole network of unbelievers. I don't know what will happen but I am praying that through our friend's witness many will be set free, experience the riches of God's grace, the fullness of the Spirit and serve Christ.[37]

---

37 Email used with permission.

This ARC leader and his wife personify the paradox that being a safe place makes us at the same time dangerous for the kingdom of God. They were a safe place for their neighbor when they took the initiative to reach out and build a friendship with her, a friendship marked by God's unconditional love and acceptance, by his grace and truth. The woman began to trust them as evidenced by her vulnerability and transparency regarding a very private matter. My friend and his wife were a safe-place people who listened to this woman with no hint of ridicule, judgment, or shame.

Being a safe place for their neighbor made them at the same time dangerous for God's kingdom purposes in this woman's life and a real threat to the dominion and purposes of the enemy. They were dangerous as they boldly shared the truth of the gospel. They were a real threat to the devil's dominion and purposes as they prayed with the woman to receive Jesus as Savior and Lord, and as they exercised the authority and power they had in Jesus' name to cleanse her property of demonic spirits. My friend and his wife were living examples of a safe-place people who at the same time were followers of Christ being dangerous for his kingdom and to the enemy. The outcome? A precious soul transferred from the enemy's dominion of darkness into God's glorious kingdom of light.

Being a safe place for the dangerous kind is about wanting to be transformed and empowered by the Holy Spirit to think, speak, and act more like Jesus Christ. Nothing more. Nothing less. Nothing else. The dangerous kind are followers of Christ who refuse to settle for anything less than all God has for them. They long for the Lord to do whatever he needs to do in them so he can do whatever he wants to do through them that the works and words of Jesus might continue in the world today.

In the exercise below you'll read of two men in Scripture who are more than merely nice and moral people. They are dangerous for the kingdom purposes of God in another man's life and as such, are a real threat to the dominion and purposes of the enemy. As you read this passage, ask the Holy Spirit to reveal to you what makes them the dangerous kind.

DANGEROUS KIND EXERCISE

Read Acts 3:1–8 and answer the following questions. Record your thoughts and answers to both questions in the space provided.

1. What is it about *who* Peter and John were as persons that made them dangerous for the kingdom of God and to the dominion of the enemy?

2. What is it that Peter and John *did* that made them dangerous for God's kingdom purposes and to the purposes of the enemy?

Following are some insights God has given me from doing this exercise over the years, insights into what made Peter and John followers of Christ who were dangerous for and to. Perhaps you saw the same things as you did the exercise. If not, add these dangerous kind characteristics to your list.

They lived out of a settled sense of identity and stayed focused on their calling. Peter and John knew they were sons of God, friends of Jesus, and living temples of the Holy Spirit. Their sense of identity and God-given needs were settled in their relationship with the Lord. They did not need to perform in any way to earn or meet their need to feel loved, valued, and significant. They already knew they were all of that because they were sons of God (see John 1:12). Their identity was settled. Their calling was sure. Thus, they lived out of a sense of peace and gratitude toward the Lord rather than from a place of striving and drivenness. They were, we might say today, comfortable in their own skin, easy to be around and not high maintenance. They didn't need a lot of attention drawn to them, so it was easy for them to direct people's attention to the Lord. And knowing that their identity as sons of God already made them worthwhile and significant set both of them free from any competitive spirit with the other disciples.

Peter and John also knew their calling from God. They knew they had been called to go into the world and make disciples (see Matthew 28:18–20). Peter and John knew they were called to declare and demonstrate that the kingdom of God could be experienced here and now, not just in the life hereafter. Knowing what they were called to do protected them from being tempted to focus their attention on anything less than declaring and demonstrating the good news of the gospel of the kingdom of God. They knew their mission and stayed focused on it.

They lived and ministered with a sense of expectancy. Peter and John expected God to be at work in the world. They believed God wanted them to partner with him in his work, and they expected something to happen when they ministered in the name of Jesus Christ. Their God-inspired sense of expectancy compelled them to refuse hiding behind any rationalized stronghold of caution or fear. Instead, they chose to do and say what God called them to, expecting that kingdom fruit would result.

They had a biblical worldview. Peter and John believed in a spirit realm that was real and had power to impact the physical realm. They believed spiritual beings could interact with and affect human beings. They witnessed the reality of this worldview time and again as they followed Jesus. For instance, they were there when a distressed father told Jesus that a spirit made his son mute and seized him and threw him down (see Mark 9).

Experiences such as this influenced Peter and John's belief in a spirit realm that can affect human beings. Thus, it was easy for them to believe God's supernatural power could also impact people's lives for good here and now, not just in the world to come. Not every person, not even every Christian, holds to such a worldview today. The dangerous kind, however, believe in and act out of a worldview that makes room for the reality of God's supernatural power to very naturally affect human beings for his good purposes.

They had a healthy disregard for the impossible. The dangerous kind have a healthy disregard for the impossible because they believe that God's power is real and that what he says is the truest thing. They do not deny reality, but believe there is a superior reality that can supersede the one they know. So, when they encounter the lame man, Peter and John do not deny the reality that he is lame; they do, however, believe there is a superior reality that can impact and change the one he knows. The words they speak and the action they take (Peter reaches out his right hand in expectancy) are based on a belief in a worldview where ordinary people can act naturally supernatural as they exercise the authority and power God has given them.

They are filled with the presence and power of the Holy Spirit. The dangerous kind refuse to settle for simply giving creedal assent to the Holy Spirit's presence in a disciple's life. Instead, they seek to keep on being filled with his presence and power (see Acts 2; Acts 10:38; Ephesians 5:18). Theologian Gordon Fee writes,

> If the Church is going to be effective in our postmodern world, we need to stop paying mere lip service to the Spirit and recapture Paul's perspective: the Spirit as the experienced, empowering return of God's own personal presence in and among us, who enables us to live as a radically eschatological people.[38]

The Greek grammar of Ephesians 5:18 tells us the apostle Paul's exhortation, which is translated in English as "be filled with the Spirit," is more accurately translated as "*keep on* being filled." Being filled with the Holy Spirit is an ongoing, repeatable experience in the life of a follower of Christ.

However, it's not so much a matter of Christians getting more of the Holy Spirit, as it is the Holy Spirit getting more of us. The more we surrender to his presence and power in our lives the more we will experience him working in and through us just as Peter and John did. This enabled them to live dangerously for the kingdom of God as the Lord worked through them to make a difference in the lame man's life—physically, emotionally, relationally, and spiritually.

---

38 Gordon Fee, *Paul, the Spirit and the People of God* (Peabody, MA: Hendrickson Publishers, 1996), xv.

They are naturally supernatural. In their encounter with the lame man Peter and John are themselves, they did not take on a different persona when they began to minister to the lame man and his needs. They were naturally supernatural. The dangerous kind live and take action according to the leading of the Holy Spirit in a very natural way that has supernatural results in the lives of others. They do not take on a different persona any more than Peter and John did. They are simply men and women being themselves who live and act out of their experience with the same Holy Spirit who empowered Jesus to do and say all he did.

They are growing more emotionally, relationally, and spiritually whole. The Peter and John we read of in Acts 3 are different men than the ones we read of in the gospels. They have become more emotionally, relationally, and spiritually whole, which in turn enables them to discern and carry out God's kingdom purposes.

Peter, for instance, had an encounter with the Lord that transformed who he was as a person and placed him back on his destiny path after having denied knowing Jesus three times (see John 21). This denial had affected Peter's entire being in a negative way. It had left him emotionally overwhelmed with shame, distanced in relationship from the other disciples, and certain that the Lord had given up on him.

It would have been so easy for Peter to bury his pain, go back to his old way of living, and allow the shame of that day to keep him from becoming the man he would become. But when Jesus comes to him on a beach to bring healing, restoration, and transformation, Peter humbles himself and receives what Jesus has to offer. In doing so he is set free, made more whole in every way, and placed back on God's path for his life.

Peter's danger quotient for God's kingdom purposes was raised that day on the beach, raised as God transformed who he was. In the same way today, whenever followers of Christ will humble themselves before the Lord and submit to his work of transforming who they are as persons, their danger quotient will be raised as well.

They are faithful in the fundamentals. The dangerous kind are faithful in the fundamentals of the faith, fundamentals such as prayer. In Acts 3, Peter and John set out that day to simply go to the temple at the hour of prayer. They were going to church as it were, keeping an ordinary, perhaps seemingly mundane appointment. As Peter and John focused on faithfulness in the fundamentals (in this case, prayer), God's extraordinary presence and power breaks in on their very ordinary practice. An intentional appointment (going to the temple) is transformed into a divine appointment (encountering the lame man). Peter and John are faithful in the ordinary fundamentals of the faith and focusing on that makes them dangerous for the kingdom of God and a real threat to the enemy's dominion and purposes.

They allow God's agenda to bump their agenda aside. This is exactly what Peter does. They had an agenda that day. Their agenda was to go to the temple at the hour of prayer. However, as they are in the process of carrying out their agenda, God breaks in with his (see Acts 3:4–8). His agenda is to heal a man who is lame, transform his entire life, and through him impact and change the lives of others. Rather than being stubborn and ignoring God's agenda, Peter and John change theirs. This makes them dangerous in the best sense of the word.

They do not allow one another or others to settle for less. It is never God's desire that we settle for less. As Peter and John encounter the lame man and hear his request, they respond in a way the man had not asked them to. He simply wanted money. They gave him something more. Peter and John were not willing to allow him to settle for only that which he thinks he wants and needs (see Acts 3:3–7). They minister to what he truly needs. Because they do this, he receives far more than he had hoped to receive. Peter and John were not willing to allow themselves, or this man, to settle for less. That made them dangerous for and to.

They experience the relational element of courage that comes with not walking alone. The dangerous kind don't walk alone. They are always part of a team and because they are, they experience the reality that courage has a relational element to it. Jesus sent his disciples out in pairs in the gospels, and Peter and John are continuing that practice as they go to the temple at the hour of prayer. Because they don't walk alone they are able to experience the relational element that can impart courage to those who are on mission together.

In *The Fellowship of the Ring,* Frodo and Sam-wise journey together, along with the rest of their band of brothers. On the way they gave courage to one another just by being together. So too, we can give each other courage in the context of relationships that are authentic and safe. This will help us be who God has called us to be, and to do and say what he calls us to. The dangerous kind do not walk alone.

They see the ministry opportunity right in front of them. The dangerous kind realize that sometimes the ministry opportunity God provides them with may have been right in front of them all along but they just haven't seen it yet. This happens for Peter and John in Acts 3. The lame man is placed beside the gate every day. They walk by him every time they go to the temple. But this day, they see him. This day the ministry opportunity right before them finally gets their attention.

This is not to condemn Peter and John. It may have been this was a fullness of time encounter, a time when the lame man is finally ready to receive what God has to give him. Peter and John, listening to God's leading in their lives, stop and notice. Like them, the dangerous kind seek to listen to the voice and promptings of the Lord and then respond obediently. Sometimes those promptings help them see the ministry opportunities that are already in front of them, opportunities they have not yet noticed nor responded to.

They pray simply and simply pray. The dangerous kind pray, and when they pray, they pray simple, child-like prayers. Peter simply prays, "In the name of Jesus, stand up." The dangerous kind don't try to talk themselves or others into faith through long theological prayers. They simply talk to God and pray out of a conviction that the power and authority of God is at work, not their own human effort or abilities.

They are like children in this way. Children trust that what their father and mother have told them is true and then take action based on that belief. In the same way, the dangerous kind believe their Heavenly Father has said he wants them to pray and answers their prayers. The dangerous kind pray as Jesus exhorts in Luke, chapter eleven—expectantly, shamelessly, and persistently. In other words, they pray simply and simply pray, just like a child.

They refuse to allow religious leaders to determine what can and cannot be done. The dangerous kind do not allow religious leaders to set the agenda. Religious people are more concerned with outward appearances than with true, inner-life transformation. They are more concerned with keeping things the way they are and not rocking the boat than dealing with the necessary tension and unsettledness that comes with following God. The religious are more concerned with protecting their understanding of God and the truth than with letting God blow up their God-boxes where needed. And religious people are not as apt to push through boundaries that in the end are manmade boundaries, causing them to settle for less than experience the fullness of what God has for them.

CASTING A VISION FOR LIFE AS THE DANGEROUS KIND

Casting a vision for living as the dangerous kind is of essential importance in a Christian culture where there can be a subtle slide into comfortable, even complacent living, and an over-emphasis on presenting Jesus as simply a nice, gentle best friend. Jesus certainly is nice, he certainly is our friend, but he is not merely nice or gentle. Jesus is wild. He is dangerous. Author Dorothy Sayers has written that, "We have efficiently pared the claws of the Lion of Judah, and certified him as a fitting household pet for pale curates and pious old ladies."[39] Followers of Christ who want to live life as the dangerous kind will no longer be willing to know Jesus as a household pet who is under control, but as the Lion of Judah who is the King of kings and Lord of lords.

Followers of Christ who seek to live dangerously for and to, desire to think, speak, and act more like Jesus. However, if we were truthful, most of us would admit that while this may be our heart's desire, it is not yet our life experience to the degree we'd like it to be. If we were honest, we might

---

39 Dorothy L. Sayers, *Creed or Chaos?* (New York, NY: Harcourt Brace, 1949), 5.

bemoan the low level of our danger quotient, as the Bishop of Canterbury did when he said, "Everywhere Jesus went there was a riot. Everywhere I go, they make me cups of tea."[40] The dangerous kind do not want to settle for cups of tea, they want to cause a riot for good in the lives of others.

There is much more that could be said about living as followers of Christ who are the dangerous kind, and for further reading on this subject I recommend the work of Graeme Sellers. I consider his book *The Dangerous Kind* to be the seminal work on the subject. It is a thought-provoking and challenging read. Sellers's insights into Scripture and how it speaks to God's preferred design for followers of Christ to live as the dangerous kind both challenge and inspire the reader.

However, to experience that kind of transformation, we need a safe place. We need a place where people are being experientially rooted in God's grace and truth, and are creating an atmosphere of freedom for authentic living. Those are the three major characteristics of what it means to be a safe place, and examining those characteristics are the focus of the remainder of this book.

---

40 Michael Frost and Alan Hirsch, *ReJesus: A Wild Messiah for a Missional Church* (Peabody, MA: Hendrickson Publishers, Inc, 2009), 21.

Part Two

Experientially Rooted
In God's Grace

12

WHAT OUR LIVES ARE ROOTED IN MAKES A DIFFERENCE

*What our lives are rooted in will determine the nature and
condition of the fruit we bear.*

AN ESSENTIAL ELEMENT in being a safe place is to be experientially rooted in God's grace. The soil that things are rooted in makes all the difference in the world because the type of soil affects the nature and quality of the blossoms or the fruit that's produced.

My daughter and son-in-law cultivated an organic garden when they were first married. Rachel and Bert's home is located in an area that was once an orchard and has rich, dark, contaminant-free soil. The year they began gardening they planted over two hundred and fifty plants. They sold their produce to local grocery stores and to friends. Rachel and Bert told me that what the plants are rooted in is the major determinant of the both the quantity and quality of produce the plants bear. The fact their plants were rooted in contaminant-free soil gave Rachel and Bert a better chance of a good harvest than if they had planted their garden in rocky, contaminated soil.

In a similar way, what our lives are rooted in will determine the nature and condition of the fruit we bear. It will be the major determinant of how healthy we are emotionally, relationally, and spiritually. This in turn will impact whether we have a helpful or unhelpful influence in the lives of others.

EXPERIENTIALLY ROOTED

Being experientially rooted in God's grace is one of three primary characteristics of Christians who are growing in what it means to be a safe place. However, for this to become a mark of our lives, God's grace must be something we are *experiencing*, not merely something we speak to theologically. Thus the intentional use of the words *experientially rooted*.

God's grace is something that can be experienced. It is something that empowers us with a power that is not ours. Unfortunately, we too often settle for simply having a good theology and academic grasp of grace. It is in fact possible to speak about God's grace, possess a large amount of information about it, and even teach and preach about it, but not actually be experiencing it as the soil our lives are rooted in. As we go on to examine what it means to be rooted in God's grace, keep in mind that a safe-place people desire an experiential reality, not simply a theological truth.

In John 1:14 the apostle John described the contaminant-free soil in which our lives can be rooted. He writes, Jesus "came from the Father *full of grace and truth*." God's healing combination of grace and truth are the dark, rich, contaminant-free soil that will help our lives be a safe place for others. This section of the book will focus on being experientially rooted in God's grace. The next section will examine what it means to be a people who seek to be rooted in his truth. And the section following that will reflect on what it means to be a people who are cultivating an atmosphere of freedom for authentic living.

13

GRACE: THE BASIS FOR HOW GOD RELATES TO US AND HOW WE RELATE TO OTHERS

God gave his all when he sent his only begotten Son on our behalf,
and in the same way, people who are rooted in his grace will give
their all, even when others don't deserve it.

H AVE YOU EVER disappointed people so badly, so many times that they've finally given up on you? And you understand why because you've given up
on yourself. You can't stop recycling the same experience over and over again—
you commit yourself to doing the right thing but fail. Then you commit yourself
to trying harder and fail again. On and on it goes until you finally come to a
point when you realize you'll never be the person others want you to be, least of
all yourself. Its clear you'll never be able to defeat the demons that keep pulling
you down. You'll never be able to change. You're never going to be free. Never.

Have you ever had the wind completely knocked out of you when a relationship that meant everything in the world to you was ended, and not by your choice—it ended because the one you wanted to be with more than any other couldn't hang in there with you any longer? Do you remember the pain you felt in your heart? Do you recall the numbing effect it eventually had on you, how it caused you to walk around in a kind of haze where everything was gray, as gray as the gloom of a southern California day in June? You couldn't taste anything, couldn't feel any anything? You were numb, just kind of walking through life like a zombie, like the living dead.

Yet even in that state though, when you thought you'd lost all hope and had simply given up, there was still one glimmer, one shred of hope buried deep within. Even though you knew you didn't deserve it, you still hoped against all hope that there would be one person who would not give up on you. You hoped there would be someone who would refuse to be scared away. All you needed was just one person who could see the best version of who you could be and would not let you settle for less, no matter how many times you let them down. If you could find that person, there just might be the possibility that the freedom and transformation you had struggled to experience for so long would finally be yours.

But where does one find such a person? Does such a person even exist? And if this person exists, does the power to transform what seems un-transformable really exist? Is there a power that can set people free from the bondage they've never been able to get free from and authentically change who they are at their core? The answer to those questions is yes. Yes, there is such a person and power in this world. There is someone who is willing and able to not let go of you when everyone else around has. There is a power to transform the un-transformable, set free the captives, and heal and restore fractured relationships. It is real. It is the power of grace, and its source is the Creator of heaven and earth.

TALES OF GRACE

Grace. It's a simple, single syllable word, a word infused with gentleness and beauty and power, all at the same time. Tales of the power of grace to transform and set free have been among some of the most well known stories in the history of literature. Perhaps one of the most beloved of all the tales of grace is the story of Jean Valjean in the iconic novel *Les Miserables*.

Valjean is a prisoner who upon being released from jail reverts to form yet again and steals, this time from a priest, the Bishop of Digne. Upon meeting Valjean, readers see a thief who is homeless and starving. The bishop, however, sees someone else. He sees someone whom Jesus loves, and for whom he died, and he treats Valjean just as he would treat Jesus, as an honored guest. The priest offers him food, shelter, and mercy. Valjean repays him by stealing household valuables. Imagine Valjean's surprise when he is arrested and discovers the priest not only does not press charges, but also gives him the very sliver he stole so he could start a new life. And that is what Valjean does. He starts a new life, because of the power of grace to transform and set free.

Grace so transforms Valjean that he spends the rest of his life doing good, and then finally, one day he has the opportunity to do for someone else what had been done for him—to give them a gift of grace. Valjean extends the grace the bishop had extended him to a dying prostitute named Fantine. His gift of grace toward her is in the form of rescuing her daughter and raising her as his own. Like Valjean himself, his adopted daughter, Cosette, is given the power to live a new life, a life full of meaning and of joy—a life that is a gift of grace.

Yet another epic tale that captures the power of grace to transform is the story commonly known as the Prodigal Son. At least this was the title I used while teaching and preaching on it for many years as the pastor of a congregation in Rapid City. However, I am beginning to think author Timothy Keller has it right when he posits that the story should be renamed the tale of the Prodigal Father. In his book *Prodigal God* he makes a compelling case for re-titling, and understanding with new insight, this timeless tale.

First, Keller instructs us in the true meaning of the word prodigal. Rather than meaning wayward, or lost, he points out that *Merriam-Webster's Collegiate Dictionary* defines prodigal as meaning recklessly spendthrift. It means to spend until you have nothing left. As Keller points out, this term is appropriate for describing the father in the story because his welcome home of the younger son "was literally reckless, because he refused to 'reckon' or count his sin against him or demand repayment."[41]

Had the younger son lost his way in life? Yes. For that matter, it appears the older son had too. Based on this Keller makes the point that the irreligious and religious can both be lost. However, the primary focus of the story is not their "lostness," but on the father's reckless, even scandalous generosity and grace. How appropriate that we reread the words of the apostle Paul in 2 Corinthians 5:19 with those words in mind—reckless, even scandalous generosity and grace. Paul writes, "For God was in Christ, reconciling the world to himself, no longer counting people's sins against them. And he gave us this wonderful message of reconciliation" (NLT). Or, as Eugene Peterson writes in The Message, "God put the world square with himself through the Messiah, giving the world a fresh start by offering forgiveness of sins. God has given us the task of telling everyone what he is doing."

The Prodigal Father's reckless grace refuses to allow the returning son to settle for less. He refuses to allow the son to return home only to become a servant, which was the son's request. No, says the father, you are my son and to full sonship will I restore you. "Quick! Bring the finest robe in the house and put it on him. Get a ring for his finger and sandals for his feet. And kill the calf we have been fattening. We must celebrate with a feast, for this son of mine was dead and has now returned to life. He was lost, but now he is found. So the party began" (Luke 15:22–24, NLT).

So the party began. I love those words. How well they capture the father's grace toward his wayward son, a grace that refuses to let the son settle for less than all the father has in store for him, a grace that transforms the boy's life forever. It is the father who takes the initiative to reconcile the relationship. He is the one who will not be scared away and refuses to give up. It's the father that sees who his son can be and is committed to restoring his child on a path toward becoming the best version of who he can be. The boy is welcomed home and his life restored. This is the power of grace.

---

41 Timothy Keller, *The Prodigal God: Recovering the Heart of the Christian Faith* (New York, NY: Penguin Group, 2008), Kindle ed.

The tales of Jean Valjean and the Prodigal Father are tales of mythic proportions. They are stories of eternal and transcendent meaning. Most of us know these stories. Here's one you may not know. It is the lesser-known tale of a man who married the woman of his dreams, the love of his life. It's the story of the power of grace to transform a man who battled for years to be set free from an unhealthy way of expressing frustration and anger, a battle that continued into the first years of their marriage. It's the tale of a man bound by his habit of overreacting whenever tension, frustration, or anger built up to a breaking point. When they did, his pattern was to speak sharply and hurtfully to those he cared about and loved. No matter how hard he worked at ridding himself of this pattern, he could not free himself. To his great dismay he found himself even speaking this way to the love of his life, the woman of his dreams.

Oh, he would be shattered when he did. He would confess, repent, and ask her for forgiveness. Being full of grace and loving him still, she forgave. Time would go by. Things would be good. Then the same pattern would raise its ugly head again. Once more he would confess, repent, and ask for forgiveness. Once again, full of grace, she would forgive him. She loved him. She believed in him.

This lesser-known tale is one of a man repeating a cycle that he did not want to repeat. He hated it. He hated himself for it. He committed to never speaking this way to his beloved bride again, only to fail in living out this commitment time and time again. But she was the one. She was the one person who refused to be scared away, who refused to give up on her husband, even though he was ready to give up on himself.

He was so angry with himself. Why do I do this hurtful thing I don't want to do? Why can't I live out the commitment I want to live out? But even while he judged and condemned himself, she would judge and condemn him. She saw the man he could be and was committed to helping him break through and become the best version of himself. Toward that end she stayed, she loved, she prayed, and set healthy boundaries, because she was the one. She was the person of grace he needed if there was any hope for truly coming into the freedom and transformation they both longed for him to experience.

It's an epic, though lesser-known, tale of the power of grace working in and through a wife committed to seeing her husband set free to be transformed and finally become the man he had always wanted to be. And it's a story of transformation that has lasted for over three decades and counting. It's a true story. I know, because it's my story, and I'm that man. Freedom. Transformation. All made possible in my life because of the power of grace.

WHAT IS GRACE?

Grace. What is it? The Greek word used in Scripture for grace, *charis*, is a word commonly used in Greek culture at the time. The use of the word *charis* in secular Greek indicated: 1) anything that brings delight or pleasure, or that wins favor; 2) a quality of favor that gives benevolence to inferiors; 3) to give thanks; and 4) the sense of force or power.[42]

This common word from Greek culture is used in the Bible to describe the relationship between God and humankind. In Scripture, grace means: 1) favor or gifts that come as a gift from God; and 2) the sense of power that enables people to live the new life in Christ.

A definition common among Christians is that grace is undeserved favor from God. That is, whatever we receive from the Lord are gifts we have not deserved but that God chooses to give to us anyway.

GRACE IS BASED ON WHO GOD IS, NOT ON WHAT WE DESERVE

Grace happens when God gives us gifts we do not deserve and can never repay. He gives us the gift of eternal life, gifts of relationships, material gifts, and spiritual gifts. However, God's grace is not only about gifts, it is the very basis upon which he chooses to relate to us in the first place. One example of this is the story of the relationship between God and Jacob in Genesis 32:3–12:

---

42 See Geoffrey W. Bromiley, gen. ed., *The International Standard Bible Encyclopedia*, Vol. 2 (Grand Rapids, MI: William B. Eerdmans Publishing Company, 1982).

And Jacob sent messengers before him to Esau his brother in the land of Seir, the country of Edom, instructing them, "Thus you shall say to my lord Esau: Thus says your servant Jacob, 'I have sojourned with Laban and stayed until now. I have oxen, donkeys, flocks, male servants, and female servants. I have sent to tell my lord, in order that I may find favor in your sight.'" And the messengers returned to Jacob, saying, "We came to your brother Esau, and he is coming to meet you, and there are four hundred men with him." Then Jacob was greatly afraid and distressed. He divided the people who were with him, and the flocks and herds and camels, into two camps, "If Esau comes to the one camp and attacks it, then the camp that is left will escape." And Jacob said, "O God of my father Abraham and God of my father Isaac, O Lord who said to me, 'Return to your country and to your kindred, that I may do you good,' I am not worthy of the least of all the deeds of steadfast love and all the faithfulness that you have shown to your servant, for with only my staff I crossed this Jordan, and now I have become two camps. Please deliver me from the hand of my brother, from the hand of Esau, for I fear him, that he may come and attack me, the mothers with the children. But you said, 'I will surely do you good, and make your offspring as the sand of the sea, which cannot be numbered for multitude.'"

Note the basis for God's relationship with Jacob and for his activity in and through Jacob's life. It is not the young Israelite's blameless life of righteousness—far from it. He had not earned nor did he deserve God to work in and through him the way the Lord did. Nor did he deserve how faithful God remained in his relationship to him. God's grace in Jacob's life is manifested in the Lord choosing to love Jacob, and to work in and through him even though Jacob had not lived in a deserving way. God relates to Jacob based on who God is, not on what Jacob deserves. Said another way, Jacob's relationship with God is not based on Jacob's doing, but on God's being.

Another example of God's grace as the basis for how he chooses to relate to human beings is found in Matthew 5:43–45:

"You have heard that it was said, 'You shall love your neighbor and hate your enemy.' But I say to you, love your enemies and pray for those who persecute you, so that you may be sons of your Father who is in heaven. For he makes his sun rise on the evil and on the good, and sends rain on the just and on the unjust."

God causes the sun to rise on the evil and the good, and sends rain on the just and on the unjust. God calls us to love our enemies and pray for those who persecute us. In each instance, God relates to people not on the basis of their merit but on the nature of his own being as a good and just and loving God.

God's grace is experienced in the very fact that he chooses to relate to us at all, and that he chooses to relate to us based on who he is, not on what we deserve. This is confirmed in Romans 5:8. "But God showed his great love for us by sending Christ to die for us *while we were still sinners*" (NLT, emphasis mine). God's love for us is not based upon what we may deserve at any particular moment, whether that moment finds us at our best or at our worst, but upon who he is and who we are to him. God's love for us is a manifestation of his grace toward us.

God chose to relate to the apostle Paul based on who he, God, is, not what Paul deserved. God intentionally reached out to initiate a relationship with Paul even after Paul had been involved in the killing of Christians. God's relationship with Peter was based on grace too. It was based on who God is that he chose to relate to and raise up Peter as a leader for the church, even after Peter had publicly denied him three times. It was based on grace, and on who he is, that God, in Jesus, chose to relate to the woman at the well and the woman caught in adultery though they were still sinners. It was based on grace, and on who he is, that God moved powerfully in and through the Corinthian Christians even while they were being divisive and hurtful toward one another.

GRACE SHIFTS THE BASIS FOR LOVING OTHERS

To understand and experience God as a God of grace is critical because it shifts our understanding for the basis of relating to others *from the deservingness of the one being loved, to the being of the one doing the loving.* Thus, we express grace to others by relating to them, not on the basis of who they are or what they deserve, but on the basis of who we are and who our God is. So, for this book, we understand grace to mean:

- God's grace is undeserved favor from him, and because of this we receive from God that which we do not deserve and can never pay back.
- God's grace is the basis for how he chooses to relate to us. The way God relates to us is based on who he is, not on what we have earned or deserve.
- God's grace is his transforming power at work in our lives that enables us to be who he calls us to be and do what he calls us to do. It is God doing in and through us what we cannot do ourselves.

With this understanding of God's grace, questions we want to ask and begin to answer in this and following chapters include: How is grace lived out? What does it look like when it is walking around in the flesh? How will being rooted in God's empowering grace be manifested in our lives and become apparent to those around us? How will they experience grace from us and through us?

GRACE AND OTHER WORLD RELIGIONS

Before moving on to answer those questions, it is important to note that the grace of God is one of the major distinguishing characteristics between Christianity and other world religions. In other religions, the emphasis is on human effort to appease a god by one's own good works or sacrifice. In other world religions, humans do good works and work hard in order to seek out their god in the hope it will gain them attention and approval.

In Christianity, it is God who takes the initiative to seek us out first. In other world religions, people make sacrifices and work hard to appease the gods. In Christianity, it is God who makes a sacrifice for us. In other religions human beings have to work hard to earn the approval of their god, and often have to adhere to a long list of rules to do so. In biblical, not cultural,

Christianity, we do not have to work hard and follow a long list of rules in order to earn the approval of God. In his grace, God reaches out to love us, forgive us, heal us, and transform us even while we do not deserve it. As a result we live lives of love and service toward others not in an effort to be loved, to be forgiven, or to be accepted, but rather out of the realization that we already are loved, forgiven, and accepted.

God's grace is one of the major differences between biblical Christianity and other world religions. It is also one of the major differences between cultural Christianity and biblical Christianity. It is one of the primary characteristics of being a safe-place people.

GRACE CAN BE SEEN

When people are experientially rooted in God's empowering grace, it can be seen. When Barnabas came to Antioch to follow up on reports that the church was including Gentile as well as Jewish believers, he rejoiced, "because he *saw* the grace of God" (Acts 11:23, NLT). God's empowering grace is not something merely to theologize about; it is something to see and experience. So, how will we see grace in people who are experientially rooted in God's grace? More to the point, what will we look like to others when we are experientially rooted in grace? Let's begin considering these questions by getting a taste of grace from reading and reflecting on the following parable. I suggest you read it out loud (especially if you do this exercise with a small group), and then circle single words that jump out at you, words that grab your attention.

A PARABLE OF GRACE EXERCISE

One sodden September day in the year 1871, in the melancholic village of Norre Vosburg on the bleakest coast of Jutland, Babette Hersant knocked at the door of a modest cottage where two sisters, Martina and Phillipa, lived. Babette had recently been the chef of the Chez Anglais, a grand restaurant in Paris, but had fled France after her husband and child had been murdered in the civil war. Martina and Phillipa carried on the mission of their late father, leading a sect of believers on their joyless journey through this valley of pain and sorrow. Since their leader's death, the flock had become more quarrel-some and even more joyless than before, which made the work of the sisters increasingly hard. So when Babette appeared at their door and asked if she could work for them, they knew she had been blown to them by the wind of the Spirit.

"Stay with us," they said. Stay she did and became the servant of the servants of gentle misery. They practiced a religion of benign denial. For instance, they believed that they could be fit for the meat and drink of the spirit only if they rejected all pleasure in the food of the flesh. So the sisters taught Babette how to soak a flat fish overnight and then boil it thoroughly the next day. How to soak hard bread in water mixed with ale, cook it for one hour, and serve it as hot ale-bread. That was the menu, all of it, day in and day out, with no relief even on the Sabbath.

Babette gratefully accepted her servant's life among the grave folk of Norre Vosburg. The only contact that she had in France was a cousin who, every year for old time's sake, bought a lottery ticket registered in Babette's name. Some years had gone by when one day a letter arrived for Babette from Paris. It was an official notice that her ticket had won the lottery. With it came a certificate drawn on the Bank of Paris for ten thousand francs. A fortune! Babette pon-dered for a time what she should do with her unexpected wealth. She finally decided that she would use it to give a gift to the faithful of Norre Vosburg. She would give them the one gift that she had to give, just as they had given her what they had to give. She would prepare them a feast.

Babette sent a list of her requirements to her cousin in Paris. Not long af-terward two small boats arrived from France loaded with the provisions she had ordered for the feast: live squab, a huge living turtle, quail, partridge, pheasant, hams, beef, every fresh vegetable of the season, ingredients for the exquisite pastries for which she had been famous throughout Paris, herbs and spices and fine wines, along with porcelain and crystal. The feast would be served on the one-hundredth birthday of their revered spiritual leader. The entire congregation was invited. Having heard of the unheard of things that had arrived by boat, the people took counsel together as to what they should do. They decided that they would endure the feast for the sake of the memory of their master, but in loyalty to his teaching they swore to one another that they would not enjoy the eating of it.

And so, on the evening of the feast, the faithful came to the cottage, dressed in their best black, at the appointed hour. They sat down in silence at the elegant table that Babette had set for them, hands folded piously on their laps, all of them awed by the array of crystal and porcelain that had been brought from Paris. As each course of the banquet was served, they received it with no sign of delight, ate with heads down, spoke to each other only in pious phrases recalling how their late leader taught them they were unworthy of the plainest of victuals, and succeeded at the start in giving no hint that one bite or sip was giving them pleasure—but they did eat. They slurped her turtle soup; they wolfed down her delicate fowl; they sliced into her red meats; they nibbled her flaky pastry; and they even sipped her vintage wines, including a Veuve Clicquot of 1860.

As they supped, their spirits gradually mellowed, even against their wills, by the wonder of Babette's lavish gift. They were drawn by her grace to see that there was something here, after all, more to enjoy than endure. Their blushing pleasure in Babette's feast, so foreign and forbidden to them a few moments earlier, began to overflow as pleasure in one another. The talk took on a lighter tone. There were some smiles between bites. A woman burped modestly; an elder looked up at her and said, "Hallelujah." Neighbors recalled how they had now and then mistreated each other in the past, and as soon as one mentioned it, the other forgave. After coffee was taken, the congregation left, feeling lighter than when they came. They walked home arm in arm, their slow plod turned almost to a skip, and they hummed together a light tune remembered from lighter days.

Babette's reckless grace had caught them off guard, melted their resistance, made them feel as if, perhaps, after all, in spite of their undeserving, they were worthy of even so fine a gift. Their discovery made them the more grateful. Joy trickled through the crevices of their spirits when, for a moment, they opened them to the grace of Babette's lavish gift. After the feast, the sisters remarked to Babette that now that she had so much money, she would soon be returning to Paris. "Oh, but no," said Babette, "I have no money. I cannot go back." "No money? But the ten thousand francs?" "All spent on the feast." "All of it? On the feast? But it was too much for you to give!" "Ah, but an artist is never poor." I fancied that during the night an angel appeared to Babette and said to her, "Henceforth, let your name be Grace."[43]

After reading the story, ask the following questions:

- What were some of the single words you circled and why?
- What is it in your heart that this story speaks to, touches, and blesses?
- Are there any parallels between Babette's story and the story of Jesus? If so, what are they?

In doing this exercise with others in the past, some of the responses I've heard include the following: Babette's gift could appear lavish and reckless, even scandalous, to some as God's grace appears to be at times. Babette gives them the best even though they didn't deserve it, and God does the same for us. This is grace.

Babette's gift of grace finally enables them to receive from her, just as God's grace enables us to receive what he joyfully desires to give to us. God's empowering grace works. It accomplishes things. It transforms peoples' lives. It is not just a theological concept; it is a reality at work in people's lives.

Before Babette (and her grace) arrived, the people were living joyless lives. Joyless, miserable living can be a sign that people may know grace in word, but they are not experientially rooted in grace and living out of it. If

---

43 Author's adaptation from "Babette's Feast," in Isak Dinesen (Karen Blixen), *Anecdotes of Destiny* (1958).

any group I visited were as quarrelsome and joyless as these people, I would never want to become a part of it. I wonder how many people are looking at Christians and feel the same way about us? Are we like these people, living lives that appear miserable and joyless? We need to receive and experience God's grace in order to be transformed.

This group felt they had to punish themselves (eat soaked flat fish) in order to be blessed. Individuals and groups who do not know God's empowering grace in their life experience can become groups who seek to punish themselves through self-imposed denial and legalism. They seek to work hard to earn God's favor, rather than receiving it as a gift. Babette gave her all, just as God gave his all when he sent his only begotten Son on our behalf. And in the same way, people who are rooted in God's grace will give their all, even when others don't deserve it.

These are just a few of the ways people have seen grace in Babette's story; and ways they have seen God's grace at work in their own lives or the lives of others.

MY TAKEAWAYS

Over the years I have done this exercise myself multiple times. As I reflect on it I can sum up my takeaways in four ways. First, God's empowering grace is an extravagant gift we don't deserve and can never repay. Second, grace is God taking the initiative to reach out toward us. God always makes the first move and any response on our part happens because he reached out to us first. God's grace enables us to receive, experience, and respond. Some Christians speak of "making a decision for Christ" but even doing this requires God first to move upon and work in our lives, giving us the ability to respond and make that decision. People of grace will in turn, reach out to others first, taking the initiative even when the other person may not seem to deserve it, as we did not.

Third, grace works. Grace is empowering. Grace changes lives. Through grace God empowers us to be who he calls us to be and to do what he calls us to do. It will be in relating to others based on the grace we ourselves have received from God that will work in their lives, enabling and empowering them to be changed. As Michael Frost writes:

> The unrelenting kindness and grace of one person toward another is infused with the potential for transformation. When we live holy, gracious lives under the noses of our friends, neighbors, and associates, we commend an alternative reality to the one they live with every day. We don't commend a holier-than-thou attitude.[44]

Fourth, grace is opposed to earning but is not opposed to effort. Babette put an effort into getting the ingredients for the feast and in preparing the meal. Effort on her part was involved in order to position the people to receive her gift of grace. So too, we make an effort to position ourselves before the Lord in order to receive his gifts. We make the effort to meet with him in word and in prayer, to be in relationship with other brothers and sisters in Christ, and to be faithful in practicing the sacraments. As we position ourselves in these ways we can receive that which we do not deserve and can never pay back—a restored relationship with God, and his marvelous gifts of grace.

A THREE-FOLD STRAND OF GRACE

There is a three-fold strand of grace that is revealed in Scripture and affirmed whenever people reflect on the parable of grace exercise in this chapter. These three points of emphasis concerning God's grace can be seen in people's lives. I shared these strands of grace earlier in this chapter, but before we unpack them in subsequent chapters, let me share them again:

1. God's grace is undeserved favor from him toward us wherein we receive from God that which we do not deserve and can never pay back.

---

44 Michael Frost and Alan Hirsch, *The Shaping of Things to Come: Innovation and Mission for the 21st-Century Church* (Peabody, MA: Hendrickson Publishers, Inc., 2003), 104.

2. God's grace is the basis for how he chooses to relate to us. The way God relates to us is based on who he is, not on what we have earned, nor deserve.

3. God's grace is his transforming power at work in our lives that enables us to be who he calls us to be and do what he calls us to do. It is God doing in and through us what we cannot do ourselves.

A people who are being experientially rooted in this understanding of God's grace is one of the essential marks of being Christians who are growing in what it means to be a safe place. Let's move on now to identify how this understanding of grace can be seen and experienced in our lives.

14

WALKING GRACE CONNECTIONS

We can only sense ourselves valued and cherished by
God when we feel valued
and cherished by others.

— GUY CHEVREAU

ONE OF THE essential elements in being experientially rooted in God's grace is encountering people who become walking grace connections for us. To be experientially rooted in God's grace requires a profound conversion for most of us because we grow up in an environment so full of ungrace. Walking grace connections are a means through which God begins to detoxify us from the effects of ungrace, and root our lives in his empowering grace. To begin reflecting on the importance of walking grace connections in our lives, take a few moments to do the following exercise.

1. In the next 30 seconds, list in the space below the names of the top five messages you have heard preached or taught that have impacted your life for good:

2. In the next 30 seconds, list the names of five people who have impacted your life for good:

3. Now, in the next 30 seconds take the top person on your list and write down what it was about that person that enabled him or her to have such a profound and good impact on your life.

The point of this exercise is to illustrate that God's grace is more often caught that taught through our relationships with people who are themselves walking incarnations of grace. We most often experience and integrate God's grace in our lives through our relationships with people who incarnate grace, more so than when we read about in books, hear it preached about in sermons, or are taught about it in classes. This does not mean we should ignore the latter. It does mean we should not underestimate the former.

THE TRANSFORMING POWER OF GOD IS AT WORK IN RELATIONSHIPS

There is a power for impartation and transformation in our relationships with one another. In Scripture, people experienced grace and truth as they relationally encountered Jesus (see John 1:14, 8:1–11, and 4:1ff). Jesus was a walking grace connection for many of the people he encountered. In his book *Walk On,* John Goldingay writes of the potential and power we have to impact one another's lives simply through our encounters with each other. Goldingay wrote this in the wake of his wife's battle with multiple sclerosis and the emotional woundedness that accompanied their management of the disease:

There is also a theological reason for God's choosing to reach out to us through each other: Love is sacramental! We are physical people, and the physical embrace we offer each other is a sacrament of the embrace of God. God can feed us spiritually without bread and wine, but bread and wine is the normal way, because we are fleshly people. God can embrace us directly and not use other people, but using other people is the normal way, because we are fleshly people. People who hugged me in such a way as to make me feel protected became sacraments of the protectiveness of God. There was an interesting characteristic about the people who became sacraments to me like that: many of them had their own hurt.[45]

God can communicate spiritual realities through physical means. He does this in sacraments. He can also do this through prayer with laying on of hands, and through our relationships with one another. I believe we have underestimated the ability of God to impart spiritual realities through the incarnational means of life-on-life contact in the context of our relationships. Guy Chevreau writes,

Jesus perceived that the only way to help people experience life as a gracious gift, the only way to help them to prize themselves as grace and treasure, was to treat them as treasure and be gracious to them. I can be anointed, prayed over, sermonized to, dialogued with, and exposed to God's unconditional love in books, tracts, and tapes, but this marvelous revelation will fall on ears that do not hear and eyes that do not see, unless some other human being refreshes the weariness of my defeated days. We can only sense ourselves valued and cherished by God when we feel valued and cherished by others.[46]

---

45 John Goldingay, *Walk On: Life, Lost, Trust, and Other Realities* (Grand Rapids, MI: Baker Academic, 2002), 114.

46 Guy Chevreau, *Share the Fire: The Toronto Blessing and Grace-Based Evangelism* (Shippensburg, PA: Revival Press, 1997), 73.

This has certainly been my experience. God has placed men and women in my life who have been walking grace connections, and it has been through my relationships with them that I have been set free from the toxicity of ungrace and rooted in the healthy soil of God's empowering grace.

Some of my first walking grace connections included my wife; father-in-law, Armand Asper; mentors Joe Johnson and Charles Miller; and my pastor, LeRoy Flagstad. When these people walked into a room the atmosphere was immediately upgraded simply because they were there. They brought God's grace into the room with them because their lives were experientially rooted in it. How about you? Have you experienced God's grace through your relationship with someone else? Who has been a walking grace connection in your life? How has their presence in your life impacted you?

BEING WALKING GRACE CONNECTIONS FOR SOMEONE ELSE

In a similar way, God wants to transform and empower you and me to be walking grace connections in the lives of others. There are people in our families for whom God wants to empower us to be walking grace. There are people in our neighborhoods, schools, work places, and play places to whom God wants to impart an experience of grace through their relationships with us.

How can we be those walking grace connections for people? A starting place for some of us may be to repent, and to seek God's healing and transformation in our lives. Repentance was Jesus' first word in ministry (see Mark 1:15). Repentance is a good word even though today it can carry a negative connotation for some. What is repentance? It is the doorway through which we enter to live more fully into God's purposes for our lives. It is a turning from old ways of thinking and behaving and turning toward Jesus. Repentance sets us free to embrace all God has purposed for our lives. Thus, repentance is a good thing, a helpful thing. It is a gift from God.

With this in mind, for some of us a starting place to be more deeply rooted in God's grace may be to repent of thoughts of judgment and condemnation toward people for whom God is calling us to be walking grace. Who are those people? Just seek to be aware when thoughts of judgment and condemnation come to mind and make a conscious note of who it is you're observing when those thoughts raise their ugly heads. Confess them to the Lord, ask for his forgiveness and receive it knowing that you can be certain of this: As you confess such inner thoughts and attitudes, God will forgive you and cleanse you because he has promised to do so (see 1 John 1:9). We can trust God to keep his Word.

Then, ask the Lord to fill you afresh with the power of his Holy Spirit and with his love for those people. It is the power of God working in us that enables us to be who he calls us to be and do what he calls us to do. God loves to fill us with the Holy Spirit. It is his will for us. In Luke 11:13 we read, "So if you sinful people know how to give good gifts to your children, how much more will your heavenly Father give the Holy Spirit to those who ask him" (NLT). And in Ephesians 5:18 Paul exhorts us to "keep on being filled with the Holy Spirit." Asking God to fill us afresh with his Spirit is a prayer he is more ready to answer than we are ready to pray.

Another step in the process of exchanging grace for the ungrace in our lives may be an experience of healing prayer. There may be a woundedness from our past that is continuing to influence our present in unhelpful ways, and one of those unhelpful ways may be that it has us rooted us in ungrace. A major component of Jesus' job description was to bring healing to the broken-hearted (see Luke 4:18). God is not bound by time and because of this he can bring healing to those places of trauma and pain in our past that still impact our present, a healing that can pull out the weeds of judgment and condemnation that have taken root and keep us from experiencing God's grace in our own lives and in our relationships with others.

Share your desire to be more rooted in God's grace with another Christian brother or sister whom you trust and who is further along in their journey of faith and grace than you. Ask them to be praying with you that God will root you ever more deeply in his grace. In closing this chapter, the following exercise is something you may want to consider doing as a way of responding to a work of grace God wants to do in your life:

- Someone in my family, neighborhood, workplace, or play place for whom I think God may want me to be a walking grace connection is
- As needed, repent of any attitude of judgment or condemnation you may have toward that person and receive God's sure word of forgiveness
- Ask God to fill you afresh with the power of the Holy Spirit, with his grace and love (Acts 1:8)
- In prayer, bless this person in Jesus' name so they might experience God's empowering grace
- Ask God to use you as a vessel through which they can experience God's grace and ask him to reveal to you how you might be a walking grace connection in this person's life
- Thank the Lord for what he is going to reveal to you and what he is going to do in and through you

One of the essential elements in being rooted in God's grace is to go beyond knowing grace in more than an intellectual or theological way, but as something that is part of your ongoing life experience. Toward that end, God can use other people as walking grace connections in our lives, and empower us then to be that for others.

15

GOD'S GIFT OF SALVATION

Because God in his grace chose to relate to us, love us, and save us before we deserved it, let us now relate to, love, and serve others in the same way.

BEING EXPERIENTIALLY ROOTED in God's grace is to realize we receive that which we do not deserve and can never repay—God's gift of salvation. Woody Allen once said, "I don't believe in an afterlife, although I am bringing a change of underwear."[47] If you were to press people, most would admit they hope, or even believe, there is some kind of life after death; they are just not sure what it's like. The Christian faith believes there is life after death, and that it is life that will be lived in a very real place:

> But the day of the Lord will come as unexpectedly as a thief. Then the heavens will pass away with a terrible noise, and the very elements themselves will disappear in fire, the earth and everything on

---

47 See Woody Allen, *Getting Even* (New York: Random House, 1971, 1978; audiobook, 2010).

it will be found to deserve judgment. Since everything around us is going to be destroyed like this, what holy and godly lives you should live, looking forward to the day of God, and hurrying it along. On that day, he will set the heavens on fire, and the elements will melt away in the flames. But we are looking forward to the new heavens and *new earth* he has promised, a world filled with God's righteousness [2 Peter 3:10–13, NLT, emphasis mine].

This new life is made possible by the sacrifice Jesus Christ made on our behalf. John 3:16–18 declares, "For God so loved the world that he gave his only Son, that whoever believes in him should not perish but have eternal life. For God did not send his Son into the world to condemn the world, but in order that the world might be saved through him." Jesus chose willingly, not begrudgingly, to give his life for ours so we might be restored in our relationship with God and live the life we were originally created to experience. Jesus said,

> Truly, truly, I say to you, I am the door of the sheep. All who came before me are thieves and robbers, but the sheep did not listen to them. I am the door. If anyone enters by me, he will be saved and will go in and out and find pasture. The thief comes only to steal and kill and destroy. I came that they may have life and have it abundantly. I am the good shepherd. The good shepherd lays down his life for the sheep. He who is a hired hand and not a shepherd, who does not own the sheep, sees the wolf coming and leaves the sheep and flees, and the wolf snatches them and scatters them. He flees because he is a hired hand and cares nothing for the sheep. I am the good shepherd. I know my own and my own know me, just as the Father knows me and I know the Father; and I lay down my life for the sheep. And I have other sheep that are not of this fold. I must bring them also, and they will listen to my voice. So there will be one flock, one shepherd. For this reason the Father loves me, because I lay down my life that I may take it up again. No one takes it from me, but I lay it down of my own accord. I have authority to lay

it down, and I have authority to take it up again. This charge I have received from my Father (John 10:7–18, ESV).

This is absolutely amazing to me. Jesus willingly sacrificed his life for me, for us! What's more, he did it even while we were misbehaving, even while we were still sinners (see Romans 5:8). He gave his life to save us even when we did not deserve it. I am always reminded of this when I listen to the words of institution preceding our celebration of the Lord's Supper—the words, "on the night in which he was betrayed." It wasn't on a good night that Jesus took bread and took the wine; it was on the night in which he was betrayed. Amazing. And it is for we who are sinners, we who have betrayed him, we who have ignored him, we who have denied him, we who have reviled and ridiculed him, that he willingly gave his life so that we could live!

On our own, we don't deserve the gift of salvation. Ever since the Garden of Eden humankind has consistently turned away from God and sought to live life our own way. "We're all like sheep who've wandered off and gotten lost. We've all done our own thing, gone our own way. And God has piled all our sins, everything we've done wrong, on him" (Isaiah 53:6, The Message). In trying to live life our own way we have fallen short of what is needed to experience a restored relationship with God and live life in a restored heaven and earth after death. Romans 3:23 declares, "For all have sinned and fallen short of the glory of God." We have all sinned, every one of us, and we have all missed the mark. But because of who God is—he is love and full of grace and mercy—and because of who we are to him, he chose to do whatever it would take to save us.

Even though we were hell-bent on living life our own way, thinking we know better than the one who created us and created life itself, he still chose to offer us a gift—new life, eternal life through faith in Jesus Christ. "For the wages of sin is death, *but the free gift* of God is eternal life in Christ Jesus our Lord" (Romans 6:23, NLT, emphasis mine). "For by grace you have been saved, through faith. And this is not your own doing, it is the gift of God, not a result of works, so that no one can boast" (Ephesians 2:8–9, ESV). God's salvation is most certainly a gift we do not deserve and can never pay back. This is grace.

GOD DID NOT DEMAND LIFE CHANGE FIRST, LET US NOT DEMAND IT EITHER

We have not received God's gift of salvation because we are living good enough or right enough that we have earned another chance. Rather, Jesus took the initiative to do whatever it took to save us because he loves us, and he knew we would never be able to live good enough or right enough on our own. And if we stop to really think about this for a moment, what is really amazing is that God did not demand life change on our part before he sent Jesus. God did not demand we change our way of thinking or behaving before he chose to relate to us and love us. He did not demand a demonstrated deservedness on our part before reaching out to us. The fact is our Heavenly Father took the initiative to reach out to us through Jesus while we were still undeserving, and he still does this today.

If God has not demanded any of these things from us, then let us not demand them from others. Because God in his grace chose to relate to us, love us, and save us before we deserved it, let us now relate to, love, and serve others in the same way. Let's take the initiative to reach out to them and love them even though they may not be deserving of it right now. Let's do for others what God in Jesus has done for us. Let's relate to them based on who God is for us and who we are as his sons and daughters, not on what they may seem to deserve in the present moment.

EVERY GENERATION MUST FIGHT THIS BATTLE

One last point regarding God's gift of salvation: Every generation will need to fight the good fight of remaining faithful to this biblical truth that salvation is God's work, not ours. Salvation is a work of God that he accomplishes through the life, death, and resurrection of Jesus. Then he offers it to us as a gift to be received by his grace through faith. We will need to fight to remain faithful to this truth because it is attacked in every generation. There is a constant attempt to water down this truth of the gospel, to turn it into something to be earned through good works, rather than received as a gift of grace. To be champions for this truth is part of our Lutheran-Christian heritage. As Martin Luther writes of grace in his *Preface to the Acts of the Apostles*,

> It should be noted that by this book St. Luke teaches that the true and chief article of Christian doctrine is this: we must be justified alone by faith in Jesus Christ, without any contribution from the law or help from our good works. It all adds up to one thing: we must come into grace.[48]

Being experientially rooted in God's grace is to realize we receive that which we do not deserve and can never repay—*God's gift of salvation!* Let us fight the good fight to hang on to this foundational doctrine of the historic, orthodox Christian faith.

---

48 Martin Luther, *Preface to the Acts of the Apostles* (Grand Rapids, MI: Kregel Publications, 1976), 17.

16

ORDINARY BLESSINGS OF GRACE

*As Christians we've somehow become addicted to drama and allergic
to the ordinary.*

— JIM HENDERSON
Evangelism Without Additives

B EING EXPERIENTIALLY ROOTED in God's grace is to realize we have received
that which we do not deserve and can never repay—the ordinary blessings
of life. In Matthew 5:45 we read, "He gives his sunlight to both the evil and the
good, and he sends rain on the just and unjust alike." God's grace toward us can
be seen in the simple, ordinary blessings of life and those simple ordinary blessings fall upon us even when we don't deserve them to.

We only need look around us with eyes wide open to see the grace and
blessings of God in what we too often take for granted. Michael Frost writes,

I do believe in the supernatural and its power. But I wonder whether
we're missing out on too much in pursuing only such expressions of

the divine. Is God not to be seen in Vincent Van Gogh's *Sunflowers?* Is God not to be seen in the crashing sea? Is God not to be seen in the innocence of a newborn baby's eyes? Or in a rosebud or a character in a film or a book, in a song or in the change of seasons? Can't we hear God in the expressions of the love of our friends? Or taste God in good food and conversation. Let's open our eyes to the so-called mundane expressions of God's grace as much as to the spectacular. You'll find them just as breathtaking.[49]

John and Stasi Eldredge write of some of the ordinary, yet breathtaking, blessings we receive as an expression of God's grace in *Love and War,*

> You can see the tenderness and love of God through all creation—he made grass just firm enough that it stands up straight like a carpet, but not too firm that it hurts you when you run on it with bare feet. And he makes snow just firm enough for snowballs and sledding, but not so firm that it hurts us when it falls; it falls so softly. He makes birds and their songs just loud enough to be delightful, and he creates our ear to delight in the sound.[50]

Slowing down long enough to notice and be grateful for the ordinary blessings of life can help experientially root us in the grace of God. It's in the simple breath we take, the friendship we too often take for granted, the coo of a baby's voice, or the blessing of rain just when its needed that we can be more aware of the grace of God at work. It's in pausing to appreciate anew the beauty of nature around us, whether the awe-inspiring crash of ocean waves, majestic mountains and forests, or the beauty of a painted desert sky that the grace of God can be experienced and received. It can be in seeing God's grace in the ordinary, seemingly mundane things of life

---

49 Michael Frost, *Seeing God in the Ordinary: A Theology of the Everyday* (Peabody, MA: Hendrickson Publishers, Inc., 2000) 5.

50 John and Stasi Eldredge, *Love and War: Finding the Marriage You've Dreamed Of* (New York, NY: Doubleday Religion, 2010), Kindle ed.

that we drink in even more of God's grace and in turn, impart that grace to others.

Author Anne Lamott writes of the ordinary blessings of God's grace that are everywhere to be seen and become apparent when we share the holy experience of walking alongside our friends and loved ones who are facing death square in the eyes:

> The worst possible thing you can do when you're down in the dumps, tweaking, vaporous with victimized self-righteousness, or bored, is to take a walk with dying friends. They will ruin everything for you. First of all, friends like this may not even think of themselves as dying, although they clearly are, according to recent scans and gentle doctors' reports. But no, they see themselves as fully alive. They are living and doing as much as they can, as well as they can, for as long as they can. They ruin your multitasking high, the bath of agitation, rumination, and judgment you wallow in, without the decency to come out and just say anything. They bust you by being grateful for the day, while you are obsessed with how thin your lashes have become and how wide your bottom. When you are on the knife's edge—when nobody knows exactly what is going to happen next, only that it will be worse—you take in today.[51]

As I look back over my life, some of the ordinary blessings through which I've received and been further rooted in God's grace are things like:

- Taking time to notice and give thanks for breathing in and breathing out
- Looking at my wife sipping her coffee in the early morning hours with our two Cairn terriers, Molly and Tillie, sitting on her lap
- Backpacking with my kids in the Big Horn Mountains of Wyoming

---

51 Anne Lamott, *Small Victories: Spotting Improbable Moments of Grace,* (New York, NY: Riverhead Books, 2014), Kindle ed.

- Sitting on my back porch in the early morning hours when all is still quiet in the neighborhood, breathing in the aroma of a fresh brew of Sumatra coffee
- Sitting in the same room with all our children, watching them enjoying each other's company
- Enjoying the company of a male best friend who is closer than a brother
- Being able to relax by taking a bath and soaking in clean, warm water anytime I want to
- Being able to go to my refrigerator without even thinking about it and pour myself a glass of cool, clean drinking water after being outside in the sun, mowing my lawn
- Sharing the joy of being on a beautiful golf course with good friends
- Being able to put one foot in front of the other and walk

I'd like to ask you to close your eyes for a moment. Think back on this past week. Recall where you went and what you saw. Now, write down in the space below, one at a time, the ordinary blessings that have been part of your week.

Now, speak out loud to God, giving thanks for those blessings as a way of giving witness to his simple, ordinary blessings you saw, smelled, touched, and experienced this past week—all of them manifestations of his amazing grace toward you. It is most certainly true: Being experientially rooted in God's empowering grace is to realize that we have received that which we do not deserve and can never repay—the ordinary blessings of life!

17

THE UNCONDITIONAL AND UNSHAKABLE LOVE OF GOD

If you want to impact someone's life, love them when
they least deserve it.

— MARK BATTERSON
Wild Goose Chase: Reclaim the Adventure of Pursuing God

In this fallen, Satan-oppressed world we live in, there will certainly be
many occasions for us to doubt God. For this reason we must be rooted
and grounded in God's love as revealed in Jesus Christ, and in nothing
else.

— GREGORY A. BOYD
Repenting Of Religion

BEING EXPERIENTIALLY ROOTED in God's grace is to realize we have received that which we do not deserve and can never repay—the unconditional and unshakable love of God. Christians who are growing in what it means to be a safe-place people will know this extravagant love in more than an intellectual or theological manner, they will know it experientially. To know such love is amazing. It is something we all hunger and search for. Chuck Swindoll attests to our universal hunger for love in *Grace Awakening*:

> The neighborhood bar is possibly the best counterfeit there is to the fellowship Christ wants to give his church. It's an imitation, dispensing liquor instead of grace, escape rather than reality, but it is a permissive, accepting, and inclusive fellowship. It is unshockable. The bar flourishes not because most people are alcoholics, but because God has put into the human heart the desire to know and be known, to love and be loved.[52]

TOO EASILY TAKEN FOR GRANTED

Being loved and loving others is a universal hunger and need. It is also something too easily taken for granted once we have experienced it. I believe this is a common experience for most Christians all the way back to those first followers in the early church. Too easily taking God's love for granted is why the Christians in Ephesus were called to repent:

> To the angel of the church in Ephesus write: "The words of him who holds the seven stars in his right hand, who walks among the seven golden lamp stands. I know your works, your toil and your patient endurance, and how you cannot bear with those who are evil, but have tested those who call themselves apostles and are not, and found them to be false. I know you are enduring patiently and bearing up for my name's sake, and you have not grown weary. But I have

---

52   Chuck Swindoll, *Grace Awakening* (Dallas, TX: Word Publishing, 1990), 128.

this against you, that you have abandoned the love you had at first" (Revelation 2:1-3, ESV).

Taking for granted something so powerful and so meaningful is not endemic to Christians in general or the Ephesians in particular. It is a human propensity to quickly forget that which once amazed us. When I think of this, I am reminded of the first time I saw the movie *Raider's of the Lost Ark*. In an opening scene, archeologist-adventurer Indiana Jones is leaving a cave in which he had recovered a rare artifact that he had risked his life searching for. As he moves toward the cave's entrance, he senses something behind him; he senses danger. He stops and slowly turns. Then ever so slowly he lifts his gaze, looking upward. Out of nowhere a boulder larger and wider than he is tall appears and begins picking up speed right toward him. Indiana begins to run, the boulder right behind him and gaining ground. Everyone in the theater was literally on the edge of their seats. Collectively we held our breath as the boulder drew closer and closer to crushing Indiana Jones. At the last minute he leaps to the side as he exits the mouth of the cave and the boulder crashes into the jungle destroying every bush and tree in its path. The sigh of relief in the theater was audible.

I can still remember that feeling of shock and awe in the movie theater that day. But I also remember the times I have seen the movie since, and my experience is no longer the same. Familiarity has robbed me of the surprise and wonder I felt when I first saw the movie. Too often I think we can lose the sense of awe and wonder that knowing we are loved by God elicits when its first experienced. After a while we forget that which is built by design into every human heart—the longing to know and be known, to love and be loved, especially with a love like God's.

LOVED WITH A LOVE THAT IS UNCONDITIONAL AND UNSHAKABLE

God's love is unconditional, unshakable, and extravagant. To be loved in this way is one of the most powerful things that can happen in a person's life. His love for us is illustrated in the following story:

A five-year-old boy came to visit his grandfather's farm, which had a cesspool. For those who don't know what those are, they're the big holes in the ground where the water and all the fluids from the house go, the toilet stuff and all that other stuff. This one was covered by wood. The first thing the grandfather told the grandson was he could go wherever he wanted on the farm, but the one thing he couldn't do is go near the cesspool.

Well, the grandson is just walking around outside and he notices this wood. You know a five-year-old boy—he starts jumping up and down. It's fun as he springs up and down in the air, but before he knows it, he's jumping so high that when he comes down he goes right through the boards. Needless to say, this isn't a good spot to be in. Immediately he's in so deep he can't even holler. He's frantic as he tries to swim in the midst of all this stuff from the toilet, all the while splashing it in his eyes, up his nose and in his mouth. Can you imagine what that might be like?

Suddenly an arm reaches down into all that stuff, grabs him by the shoulder, pulling him out, saving his life. It was his grandfather. Do you know what the grandfather did next after he gets his grandson to safety? He kisses his grandson. He doesn't even wipe his face off; he just kisses it while it's still covered with all the muck. He doesn't scold him or lecture him. He doesn't tell him, "I told you so," he just hugs his grandson, calming his fear, reassuring him that he's safe.[53]

That five-year-old boy is you and me, and that grandfather is our Father God. The grandson has an entire farm to explore and enjoy. The grandfather tells him there is only one thing he needs to avoid. That's all, just one thing. The rest of the farm is his to explore and enjoy to the fullest. But the grandson chooses not to heed his grandfather's wise counsel. Whether consciously or not, he refuses to believe his grandpa knows how he can best enjoy his time

---

53 Author unknown.

on the farm to its fullest. Instead, the boy is foolishly overcome by the temptation to try out the one thing he was told not to. In this story, the history of humankind is re-enacted.

Adam and Eve were once that grandson. They were given an entire garden of perfection to explore, enjoy, and work in. They too were instructed that out of all they were given, there was just one thing to avoid. But they did not heed the wise counsel of the father figure who loved them either. They were tempted and drawn to the one thing they'd been warned away from, the one thing that would put them in harm's way. And since that day humankind has continued to be tempted and drawn toward things that harm us rather than run toward the rest of creation we've been given to steward and enjoy.

For being creatures that can be so smart in so many ways, we humans can be so equally clueless. We just don't seem to get it. There are things in life that will harm us, not help us. And there is one who knows better than we what those things are. We are highly intelligent beings. We're just not always wise, and there is a difference.

We just don't seem to get it. There is someone who really does know better than we how life was designed to be lived it to its fullest. That someone in the story was the grandfather, that someone for us is God. Like the grandfather, our Heavenly Father warns us what to avoid, not because he is some kind of cosmic killjoy, but because he loves us, is for us, and is against anything that would harm us. But like the grandson, we seem to continue choosing the cesspools in life. Time and time again we find ourselves up to our necks in it. We don't seem to truly believe there is someone who knows better than we how life can be lived to its fullest, and that that someone loves us.

We choose the cesspools. We get up to our necks in it. At that moment, when we may least deserve being helped, a hand reaches out and grabs hold. In the very moment of our stubbornness, disobedience, and rebellion, God is there, just like the grandfather. God is there, reaching out a hand to grab hold and pull us to safety. What the grandfather did for the grandson, God has done for us. He took the initiative to reach down and grab hold of us by sending his only begotten Son to die for us and save us: "For God loved the world *so much* that he gave his one and only Son, so that everyone believes in him will not perish, but have eternal life" (John 3:16, NLT).

And there it is again, the familiarity. Most of you may have even skipped over reading that verse because that's what we often do when we read books like this. We read what the authors have written but we skip the bible verses because we've heard them before, we're familiar with them, and they've lost their power. This verse, in fact, is so familiar that we expect to see it on a poster behind the goalposts in a football game as much as we read it or hear it quoted in church. That's all it's become for many of us— fodder for a poster. But oh, how amazing that God has loved us *so much*. Being rooted in it is one of the essential keys to living lives of freedom, purpose, and meaning. It is an essential element for living life as someone who, like Jesus, is safe.

Being saved from the stuff of the cesspools of life is amazing enough. But what amazes me even more is what happens next. Like the grandfather in the story, God's first act after he reaches down and pulls us out of the mess we've gotten ourselves into is not to lecture, scold, or punish us, but to grab us, hug us, and kiss us. God's first act is to love, always has been, always will be. And what a love! It is a love that is unconditional, unshakable, and amazingly extravagant. Think not? Listen again to the story of the Running Father (the story we call the Prodigal Son) in the gospel of Luke:

> But when he came to himself, he said, "How many of my father's hired servants have more than enough bread, but I perish here with hunger! I will arise and go to my father, and I will say to him, 'Father, I have sinned against heaven and before you. I am no longer worthy to be called your son. Treat me as one of your hired servants.'" And he arose and came to his father. But while he was still a long way off, his father saw him and felt compassion, and ran and embraced him and kissed him. And the son said to him, "Father, I have sinned against heaven and before you. I am no longer worthy to be called your son." But the father said to his servants, "Bring quickly the best robe, and

put it on him, and put a ring on his hand, and shoes on his feet. And bring the fattened calf and kill it, and let us eat and celebrate. For this my son was dead, and is alive again; he was lost, and is found." And they began to celebrate (Luke 15:17–24, ESV).

This son may have had great intelligence, but he did not have wisdom. In his pride and stubbornness, his disobedience and rebellion, he had gotten himself into it up to his neck. The father would have been justified in turning his back on his son. But he doesn't. Every day he is watching, waiting, hoping for the son's return. Then in the distance there's a glimpse that catches the father's eye. Could it be? He holds his breath. Then he begins to run. This father, knowing full well that in this Middle-Eastern culture it is considered a shameful thing for a father to run, lifts his robe and does just that, he runs. Oh, how he runs. Rather than standing his ground and making the son come to him, he runs, refusing to be bound by the cultural taboos of what is and is not appropriate. Even in this seemingly small detail of the story there is great meaning, because in his running the father takes on the humiliation and shame that rightfully should have been his son's. In compassion and in love the father's movement is toward the son, not away from him; and that is always God's movement toward us.

It amazes me every time I read this story in Luke that like the grandfather in our earlier story, the father's first emotion at the disobedient son's return is compassion, not anger; his first act is to lovingly restore the boy to complete sonship, not to lecture or punish him. God's love for us is so unconditional that he does not demand something in return from us before he acts. He acts first and he acts to love, not to lecture, scold, or punish. This is grace. It is something we do not deserve and can never repay.

Grace can be seen when we, like the Lord, take the initiative to move toward people, not away from them, and love them when they are up to their necks in the stuff, loving them in the very moments they do not deserve it, loving them as God in Christ first loved us. Grace can be seen when we do this and do not demand something from them before we act.

THERE IS NOTHING WE HAVE TO DO

The experience of God's love can take our breath away if we've never experienced it before. Words fail me in an attempt to describe how amazing, how wonderful it is to know the love of God. Like a diamond, the Lord's love refracts an embarrassment of rays, and aspects of light and beauty that can leave us dumfounded and in awe. There are two things in particular that are amazing to me when we consider what it means to be rooted in God's unshakable love and grace.

The first is when we discover there is nothing we have to do to get God to love us. We do not have to coerce him or appease him in some way to make us worthy of his love, because we already are loved. The bible says so: "For God so loved the world" (John 3:16, NLT). "But God showed his great love for by sending Christ to die for us while we were still sinners" (Romans 5:8, NLT). While we were still sinners! Not after we have coerced him, not after we have appeased him, not after we've worked hard enough and are living right enough! He loves us just as we are. We are of such great worth to God that he sent his son, his only begotten son, to die on our behalf so we might experientially know his father-love for us and be restored to a very real, intimate relationship with him. This is just one of the ways we experience being experientially rooted in God's grace, and it is one of the things that separates the Christian faith from other world religions.

Unlike most world religions, Christianity teaches that we do not have to work hard in our own efforts to get God to love us or look upon us with favor. Rather, Christianity teaches that God already loves us and looks upon us with favor simply because we are his creation. This reality is wonderfully illustrated in Gavin's story. Gavin was the son of my friends John and Dawn Huntley, parents of two beautiful little girls in addition to being Gavin's mom and dad. Dawn writes,

> During labor with Gavin, my water broke at home and the cord came out. Gavin was deprived of oxygen for approximately thirty minutes from the time it took the ambulance to get me to the hospital and the doctor to perform an emergency c-section. He had

to be resuscitated and right away was having severe seizures and many other problems. After three and a half weeks in the neonatal intensive care unit, the final prognosis was that his brain stem was severely damaged which caused him to not be able to have reflexes like blinking, crying, sucking, swallowing, gagging, and he would have long periods of apnea. We believe he was at least partially blind since he didn't ever look at us. In fact, he couldn't even move for the most part. He was a severely hurt little boy. We couldn't leave him alone for even the briefest time. He required constant attention and we had to suction him out around the clock so that he didn't choke on his secretions. He had to be fed with a feeding tube.

In and of himself, he did nothing to "make" us love him. He didn't coo or smile or even look at us. He couldn't do anything that our other babies did that were so adorable. And _yet, I couldn't have loved that precious little boy more._ My heart overflowed and I could feel it almost bursting at times over how much I wanted and loved this child. It gave me a good glimpse of how it must be with God. We are pitiful humans that are filthy in comparison to the Holy God, and yet he just couldn't love us more. He doesn't love us because we can *do* or *be* anything for or to him. He loves us because we are his children.[54]

Little Gavin could not do anything and did not have to do anything to get Dawn and John to love him. They loved him because he was their son. Their hearts filled with love for him the moment he was born, almost to the point of bursting. God's heart is filled to the point of almost bursting with love for you and me simply because we are his sons and daughters. We don't have to do anything to get God to love us because he already does!

---

54 John and Dawn Huntley (January, 2015), used with permission via email.

NOTHING IN OUR DARK AND SECRET PLACES SCARES GOD AWAY

There is a second aspect of God's love that still amazes me and fills my heart with so much gratitude that I don't have the words to adequately say thank you to him, even after walking in relationship with him for forty years. That aspect is this—there is nothing about us that will scare his love away.

To be experientially rooted in God's grace is to know we are already as loved and accepted as we ever will be by Abba Father, and there is nothing about us, not even the things hidden in our dark and secret places, that will scare him and make him stop loving us. Henri Nouwen speaks of this reality as he writes of Mary Magdalene,

> This simple and deeply moving story brings me in touch with my fear as well as my desire to be known. When Jesus calls Mary by her name, He is doing much more than speaking the word by which everybody knows her, for her name signifies her whole being. Jesus knows Mary of Magdala. He knows her story: her sin and her virtue, her fears and her love, her anguish and her hope. He knows every part of her heart. Nothing in her is hidden from Him. He knows her even more deeply and more fully than she knows herself. Therefore, when He utters her name He brings about a profound event. Mary suddenly realizes that the One who truly knows her, truly loves her!

> I am always wondering if people who know every part of me, including my deepest, most hidden thoughts and feelings, really do love me. Often I am tempted to think that I am loved only as long as I remain partially unknown. I fear that the love I receive is conditional and then say to myself, "if they really knew me, they would not love me." But when Jesus calls Mary by name He speaks to her entire being. She realizes that the One who knows her most deeply is not moving away from her, but is coming to her, offering her his unconditional love![55]

---

55   Henri Nouwen in Philip Yancey, *Prayer: Does It Make Any Difference?* (Grand Rapids, MI: Zondervan, 2006), 34–35.

There is nothing about you and me that scares God and is going to make him stop loving us. The grace of God is seen and experienced when we refuse to be scared away from being loved by God, and when we refuse to be scared away from loving others, even when we all are at our worst.

THE IMPORTANCE OF KNOWING EXPERIENTIALLY THAT WE ARE LOVED

We cannot overstate the importance of knowing experientially that God loves us. It is much too easy to know this only as an intellectual or theological truth. Jesus loves me, this I know, for the Bible tells me so, goes the old Sunday school song. We sing it so easily. We know it in our minds, yet how few of us know it so deeply within our hearts that it is our default position for living life. When we know deep within our hearts, not merely in our minds, that God loves us, it will change how we experience and deal with all the issues of life; and it will change how we experience and deal with others. Being a safe-place people is to be a people who experientially know God loves us, and seek to connect others to that same life-giving love.

Being experientially rooted in God's unconditional and unshakable love is an essential key in living a life of true freedom this side of heaven. Without this as our rock-solid foundation, we will be susceptible to the attacks, accusations, and deceptions of our enemy. Gregory Boyd writes,

> We may see glimmers of the glory of God in the starry night, beautiful sunsets, and majestic mountains. But our view of God and our trust in Him must not be rooted in such things, for the fallen world is also full of tornadoes, disease, famines, earthquakes and the like. We may thank God for our health, financial blessing, and intimate friends. But if our trust is based on these things, it can be no more stable than they are—and, sorry to say, these things are not stable! Friends may betray you, your boss may fire you, and your health may quickly leave you. If we are not rooted and grounded in the revelation of God's love in Jesus Christ, the Accuser will rise up whenever

misfortune strikes to turn us into accusers of God, and thus of ourselves and other people.[56]

As we seek to live life as followers of Christ who are a safe-place people for fellow Christians and non-Christians alike, it is important to remember the one purpose of our enemy is to separate us from the Father, and from experientially knowing his love for us. This is so central that stories have revolved around it for centuries, beginning with the story of Adam and Eve.

The story of an enemy trying to separate us from the assurance of a father's love is so central to our existence it is even retold in animation stories such as *The Lion King*. In this mythic story, the lion cub Simba is separated in his youth from his father through a murder engineered by his uncle, Scar, the character symbolizing the evil one in the story of humankind. Scar arranges for the cub to be caught in a stampede of wildebeests, knowing his father, Mufasa, will risk his life to save his son. Mufasa does, and Simba is saved, but his father is killed. Scar then turns on Simba and accuses him, in a very vulnerable and desperate moment, of causing his father's death. This is always the way of our enemy, to attack us with doubt and deceit in our most vulnerable and desperate moments. Brokenhearted, frightened, and racked with guilt, Simba runs away from home. It's a win-win for Scar. He separates young Simba from his father and wounds Simba emotionally, hindering him from living fully into his destiny. In the end however, someone takes the initiative to intervene in Simba's life—the wise Rafiki—and it is his intervention that helps bring healing to Simba's emotional wound and puts him back on the destiny path for his life.

In a more real and powerful way we, like Simba, have one who intervenes in our lives, heals us, and restores to our destiny path—Jesus Christ. Like Simba, we have an enemy who will do anything to separate us from the love of our earthly fathers and mothers, and especially from the love of our Heavenly Father. It was for this very reason that Jesus came into the world and gave all humankind an incarnational revelation of the Father's heart for us. He showed

---

56   Gregory A. Boyd, *Repenting of Religion: Turning from Judgment to the Love of God* (Grand Rapids, MI: Baker Books, 2004), 135.

us that God's heart was still toward us, showed us that God was for us and against anything and everything that would harm us. Jesus had been with the Father, had seen the Father, and came to tell us about him, and more than that, to show us what our Heavenly Father looks like (John 14:5–9, NLT):

> Thomas said, "We haven't any idea where you are going, so how can we know the way?" Jesus told him, "I am the way, the truth, and the life. No one can come to the Father except through me. If you had known who I am, then you would have known who my Father is. From now on you know him and have seen him!" Philip said, "Lord, show us the Father and we will be satisfied." Jesus replied, "Philip, don't you even yet know who I am, even after all the time I have been with you? Anyone who has seen me has seen the Father!"

Scratch the most vigorous, authentic Christian you know, and he or she will bleed love—love for God, love for others, and a deep conviction about God's love for him or her. Do the opposite: scratch the sourest, most sedentary Christian you know, and he or she will bleed guilt or toxic shame.

Being experientially rooted in God's empowering grace is seen and experienced as we come to realize we have received that which we do not deserve and can never repay—the unconditional, unshakable, and extravagant love of Father God! And then, through his grace and the empowering presence of the Holy Spirit, being an incarnational revelation of that love to others by loving them in the same way, with the same love—even in those moments when they are up to their necks in it!

SOME WAYS TO RESPOND

Before moving on, take a moment to respond to this word of God's love for you, and through you to others. Following are two prayers you might consider praying as a way of responding. First, consider praying the following alone, or with someone else who will agree with you in prayer:

Dear Father, it's sometimes hard for me to think that I am important to you. It is hard for me to believe I matter as much to you as your Word says I do. I am sorry, but I have learned to trust my experience more than the Bible. Please do a healing work in my life. Heal my heart and set me free from the experiences I have had in life that keep me from believing, truly believing, that you love me in a way that is unconditional, unshakable, and extravagant. Do your work of healing in my life, so I can receive the love you have for me. Father, do whatever you need to do in me so I can hear with the ears of my heart you saying to me, "You are my beloved." Father do whatever you need to do in me so I can experience this and then experience being set free to love others in the same way. In Jesus' name, amen!

Second, in prayer ask, "Father, who is it you want to give me a 'Hosea love' for?" A "Hosea love" is a love for others precisely when they are at their worst. As God brings to mind the names of those for whom he wants to give you that "Hosea love," ask him to fill you afresh with the Holy Spirit and empower you with a boldness and love for them. Then go in the power of the Holy Spirit to love them even though they're up to their necks in it.

A safe-place people are experientially rooted in God's grace, and one of the primary aspects of how that grace has been received in their lives is by being experientially rooted in the love of God. As they are, a safe-place people then willingly and joyfully go wherever in the world God sends them to love others in the same way, with the same love. God's love becomes the gold standard through which every issue they face and every relationship they develop is viewed.

18

FORGIVENESS OF SIN AND HEALING FOR SHAME

*Our Heavenly Father loves to forgive. You and I act like Jesus when
we forgive.*

— JOE JOHNSON

*The gospel of the kingdom of God not only declares forgiveness of
sin but also offers healing from shame. Shame afflicts the poor and
the affluent, the young and the old, every ethnicity, every culture,
every country. In short, shame afflicts all of humankind; always has,
always will.*

B EING EXPERIENTIALLY ROOTED in God's grace is to experientially know
his forgiveness of sin and healing for shame. When teaching on being a safe place I often make the following pledge: If you set your hearts
on being a safe place I can promise you one thing—you will fail, and fail

badly. You will at some point be unsafe for someone. However, it is in those moments of failure, perhaps most especially in those moments, that we can experience the transforming power of God's forgiveness and healing, a transformation that will help us grow in Christ-likeness, help us grow in being a safe place.

In order to experience this growth and transformation it is important we learn to differentiate between what forgiveness is and what it is not, and how we can create shame-free zones in our own lives and in our churches. First let's consider some of the things forgiveness is not.

WHAT FORGIVENESS IS NOT

Forgiveness is not always easy. Noted theologian and author R. T. Kendall, former pastor of Westminster Chapel in London for twenty-five years, had been hurt badly. The thought of forgiving those who had hurt him was difficult to embrace, even though he knew it was what he needed to do. One night, a good friend spoke hard but helpful words to him, "R. T., you must totally forgive them. Until you totally forgive them you will be in chains. Release them, and you will be released." Kendall writes,

> No one had ever talked to me like that in my life. But those words, spoken to me unexpectedly by my friend Josif Tson of Romania, are among the most important words anybody has ever personally shared with me. Mercifully the Holy Spirit spoke to me that day through Josif's words. At first I was angry; I felt hemmed in. But it was a pivotal moment for me, and it changed my life. I was never the same again.[57]

Forgiveness is not always easy. It is not always accompanied with warm feelings. There will be times when it is a difficult choice we make because we know it is right and that it truly is the best thing we can do for ourselves as well as for the person(s) we need to forgive.

---

57 R. T. Kendall, *Total Forgiveness* (Lake Mary, FL: Charisma House, 2007), Kindle ed.

Forgiveness is not forgetting. People who try to forgive by forgetting usually fail on both counts. Forgiving and forgetting are not the same. When we forgive someone we don't forget what he or she did to us. Forgetting, in fact, may be dangerous if it become a way to avoid doing the sometimes hard but necessary work of forgiving. Though we may not forget what someone did, forgiveness releases the power of God to break the bondage and pain of the memory.

Forgiveness is not tolerance. You can forgive someone, but that does not mean you should tolerate what he or she does. It does not mean we must tolerate sin. There may be times when you must lovingly, yet very firmly, establish boundaries whereby you forgive a person's past sins while at the same time take a stand against future sinful behavior.

Forgiveness is not the same as trust. Forgiveness does not mean you have to trust the person and expose yourself to being hurt again. Once we have forgiven someone, wisdom demands that we also establish healthy boundaries. Forgiving someone does not mean you have to trust them and thereby place yourself in a position of being hurt or even abused again. Though you may forgive them, trust is something that is earned over time—if ever again.

Forgiveness is not the same as restoration. Forgiveness does not mean the relationship will always be completely restored to the same state as it was prior to the offense. Romans 12:18 says, "If possible, so far as it depends on you, live peaceably with all." Restoration requires the full participation of two people. The person you forgive may not want to see or talk to you. Or they may have passed away since the time of the offense. Moreover, you may not want to maintain a close relationship with the person you forgive because they are still an unhealthy person. Forgiving someone doesn't necessarily mean we will want to renew our relationship with them, but it does mean that we release the bitterness and unforgiveness in our hearts concerning what they have done.

WHAT FORGIVENESS IS

Two different Greek words are used for forgiveness in the Bible. The first is *aphiemi,* which means, "to let go, send away, or release" (Hebrews 9:22). The second is *charizomai,* which has *charis* (grace) as its root. This word means, "to give freely, grant forgiveness, show kindness unconditionally" (Ephesians 4:32; Colossians 1:13). Now let's consider some of the things forgiveness is.

Forgiveness is acting like Jesus. When we forgive we act like Jesus. The apostle Paul tells us in Romans 5:8 that "God demonstrates his own love for us in this: *While we were still sinners,* Christ died for us" (emphasis mine). Jesus did not wait until we cleaned up our act to love and forgive us. He loved and forgave us while we still were in a state of not deserving it.

When we forgive others, even when they may not deserve it, we act like Jesus. Joe Johnson reminds us, "Our Heavenly Father loves to forgive. You and I act like Jesus when we forgive. First we receive God's forgiveness, and then we can share the gift of forgiveness with others."[58]

We act like Jesus when we lay down what we think are our rights. Too often we choose to believe we have a right to hang on to unforgiveness toward someone and in doing so, are more like the unforgiving servant the apostle Matthew tells us about in Matthew 18:21–35: "The king was angry with the unforgiving servant and said, 'You worthless wretch! I canceled your entire debt when you pleaded with me. Should you not have dealt mercifully with your fellow servant, as I have dealt with you?'" Too often we convince ourselves we are justified in remaining angry and unforgiving toward someone because they have treated us so unfairly or have betrayed us. Isaias Powers speaks to this in the following reflection from his book *Healing Words From Jesus:*

> So often we feel that we have a right to our anger at the injustices—
> great or small—committed against us. But dealing mercifully with
> others has nothing to do with rights; Jesus said as much in this parable. To be merciful is to act out of compassion, with regard for the
> needs of another. When we show mercy to others, we are modeling
> the action of God in our lives who overlooks our debts each and
> every day. We can do no less than what has been done for us! Only
> when we remember how immeasurably God loves us will we be

---

58 Joe Johnson, used with permission.

able to stop living a life based on rights rather than on compassion and love.[59]

A safe-place people are committed to living lives based on compassion and love, not on stubbornly holding on to their rights. I am not saying this is easy to do. And I do not want to make light of how grievously and unfairly you may have been hurt or betrayed. However, choosing to hold on to what you may think is your right to not forgive in the end will hurt you.

It was not fair or right that Jesus should have had to die on our behalf, but he did. He laid down his rights when he left heaven to come to earth. And now he calls us to follow his example and lay down what we think is our right—to not forgive—so that we might be set free to live the life he has purposed for us. When we forgive, we are acting like Jesus.

Forgiveness can be one of the hardest things you've ever done. In the previous section we noted that forgiveness is not always easy. It stands to reason then that it can be one of the hardest things we're called to do in life, especially when we have been grievously and legitimately hurt or betrayed. R. T. Kendall continues his story of total forgiveness as he writes,

> It was the hardest thing I had ever been asked to do, but it was also the greatest thing I had ever been asked to do. However, if I allowed myself to think about what those people did, I would get churned up inside. I would say to myself: "They are going to get away with this. This is not fair! They won't get caught. They won't be found out. Nobody will know. This is not right! And then the sweet peace of the Lord left." I had to make an important decision: Which do I prefer—the peace or the bitterness? I couldn't have it both ways. I began to see that I was the one who was losing by nursing my attitude of unforgiveness. My bitterness wasn't damaging anyone but myself."[60]

---

59 Isaias Powers, *Healing Words from Jesus* (New London, CT Twenty-third Publications, 1996), 17.

60 Kendall, *Total Forgiveness*, Kindle ed.

Kendall presents us with a powerful choice: Do we want the peace or bitterness? Do we want prison or freedom? Forgiveness can be hard work, but it will be worth it in the end. Forgiveness can be hard, but because of what Jesus has done on our behalf, and because of how he has forgiven us when we have not earned it nor deserve it, he can empower us to forgive others.

Forgiveness is our only way out of our own prison. I cannot underscore this enough. No matter how badly we have been wounded—and I speak as one who has experienced great pain and betrayal in some of the relationships in my life—in the end unforgiveness will only hurt us and keep us imprisoned for the rest of our lives. When we choose to not forgive, we become prisoners of our own making. We become the ones who continue to be hurt and held in bondage, and when that is the case the enemy wins by distracting us and misdirecting us from God's purposes for our lives.

To not forgive is to remain tied to the person we refuse to forgive for the rest of our lives. Picture a person who has a heavy chain attached to their ankle. The other end of the chain is attached to the wrist of another person. The first person must drag that other individual everywhere they go. Can you imagine how weary the first person gets dragging the other? Can you imagine the pain as the chain cuts into their ankle? This is the weariness and the pain of unforgiveness. And it hinders the first person from experiencing more of the freedom that life could hold for them.

Now, imagine that chain being broken and that person being set free. What a feeling of freedom that would be. What a relief. The burden is finally gone. That's what forgiveness can mean for us. It can mean that as we "cut that person loose" they no longer have the right to follow us into the rest of our lives and harass us and hold us back from whatever it is God has for us.

Forgiveness is validating that the offense did occur. Forgiveness does not ignore the reality of an offense. In fact, forgiving someone validates that the offense did indeed occur. Joseph's response in the Old Testament is an example of this. In Genesis 50:20 he told his brothers that he knew they had intentionally chosen to hurt him. Joseph then forgave his brothers. In forgiving them he did not rationalize, minimize, or deny what they had done to him. He actually acknowledged it, and in doing so validated that the offense did occur.

Validation of this sort is an essential element of true forgiveness and a key to living life free of the offense and in right relationship with other people, in so far as it is up to us.

Forgiveness is releasing someone who has wronged you to God. Forgiveness in Scripture is a legal matter, not just an emotional one. In a sense, it has to do with dropping the legal charges against someone. It is trusting eternal judgment to God. Forgiveness is recognizing the debt the other person owes us and making an internal personal decision to release the offender from their indebtedness to us, and releasing them instead to God.

Forgiveness can be a process. Forgiving someone can be a process, not just a one-moment event. Especially in cases of great trauma, forgiveness may be a process of healing, which, if rushed too quickly can be harmful. We can learn a lesson about not prematurely rushing forgiveness from the healing process built into our physical bodies by God. There are some wounds that can be fixed quickly and easily. However, there are other, more serious wounds that are different. Of such wounds Peter Steinke writes,

> They are wider and deeper, with jagged edges and debris. No suture could tie them together and make them tight. This kind of wound has to heal by a process called "granulation." It is a slow process, the healing happens from the inside out. Care must be taken to protect the raw, open tissue from further injury. Slowly, the wound heals, becoming smaller and more shallow. Many processes are at work at once. The new skin is pink and fresh. As the evidence of the old wound passes away, behold, there is a "new creation."

Sometimes people want to save time or desire a quick fix. They use sutures to bring the offense together tightly, to make the edges fit together. They pull harder. All too often, though, these wounds buckle. When a wound is prematurely closed the edges never come together appropriately. The wound festers within, even though it appears to be well. Eventually cells die from infection, lack of oxygen, poor circulation, or isolation. There is no community. The cells do not come together to heal. Then everything starts to erode, and sometimes the disease goes deeper into a bone or blood.[61]

The healing of physical bodies and the healing of relationships and our soul through forgiveness are both best done as a process in certain cases. As we work out the process of forgiving in a safe-place community, there comes a day when you realize that you are no longer hoping the other person fails or that something bad happens for them. And you rejoice because you know God's forgiving power has been at work in your life.

There may be times when you, or someone you are seeking to help, do not feel ready to forgive those who have hurt them so badly. Rather than demanding immediate forgiveness on the spot, this might be helpful to ask: Even if you don't feel like you could forgive that person or persons right now, would you like to some day? Would you like to move toward being able to forgive them? Then pray with them for that desire to be birthed in their hearts and continue to work out the process of forgiveness.

Forgiveness can save us from grieving the Holy Spirit. "And do not grieve the Holy Spirit of God, by whom you were sealed for the day of redemption. Let all bitterness and wrath and anger and clamor and slander be put away from you, along with all malice. Be kind to one another, tenderhearted, forgiving one another, as God in Christ forgave you" (Ephesians 4:30–32, ESV). It is clear from this passage, that one of the ways we can sadden the Holy Spirit is by not forgiving one another.

Have you ever stopped to wonder about the severity of what it means to grieve the Holy Spirit? Have you ever felt deeply hurt by something or someone? Have you known someone who has? To cause others such sadness in their hearts is not a small matter. Some of the other meanings for the Greek word for grieve—*lypeoœ*—give us more insight into the seriousness of this action. It means to be pained, distressed, or sorrowful. The heartache of these words cannot be fully understood unless one has actually experienced being grieved by the thoughts, words, or actions of another.

---

61 Peter L. Steinke, *How Your Church Works: Understanding Congregations as Emotional Systems* (Herndon, VA: The Alban Institute, 1993), 33–34.

I think we would do well to try and understand how badly we can hurt God with our thoughts, words, and deeds. When we gossip, slander, accuse, and tear apart our relationships with one another it hurts our Heavenly Father. This is a grave issue that I am certain we will regret one day as much or more than anything we have ever done. Let's commit now to doing whatever we can to avoid grieving the Holy Spirit. Let's choose to forgive. And then let's act on that choice and forgive those toward whom we are holding onto unforgiveness toward.

Forgiveness can help us avoid demonic deception and influence in our lives. In Acts we are told that Simon the Sorcerer was in bondage to bitterness (Acts 8:23). Was this perhaps the open door through which a demonic spirit gained influence in his life? Being in bondage to bitterness and unforgiveness can make us vulnerable to being influenced and deceived by unclean spirits. The apostle Paul counseled the Corinthian Christians, "If you forgive anyone, I also forgive him. And what I have forgiven—if there was anything to forgive—I have forgiven in the sight of Christ for your sake, in order that Satan might not outwit us. For we are not unaware of his schemes" (2 Corinthians 10:11). And he counseled the Christians in Ephesus, "In your anger do not sin. Do not let the sun go down while you are still angry, and do not give the devil a foothold" (Ephesians 4:26–27).

Our enemy, the devil, does scheme against us and does seek to gain a foothold in our lives. A foothold is a place of influence. In addition to being influenced by God, Christians can be influenced by the world, the flesh, and the devil. Refusing to forgive provides the enemy an opportunity to influence our lives, and when that happens we are in danger of being distracted and diverted from the paths of God for us individually or corporately. As badly as we may have been hurt, we do not want to give the enemy any opening whereby he can harass us and distract us from the purposes God has for us.

These are some of the things forgiveness is and is not. If we are to grow in what it means to be a safe place as an individual or as a congregation, we must learn to discern between the two, and lovingly help one another toward releasing forgiveness toward those who have hurt and betrayed us.

A SHAME-FREE ZONE

The gospel of the kingdom of God not only declares forgiveness of sin but also offers healing from shame. Shame afflicts the poor and the affluent, the young and the old, every ethnicity, every culture, every country. In short, shame afflicts all of humankind; always has, always will. It first came into the world when Adam and Eve disobeyed God in the Garden of Eden and humanity has suffered its effects ever since.

What is shame? Author Robert Walter writes, "Shame is a painful sense of being fundamentally flawed that comes with a deep conviction that I am not only unacceptable, but hopeless because I am powerless to change."[62] Shame is thinking that we *are* a mistake rather than we *made* a mistake. Guilt comes with realizing we failed, shame is the belief that we are a failure. Guilt is related to action. Shame is related to identity. Those who are in bondage to shame believe they are flawed, unacceptable, and will always be that way. They even beat themselves up for having shame.

Creating a shame-free zone is an essential element in being an individual or church that is growing in what it means to be a safe place. Its critical nature is apparent when we think of the pervasive effects shame has. Walter writes,

> Shame is considered to be one of the driving forces behind a myriad of personal problems—addiction, depression, promiscuity, violence, suicide, eating disorders, and bullying. But it's not just a root to the obvious problems; it's also behind "acceptable" excesses like perfectionism and workaholism. These traits might serve us well in the short term but eventually we become their slaves if the compulsion is not tamed. Shame strangles us spiritually; it poisons our relationships and makes us obsessively self absorbed."[63]

Shame is nothing new. It is a concept we find throughout the Bible. Walter notes, "The word shame occurs more than twice as many times as the word

---

62 Robert Walter, *Grace for Shame*, a workbook for a class taught at The Master's Institute Seminary (September 2011), 6.

63 Ibid., 3.

guilt in a multi translation concordance."[64] The debilitating message of shame is "you are not enough, God is not enough to make you enough, and you need something else from the world to make you enough"[65] It is absolutely essential therefore, that safe-place people and churches commit themselves to creating shame-free zones so that people are breathing in an emotional, relational, and spiritual air that tells them that in Christ they are more than enough.

CREATING A SHAME-FREE ZONE

How can we create and sustain a shame-free zone? For a more in-depth treatment of that question I commend the work of Robert Walter to you (www. ongodstrail.com). His writings and seminars address this topic in much greater detail than I am able. Walter's expertise and insights on this topic, along with his practice in inner healing prayer, can help you better identify and deal with the issue of shame in your own life, your home, and your church. With that in mind, following are a few of the important things to be aware of in creating a shame-free zone.

Indicatives before imperatives. An important starting point in creating a shame-free zone is to examine, and where needed to change, how we preach, teach, and counsel. In each of these areas it is important we remember to tell our congregations and ourselves that in Scripture, the work of God always precedes the our response to that work. Exhorting one another with commands is most often well intentioned. However, when we challenge each other with even the most inspirational of exhortations without first recalling the indicatives given in the Bible, we place a heavy load on each other. We make ourselves and our strength and ability the focus, rather than God's strength and ability. Remembering that God's enabling work precedes any response on our part reminds us that we can only carry out every God-given command we are given because of what God in Christ has already done for us.

Author Bill Jackson notes this in his book *The Quest for the Radical Middle,* a look back at the Vineyard Christian movement. Jackson writes, "The Vineyard

---

64 Ibid., 4.

65 Ibid., 11.

has put the weight on what are called 'indicatives' in the New Testament—statements of fact, i.e., Christ died for your sins. In the New Testament indicatives always come before the imperatives, i.e., Christ died for your sins; therefore repent."[66] Keeping the statements of fact concerning God's work in front of our exhortations when we preach, teach, and counsel will help create a shame-free zone because it will remind us and those we are ministering to that God always gives us the grace to be who he calls us to be and to do what he calls us to do. Neither they nor we have to rely on our own strength, but on God's strength and on his promises.

Grace-infused language. Another aspect related to our preaching, teaching, and counseling is being intentional in using grace-infused language. When we use words such as ought, should, need to, and have to in regards to our relationship with Christ and our lives as Christians we can unwittingly deepen any sense of shame someone might be carrying because we only reinforce what they already know to be true—they are not enough and never will be. Seeking to be experientially rooted in God's grace will give us a new vocabulary. In place of the old will be new words like enjoy, love to, want to, get to, and more when it comes to our relationship with the Lord and in our practice of fundamentals of the faith.

You are enough because of Christ in you. Another essential element in creating a shame-free atmosphere is to speak and teach the truth from God's Word that contradicts the message of shame—the message that you are not enough, God is not enough to make you enough, and you need something else from the world to make you enough. The truth that contradicts this lie is that Jesus not only forgives our sin, and heals and sets people free in Scripture, but that he also heals the shame that accompanies their sin, disease, or bondage to demonic forces—and in doing so makes their not enough more than enough.

We can see this in stories such as the man freed from his chains in Mark 5:1–20, the woman who struggled with the issue of blood in Mark 5:21–34, the woman caught in adultery in John 8:1–11, and the son who comes home after shaming his father as well as himself in Luke 15:1–32. In each case the

---

66 Bill Jackson, *The Quest for the Radical Middle: A History of the Vineyard* (Cape Town, South Africa: Vineyard International Publishing, 1999), 221.

person involved experienced a healing from shame, not only forgiveness of sin. As a result, each of them was amazingly transformed and would most certainly go on to impact the lives of others.

Proclaiming the truth that Jesus died to heal our shame as well as forgive our sins can have a transformational effect as the Holy Spirit works in power through the proclamation of the Word of God—"Faith comes from hearing and hearing through the Word of Christ" (Romans 10:17, ESV). Each follower of Christ is enough because Christ in us is more than enough; Christ in us is the hope of glory (see Colossians 1:27).

Simply declaring this biblical truth and reality may not always set people free from the cloud of shame that has enveloped their lives, yet for some it might be a contributing factor for freedom because of the ability of Holy Spirit to work powerfully through the declared and preached Word of God. At the very least, it may be an important part of God's process of delivering them from the debilitating hold of shame on their life.

Perhaps one practical thing we could do in our churches would be to create orders of confession that declare who God is for us and what our new identity in Christ is, rather than only confessing our sin. While we must never do away with the latter, adding the former to our orders of worship might help some people expel the toxic fumes of shame they have been breathing in and fill them with the cleansing breath of God's grace. Orders of confession of who God is and who we are in him can affect what's in the air.

You are the one. Another element in creating a shame-free zone is to expose the lie of the enemy that says to an individual or church, you are not the one God can use and can never be the one. The truth is that in the kingdom of God it is often those who appear to us as having no hope of being the one who are in fact the one through whom God moves in significant and powerful ways. Oh, their impact may not garner nationwide attention on CNN or Fox, but in their own way, no, in God's way, they are making a difference that forever transforms the lives of others.

In the kingdom of God it's often that person who looks more like a hafling in the shire or the little church in the city or countryside that doesn't have the greatest orator for a pastor and certainly can't put on the big show that impacts people with God's power and love as their members faithfully pray, love, and serve others.

That people hunger for such a message is evident in the epic tales of movie trilogies that have captured our attention worldwide over the past four decades. Remember with me for a moment: Luke Skywalker was just a young farmer, Thomas Anderson only a computer software programmer, and Frodo, well he was a hafling, literally half the size of the returning king. But we reveled in the fact that Luke became the Jedi knight who was the one to lead the victory over the evil empire. We cheered as Thomas Anderson was revealed to be Neo, the bringer of freedom in the Matrix. And we loved the fact that it was Frodo, along with his own personal Barnabas, Sam-Wise Gamgee, and not the strong and handsome Aragon, who was the one called to destroy the ring and break the power of evil over the land.

The truth of Scripture is that you *are* the one, you are a key player in God's kingdom purposes in the very places you are positioned—the place where you work, the neighborhood in which you live, the places where you play and relax, and in the family you have, immediate and extended. It's critical that we proclaim this truth to people: It is essential we all understand how important we are in the place we are because God can impact others through us because of the presence of his Spirit in us.

You are the one who can contend in prayer for God's will to come on earth as it is in heaven for the people and places God sends you to. You are the one who can make a difference for the kingdom of God at home, in your neighborhood, at work, where you play, and in your church. The lie of the enemy is that you are not the one. The truth of God is that you *are* the one, and the enemy who is the father of all lies knows this better than you and me. He fears our discovery of the truth and the healing of our shame because that will enable us to lay down the distorted pictures of God and of ourselves that we have been holding onto. He knows the discovery of truth and healing of shame will set us free to live as who we really are—ordinary men or women, who know, love, and serve an extraordinary God.

Joy. Filling the air with joy is another essential element in creating a shame-free zone. Walter notes that shame, like anger or depression can have an extremely powerful influence on our thinking. But, he notes, "Brain scientists have discovered that the emotional center of our brain has control over the rest of the brain. When we are upset, our emotional center takes over and shuts down our relational and rational functions as we move into 'fight, flight or freeze' mode. But amazingly, our emotional center doesn't have ultimate control. God made our emotions subject to the joy center in our brain. If we can tap into joy, we can break free of shame and re-engage with our right mind."[67] Here's how Christian psychologist James Wilder explains it,

> Having enough joy strength is fundamental to a person's well being. We now know that a "joy center" exists in the right orbital prefrontal cortex of the brain. It has executive control over the entire emotional system. When the joy center has been sufficiently developed, it guides us to act like ourselves: it releases neurotransmitters like dopamine and serotonin; and it is the only part of the brain that overrides the main drive centers— food and sexual impulses, terror and rage.[68]

Joy can be restored through the relational connection we have with God, which in turn can be experienced a number of ways: in fellowship with others who incarnate the joy of the Lord; joy-filled freedom in worship; inner healing prayer and sovereign downloads of God's freedom and healing presence. Joy can also be restored as one of the manifestations of praying to be filled with the Holy Spirit.

Praying to be filled with the Holy Spirit. When I think of praying for the filling of the Holy Spirit being accompanied by a manifestation of joy, I cannot help but remember the true account about one of my sons. Debi and I were attending a Bible camp with our family in Alberta, Canada. One night, as our eight-year-old son was walking along with Debi, he asked her out of the blue if he could pray for God to fill him with the Holy Spirit from the top of his head to the bottom of his feet. "Of course," she replied and they walked to a cabin

---

67 Walter, *Grace for Shame*, 32–33.

68 James Wilder in Robert Walter, *If I Am Forgiven, Why Do I Still Feel So Bad?* (Robert Walter, 2014), 33.

that was being used for Bible classes during the day. They prayed together, and as they prayed our son began to cry a bit. "Why are you crying?" Debi asked. "Because I'm so happy," he answered with a smile on his face and tears continuing to stream down his cheeks. As the presence of the Holy Spirit was being stirred up within him, an impartation of God's joy was flooding his being, touching him in such a deep place that the natural response of his body was to cry. To cry tears of joy!

This was also the experience of Charles Finney, one of the leaders of the Second Great Awakening in the late eighteenth and early nineteenth centuries:

> The Holy Spirit descended upon me in a manner that seemed to go through me, body and soul. I could feel the impression, like a wave of electricity, going through and through me. Indeed it seemed to come in waves and waves of liquid love. It seemed like the very breath of God. I wept aloud with joy and love; and I do not know but I should say, I literally bellowed out the unutterable gushings of my heart.[69]

Perhaps one of the most fascinating accounts of lost joy being restored when we are filled with the Holy Spirit comes from my good friend, Pastor Glen Carlson of Alberta, Canada. Glen went through a long, hard season in which he lost his sense of joy. He graciously shares his story with us:

> My wife and I attended the International Charismatic Conference on the Holy Spirit in Brighton, England. This was a conference that had people from over a hundred different countries and people from most denominations. It was an exciting event that was not only informative but spiritually uplifting. About the third day into the conference, my wife and I took our regular seats in the first row of the balcony of the conference center for the evening meeting. The service began with much singing and rejoicing and dancing as we often had at our

---

69   Rich Nathan and Ken Wilson, *Empowered Evangelicals: Bringing Together the Best of the Evangelical and Charismatic Worlds* (Ann Arbor, MI: Servant Publications, 1995), 40.

worship services. It was good to see all the people from so many ethnic backgrounds celebrating and worshipping together.

The speaker than evening was Bishop Chitimo from Kenya in Africa, who introduced himself as the laughing Bishop. I thought this was a neat title and as he spoke it was certainly evident that he was filled with the joy of the Lord. About halfway through his message I began a laughter that formed deep in my gut and seemed to well up within me. It was something that I didn't seem to have any control over, except I tried my hardest to prevent it. It seemed to get worse and worse to the point where my wife nudged me and told me to be quiet. I apologized for my behavior but I couldn't seem to prevent it. The people behind me tapped me on the shoulder and told me to stop because they in turn were getting the same kind of laughter. Because of my nature I was embarrassed over it for I don't like to make a scene, however, it continued.

After the service was over I still had this laughter that was being produced from within and all the way to the hotel I kept laughing. We went for tea with another couple, but I ended up excusing myself in order to go back to my room because of the laughter. That evening when I went to bed I literally laughed myself to sleep. This laughter was not a boisterous laughter, but it just came from within. It wasn't until the next morning that I began to realize, through the guidance of the Holy Spirit, what this was all about. It became very clear to me that God *was restoring the joy of the Lord* into my life and ministry. It wasn't that I was not happy before, but I knew that *there was something missing.* As I reflected on this I began to realize that a year or so prior to this event I had been involved with a deliverance ministry that I did not have the prayer protection that I usually insist on. In this deliverance ministry I know something came over me that brought a fear within me and from that point on I avoided anything that had to do with deliverance ministry. What God was doing through this manifestation of the spirit of laughter was restoring the joy of the Lord, and as a result was taking away the fear that had come upon me during that deliverance ministry. Through this experience I have discovered that God manifests His Holy Spirit in ways we do not always understand [emphasis mine].[70]

Inner healing prayer. Another way God can restore our joy and heal our shame is by the work of his presence and power through inner healing prayer. This is a form of prayer in which God can bring healing to wounded emotions or memories from the past that are still influencing our present in unhelpful ways. A particularly powerful school of inner healing prayer is called the Immanuel approach. In the Immanuel approach, God reveals himself to the person being prayed for. Robert Walter, a practitioner, teacher, and advocate of this inner healing prayer model writes, "When God reveals the truth of who we are to the person being prayed for, he steals shame's script. Words of condemnation no longer define us. Because our world makes love conditional, it's hard to grasp how God could love us so unconditionally. But when his love and care are revealed to you personally you not only discover the truth about God, you discover the truth about yourself. In the process shame is scattered."[71]

I am writing this chapter the day after teaching in a school of ministry at Penasquitos Lutheran Church in San Diego, California. The evening before, one of the students recounted her experience of Immanuel prayer at the national gathering for the Alliance of Renewal Churches network the previous summer. As she was being prayed for, Jesus restored her joy and healed her shame. She walked away with a new, experiential sense of her identity as God's beloved daughter. She no longer knew it in a merely theological or intellectual way; she now knew it in her heart of hearts. The power of God working through the Immanuel approach to inner healing prayer can restore our joy and in doing so, break the power of shame over our lives.

---

70 Glen Carlson, in an email to the author (December 14, 2014), used with permission.
71 Walter, *If I Am Forgiven*, 38.

Intentional cultivation. Yet another way to restore joy in our lives and break the power of shame is to intentionally cultivate joy. Walter writes, "Joy is fundamental to a person's well being. Figure out what stimulates joy for you and write yourself a daily prescription. Spend time with people that bring you joy. Spend time doing what brings you joy. After (or during) every episode of shame deliberately try to return to joy. Train your brain to return to joy each time."[72] Restoring joy is something we can intentionally position ourselves to cultivate.

CLOSING

Being experientially rooted in God's grace is to realize we receive that which we do not deserve and can never repay—God's gift of forgiveness of sin and healing for shame A safe-place people will seek to discern the difference between what biblical forgiveness is and is not, and they will be intentional to not only declare the gospel as forgiveness of sin, but also as healing for shame.

---

72 Ibid., 22.

19

GOD DELIGHTS IN US

Some neurologists now say that the basic human need is to be the
sparkle in someone's eyes.

—— JAMES G. FRIESEN
The Life Model: Living From the Heart Jesus Gave You

He led me to a place of safety; he rescued me
because he delights in me.

—— PSALM 18:19, NLT

H AVE YOU EVER noticed the power of being delighted in? My grandson, Michael, is two years old. Lately, when my Debi and I video Skype with Michel and his mom (our daughter, Rachel), one of the things he likes to do for us is sing his ABCs. As I write this, Michael knows how to sing the tune, but does not know all of the letters yet. So, rather than singing, "A, B, C," many of the letters come out, "E, E, E." What's really great about his rendition of this classic song is his ending. When he is finished singing, we begin to clap and cheer for him, and he joins right in. Michael gets this great smile on his face (he *is* the cutest grandchild ever) and cheers for himself too. Our grandson loves it when we delight in him.

Being experientially rooted in God's grace is to know not only that God loves us, but that he also delights in us! The bible tells us so:

> Sing, O daughter of Zion; shout aloud, O Israel! Be glad and rejoice with all your heart, O daughter of Jerusalem. For the Lord will remove his hand of judgment and will disperse the armies of your enemy. And the Lord himself, the King of Israel will live among you! At last your troubles will be over, and you will never again fear disaster. On that day the announcement to Jerusalem will be, "Cheer up, Zion! Don't be afraid! For the Lord your God is living among you. He is a mighty savior. *He will take delight in you* with gladness. With his love, he will calm all your fears. He will rejoice over you with joyful songs" [Zephaniah 3:14–17, NLT, emphasis mine].

> Yet Jerusalem says, "The Lord has deserted us; the Lord has forgotten us." "Never! Can a mother forget her nursing child? Can she feel no love for the child she has borne? But even if that were possible, I would not forget you! See, I have *written your name on the palms of my hands*"[Isaiah 49:14–16a, NLT, emphasis mine].

God loves and delights in his children, so much so that he got a tattoo, as it were, to remind us all. God loves and delights in us so much that the Bible book *Song of Songs* is an entire hymn to the divine romance of God's passionate desire and delight in his bride—you and me.

Remember our working definition of grace? God's grace is experienced in how he chooses to relate to us; he chooses to relate to us based on who he is, not on what we deserve.

There may be moments we do not feel we deserve God's delight in us, and in fact, we may not. There may be moments when God does not delight in our choices, actions, or beliefs, particularly when we're believing a lie as if it's truth. But he still delights in *us*.

THERE IS POWER IN DELIGHTING

There is power in delighting in another person. We can have a profound impact on others merely by being present with them and taking delight in them, even though at times we know they misbehave. In those moments when their behavior does not deserve being delighted in, but we still delight in who they are as persons, grace is seen, grace is experienced.

The delight of a parent or grandparent is not based on *doing;* it is based on *being.* As a father, I do not delight in my children because they always behave or believe properly. I delight in them because they are my children. I delight in them as I watch them exploring and navigating life, making discoveries, growing, maturing, and blossoming into the people God has created them to become.

One of my fondest memories of my own dad, Darwin (Brad) Bradley, and of Debi's dad, Armand (Al) Asper, was watching these two grandfathers when they were in the presence of our children. Al met only our oldest son, Andy, before he (Al) died in 1980. But oh, how Al's face would light up when he watched Andy, and held him. His grandfather-heart delighted in his grandson.

Brad absolutely delighted in our children. Did he see them misbehave at times? You bet, but that didn't keep him from delighting in his grandkids. My dad's eyes would light up when he was with them. Even though he was battling Parkinson's disease, bone cancer, and heart disease, he would get this twinkle of delight in his eyes as he watched our kids—all the while knowing they weren't perfect. And this grandfather's delight impacted our children. Even though my dad couldn't *do* much with our kids toward the end of his life because of his battle with those diseases, he still impacted them and affected them for good just by being present and delighting in them. They knew they were loved and delighted in because that's what their grandpa communicated through his presence and demeanor.

Have you ever noticed the delight in a child's eyes when, like my grandson, they experience a parent or grandparent taking delight in them? It has been said that, "In a child's first two years, the desire to experience joy or delight in loving relationships is the most powerful force in life. In fact, some neurologists now say that the basic human need is to be the sparkle in someone's eyes."[73] When you catch a glimpse of a child's face as he or she runs toward a waiting parent or grandparent with arms outstretched in unrestrained joy, you can witness firsthand the incredible power that comes from "being the sparkle in someone's eyes." Whose eye are you the sparkle in? Who is it that looks to be the sparkle in your eye?

SIN DOES NOT MAKE US WORTHLESS, ONLY LOST

To be able to delight in others, even while we are fully aware of how imperfect they may be, is possible when we realize that sin does not make us worthless, only lost![74] To delight in others, especially in the midst of their moments of imperfection, can be one of the most healing things they may experience, and need.

Unfortunately, not even every Christian, let alone non-Christian, has this sense of being delighted in by their Heavenly Father because they have not been loved or delighted in by their earthly father or mother, or anyone else for that matter. This is why God's desire in the lives of so many is to break through with what author Brennan Manning calls the "Abba Experience":

The greatest gift I have ever received from Jesus Christ has been the Abba experience. My dignity as Abba's child is my most coherent sense of self. Only a sense of self that is rooted in the deep assurance that I am completely and unconditionally loved by my Daddy God

73 James G. Friesen, et al., *The Life Model: Living from the Heart Jesus Gave You* (Pasadena, CA: Shepherd's House, Inc., 2000), 11.
74 Dallas Willard, *Renovation of the Heart: Putting on the Character of Christ* (Colorado Springs, CO: NavPress, 2002), Kindle ed.

already, will result in a tender, confident, bold and effective living for the Lord in this world. Tenderness awakens with the security of knowing we are thoroughly and sincerely liked by someone. The mere presence of that special someone in a crowded room brings an inward sigh of relief and a strong sense of feeling safe. We become more open, real, vulnerable, and affectionate. We grow tender.[75]

Being delighted in by another person is one of the greatest gifts we can have in life because "not many people feel celebrated and a relationship that offers celebration heals the soul.[76] As Manning stated, to be in a crowded room and know there is someone special there who thoroughly and sincerely likes us and delights in us sets us free to discover and live out of the most essential sense of self we can have. And living out of that settled sense of identity gives us a peace that others sense. We become those people of whom they say, "They are comfortable in their own skin."

Being people who live knowing they are already delighted in by someone special can be a powerful and incredible gift to those around us. Being experientially rooted in God's grace is to know God not only loves us, he also delights in us! Being a safe-place people is to not only know this is how God views us, but it is to then be that someone who has a sparkle in their eye for others. Who is it God wants you and me to have a sparkle in our eye for? A sparkle, a delight, that is not merely some nice feeling, but is a powerful source of healing and transformation?

Before you read on, can I ask you a question? Have you ever felt the absence of having someone delight in who you are? Are you, or have you ever been, the sparkle in someone else's eye? If not, I wish I were there to be that for you. If not, I wish God would send someone into your presence right now to be that source of God's delight for you. But since I cannot be physically

---

75 Brennan Manning, *Abba's Child: The Cry of the Heart for Intimate Belonging* (Colorado Springs, CO: NavPress, 1994), Kindle ed.

76 Larry Crabb, *Becoming a True Spiritual Community: A Profound Vision of What the Church Can Be* (Nashville, TN: Thomas Nelson Inc., 2007), 11.

present with you, can I pray for you? Here is my prayer. Please read it, hear it, and receive it just as surely as if I were sitting right there with you:

Abba Father, come right now to this beloved one and delight in them through your Holy Spirit. Fill the atmosphere of the place where they are, as they read, this with a rich and tangible sense of your presence. And Father, send them someone, no send them two, no make that three people, who will be "Jesus in the flesh" and will delight in them with your delight! And so heal and transform their hearts through this gift of your delight in them that they are set free and empowered to go and delight in others. In your name we pray. Amen!

Being experientially rooted in God's grace is to know that we receive that which we do not deserve and can never repay—*his delight in us!* Let us now go and give to others that which they may not deserve either—God's gift of delight in them.

20

GOD'S GIFTS OF BEING INCLUDED AND ACCEPTED

*Therefore, accept each other just as Christ has accepted you so that
God will be given glory.*

— ROMANS 15:7, NLT

*Including and accepting someone is not the same as approving of
their choices, beliefs, or behaviors. To include and accept people is
to do what Jesus did—to be for them
and to speak to their potential.*

"HE JUST LOVES being included." This is what my daughter, Rachel, told
me after I shared with her how my grandson had helped his dad and
me unload a pickup truck full of wood planks. Bert was building a privacy
fence around their property and we were stacking the wood in the backyard.
Michael wanted to help, so we found a couple of small pieces of scrap wood

he could carry from the truck to where we were stacking the wood. When he placed his piece of scrap wood on the pile, I'd reach down and grab it as soon as he headed back to the pickup. Once at the truck, I'd take that same piece of scrap wood, hand it to him, and he joyfully carried it to the backyard and carefully placed it on the stack. He loved helping his dad and me. He loved, as my daughter said, *being included.*

I've thought about that ever since. And I've wondered; where does that childlike joy of being included go? When does it disappear? How do we lose it along the way of our journey in life? I wonder about that because it seems like it becomes one of the things we work really hard to reacquire in life—the sense that we're included, that we belong, and are accepted. Being people who are experientially rooted in God's grace is to receive that which we do not deserve and can never repay—God's gifts of being included and accepted.

WHAT DOES IT MEAN THAT WE ACCEPT SOMEONE?

Acceptance. What do we mean when we say we accept someone? To accept a person is to be *for* them, even while knowing their imperfections and their sin. To accept people is to do what Jesus did—including and accepting people while their lives were a mess. Jesus did this, sometimes to the point they felt they belonged before they even believed. We see this in the story of Zacchaeus in Luke 19:1–7:

> Jesus entered Jericho and made his way through the town. There was a man there named Zacchaeus. He was one of the most influential Jews in the Roman tax-collecting business, and he had become very rich. He tried to get a look at Jesus, but he was too short to see over the crowds. So he ran ahead and climbed a sycamore tree beside the road, so he could watch from there. When Jesus came by, he looked up at Zacchaeus and called him by name. "Zacchaeus!" he said. "Quick, come down! For I must be a guest in your home today." Zacchaeus quickly climbed down and took

Jesus to his house in great excitement and joy. But the crowds were displeased. "He has gone to be the guest of a notorious sinner," they grumbled (NLT).

The crowds grumbled, they murmured say other translations. But Jesus did not. Instead, he extends his gifts of including and accepting toward one who is neither included nor accepted. Jesus wants to be a guest in Zacchaeus' home. The Lord wants to spend time with him and just be with him. Unlike the crowd, Jesus relates to Zacchaeus based on who he, Jesus, was, not on the basis of what Zacchaeus may have deserved or based on what other people thought. One of the great things about Jesus is that he is always more concerned about other people than with his own reputation!

The people viewed Zacchaeus as a notorious sinner, as opposed to a "run-of-the-mill" sinner, as if there were truly such a category with God. But to them, this is who Zacchaeus was, a notorious sinner. He was the chief tax collector, which meant he stood at the top of a collection pyramid scheme that was unfair and oppressive. Their reaction to him was understandable.

Jesus, however, extended Zacchaeus the gift of being welcomed. He extended him grace. Jesus accepted Zacchaeus because he was *for* him, and against anything that would harm him. Jesus came alongside this "notorious sinner" even though he did not approve of what he had been doing up to that point in his life. Jesus shows us—in how he related to people like Zacchaeus—that including and accepting someone is not the same as approving of their choices, beliefs, or behaviors. Rather, to do what Jesus did is to be for them and to speak to their potential.

THE POWER OF INCLUDING AND ACCEPTING

There is a power in including and accepting someone. It can have so much more than merely the effect of experiencing someone being nice to us; it can set free the transforming power of God to change the trajectory of the rest of our lives.

As Jesus walked through Jericho, he had the option to eat with anyone there. So whom did he choose? The one man everyone hated. "Zacchaeus,"

Jesus said, "hurry and come down, for today I must stay at your home." That very public display of welcoming someone whom others would not began the process of a remarkable change in Zacchaeus' life.

Jesus does not lecture Zacchaeus, or prophesy his sin to him right away. Instead, he loves and comes alongside Zacchaeus. Remember, love is the gold standard for those who want to live as a safe place for the dangerous kind; God's love is the filter through which every issue we deal with and every relationship we develop will be viewed. And this powerful gift of love, inclusion, and acceptance is one of the manifestations of those who are experientially rooted in God's grace and experientially know his unconditional, unshakable, and extravagant love in their own lives.

The fruit of this encounter was the beginnings of a transformation in Zacchaeus's life. According to Luke 19:8 he said, "Behold, Lord, half of my possessions I will give to the poor. And if I have defrauded anyone of anything, I will give back four times as much." All Jesus did was ask Zacchaeus if he could dine at his house, if he could be with him and spend time with him. All Jesus did, in a very public setting, was extend Zacchaeus the gift of being included and accepted. But in doing something that seems so simple and basic, he begins to fill Zacchaeus's need to be loved and to belong. In all of this, Zacchaeus actually begins to believe that he belongs, and this begins to transform his thinking, and heal the pain of rejection he'd probably experienced most of his adult life.

REFUSING THE LIE

This encounter of acceptance reveals to us the essential importance of refusing the lie that we can and must fix ourselves *before* God will come alongside us. Mike Yaconelli writes,

> We talk our way out of the spiritual life by *refusing to come to God as we are.* Instead, we decide to wait until we are ready to come to God as we aren't. We decide that the way we lived yesterday, last week, or last year makes us "damaged goods" and that until we start living

"right," we're not "God material." Some of us actually believe that until we choose the correct way to live, we aren't chooseable, that until we clean up the mess, Jesus won't have anything to do with us. The opposite is true. Until we admit we are a mess, Jesus won't have anything to do with us. Once we admit how unlovely we are, how unattractive we are, how lost we are, Jesus shows up unexpectedly [emphasis mine].[77]

Why don't we extend this wonderful gift of God to others more often? Many of us do not know how to extend this gift because it's never been extended to us. Others of us resist extending the gift of being including and accepting toward people because we believe it means we are condoning their choices, beliefs, and behaviors. However, to accept someone does *not* mean to approve of everything they choose, believe, or do. C. S. Lewis writes of his hesitancy to extend acceptance toward someone he didn't always agree with or approve of—himself:

There is someone I love, even though I don't approve of what he does. There is someone I accept, though some of his thoughts and actions revolt me. There is someone I forgive, though he hurts the people I love the most. That person is me. There are plenty of things I do that I don't like, but if I can love myself without approving of all that I do, I can also love others without approving of all they do. As that truth has been absorbed into my life, it has changed the way I view others.[78]

To include and accept someone means we welcome and come alongside them as persons in order to convey God's stance toward them—we are for you and against anything that will harm you. To relate to others in this way is to let them know we desire what is best for their souls.

To experience being welcomed and to belong when we least deserve can be a key to unlocking the freedom God wants us to live in. Larry Crabb

---

77 Mike Yaconelli, *Messy Spirituality*, 37.
78 Lewis, *Mere Christianity*, 44.

writes that "we cannot know the freedom to be who we truly are *until we yield who we really are to another and experience that person's acceptance*" (emphasis mine).[79] When we experience another's acceptance that we do not deserve, when we know they are for us even when we do not deserve it, it can give us the courage to face realities about ourselves that we need to face in order to be set free. Crabb writes,

> What do we believe about each other, not only when we're on our best behavior, but when we're irritating and demanding? *Realistically appraising the evil in my Lower Room is terrifying.* As I uncover what's bad within me, a spiritual friend stays relaxed. He sees something else. I know of little else so powerful as confessing wretched failure and having a friend look on you with great delight. The more I see my sin in the presence of a spiritual community, the more I see Christ and celebrate Him and long to know Him and be like Him. The safety necessary to own my badness comes when someone believes that I am in Christ and that He is in me. Then anything can be faced *without fear of being discarded*" [emphasis mine].[80]

Being experientially rooted in God's grace is to know we have received that which we do not deserve and can never repay—God's gift of being included and accepted. And including and accepting others as the Lord has us is one of the essential ways others can see and experience God's grace in our lives.

---

79 Larry Crabb, *Soul Talk: The Language God Longs for Us to Speak* (Nashville, TN: Integrity Publishing, 2003) 17.

80 Crabb, *The Safest Place On Earth*, 98–99.

21

GOD WORKS THROUGH US EVEN
WHEN WE DON'T DESERVE HIM TO

*It is not that we think we are qualified to do anything on our
own. Our qualification comes from God. He has enabled us to be
ministers of his new covenant.*

—— THE APOSTLE PAUL
2 CORINTHIANS 3:5–6

I T WAS SUNDAY morning. I was up early, getting ready to head to church. I
had to be there. After all, I was one of the pastors—the youth pastor and
worship leader actually. To this day I don't know what set me off or what the
issue was, but when my wife got up to start getting our five young children
ready to go I was irritable and acted like a jerk. We got into an argument.
Even as we were arguing I could see the fault was mine, yet I kept on talking. My words were short, sharp, and hurtful. I felt terrible to be treating the

woman I loved more than any other person on this earth the way I was. But did that stop me? No!

Then suddenly, it was time to go. If I didn't leave the house right then I would be late. There was no time to reconcile, no time to make it right before I left. On the drive to the church there were voices inside my head, haunting me with loud accusations. Who do you think you are? Do you really believe God can use you to lead this congregation in worship today? Look at all your faults! Look at how you treated your wife! And what about all your other sins? All your hidden stuff! Who *do you* think you are to imagine God could use someone like you?

I was so tempted to pull out my phone, call my senior pastor, and with a sickly-sounding voice tell him I was ill and couldn't make it to church that morning. But I couldn't do it. On I drove. And what a morning it was. The worship was beautiful. The lyrics of songs were so meaningful to so many people that some actually took the time to tell me about it before they went down to the fellowship hall to have coffee and doughnuts. To top it off, God had prompted me to speak a prophetic word that morning, which seemed to be spot-on for quite a few people, a word of encouragement that seemed to speak directly to the hearts of many who then wanted to have prayer from our prayer ministry teams before the service was over.

All through the morning though, the voices persisted. Who do you think you are? Do you really believe God used you for good this morning? Look at how you treated your wife! Who *do you* think you are? Was there any basis for any or all of those thoughts? Oh, most certainly. And as soon as I could, I did remember to repent, ask forgiveness, and reconcile with my wife that afternoon when we had time to sit down and talk. Debi is so gracious; she was quick to forgive me and give me a reassuring hug and kiss. But still the thoughts persisted, and they try to come back to haunt me again, even to this day.

One of the hardest lessons for me to learn about what it means to be experientially rooted in God's grace is to realize that the Lord works through us even when we don't deserve him to. Like many of you, I find it easier to walk with more confidence and believe God can use me on good days than on the bad, on the days when I have had my daily quiet time, feel full of enough faith, and haven't behaved poorly toward anyone. In fact, on the bad days, I'm certain there is no way he would even want to work through me to impact others with his power and love because I know I don't deserve him to.

Why is it that so many of us struggle with thoughts like this? For many, perhaps the reason is that while we're certain we're saved by grace, we're not so sure that's how God works with us in life and ministry. But the reality is, that is exactly how he works. We are not only saved by grace, we live and minister according to his undeserved favor too. Being experientially rooted in his grace is to experience God working through us even when we don't deserve him to!

HAVE YOU DONE ENOUGH?

There is a school of thought within Christendom that you cannot be used by God until you have done enough—repented enough, studied enough, worshipped enough, are prayed up enough, and have done enough spiritual warfare. However, there's a problem with this line of thinking—how do we know when we have done enough? And who determines what is enough and when it's enough?

When this cycle of doing enough begins to wrap its tentacles around our minds and hearts the enemy wins. He wins because those questions and doubts we hear within choke off our faith and we draw back from stepping out to serve the Lord. We have to. The voices are right. We don't deserve to have the Lord use us for good in the lives of others in the ways that he does. Who *do* we think we are? And the enemy wins when we notice we're drawing back and then double and triple our efforts to do all "the enoughs." The result? We either burn out, or we become highly judgmental and condemning toward others, expecting them to be doubling and tripling their efforts too. And all the while we are judging and condemning others for not giving enough effort, or not being "committed enough" to the Lord, we are judging and condemning ourselves even more.

GOD WORKS THROUGH PEOPLE
WHO HAVEN'T DONE ENOUGH

When the doubts and questions assail us we need to be reminded of what is true in God's Word. The truth is that the Lord often works through people who do not deserve it and have not done enough. This is one way we experience and see God's grace in our lives. This was certainly illustrated in the life of the apostle Paul. If it's really true that God cannot work through us until we "measure up" and have "done enough," Paul would have been up the proverbial creek without the proverbial paddle. Consider the following testimony from Paul himself:

> I don't really understand myself, for I want to do what is right, but I don't do it. Instead, I do what I hate. But if I know that what I am doing is wrong, this shows that I agree that the law is good. So I am not the one doing wrong; it is sin living in me that does it. And I know that nothing good lives in me, that is, in my sinful nature. I want to do what is right, but I can't. I want to do what is good, but I don't. I don't want to do what is wrong, but I do it anyway. But if I do what I don't want to do, I am not really the one doing wrong; it is sin living in me that does it. I have discovered this principle of life—that when I want to do what is right, I inevitably do what is wrong. I love God's law with all my heart. But there is another power within me that is at war with my mind. This power makes me a slave to the sin that is still within me. Oh, what a miserable person I am! Who will free me from this life that is dominated by sin and death (Romans 7:15–24, NLT)?

Paul knew what it was to wrestle with the inner accusations that you haven't done enough and don't deserve to be used by God for good. And it wasn't only Paul who experienced God working through him expressly when he had done nothing to warrant it. Just think of the litany of people in scripture that God used for good even though they didn't deserve him to: Moses, Jacob, David, and Peter just to name a few. In themselves, none of them deserved God to work through him, yet the Lord did, and he did it in some amazing ways.

IT'S ALL ABOUT GRACE

It is not doing "enough" that makes us worthy of God using us to impact others with his power and love. It is not having jumped through all the right religious hoops that makes us competent for ministry. It is God and his grace that enable us to experience him moving in and through us when we least expect it or think we deserve it. The apostle Paul realized this, the very man who struggled with not doing enough. He realized that in the end, it was not his "enoughs" that would determine whether or not God would work through him for good. It was God, in his grace, who would make him competent for the task at hand. "It is not that we think we are qualified to do anything on our own. Our qualification comes from God. He has enabled us to be ministers of his new covenant" (2 Corinthians 3:5–6, NLT).

Does this truth negate any need to desire growing in holiness and righteousness (see Romans 8:28–29, 12:1–2; 2 Corinthians 3:18)? No. Our God is a holy God and it is his desire that our lives increasingly reflect his righteousness. The Lord invites us to turn to him in repentance when we need to, ask for forgiveness, and then impart that same forgiveness and freedom to others. It is his will that we seek to cast off every sin and anything else that weighs us down so we can live life less hindered (see Hebrews 12:1–2).

However, this does not mean we have to wait until we get "clean enough" or become "mature enough" or have "enough" faith before God can use us. Being experientially rooted in his empowering grace means realizing there are times when God will choose to use us to accomplish his purposes in the very moments we least expect him to or deserve him to.

Can you recall a time when God used you for his purposes, even though you did not deserve him to? If so, describe that time in the space below:

Take a few moments before you read on and thank God again for using you in that way at that time. Then ask him to continue using you and rooting you so deeply in his grace that the tentacles of accusation can no longer grab hold.

Let us all remember—our worst days are never so bad that we are beyond the reach of God's grace, and our best days are never so good that we are beyond our need for his grace! The truth is, we are not only saved by grace, *we live and minister by his grace too!* Being experientially rooted in God's grace is to experience God working through us even when we don't deserve him to!

22

SET FREE TO DO BECAUSE
WE ALREADY ARE

*To be people who do because they already are, sets us free to live
our Christian lives out of a response of joy-filled love, rather than a
joyless sense of duty.*

BEING EXPERIENTIALLY ROOTED in God's grace is to be set free *to do* because *we already are*. In God's kingdom economy we do not have to do in order to be. We do not *do* in order to *be* loved or accepted. We do not have to do in order to be significant or to belong. Rather, we do because we already are fully and unconditionally loved, fully and unconditionally accepted by Abba Father. We already are significant by virtue of the fact that we are his sons and daughters.

To be people who do because they already are, sets us free to live our Christian lives out of a response of joy-filled love, rather than out of a joyless sense of duty that makes us appear to be miserable people. To be a safe-place people who are experientially rooted in God's grace is to know that we do because we already are, and knowing this enables us to live as working lovers rather than loving workers; and the former will always outwork and outlast the latter. Consider the following story of Alice who discovered the power of being a working lover:

> Alice was very young when she married. Her husband was much older. When they returned from the honeymoon he gave her a long list. She had to get up at a certain time, prepare his meals at a certain time, wash his clothes on a certain day, and listed all of the other things she had to do to make him happy. After a few months Alice began to hate that list. She also began to resent the domineering man she had married. But when they had been married for a few years her husband became sick and died. About a year later Alice met a man who really loved her. She fell in love with him, and they were married. One day, after they had been married for a few years, Alice ran across that hated list given by her first husband. And when she looked at it she was amazed to discover that she was doing hundreds of things more, out of love for the man who loved her. By faith in Christ we are free from the restrictive rules and regulations of the Law, free to step out in faith and follow Christ for no other reason than love. Christ was righteous for you and for me.[81]

It was out of her relationship of love that the desire *to do* those things grew best in Alice and the same is true for us. A domineering form of Christianity that demands we do in order to be loved and accepted by God may work for a time, but it will rarely result in a lifetime of serving the Lord that is marked by gratitude and joy rather than sour duty.

A NEW LANGUAGE

In a Christian setting that is a safe place, a new language begins to emerge. Words and phrases such as "have to, need to, must, ought, and should," begin

---

81 Original source unknown.

to increasingly disappear from our vocabulary. They begin to be replaced by words and phrases such as "want to, desire to, love to." For instance, in a safe place, "I have to read my Bible" begins to be replaced by "I want to read my Bible, I can't wait to read my Bible." This new language begins to emerge because the Bible is no longer a book I have to read or study; it becomes a place where I get to go to meet Jesus. It's a place where I can learn more about him and hear him speak to me. And because I know I am already loved, accepted, and significant, I am set free from having to read my Bible in order to feel all of those things; so reading it becomes something other than duty.

Knowing we "already are" will set us free to live lives marked by peace, joy, and love. Lives like that will draw people toward us rather than repel them from us. Lives lived to do because we already are will be one of the marks of a safe-place people who are experientially rooted in God's empowering grace.

23

HAVING SOMEONE WHO
BELIEVES IN US
BEFORE WE EVEN BELIEVE
IN OURSELVES

We are not our problems. We are not our wounds.
We are not our sins.
We are persons of radical worth and unrevealed beauty.

— LARRY CRABB
The Safest Place on Earth

WE ALL NEED someone who believes in us before we even believe in ourselves. We need someone who has the willingness and ability to see
beyond who we are in the present, someone who sees the person we can be
and dares to call it out of us. Not everyone who has this ability is a safe-place

person, but when they are, they become one of the keys God uses to experientially root us in his grace.

In the Gospels we see Jesus doing this. He often believed in people before they ever believed in themselves. For instance, in John 1:42 we read, "Then Andrew brought Simon to meet Jesus. Looking intently at Simon, Jesus said, 'You are Simon, the son of John—but you will be called Cephas (which means Peter).'" Jesus was not blind to who Peter actually was when they first met and how he would misbehave later on. He simply had the ability to see Peter for who he could be and to believe in Peter before he believed in himself. As a result Simon does become Peter. He is transformed and empowered to live out the purposes of God for his life, because Jesus saw the man he was created to be.

WE ARE PEOPLE OF RADICAL WORTH AND UNREVEALED BEAUTY

We all need someone who has the ability to believe in us even while we have behaviors, beliefs, and attitudes that need to be transformed. We need someone who can see beyond the mud to the masterpiece as it were. John Burke speaks to this in his book by that title, *Mud and the Masterpiece: Seeing Yourself and Others through the Eyes of Jesus*. Burke draws our attention to the definition of the Greek word used for *workmanship* in Ephesians 2:10, where the apostle Paul writes, "For we are his workmanship, created in Christ Jesus for good works, which God prepared beforehand, that we should walk in them." Burke says, "The word translated 'masterpiece' or 'workmanship' is the Greek word *poiema* from which we get the word poem. It's a work of art—the work of a Master Artist."[82]

Do you realize that you are a work of art, a masterpiece? If we honestly answered that question most of us would probably say no, I don't realize that. We might even say something like, "I know I'm a piece of work, but it's not art. That's not my reality." However, that is the reality God purposes for us

---

82   John Burke, *Mud and the Masterpiece: Seeing Yourself and Others through the Eyes of Jesus* (Grand Rapids, MI: BakerBooks, 2013), Kindle ed.

to know and to live out of. Toward that end one of his great grace-gifts in our lives can be that person who is able to look beyond the stuff of our mud to the masterpiece God has created us to be, someone who can help us begin to see and experience the person the Lord sees we can be and helps to create opportunities and platforms for us to begin being that person.

Having someone who believes in us before we even believe in ourselves is to know something of the experience of a master artist such as Michelangelo. Perhaps one of his greatest and most recognizable works is the statue of David. Over a million tourists a year come to gaze on this seventeen-foot high block of white marble that Michelangelo carved into an image of David with a sling over his shoulder, ready to do battle with the giant Goliath. What an amazing achievement this sculpture was. Who could have seen the image of David in this large, solid block of granite? Well, Michelangelo did. Of him Burke writes,

> Michelangelo thought of sculpting as the highest form of art because it mimicked divine creation. He worked under the premise that the image of David was already in the block of stone, and his task was simply to reveal the masterpiece underneath the rough, jagged edges. Michelangelo explained, "In every block of marble I see a statue as plain as though it stood before me, shaped and perfect in attitude and action. I have only to hew away the rough walls that imprison the lovely apparition to reveal it to the other eyes as mine see it. What we often see in ourselves and in others around us is just an unimpressive block of marble with rough, jagged edges protruding.[83]

Michelangelo's gift is just a reflection of the work that Jesus, the Master Artist can do. He can see the masterpiece that is hidden within each one of us when all we see ourselves as is an unimpressive block of marble. I love what Larry Crabb writes,

---

83 Ibid.

We are not our problems. We are not our wounds. We are not our sins. We are persons of radical worth and unrevealed beauty. If we face ourselves fully, we will be broken by what we see, by the self-ishness and fear and rage and lust that cover our spiritual beauty like tarnish on silver. But the silver is there, something brilliant and intact gleams through the stain of our brokenness.[84]

The silver is there in each one of us, but it's often covered with the tarnish of living as fallen and broken beings in a fallen and broken world. We need God's grace gift in the form of others who can see the something brilliant and intact that gleams through the stain of our brokenness. We need others who believe in the Lord's gifts and call upon our lives before we even see them ourselves. We all need safe-place people whom God can use to call forth who he has created and gifted us to be—his work of art, his masterpiece, his shining silver vessel.

GOD'S ANSWER TO MY PRAYER

Some of the greatest blessings in my life have been the people who believed in me before I believed in myself, people who helped call forth the person God had designed and gifted me to be. Charles Miller is one of those people. I first met Charles as I was praying for someone to disciple me. Today we call it men-toring, but in the mid-1980s we called it discipling. I knew his son through a ministry we were both involved with called Inter-Collegiate Fellowship Renewal (ICFR), a ministry focused on helping impact teens and young adults with God's power and love. I knew his father was a Lutheran pastor who had been tasked by the Lutheran Church in America (LCA) to facilitate charis-matic renewal amongst Lutherans. My best description of Charles Miller at the time was that he was the most gently powerful man in the Holy Spirit I had ever seen. He manifested the fruit of the Spirit and moved powerfully in the gifts of the Spirit but in a gentle way and with great integrity.

---

84 Crabb, *The Safest Place on Earth*, 34.

"That's who I want to disciple me," I thought and I told that to God in prayer. "Oh, not Charles himself of course, Lord, but someone like him. Charles is too busy traveling internationally to have time for a young youth pastor-worship leader like me who lives all the way out here in Rapid City, South Dakota," I believed. Then one year our senior pastor invited Charles to minister at our church. A few of the days he was with us were spent at the Kelly Inn in Keystone near Mount Rushmore. We were there with the church council, elders, and staff of Trinity Lutheran as Charles taught and ministered.

I sat next to Charles because I was leading worship, playing my wife's Lyle guitar, a Gibson look alike. During a break he turned to me and asked, "Mike, do you have anyone discipling you?" I laughed nervously and told him, "Not right now but I've actually been praying about that. In fact, you'll get a kick out of this. I've actually been telling the Lord I'd love for someone like you to disciple me. Now, not *you* of course, because you're an international traveler, teacher, and minister, but someone *like* you." After a few moments of silence (it seemed like a long time to me), Charles gently and thoughtfully asked, "Why not me? What's wrong with me?" I was so shocked I didn't know what to say at first, but then, as if to quickly seal the deal before Charles changed his mind I blurted out, "I'd *love* to have you disciple me. When can we start?" And start we did.

Over the next ten years Charles Miller and I visited over the phone and in person (he would come to Rapid City a couple of times a year), and I would travel once or twice a year with him and his wife, Ann. We didn't have a curriculum as it were. We didn't have a book on discipleship that we were working through. Our curriculum was being *with* one another. Kind of like Jesus calling his disciples to be *with* him (see Mark 3:14).

I learned by being with Charles, watching him in action, and talking and praying with him. Oh, before anyone reading this gets unnecessarily upset, let me be quick to say that this was not all about Charles. I did not worship him nor was I substituting him for Jesus. You see this is how Jesus works. He works through his Word and by his Spirit directly in our lives, and he impacts us by working through his Word alive and his Spirit present in other flesh-and-blood people, just as he worked in Timothy's life through the apostle Paul. Furthermore, it was how Charles worked. He never made things about himself; he always pointed others and me to Jesus.

As I traveled and spent time with Charles and Ann, I continued to serve as youth pastor and worship leader at Trinity Lutheran Church. But God began to expand my sphere of influence beyond working with teens and their parents. He began to provide opportunities for me to speak, teach, preach, and minister to adults, and that ministry was bearing good fruit.

However, I was fighting it because I saw myself as simply a youth pastor. Now, being a youth pastor is a highly significant ministry. It is not that this form of ministry is unimportant, it's just that something within would not give me permission to see myself as the something other than, not better than, which God was wanting to transform and release me into. But Charles saw it. He saw the call of God on my life. He saw the God-given gifts in my life. Charles saw the wholeness and character God was developing in me. In short, Charles Miller *believed in me before I ever believed in myself.* Then one day he chose to do something about it.

We were in Alberta, Canada, where he was the keynote speaker and minister for a group of charismatic Lutheran pastors and seminary students at an event called the Leadership Training Institute (LTI), led by our dear friend, Pastor Glen Carlson. We called Glen "Bishop Blaze" because of his influence in leaders' lives and because of the wonderful shade of red he turned when you teased him. I led worship and Charles taught the morning sessions on the first day of the LTI, then we broke for lunch.

After lunch the first session was to be a teaching on how to seek God for his vision for your congregation. Charles and I had been talking about this because I had been reading, writing, and teaching on it with my youth staff— a staff of thirty volunteers who worked with our youth ministry of around three hundred teenagers. We returned from lunch. Charles opened the session on vision with these words, "Our session this afternoon from now until we break for dinner at 5 p.m. is on how to seek God's leading in discerning his vision for your congregation. I could teach on it but there is someone here who is better versed in this than me, so I would like him to come up and lead the session this afternoon. Mike, come on up and share with us what God has been teaching you about seeking him for a vision for ministry."

I laughed at Charles' joke, and so did the pastors and seminary students. Charles didn't laugh. Instead, he began walking from the front of the room back to where I was seated. I laughed at his humor some more and everyone else joined in. Charles still didn't laugh. Then suddenly he was standing beside me. Leaning over he whispered, "Just go up and share with them the things you've been sharing with me."

By now, everyone else had figured out Charles was not joking, he was serious. I stood up on legs wiggling like Jell-O, walked to the front, and stood behind the music stand we were using for a podium. I looked out at the pastors and seminary students and said, "Well, I guess we'd really better pray." They laughed. We prayed. I thought of one sentence to open with and the next thing I knew, it was 5 p.m. I had shared and taught, they had asked questions. I had led them in an exercise or two, we had prayed, and now it was 5 p.m., time for dinner.

Over dinner many of the pastors and seminary students thanked me for the teaching, some even wanted my phone number and email address so they could follow up with questions and receive coaching in this thing of seeking God for his vision for your ministry. I don't remember ever being as scared in a ministry setting as I was standing behind that music stand. And I don't remember ever being as thankful as I was after that day of stretching. As a friend of mine would tell us, Charles had spontaneously given me a challenging assignment, one that stretched me, an assignment that opened the door for me to step into the next season of life and ministry God had in store for me. I couldn't see it. Charles could. He was God's grace-gift to me. Charles Miller believed in me before I even believed in myself. If you're reading this, "Thank you, Charles. I love you my friend, my brother, my mentor."

GRACE-GIFTS

Receiving this grace-gift that we do not deserve, this gift of someone who believes in us before we even believe in ourselves, is an important aspect of what it means to be experientially rooted in God's grace. It can have an amazing, transforming impact in your life. Jesus sees us for who he knows we can be, not just who we are, and then he sends grace-gifts in the flesh to believe in us and help stir and prod us toward the new season he has in store for us.

Some of you need a mentor who has the ability to believe in you before you even believe in yourself. Is that you? Do you need a grace-gift like this in your life? If so, do what I did—simply pray. I'm not being trite when I write that. Pray. I did. And God answered that prayer. Boy, did he answer that prayer! Pray and ask God to send you a mentor who will see you for who you can be, not just who you are. God loves to answer prayers like that.

Others of you need to be that kind of mentor. Your prayer may be that God will do whatever he needs to do in you, so he can do what he wants to do through you in the life of another. He wants to use you as a Charles Miller in someone's life. He wants to use you to answer someone's prayer for a mentor who will see him or her for who they can be. Please allow God to do whatever he needs to do in you so you can be the answer to that prayer. Let him change you, heal you, mature you, and set you free in any way he needs to so you can be that grace-gift for someone. His answer for me through Charles changed the trajectory of my life. His answer through you will change someone else's trajectory.

Dare to seek out a safe-place mentor, or be that for someone else in the same way Charles Miller was for me. If you will, it can be one of the ways you will experience being rooted in God's grace, and one of the ways others will see walking grace that is tangible and real.

24

PEOPLE WHO REFUSE TO JUDGE OTHERS

God is for us and against anything that will harm us.

SAFE-PLACE PEOPLE WHO are experientially rooted in God's grace refuse to judge others. They refuse to get a sense of worth and significance for their own lives by judging and condemning others. A friend of mine, Gregory Boyd, had an awakening of grace while at The Mall of America in Minneapolis, Minnesota, an awakening that left him convicted that he had been judging others as surely as the judges on *American Idol* judge and critique those contestants. Only, in his case, God revealed this was not something good. The Lord showed Boyd how he was getting a sense of life, worth, and significance from judging others rather than getting it from his relationship with God himself. Here is Boyd's account from his book *Repenting from Religion:*

I am sitting in a mall on a Saturday afternoon. As I sip my coke and relax, I study people. I notice some are pretty and some are not. Some are slender; some are obese. On the basis of what they wear, their facial expressions, the way they relate to their spouses, friends or kids, I conclude some are "godly" while others are "ungodly." Some give me a warm feeling as I watch their tenderness toward their children. Others make me angry or disgusted.

Then suddenly I notice I'm noticing all this. Believing as I do that every activity we engage in, including our thinking, is for a purpose, I begin to wonder what purpose this silent commentary about other people is serving. After a moment's introspection I realize it is on some level making me feel good. It is in a sense feeding me. It's satisfying some need I have to stand in judgment over people. Deep down, I enjoy being the one who at least before the tribunal of my own mind gets to pronounce the verdict: Pretty. Ugly. Good figure. Fat. Ungodly. Disgusting. Cute. And so on.

With this insight came another one, this one, I am sure, prompted by the Holy Spirit. I recalled that Jesus taught wherever we go, our first responsibility is to bless people (Luke 10:5). I recalled Scripture teaches us to think and speak evil of no one (Titus 3:2; James 4:11). Instantly I was convicted by how many non-blessing thoughts—indeed, how many cursing thoughts—I had been entertaining without even being aware of it.

So I stopped. I determined to have one thought, and one though only, about every person I saw in the mall on that afternoon: it was to love them and bless them as people uniquely created by God who have infinite worth because Jesus died for them. As I replaced judgmental thoughts with loving thoughts and prayers of blessing, something extraordinary began to happen. I began to see the worth I was ascribing to people, and I began to feel the love I was giving to them. It felt like finding home after having been lost for a long while. It was like waking up from a coma. I was filled with a profound sense of compassion for people.[85]

By his own admission, Boyd was judging people, something Jesus clearly tells his followers not to do: "Judge not, that you be not judged. For with the judgment you pronounce you will be judged, and with the measure you use it will be measured to you (Matthew 7:1–2, ESV). Or, as translated in The Message: "Don't pick on people, jump on their failures, criticize their faults—unless, of course, you want the same treatment. That critical spirit has a way of boomeranging."

The Greek word Jesus uses for judging others is κρίνετε (krinete). It comes from the root word κρίνω (krino), which means, "to judge, to decide." In Matthew 7, the word krinete is a verb that is in the second person, plural, which means it is not just addressed to an individual, but to all. And grammatically it is a present, active, imperative verb. In his book *Basics of Biblical Greek* William D. Mounce writes,

> There is no more forceful way in the Greek language to tell someone to do something than a simple imperative—particularly the second person imperative. The one giving that command sees himself as an authority figure. He expects those addressed to do exactly as he has ordered.[86]

According to Greek grammar, what Jesus says in Matthew 7 is a command, not an opinion, suggestion, or just good advice. Jesus really expects us to do this. He really expects us to obey him and to not judge others! Why? Because Jesus knows judging people has a harmful effect on us, and on our

---

85 Boyd, *Repenting From Religion*, 13–14.
86 William D. Mounce, *Basics of Biblical Greek* (Grand Rapids, MI: Zondervan, 1993), 302.

relationships with others, most of all with God himself; and God is for us and against anything that will harm us. Judging people harms us because we cannot judge others and fulfill the Great Commandment:

"Teacher, which is the great commandment in the Law?" And he (Jesus) said to him, "You shall love the Lord your God with all your heart and with all your soul and with all your mind. This is the great and first commandment. And a second is like it: You shall love your neighbor as yourself. On these two commandments depend all the Law and the Prophets" (Matthew 22:36–40, ESV).

When we judge others, rather than loving them as Jesus commands, we separate ourselves from them, we create distance between them and us. To judge and condemn others is to break the Great Commandment and disobey God. Judging others also damages our witness to the world because it only reinforces the negative stereotype many already hold of followers of Christ—that we are arrogant and angry, judgmental and condemning.

ERRORS IN JUDGMENT: WRONG VERDICTS

In their book *unChristian*, David Kinnaman and Gabe Lyons note two types of errors Christians make when we judge others—wrong verdict and wrong motivation. The first error is when Christians declare a wrong verdict. A wrong verdict occurs when we judge others and jump to a wrong conclusion about them. God's judgments about people are perfect; ours are imperfect. When we reach the wrong verdict, it is typically because of our own biases, assumptions, or stereotypes about others, or the lack of having all the information in any given situation.

One Christian told Kinnaman, "Yeah, I know what you mean about stereotypes. When I see a person who is tattooed or pierced up, I try not to judge them based on their outward appearance. I realize that their appearance is probably just a symptom."[87] Did you notice what that person did? He

---

87   Kinnaman and Lyons, *unChristian*, 187.

jumped to a wrong conclusion even though it sounded like he was trying to be vulnerable about his struggle with a temptation to judge. He actually goes on to make a judgment, that if someone has a tattoo it indicates "a symptom" that something is wrong with him or her. This man may as well have said, "I wouldn't judge based on outward appearance, but there is something wrong with these people on the inside." This is a more subtle way of declaring a wrong verdict because this man has no way whatsoever of knowing what is on the inside of a person.

Over the years I've had multiple experiences with Christians who declared a wrong verdict regarding someone who did not look the way they thought Christians should look. One particular experience involved a teenage girl who was in the youth group I pastored in the 1980s. She had her hair spiked in a Mohawk. It was a different color just about every week, and one side of her head was shaved. She looked like she was probably a rebellious teenager, which is exactly what many of the adults in our church believed to be true about her. However, I had gotten to know her and knew how much she loved Jesus. Oh, how she loved the Lord!

She also had a great love for marginalized teens in our community. She was able to be like Jesus with those Jesus would have been with—these marginalized ones. She spent time with them, loved them with God's love, and when appropriate, spoke God's grace and truth into their lives. These were young people that I, as a pastor, and the adult members of my congregation, were never going to be able to reach. She could though, and she did.

One week I asked her to help us serve communion during a Sunday morning worship service. As people came and knelt at the communion rail and bowed their heads, they saw her feet pass by as they placed the communion cup back in the tray she carried. As they looked back down—supposedly to pray—they saw her toenails because she was wearing sandals, and what they saw was a beautiful work of art. Every toenail was painted in different colors and different artistic patterns. This girl was, and still is, a gifted artist. When I got home the phone began to ring. A few angry church members wanted to know why I let a girl "like that" help serve communion. They demanded it never happen again. I tried to explain but they didn't want to listen. It broke my heart, but it didn't influence my decision. I still had her continue to help serve communion, and, by the way, our wise and caring senior pastor backed me up all the way.

What these people did not know is that this teenage girl had a heart for the Lord that was as big as the Black Hills of South Dakota where we lived. She not only had a heart for the Lord, but also had God's heart for the marginalized teens in our city. She talked about the Lord to young people that other members of my church would only look at with disdain and judge and condemn from a distance. What those "faithful church members" were not remembering is that these young people they were so critical of were people precious to the Lord, people for whom Jesus poured out his blood on the cross at Calvary. This young teen loved Jesus, she loved those marginalized teens, and she loved our church. She even loved those older, faithful members of our congregation when they did not love her. It's sad they didn't love her back. They missed out on an opportunity to get to know a really great person. Instead they made, and spoke, a wrong verdict. As a postscript to the story, this young girl so precious to the Lord is now married, the mother of beloved children of her own, and still impacting people with God's love by the way that she lives and loves.

When we make a wrong verdict in our hearts, or speak it with our lips, we are rightly viewed as being judgmental and condemning because that is exactly what we are doing. When we think or speak a wrong verdict we give life to the negative stereotype of Christians many people hold and we drive people away from the Lord rather than woo them toward him.

ERRORS IN JUDGMENT: WRONG MOTIVATIONS

Another type of judgmental error is wrong motivation. There are times we have the right discernment concerning someone, but act on it with a wrong motivation. When Jesus encounters the woman accused of adultery in John 8, we see her accusers driven by the wrong motivation. Was their discernment that she was involved in sin correct? Yes, she was involved in sin, and so was the man she had been with. Her offense was clear, but people's motivation for wanting her punished was wrong. It was a wrong motivation; it was vindictive and self-righteous.

Jesus is a safe place for her though as he turns their wrong motivations back on the people: "If any one of you is without sin, let him be the first to throw a stone at her" (John 8:7, ESV). Can you imagine that moment when Jesus, in perfect union with God's plan, broke ranks with centuries of religious teaching within Jewish law and custom? He challenged the accusers to choose compassion over retribution by considering the impurity in their own lives before passing judgment on someone else. And don't forget the end of the story. Jesus, the perfect judge, tells the woman to abandon her self-destructive behaviors: "Go and sin no more" (John 8:11, ESV). Jesus is a safe place for this woman, responding to her in both grace and truth.

GOOD JUDGMENT AS OPPOSED TO SINFUL JUDGMENT

Jesus tells us not to judge, and Kinnaman and Lyons encourage us to avoid errors of being judgmental. But then, along comes the apostle Paul and tells us that we *are* to judge. He writes to the Corinthians,

> I can hardly believe the report about the sexual immorality going on among you, something so evil that even the pagans don't do it. I am told that you have a man in your church who is living in sin with his father's wife. And you are so proud of yourselves! Why aren't you mourning in sorrow and shame? And why haven't you removed this man from your fellowship? Even though I am not there with you in person, I am with you in the Spirit. Concerning the one who has done this, I have *already passed judgment* [1 Corinthians 5:1–4a, ESV, emphasis mine].

> I am not overstating it when I say that the man who caused all the trouble hurt your entire church more than he hurt me. He

was punished enough when most of you were united *in your judgment against him*. Otherwise he may become so discouraged that he won't be able to recover. Now show him that you still love him [2 Corinthians 5:5–8, ESV, emphasis mine].

What's going on, Paul? Are you actually taking a different stand than Jesus did? He said don't judge. You say we are to judge. What's up with this?

CONTEXT, CONTEXT, CONTEXT

There is an important role to be played in the body of Christ by those who are trained in the original languages of scripture and in good practices of exegesis because this kind of training helps us read, interpret, and apply God's word in a responsible and healthy way. Good exegetical practices always tell us not to lift any one verse or passage of scripture out of context and build a complete doctrine around it.

The phrase students in hermeneutics classes hear ad nauseam is context, context, context. They are drilled to always be aware of the context within which a particular scripture verse or passage is set because that can influence the interpretation and application of that verse or text. This is true in the case of judging, because if we were to only lift Jesus' words in Matthew, chapter 7, out of the Bible, we would have basis for building a doctrine that says judging is always wrong, while not taking into account that there may be another form or meaning of judging that God wants us to be aware of. There is in fact more than one form and meaning.

LOVING *KRINO*, UNLOVING *KRINO*

There is a good and right judging, and there is a sinful judging. In the Greek, the root word for the verb form of judging is *krino*, which literally means *to separate*. The English word *critic* comes from this word. A movie critic, for instance, is one who helps us separate good movies from bad movies (though I often don't agree with the movie critics).

In Scripture, as in life, there is a loving *krino,* and an unloving *krino.* Although there can be a sinful, hurtful kind of judging, there is also a positive kind that Christians are supposed to practice. In this positive kind of judging we are called to be "critics" or "separators" on behalf of one another in a loving manner. We are to help one another critique, separate, or discern good and wise beliefs and behaviors from ones that are unhealthy and harmful.

This sort of discernment and loving feedback is obviously not what Jesus is referring to in Matthew, chapter 7—that type of judging is clearly forbidden. Most fundamentally, the form that Jesus prohibits is *about separating people.* More specifically, the one doing the judging is separating themselves from the one they are judging, and placing themselves above that person. The judgment Jesus prohibits is about trying to gain a sense of worth or significance for oneself by detracting from others' sense of worth. The positive type of judging Paul advocates is about discernment regarding beliefs, issues, and behaviors, not persons. We are to discern those that are helpful to us as opposed those that would place us in harm's way.

How do we know when we have crossed over from critique and discernment to prohibited judgment? Jack Deere shared the following list at a Lutheran Renewal conference in St. Paul some years ago. I have found it helpful in differentiating between sinful judgment of others, and the critique and discernment of beliefs and behaviors. The judgment Deere refers to below is the former:

- We have crossed from evaluation to judgment when there is no mercy
- We have crossed from evaluation to judgment when we feel superior to others (see Luke 18:9–14)
- We have crossed from evaluation to judgment when it is in some sense "feeding us"
- We have crossed from evaluation to judgment when we desire the other person to fail or wish them harm
- We have crossed from discernment to judgment when we get pleasure (and there is a false pleasure) when we see another person fail
- We have crossed from critique to judgment when we see another person's weaknesses as permanent flaws rather than being in process

Deere exhorted us to be careful not to judge others because:

- It guarantees our own judgment (see Matthew 7:1–3)
- It makes us hypocrites (see Romans 2:1–4)
- It causes us to live in the past; it ties us to the past
- It robs us of joy
- It grieves the Holy Spirit (Ephesians 4:29ff)

Deere then gave the following counsel to help free us from the temptation to judge and condemn others:

- Surrender to the power of Christ—without Christ we are in bondage to sin and cannot free ourselves
- Realize the freedom that ceasing from judgment can bring (see Luke 6:37ff); realize that judging takes a lot of energy
- Ask God to give you a passion for something else

That latter word of counsel can be true for an individual or for a congregation. As long as we are focused on the past and not on the future, we can be stuck in a negative identity. For a corporate body, a temptation can be to state an identity based on "who you are not," or "what you are against," rather than on "who you are," "what you're for," and "what you've been called to do."

In order to be a safe-place person, family, or church, we must be so experientially rooted in God's grace that we become a people who refuse to get our sense of identity, worth, or significance from judging others. As mentioned in the chapter on being a safe place to grow and be transformed, the issue of judging may be connected to a wholeness issue. That is, there may be a deeper root issue or wound that is giving life to your propensity to judge others. Let's seek to experience God's freedom and healing so we aren't driven to gain our sense of identity, worth, or significance from judging others. If we'll do that, we will be experienced as men and women who are a safe place for others, men and women who are loving and encouraging, not judgmental and condemning.

25

GRACE AND EFFORT ARE NOT OPPOSITES; GRACE AND EARNING ARE

A safe-place people will say yes to costly grace and no to cheap grace. They will not seek to earn God's grace, but they will make every effort to position themselves to receive and grow in it.

WE CAN GROW in being experientially rooted in God's grace through the practice of holy habits. A holy habit is another name for the centuries-old practice of the disciplines of the faith in the Christian church. Those disciplines include things such as prayer, reading God's Word, worship, meditating, fasting, receiving the Lord's Supper, and more. It is not God's heart that we practice holy habits in a legalistic manner as a way to earn his love, acceptance, or favor. We can practice holy habits in that way if we do not guard against it, but at its best, practicing holy habits positions us to receive and grow in the grace of God. It is absolutely critical we be aware that grace and effort are not opposites; grace and earning are.

REPOSITIONING OURSELVES

The importance of making an effort to reposition ourselves to receive all that God has for us is wonderfully illustrated in the story of Jesus, Mary, and Martha in Luke 10:38–42. When Jesus comes to visit Mary and Martha, Martha goes into the kitchen to prepare the dinner, which is in fact, a normal and culturally appropriate thing for her to do. Mary on the other hand, makes an effort to reposition herself. She does not go into the kitchen. Instead, she repositions herself at the feet of Jesus, "listening to what he taught" (10:39). Mary made an effort. She had not earned the right to sit at Jesus' feet, but she did make the effort to reposition herself there. Because she does, she is able to receive what the Lord has to teach her.

While on vacation with Debi some years ago in Manzanillo, Mexico, I had the thought that I was to finish a book I'd been reading by Mark Buchanan. Unfortunately, I had left it at home in Minnesota. However, once we returned from vacation, I picked it up and began reading right where I'd left off in chapter thirteen, the chapter on holy habits. Buchanan writes about the passage in Mark 9:14–29 where the disciples are having trouble casting out a demon. He points out that Jesus emphasizes that the reason they can't cast out the demon is that "such as these" only come out by prayer and fasting. In other words, they come out by making an effort to practice holy habits.[88]

Jesus himself made an effort to practice holy habits. This is most likely why he was able, when the disciples were not, to cast out this demon. Jesus had a well-established practice of prayer, and most likely fasting, in his life. For instance, Mark 1:35 tells us, "Very early in the morning, while it was still dark, Jesus got up, left the house and went off to a solitary place, where he prayed." Jesus made the effort to get up early and made the effort to pray. This effort positioned him to receive God's grace, which empowered him to do all he did and say all he said.

---

88 Mark Buchanan, *Your God is Too Safe: Rediscovering the Wonder of a God You Can't Control* (Grand Rapids, MI: Multnomah Books 2001), 193.

Unlike Jesus, we often seem to lack spiritual power. We often seem helpless and hapless in the face of the evil in this world. Why can't we move more consistently in Jesus' power and authority? Because, Buchanan says, "we want the five easy steps, or the 30 or 40 day, fix it quick plan."[89] This just isn't working for us. Instead, we would be better suited to be intentional and consistent in our practice of the fundamentals of our faith, the disciplines of the faith, the holy habits.

Making the effort to practice is the key to almost any worthwhile endeavor in life. Athletes and musicians surely do it. They start where they are, they practice and train each day, and step-by-step they grow in their abilities. Anyone who plays the guitar or violin well started with the tedious practice of the scales. Anyone who runs marathons began by running around the block. Those who climb mountains began climbing hills first. You can't do any of this without making the effort to practice and train. Spiritual growth happens in the same way.

GRACE IS NOT OPPOSED TO EFFORT, IT IS OPPOSED TO EARNING

Grace is not opposed to effort; grace is opposed to earning. Working *for* our salvation is a heresy. Working *out* our salvation is basic biblical truth (see Philippians 1:6). Grace and effort are allies. Buchanan says there are eight New Testament scriptures that tell us that because God has already given us all things, we therefore "must make every effort to do what leads to peace and mutual edification; make every effort to enter through the narrow door; make every effort to keep unity; make every effort to be holy; make every effort to be found spotless, blameless, and at peace with him. Hebrews 4:11 is especially strong: Make every effort to enter rest."[90]

Buchanan goes on to say that the difference between working out our salvation—making every effort—and working for our salvation can be quickly and easily explained. "You can only work out of what you already

---

89 Ibid., 195.
90 Ibid., 198.

have. Everything you need, you've got. For this very reason, make every effort."[91]

To deny a place for effort in the Christian life is to be in danger of embracing a cheap grace rather than the costly grace that a life of following Jesus calls for. Perhaps some of the most insightful and powerful writing we have today that differentiates between cheap grace and costly grace comes from Lutheran theologian and pastor Dietrich Bonhoeffer. In *Discipleship* Bonhoeffer writes of cheap grace,

> Cheap grace is the mortal enemy of our church. Our struggle today is for costly grace. Cheap grace is preaching forgiveness without repentance; it is baptism without the discipline of community; it is the Lord's Supper without confession of sin; it is absolution without personal confession. Cheap grace is grace without discipleship, grace without the cross, grace without the living, incarnate Jesus Christ.[92]

Bonhoeffer then writes of costly grace,

> Costly grace is the hidden treasure in the field, for the sake of which people go and sell with joy everything they have. It is the call of Jesus Christ, which causes a disciple to leave his nets and follow him. Costly grace is the gospel, which must be sought again and again, the gift of which has to be asked for, the door at which one has to knock. It is costly, because it calls us to discipleship; it is grace, because it calls us to follow Jesus Christ.[93]

Costly grace is a biblical grace. Cheap grace is a cultural grace. A safe-place people will say yes to the former and no to the latter. They will not seek to earn God's grace, but they will make every effort to position

---

91 Ibid., 199.
92 Dietrich Bonhoeffer, *Discipleship* (Minneapolis, MN: Fortress Press, 2003), Kindle ed.
93 Ibid.

themselves to receive and grow experientially in his grace. Because of what God has already done for us in Christ Jesus, let us make every effort to position ourselves to receive all that he has for us. That kind of commitment will make us a safe place for the dangerous kind.

PART THREE

ROOTED IN GOD'S TRUTH

26

Essential for Living a
Life of Freedom

You are truly my disciples if you keep obeying my teachings.
And you will know the truth and the truth will set you free.

— Jesus Christ
John 8:31–32, NLT

A SAFE-PLACE PEOPLE will be full of both grace and truth, even as Jesus was (see John 1:14). We've seen what it means to be a people experientially rooted in God's grace, in the previous section of this book. This section will examine what it means to be a people who seek to be rooted in God's truth.

ESSENTIAL FOR LIVING A LIFE OF FREEDOM
Being rooted in truth is essential for living a life that is truly free. The hunger for freedom has been a primordial desire deep within the heart of human

beings since the beginning of time. There has always been something in us that refuses bondage, resists captivity, throws off oppression, and yearns for freedom. And it may only be in contexts where freedom has been taken away from us that we truly realize what a precious gift it is.

One of my favorite movies, *Braveheart,* not only paints a picture of the human longing for freedom, but of the courage and willingness on the part of some to die for it so that others might live in it. In the movie, historic Scottish freedom fighter William Wallace calls his army to battle with the passion-igniting cry, "They can never take our freedom!" A byline on a poster for the movie declared, "Every man dies, not every man really lives."

This is what freedom is about: *really* living. And really living is God's desire for us. Jesus told us this in the gospel of John, "The thief's purpose is to steal and kill and destroy. My purpose is to give them a rich and satisfying life." In The Message it reads, "A thief is only there to steal and kill and destroy. I came so they can have real and eternal life, more and better life than they ever dreamed of," and in the English Standard Version, "The thief comes only to steal and kill and destroy. I came that they may have life and have it abundantly."

The desire in every human hearts is to live a rich and satisfying life, a life that is better than any we've ever dreamed of, a life that is abundant. We all want to *truly* live. We all want to be truly free. But what does being truly free so we can truly live mean? When I was a teenager I knew the answer to that question. In fact, it was pretty obvious to me. Being truly free meant I could do whatever I wanted, whenever I wanted, and however I wanted to do it. How hard is that to understand? Of course, I'm older now, and as I've gotten older I realize my teenage definition for freedom was actually just a lack of impulse control.

Webster's dictionary defines freedom as 1) a state of being at liberty rather than in confinement; 2) exemption from external control; 3) power of determining one's own action; and 4) power to make one's own choices.[94] Many people think living a life of freedom is living free from external control of any kind by anyone else. Furthermore, most people seem to think of freedom in

---

94 www.merriam-webster.com/dictionary/freedom.

terms of what they are free from, rather than what they are free for. In his landmark study *Habits of the Heart,* Robert Bellah wrote that Americans want freedom *from* rather than freedom *for.*[95] Americans generally want to be free from external control and from anyone telling them what to do, rather than living lives of freedom for someone else, or for some ideal or cause.

NOT REALLY FREE TO BEGIN WITH

Eventually most of us realize that being free to do whatever we want, whenever we want, however we want, is an illusion because most of us aren't really free to do that anyway. As we grow older we become more and more aware that there is something internal in us, not something or someone external, that hinders us from doing whatever we want, whenever we want. As life goes on we are confronted with the reality that we do things that we don't want to do, while struggling to do things we do want to do. The apostle Paul wrestled with this reality and writes of it this way,

> I do not understand what I do. For what I want to do I do not do, but what I hate I do. I have the desire to do what is good, but I cannot carry it out. For what I do is not the good I want to do; no, the evil I do not want to do—this I keep on doing. Now if I do what I do not want to do, it is no longer I who do it, but it is sin living in me that does it (Romans 7:15, 18–20, NIV).

Christians and non-Christians experience this inner battle of not being very good at doing what we want to do, but being really good at doing what we don't want to do. We all have this in common, and it is not only true of people in Western Europe and the United States, it is endemic to human beings around the globe. This is a struggle for every people everywhere.

---

95   See Robert N. Bellah, *Habits of the Heart: Individualism and Commitment in American Life* (Berkeley: University of California Press, 1985, 2008).

DEFINING FREEDOM

So, if doing whatever you want whenever you want is not true freedom, what is? Following are some definitions I have come to appreciate over the years. First: true freedom is having the ability to say yes to what is right and no to what is not. Second, Graeme Sellers, of the Alliance of Renewal Churches, defines freedom as, "the ability to think according to what is really true; the ability to think, act, and function according to the way that you were originally designed."[96]

Based on these definitions, being a people who are living lives of true freedom can mean the following: 1) People who are truly free are growing in their ability to say yes to what is right and no to what is wrong; and 2) People who are truly free are growing in their ability to think, act, and function according to the way they were originally designed so they can grow in being who they were meant to be.

If we are to live lives in which we are truly free to say yes to what is right and no to what is wrong, we first need some sense of what is right and wrong. For the Christian, the source of that sense is the One who created us. Jesus said, "I am the way, the truth, and the life" (John 14:6, ESV). We believe truth can be seen in the life Jesus lived here on earth, and can be learned by reading, studying, and meditating and reflecting on the truth as revealed in his Word, the Bible, which is God-breathed (2 Timothy 3:16). Truth as revealed in Scripture can be the rock-solid foundation for living a life that is truly free and abundant. It is such a strong foundation that it even enables those who are under the oppression of a government that is antagonistic toward Christians, or those who have found themselves literally in prison, to live lives of inner freedom that no external force can take away. This is the power of being a people rooted in the truth as revealed in God's Word.

Being a people who are experientially rooted in God's truth will be one of the major characteristics of any individual, group, or church that desires to grow in what it means to be a safe place. This is so important that the apostle

---

96   Shared with permission from Graeme Sellers, originally used in a sermon at Wonderful Mercy Church, Gilbert, AZ.

Paul gives us more than one warning to be on guard lest we be deceived into believing lies to be truth:

> Pay careful attention to yourselves and to all the flock, in which the Holy Spirit has made you overseers, to care for the church of God, which he obtained with his own blood. I know that after my departure fierce wolves will come in among you, not sparing the flock; and from among your own selves will arise men speaking twisted things, to draw away the disciples after them. Therefore, be alert (Acts 20:28–30, ESV).

> Then we will no longer be immature like children. We won't be tossed and blown about by every wind of new teaching. We will not be influenced when people try to trick us with lies so clever they sound like truth (Ephesians 4:14, NLT).

Being a people rooted in truth is essential for living lives of true freedom, and to live in that freedom we must be ever vigilant to identify and guard against the preaching and teaching of lies, dressed up so they are presented, and even appear at times, to be truth. What does it look like to be a people rooted in the God's truth? That will be the subject of the following chapters, but before moving on to read them, take some time to do the following exercise.

PEOPLE OF TRUTH REFLECTION

- Think of times when people have shared truth with you in helpful ways and identify:
  - What it was about *who* they are as persons that made it possible to receive what they had to share?
  - What was it about *how* they communicated truth that made it possible to receive what they had to share?

2. Think of times when people have shared truth with you in ways there were not helpful and identify:

    a.   What is it about *who* they are as persons that made it difficult to receive what they had to share?

    b.   What is it about *how* they communicated truth that made it difficult to receive what they had to share?

27

ROOTED IN A RELATIONSHIP THAT
LEADS TOWARD TRANSFORMATION

The Word of God is a meeting place—a place where we meet
with God and experience his presence, hear his voice, and grow in
knowing his nature and will.

The Bible is alive, it speaks to me; it has feet, it runs after me; it
has hands, it lays hold of me!

— MARTIN LUTHER
The Table Talk of Martin Luther

BEING A PEOPLE rooted in truth is more about transformation than information, more about relationship than religion and rules. A safe-place people
seeking to be rooted in truth refuse to settle for merely accumulating more
information about God. Instead, they focus on growing in a relationship with

him so that they can become more like him. What good is it to know information about God but not think, speak, and act more like him?

There is a knowledge that is intellectual, academic, and theological in nature, the world of concepts, ideas, and philosophies. There is a knowledge that is intellectual, academic, and theological in nature, the world of concepts, ideas, and philosophies. There is another knowledge however, that is experiential in nature—it impacts and changes who we are. Graham Cooke counsels us, "Never trust a theologian who has not experienced the truth him/herself. Logical, rational and intellectual appreciation of scripture will not take us into the high places of faith and breakthrough." Without this appreciation "we are reduced to explaining God rather than experiencing him."[97] A safe-place people do not want only to explain God to others.

They want to experience God in their own lives and they want others to experience his presence and his love and power through them.

TRUTH IS A PERSON

John 8:32 tells us that truth will set us free. Verse 36 tells us that the truth that will set us free is a person. Truth is more than simply a proposition, idea, or concept, it is a person, and that person is Jesus Christ. As one author writes,

> We're not pursuing a truth that is figured in historical facts and debates or doctrines or questions of whether something happened of not. We're pursing a truth that is a person—a living God. We are not after right answers; we're after the right person. Our faith rests in Father, Son, and Holy Spirit. It's not the information from God that satisfies. It's his presence that satisfies. He himself is the

---

97 Graham Cooke, *The Qualities of a Spiritual Warrior* (Vacaville, CA: Brilliant Books, 2008), 136, 137.

answer to all fears—losing money, being persecuted, losing out on opportunities.[98]

It is not merely knowledge about God that can be the answer to the fears and anxieties we may experience, it is a relationship with him. It is so easy in this information age to become "professional Christians" who read and study the Word of God to prepare bible studies, teachings, and sermons, and in doing so become subtly lulled into a relationship with knowledge (even if it is great, biblical knowledge) rather than with a person.

The Word of God was not given to humankind just to be a book of knowledge about God to be parsed and studied, preached and taught. The Word of God is a meeting place—a place where we meet with God and experience his presence, hear his voice, and grow in knowing his nature and will. The Bible is a place where we can meet with the One who is truth and grow in a very real relationship with him. Will we receive him? Will we receive the truth he embodied when he walked the earth and speaks into our lives today? Will we allow this truth to transform us? These are important questions to consider, and our answer to them will determine the destiny path for our lives.

A Great, but Sometimes Mixed, Blessing

As God's written word the Scriptures are a great, but sometimes mixed, blessing. They are a blessing because each new generation of Christians has access to the fact that God speaks through the Scriptures. They can become a mixed blessing, however, the moment the words are reduced to something that is looked at, studied, interpreted, but not heard personally.

In John 5:39–40, Jesus says, "You search the Scriptures because you think that in them you have eternal life; and it is they that bear witness about me, yet you *refuse to come to me* that you may have life" (emphasis mine). Here Jesus is speaking to the religious leaders. And Jesus would speak this warning to us today: Do not be people who just read, study, and parse my Word, but

---

98   Charles Park, "Biblical Authority in a Postmodern World," *Cutting Edge Magazine* 15, no. 2 (Fall 2011): 7.

be people who come to my Word to *meet and be with me;* be people who want to listen to my voice and hear my heart, and then respond to what they hear in humility, faith, and obedience.

God has given us the written Word that we might meet with him, hear him, and come to know him. The following story illustrates how one can read the Scriptures, but not hear them speaking to him or her, or come to truly know and enter into a relationship of faith with God:

The prince of Grenada, an heir to the Spanish Crown, was sentenced to life in solitary confinement in Madrid's ancient prison. The dreadful, dirty, and dreary nature of the place earned it the name, "The Place Of The Skull." Everyone knew that once you were in, you would never come out alive. The prince was given one book to read the entire time . . . the Bible. With only one book to read, he read it over hundreds and hundreds of times.

The book became his constant companion. After 33 years of imprisonment, he died. When they came to clean out his cell, they found some notes he had written using nails to mark the soft stone of the prison walls. The notations were of this sort: Psalm 118:8 is the middle verse of the Bible; Ezra 7:21 contains all the letters of the alphabet except the letter J; the ninth verse of the eighth chapter of Esther is the longest verse in the Bible; no word or name of more than six syllables can be found in the Bible.

The individual spent 33 years of his life *studying* what some have described as the greatest book of all time. Yet he could only glean trivia. From all we know, he *never made any religious or spiritual commitment to Christ.* He simply became an expert at Bible trivia [emphasis mine].[99]

---

99 Leonard Sweet, *Aqua Church: Essential Leadership Arts for Piloting Your Church in Today's Fluid Culture* (Loveland, CO: Group Publishing, 1999), 58–59.

God's gracious purpose in giving us his Word in written form is not to turn us into Bible students, but to provide a means by which we can hear him speak and be turned into followers of Christ who are committed to growing more like Jesus and living lives of service and mission.

A Meeting Place

Over the years my Bible has become my coffee shop as it were. When I lived in Pasadena, California, I could not throw a stick without hitting a Starbucks or Coffee Bean—my bank even had a Starbucks in it! I noticed that the Starbucks and Coffee Bean shops in Pasadena were always full of people. And I noticed that people gathered there in order to be together, to *be with* each other, to hear one another, and to connect with each other. This is what our time in the Word can be with the Lord. The Bible is not meant to be just a book we read, but a place where we meet with God, where we hear God, and where God encounters us. Martin Luther knew this when he wrote, "The Bible is alive, it speaks to me; it has feet, it runs after me; it has hands, it lays hold of me!"[100]

If need be, ask God to help change your paradigm of what reading, studying, and praying his Word is so that it becomes a meeting place for you. As you do you will discover yourself looking forward to meeting the Lord there and just spending time with him. After all, isn't this what Jesus invited the disciples to do, to be with him? (See Mark 3:14.) He did not invite them to study him, but to be with him. Let's ask God to make this our experience as we come to his Word. If we will ask, he will answer, and our times of being in his Word, in prayer, and in worship will become rich with a tangible sense of his presence.

We Become Like the People We Spend Time With

We tend to become like the people we spend time with. "When you make that face you look just like your mom!" "When you say that, you sound just

---

100 Martin Luther, *The Table Talk of Martin Luther* (Mineola, NY: Dover Publications, 2005), Kindle ed.

like your dad!" I am the proud godfather for Samuel Michael Sellers, son of my best friend, Graeme Sellers. As I write this chapter Sam will soon turn six years old. Ever since he was about two, he could play both guitar and drums with an amazing sense of rhythm. Often when I visited he would put on a concert for me, playing on one or both. One of my favorite Samuel Michael songs was his rendition of the great rock 'n' roll classic *Old Time Rock and Roll* by legendary rocker Bob Seger.

Sam was only two years old! How did he learn that song at this age, and learn it so well, I wondered. Then it dawned on me, he knows it and loves it because his dad knows it and loves it. Sam was becoming like his dad because his dad was the person he spent time with. In fact, just recently we visited Sam's new school on first grade orientation night, and when asked on an information form what his favorite thing to do was, he wrote, "Play with my dad." We become like the people we spend time with. It is no different with the Lord and his kids. When we spend time with God, being with him and not just reading about him or studying him, we tend to become more like him. And when we become more like him we grow in what it means to be a people who are safe.

Growing in what it means to be a safe place requires becoming a people who seek to be rooted in God's life-giving truth by coming to meet with him in his Word and grow in our relationship with him. Growing in our relationship with a person who is truth, rather than merely understanding truth as information, will lead to a transformation in our lives that finds us thinking, speaking, and acting more like Jesus. And to be more like Jesus is to be a people who are safe, rather than unsafe, for those around them.

28

OFFERING VINTAGE WINE

The truth that a safe place offers is the vintage teaching of Jesus Christ, the apostles, and historic, orthodox Christianity. This is the truth that a post-Christian, postmodern culture still needs if it is to experience what it means to truly live free.

GOOD HOSTS OFFER the best wine. Those more knowledgeable than I concerning wine tell me they most often prefer vintage wine to new wine. In Scripture, wine is often a metaphor for truth. Realizing this, safe-place people seek to be experientially rooted in the vintage wine of truth as revealed in God's Word. This is one of the hallmarks of being a safe place, even while a growing number of people, including some Christians, are calling for the church to offer new wine for a new age.

NEW TIMES CALL FOR NEW TRUTH
We live in a new, postmodern era. Therefore, say some, the church needs to change with the times and offer new wine for the new era, rather than offering

old, outdated wine. Rather than continuing to teach and preach the truth we have preached and taught for millennia, some are calling the Christian church to change our interpretation and application of God's Word, particularly as it affects multiple social and lifestyle choices. For them, the vintage wine of past ages is no longer viewed as applicable or relevant in the new era.

A new age, they advocate, requires a new wine. Theologian Rudolf Bultmann presents an example of what discarding vintage wine in favor of something new looks like, when he writes, "We can't recover the historical Jesus. Therefore, we must reinterpret the mythology of the New Testament to rescue its significance to modern people."[101] In other words, say Bultmann and others of his ilk, because our life experiences do not always match the vintage truth we claim to believe, let's change our interpretation and application of that truth to match our experience—or lack thereof. Bultmann and others like him believe that if what we have considered to be true does not match our experience, we should reinterpret and present truth in a new way so it matches our experience. But others of us who prefer vintage wine to new wine have a different view and offer a different solution—we ask God to change our experiences so we come into alignment with the vintage truth of his Word.

There is a time and place when responsible hermeneutics and exegesis should lead us to question our experiences and practices. For example, critically examining biblical texts helped William Wilberforce and others realize that while certain Scriptures seem, at first glance, to accept the practice of slavery in biblical culture, this did not justify continuing its practice. The responsible use of hermeneutics and exegesis helped the opponents of slavery come to realize those Scriptures that seemed to simply accept its practice as a norm for all time were not God's highest ideals. Instead, those hermeneutical principles informed them to reject slavery as a norm for all time, and to live according to God's higher ideal of freedom for all peoples. In this case, those Scriptures that seemed to accept the practice of slavery rightly needed to be re-examined in the light of this higher hermeneutical and exegetical priority.

---

101   Rudolf Bultmann, in *Kerygma and Myth* by Rudolf Bultmann and Five Critics (London: SPCK, 1953), available at www.religion-online.org/showchapter.asp

However, it is one thing when responsible hermeneutics and exegesis cause us to rightly question and reconsider our understanding of certain Scripture passages, but it is quite another to discount portions of Scripture as being myth or fable simply because they do not seem to match our current experience or worldview. A danger of interpretations such as Bultmann's is that it will embolden leaders and the people of God to deal with any lack of experiencing a biblical worldview or truth by changing and reinterpreting God's Word. What we need instead is an experience of a worldview and truth that is more aligned with the truth of God's Word.

GOD-BREATHED

At the foundation of a safe-place people's commitment to adhere to truth as revealed in the Word of God is a conviction that all scripture is *God-breathed*. The apostle Paul wrote to his disciple Timothy that, "Every part of Scripture is God-breathed and useful one way or another—showing us truth, exposing our rebellion, correcting our mistakes, training us to live God's way" (The Message). Other versions of the Bible translate the term God-breathed as "inspired by God" or as "divine inspiration." However, Gregory A. Boyd writes the following concerning translating that phrase in such a manner:

> I should also register my conviction, shared by a number of others, that the more literal translation of *theopneustos* as "God-breathed" is preferable to its more customary translation as "divine inspiration," despite the fact that "God-breathed" undoubtedly sounds wooden and/or idiosyncratic to some readers. Among my reasons for this preference is the fact that "inspired" tends to either misplace the focal point of God's revelatory activity within Scripture's *human authors*— as though God breathed *into* them —or it misplaces the focus on the effect Scripture has upon readers (i.e., we find it "inspiring"). I would rather argue that *theopneustos* suggests that the focal point of God's activity is on *the biblical texts themselves*, which this term indicates were "expired" by God.

By placing the focus on biblical texts that God "expired" rather than on the human authors whom God "inspired," we are freed from becoming preoccupied with the futile project of trying to parse out the mysterious God-human interaction that led to the production of these texts. As Kenton Sparks notes, while *theopneustos* grants divine authority to the canonical texts, "the Greek word itself does not really imply anything in particular about how the transaction between God and the human authors took place."[102]

A safe-place people are not so concerned in getting caught up in a fruitless debate about how the transaction of inspiration between God and the human authors took place, but rather are more concerned with the sure knowledge that the Scriptures as written have divine authority in our lives as individuals and as corporate bodies. Therefore, if there is a discrepancy between truth as revealed in the Bible and our own life experience, it is our life experience that needs to be changed, not the Scriptures.

DOING CHURCH DIFFERENTLY

Another contributing factor to the call by some for a change in the interpretation and application of God's Word has been the theme of doing church differently, because now we live in a postmodern rather than modern era. There has been much talk for a number of years about the need to structure churches differently from the way they were in the modern era. I truly appreciate many of the questions the postmodern movement asks and the points that postmodernity makes. It is always good to critique what we're doing in light of both Scripture and the cultural contexts in which we live to ensure we are sharing God's truth in the most effective means possible. However, what I do not agree with is talk of being contextual or missional beyond the scope of different wineskins, structures, or models of churches, to the point of suggesting that we need new truth to go along with new structures or practices.

---

102 Boyd, *The Crucifixion of the Warrior God*, 4.

To consider new structures and practices for doing church is one thing. Believing the truth we share needs to change is something altogether different. I am not opposed to considering new structures and ways of church practice. Scripture does not provide us a one size fits all template for how to structure or do church. In many ways, for those who come out of a Lutheran-Christian heritage as I do, our Reformation heritage was a new wineskin movement in its day, as calls were made to change how they practiced being the church. For instance, one way the Reformers did church differently was to translate the Word of God into the language of the people and put it in their hands to read and study for themselves. They also introduced new music and hymnology. These were very significant, new, and different ways of doing church at that time.

However, being a people seeking to be rooted in God's truth in a postmodern, post-Christian culture that is open to developing "new wineskins" does not mean we must present some kind of new truth. While the structures, styles, and practices of the church may change, the truth of the Gospel of Jesus Christ never does. In fact, when it comes to the wine of *truth*, it is the old wine that people will ultimately like best. Those who experience the healing, freedom, and purpose that the vintage wine of biblical truth brings to bear on their lives testify to its preference over the new wine being offered by some theologians today. It is the old wine that people still need, even if it may need to be presented in the context of new containers. As Ray Anderson writes,

> The gospel is itself "old wine" that has gone through the fermentation process and has acquired a taste and character that satisfies the most discerning and demanding palate! It is the vintage gospel. And in what do you serve old wine? In any kind of vessel that you want! For old wine does not demand that which is merely new, but that by which the wine may be served. The gospel of the emerging church is vintage wine . . . Older wineskins have carried it forward in history, but these are disposable when they have served their purpose.

The gospel was rediscovered by Luther and the other reformers, served in vessels and carried forward with institutional structures, church polities, and liturgical rules and regulations. But these are merely the wineskins and when they have served their purpose, the original, vintage gospel can be served and tasted in new ecclesial forms. What Luther discovered and set in motion was not Lutheranism but the gospel.[103]

The truth that a safe place offers is the vintage teaching of Jesus Christ, the apostles, and historic, orthodox Christianity. This is the truth that a post-Christian, postmodern culture still needs if it is to experience what it means to truly live free. Thus, one of the chief characteristics of a safe-place people will be that they seek to be rooted in the vintage truth as revealed in the Word of God.

---

103   Ray Anderson, *An Emergent Theology for the Emerging Church* (Grand Rapids, MI: Zondervan, 2005), 74–75.

29

SAYING NO TO WATERING DOWN THE TRUTH

Therefore each of you must put off falsehood and speak truthfully to his neighbor,
for we are all members of one body.

— EPHESIANS 4:25

BEING A SAFE-PLACE people requires that we say no to any and all temptations to water down the truth as presented in the Word of God. We have spoken previously of the importance of being a people who are experientially rooted in God's grace. There are some Christians who misunderstand how being a people rooted in grace and truth can go together. Because they misunderstand, they are succumbing to the temptation to water down the truth of God's Word in order to appear more accepting and full of grace toward people. In doing this, however, they are actually placing people in harm's way. Rather than giving in to this temptation to water down the truth, followers of Christ would be better served by learning when, where, and how to share the truth, and by discerning when it is the second word rather than the first God wants us to speak.

GOD'S GRACE IMPACTS WHEN AND HOW WE SHARE TRUTH

To be grace-filled toward others does not require that we water down the truth of God's Word. It is not a matter of choosing one or the other. Jesus himself is full of both grace and truth (see John 1:14) and models the ability to relate to people in grace while at the same time not watering down the truth. We see this in his encounters with the woman at the well in John 4 and with Zaccheaus in Luke 19, just to name two.

Rather that watering down God's truth, being a people rooted in God's grace impacts when, where, and how we communicate that truth. Grace and truth are never to be divorced from one another. Together, grace and truth are God's healing combination. Joe Johnson writes,

> Jesus' presence with us enables us to risk facing the truth. To be safe we do not protect others from facing the truth because truth sets us free. Safety does not mean denying the truth. God protects us from harm by revealing the truth about our brokenness or sin, which is wounding us.[104]

A wonderful example of the impact the healing combination of grace and truth can have in someone's life is how Jesus relates to the woman caught in adultery in John 8:3–11. In this encounter Jesus offered the woman grace in the form of forgiveness and acceptance. The power and scope of God's grace is demonstrated in the fact that Jesus accepted her with full realization that she was an adulteress.

---

104 Originally published in a church newsletter and shared with permission from Joe Johnson.

Jesus does not stop, however, at only offering this woman grace. He also offers her truth and freedom. God's truth and freedom are imparted to her in Jesus' words, "Go now and leave your life of sin." These two ingredients together—grace and truth, acceptance and direction for new life—serve to bring this woman into right relationship with God. This is the only way that true, deep healing can ever take place.

SHARING TRUTH IN A GRACELESS MANNER

To be a people who are safe requires an awareness that it is possible to speak words of truth in a graceless manner. We can speak the truth in a manner that is arrogant and angry, judgmental and condemning. But we are not called by God to speak in that manner. Jesus modeled God's desire for us to speak truth, but to do so in grace. The absence of either grace or truth can be damaging to those we want to impact with God's power and love. Therefore, a safe-place people, knowing we are not justified in sharing the timeless truths of God in a graceless manner, will seek to allow God's grace to inform them of where, when, and how to share words of truth.

30

BLOWING UP OUR GOD-BOXES: SAYING NO TO SIMPLY BEING SINCERE

There are times when merely being sincere about what we believe is not enough. The content of what we are sincere about is important too because we can be sincerely wrong.

B EING EXPERIENTIALLY ROOTED in God's truth requires more than simply being sincere about what a person believes. In our society today, it is not unusual to hear something such as this: "It doesn't matter what you believe, as long as you're sincere in your belief." But is that really true? Is it enough to simply be sincere in what we believe? Or, is it also important to consider what content we are sincere about? In response to questions such as these, one author writes,

> Sincerity is a precious thing, and arguments about who has the correct beliefs have too often led to arrogance, ugly arguments, and even

violence. But believing untrue things, however sincerely, can have its own unintended consequences. For example, try believing that God will be pleased if you fly an airplane into a tall building, that you can get away with embezzling funds, that you have a personal exemption from sexual propriety, or that your race or religion makes you superior to members of other races or religions. You will become someone nobody respects, including (eventually) you.[105]

In Acts, chapters 10 and 11, there is a story of how God speaks to Peter about what Peter sincerely believes, and how that sincere belief needs to change. Peter, like most Jewish men and leaders of his day, was sincere in his view of what food was clean and what food was unclean (see Acts 10:14ff). He was also sincere in his belief that Israel was God's chosen people. Peter is very sincere in his beliefs on these matters. God however, chooses this as the time to change the content of what Peter sincerely believes. So, he comes to Peter in a vision and we have the story of this God encounter in Acts, chapter 10.

In regards to what can be eaten, a voice in Peter's vision (which he later discerns to be God's voice) says, "What God has made clean, do not call common," and this happened three times. In this vision, the Lord challenges the content of Peter's sincerity and wants to change the belief that Peter is sincere about (see Acts 10:28). The Lord uses this vision and encounter to change the content of Peter's sincerity regarding something else—who the people are that God wants to restore in relationship to himself. God tells Peter that he wants to restore the Gentiles as well as the Jews.

BLOWING UP OUR GOD-BOXES

Now, this content that God introduces to Peter is not new content, but rather content that has been forgotten or set aside. Genesis 12:1–3 tells us that from the very beginning God has wanted to reach out to and restore all peoples to himself, not only the Jews. God, in a sense, blows up Peter's "God-box." That

---

105 Brian D. McLaren, *The Secret Message of Jesus: Uncovering the Truth That Could Change Everything* (Nashville, TN: W Publishing Group, 2006), 6.

is, God blows up Peter's limited understanding of how the Lord thinks and how he moves in the world. Peter had put his understanding of God in a box and, as Peter learned, the Lord is not content to be contained in boxes of our making.

We all have limited God-boxes that we sincerely believe to be true, and if we are to live more fully into God's purposes for our lives we need them blown up. I have had multiple God–boxes over the years, and have needed this experience of having them blown up numerous times in my journey with the Lord.

SINCERITY IS NOT ENOUGH

It has not been enough that I sincerely believed what I believed. I needed the content of what I believed and trusted in changed. First and foremost, I needed my sincere belief that I did not need God changed. There came a time when through a series of circumstances and relationships the Lord challenged my sincerely held belief and revealed to me my great need for him. There came a point in my life as a young man that I suddenly realized I needed a Savior. It became so clear to me that no matter how hard I tried to live a good life, I would still be a sinner; there would always be temptation and sin in my life no matter how good I appeared to others. I needed someone whose power was greater than mine, someone who could pay the price for the sin I had already committed and could help set me free from the temptations I still battled. God showed me my need for his Son, Jesus Christ. And at twenty-one, I said yes to a relationship with Jesus as my Savior and my Lord. He changed the content of what I had sincerely believed, and it was not long before I began to construct my first God-box.

That first God-box contained two things I sincerely believed. First was the belief that God could not really use any historical, mainline churches because they were all spiritually dead, liberal, and of no use to him. Second was the belief that anything charismatic, any Christian spiritual experience, was from the devil because God no longer moved in that way.

The discipleship group I was a part of after becoming a Christian had taught me these twin beliefs. That group was made up of wonderful people and they taught me many things I am so grateful for and hold to be true to this day. For instance, they taught me that the Bible is the Word of God, period. That has been a rock-solid foundation for me throughout my journey with Jesus. However, in this matter regarding an experience of God's supernatural power today, they taught that God had only moved in that kind of power during the "apostolic age" when the church was being birthed through the work of the apostles. They based this teaching on a combination of personal bias and poor hermeneutical work regarding a particular passage in Scripture.

Fortunately for me, there came a time when God broke in on my life and blew up my God-box in regards to both of these misbeliefs, chiefly by introducing me to a Lutheran pastor who believed the supernatural power of God was real today, and who himself exercised that power in a very natural way. His life demonstrated a great passion and witness for the Lord, and a keen intellect. This mainline, denominational church pastor was anything but spiritually dead, liberal, or of no use to God. He was spiritually alive, faithful to God's Word, and a powerful influence for the Lord in the lives of others.

And regarding my second misbelief, this pastor manifested the power of God working in and through him, even as the power of God had been manifested in and through the lives of the apostles in the early life of the church. Through my developing relationship with this charismatic Lutheran pastor the Lord blew up my God-box and helped me experience the empowering presence of his Spirit, and fanned my passion for him and his kingdom into fuller flame. Needless to say, now that I am the director for a network of churches that embraces both the sacramental and charismatic streams of the Christian faith, I am thankful that God challenged those sincere, but incorrect, beliefs I held. By the way, as a postscript, that charismatic Lutheran pastor went on to become my father-in-law. To this day, I am thankful for one of the greatest gifts God has ever given me—Pastor Armand "Al" Asper.

WE CAN BE SINCERELY WRONG

There are times when simply being sincere about what we believe is not enough. The content of what we are sincere about is important too because we can be sincerely wrong. World history bears this out, does it not? The Axis powers of World War II were sincerely wrong. Those who thought of and built the gas chambers, sending millions of innocent Jews to their death, were sincerely wrong. There have been times in history when Christians have been sincerely wrong in some of our initiatives and actions in the world. Sincerity in belief is not enough. Sincerely believing content that is right and true is important too.

What is it you have sincerely believed that God wants to challenge and change in order to bring your experience of life and of him into greater alignment with the truth as revealed in his Word? What is it God has already been speaking to you about but you have not yet allowed him to change in regards to the content of what you believe? Will you humble yourself as Peter did, and allow the Lord to change your understanding about that which he wants you to sincerely believe?

Being experientially rooted in God's truth is more than simply being sincere about what we believe. It is about being sincerely rooted in the truth as revealed in the Word of God. It is about allowing God to change that which we sincerely believe when it needs to be changed. It is *not* about changing our interpretation and application of God's Word to fit what we are sincerely wrong about. Anytime Christians begin to change what God's Word says simply because we do not like it, or our experience does not yet measure up to it, we become the very thing we do not want to become—a people who are unsafe for Christians and non-Christians alike.

So, humble yourself, and pray right now before you read on. In prayer ask God to blow up your God-box where he needs to, so that you can experience a deeper, more vital relationship with him and live more fully into all the purposes he has for your life. Allowing God to blow up our sincerely held God-boxes where needed will enable us to grow in what it means to be a safe place because it will enable us to increasingly think, speak, and act more like Jesus.

31

REFUSING TO USE SPIRITUAL LANGUAGE TO RATIONALIZE AND JUSTIFY WRONG BELIEF AND BEHAVIOR

Spiritual sounding language, including Scripture itself, can be used as a form of control, manipulation, and intimidation in an attempt to silence God's people and force them to submit to wrong belief and wrong behavior.

P EOPLE WHO SEEK to be rooted in God's truth refuse to use spiritual language to rationalize and justify wrong belief and behavior. It is possible for Christians, as well as non-Christians, to do this. An example can be found in Jesus' confrontation with the Pharisees in Mark 7:6–13:

And he (Jesus) said to them, "Well did Isaiah prophesy of you hypocrites, as it is written, 'This people honors me with their lips, but their heart is far from me; in vain do they worship me, teaching as doctrines *the commandments of men.'* You leave the commandment of God and hold to the tradition of men." And he said to them, "You have a fine way of rejecting the commandment of God in order to establish your tradition! For Moses said, 'Honor your father and your mother'; and, 'Whoever reviles father or mother must surely die.' But you say, 'If a man tells his father or his mother, "Whatever you would have gained from me is Corban"' (that is, given to God)—then you no longer permit him to do anything for his father or mother, thus making void the word of God by your tradition that you have handed down. And many such things you do" [ESV, emphasis mine].

In this passage, we learn that the religious leaders had established a rule contrary to God's will. Their rule encouraged people to take money they would have used, and according to God's will they should have used, to take care of aging parents and give it as a gift to God. In reality, it was a gift being given to the Pharisees. In their greed for money the religious leaders were teaching people they could take that money meant to be used for the care of parents and designate it to be *corban*, that is, designate it as a gift to God instead. Corban is a transliteration of a Hebrew word meaning "offering."

The religious leaders were teaching people to disobey God's will for the sake of their own monetary gain, all the while rationalizing and justifying this wrong belief and behavior by using spiritual language. Who is going to argue with "giving a gift devoted to God" if this is what is being taught and called for by the respected religious leaders in society? This is just one example in the Bible where religious leaders use spiritual language to rationalize and justify wrong behavior.

USING SPIRITUAL SOUNDING LANGUAGE DOES NOT MAKE IT RIGHT

Simply because someone uses spiritual sounding language does not mean that what they say is true or right—or that it is something that actually comes from the Lord. For instance, just because someone prefaces what he or she claims to be a prophetic word with, "Thus says the Lord," does not mean it is in fact a prophetic word from God. Or, simply because someone says, "As I was praying I heard such and such from the Lord," does not automatically mean what they thought they heard was in fact from God.

Spiritual sounding phrases can be used to rationalize and justify our own selfish desires and mask our own lack of emotional, relational, or spiritual wholeness. For instance, one of the spiritual sounding phrases on my personal top ten list of "Phrases Not to Believe In" is the Abrahamic Call. This describes something that was taught and lived out in a ministry I once served in. The Abrahamic Call. Sounds so spiritual doesn't it? In reality, it is a teaching used by leaders to rationalize and justify ignoring the assigned responsibilities of a leadership position they have been called to fill. It is used by leaders, and those who surround and support them, to rationalize and justify a propensity to neglect the care for their congregation, para-church ministry, or even their own family, while they go off to participate in activities they personally enjoy but are not part of their assigned responsibilities.

These leaders pursue these other activities because they enjoy them, and as leaders, receive a lot of attention and affirmation for participating in them. For instance, I know of a pastor who had been called to lead a multi-thousand-member church but soon after accepting the call began to be absent from his congregation during the week because he was busy serving as an "apostle" for a number of small, Pentecostal churches in the region surrounding his church. His assigned responsibilities were to be the senior pastor of this particular church, but that would mean focusing primarily on the one church and on the sometimes mundane and administrative responsibilities that being a senior leader entails. Leadership is not always fun or exciting. So instead, he decided to spend the majority of his time speaking and ministering among the Pentecostal churches in that region, endeavors that were more enjoyable for him, and he was doing all this without asking for permission from the church council of the congregation that hired him. In his way of thinking, like Abraham he had heard the call of God and he had to be obedient to follow that call.

It sounded so spiritual. Yet, in reality, it was a misuse of Scripture designed to rationalize and justify irresponsibility, selfishness, and a lack of wholeness on the part of this leader and those who supported him. Complicating such situations, leaders and their supporters using spiritual language to rationalize and justify their wrong belief and behavior are seldom questioned. Very rarely will someone in a congregation dare to question a pastor who has gone to seminary. Nor will they dare to question those who surround and support that pastor, particularly if they hold leadership positions such as being an elder or a church council member. More often than not, the run-of-the-mill church member will think, "Who am I to question someone like that?" This kind of thinking will often keep them silent until its too late. In retrospect, it is only after the damage of a leader's irresponsibility and selfishness has been done that people realize that what they sensed was wrong, was in fact wrong.

Another phrase on my top ten list of spiritual-sounding phrases used to rationalize and justify wrong beliefs and behaviors is "the main thing is taking territory for the kingdom of God." At first glance this sounds like a good phrase to use for motivating God's people to carry out the Lord's kingdom agenda in the world. However, it can become a spiritual sounding excuse used by leaders who are passionate about accomplishing something great for God but do not see (or worse, they do see) how they are using, manipulating, and wearing out God's people in the process. These leaders are so focused on the task that they willingly rationalize and justify sacrificing caring relationships, leaving a trail of worn out and wounded Christians strewn along the path behind them.

SCRIPTURE ITSELF CAN BE USED

It is possible to not only use spiritual sounding language, but to use Holy Scripture itself to rationalize and justify wrong belief and behavior. This was the devil's strategy when he came to tempt Jesus. In both accounts of the devil tempting Jesus to sin, Matthew 4 and Luke 4, the devil quotes Scriptures from the Old Testament. He takes them out of context and uses them to tempt Jesus to disobey God. We can do the same thing.

For example, in toxic faith systems it is common to hear a Scripture from the Old Testament used to control and manipulate people as a means to keep them from questioning the motives or actions of leaders who are engaging in wrong practice or even abusive behavior. They will lift the words David spoke in his refusal to kill King Saul, "I will not touch the Lord's anointed," and make it a command for God's people today. When members of a congregation might begin questioning or challenging the wrong practice or abusive behavior of a pastor or an elder in the church, they will be told, "Don't touch the Lord's anointed," or some form of that phrase. In doing this, church leaders are lifting phrases from the Bible, taking them out of their scriptural context and using the Bible's words to rationalize and justify wrong belief and behavior.

It is our responsibility as followers of Christ to discern whether Scripture is being used rightly or if it is being taken out of context, and being misinterpreted and misapplied. An example of practicing this responsibility is seen in the lives of the Christians of Berea in Acts 17. In verse eleven we read, "Now the Bereans were of more noble character than the Thessalonians, for they received the message with great eagerness and examined the Scriptures every day to see if what Paul said was true" (Acts 17:11, NLT). The apostle Paul also speaks to this responsibility for all Christians when he writes to the Thessalonian Christians, "Do not treat prophecies with contempt. Test everything. Hold on to the good. Avoid every kind of evil" (1 Thessalonians 5:20–21).

As followers of Jesus, we all are given the responsibility to examine and test in the light of Scripture what we are being taught and told because spiritual-sounding language, including Scripture itself, can be used as a form of control, manipulation, and intimidation. Growing in what it means to be a safe-place people who are rooted in God's truth means refusing to use spiritual language to rationalize and justify wrong belief and wrong behavior, and refusing to allow others, even our leaders, to do so either.

32

DISCERNING THE DIFFERENCE BETWEEN LEGALISM AND BIBLICAL TRUTH

The essence of legalism is trusting in religious activity and performance rather than trusting in God. It is putting our confidence in a practice rather than in a person. And without fail this will lead us to love the practice more than the person.

— STEVE McVEY
Grace Walk

CHRISTIANS MUST LEARN to discern the difference between legalism and biblical truth if they are to grow in what it means to be a safe-place people who are rooted in the truth of God's Word. Legalism is the human tendency to turn God's covenant of grace into a contract. Rather than understanding that the Lord loves us and chooses to relate to us based on who he is, not what we deserve, the legalist believes we must perform and live up to a certain set of standards in order to convince God to bless us with his favor. A person caught in legalism cannot feel completely right or at peace with God unless they are performing up to that certain set of standards—and those standards often differ from one group of Christians to another, from one area of the country to another.

DEFINING LEGALISM

Author Steve McVey writes that "any approach to Christian living that focuses on keeping rules as a means of experiencing victory or growing spiritually is legalism. Legalism is a system in which a person seeks to gain God's acceptance or blessings by what they do."[106] In his 1963 article *The Paralysis of Legalism,* S. Lewis Johnson put his finger on the crux of one of the major impacts of legalism in the lives of Christians:

> One of the most serious problems facing the orthodox Christian church today is the problem of legalism. One of the most serious problems facing the church in Paul's day was the problem of legalism. In every day it is the same. Legalism wrenches the joy of the Lord from the Christian Believer, and with the joy of the Lord goes his power for vital worship and vibrant service. Nothing is left but cramped, somber, dull, and listless profession. The truth is betrayed, and the glorious name of the Lord becomes a synonym for a gloomy killjoy. The Christian under law is *a miserable parody of the real thing* [emphasis mine].[107]

Christians caught in legalism will be more concerned with adherence to the standards they believe in and to outward appearances than with the inward realities of their own lives and the lives of others. Their emphasis on

---

106   Steve McVey, *Grace Walk* (Eugene, OR: Harvest House Publishers, 1995), 80.

107   S. Lewis Johnson, "The Paralysis of Legalism," *Bibliotheca Sacra* 120, no. 478 (April-June 1963): 109. Quoted in Swindoll, *The Grace Awakening*, 69.

appearances will create an atmosphere in which people will consciously or subconsciously put on a false self in order to be accepted and receive approval. They will wear masks because to be who they truly are will be to invite criticism, ridicule, and even rejection. Christians who are caught in legalism often evidence a lack of joy along with a critical spirit, giving life and power to the stereotype that to be a Christian is to be arrogant and angry, judgmental and condemning. Christians who are caught in legalism are in a word unsafe.

LEGALISM EQUATES CULTURAL STANDARDS WITH BIBLICAL STANDARDS

Followers of Christ who are captive to legalism believe cultural standards to be biblical mandates, but they are not always the same thing. When a legalistic Christian understands cultural preferences to be biblical commands—even though they are not—they will seek to live up to those standards in order to gain a sense of acceptance and approval from God, and one another. The list of the cultural standards can vary from one group of Christians to another, from one geographical area to another. They can even be different from one country to another. Following are some common examples of how cultural standards can be presented as biblical mandates in the United States. Consider them and then add to the list based on your own experience.

- Christians cannot smoke
- Christians cannot drink alcohol at all
- Christians cannot play cards
- Christians cannot dance (in my case, this is actually true, I *can't* dance)
- Christians cannot watch R-rated movies
- Christians have to listen to "Christian" music only
- Christians must vote the Republican ticket, the Independent ticket perhaps, but never the Democratic ticket
- Christian males cannot have long hair
- Christians cannot have tattoos
- Christians have to have daily devotions in the morning

In the early years of my life in Christ, I believed each one of these taboos. I had been taught that each of them was God's will for all Christians and I sought to live according to this list, and more. However, as the years went by I met fellow believers who smoked, drank alcohol in moderation, played cards, danced, watched an occasional R-rated movie that had a great story line, listened to some good old rock 'n' roll or country and western music, proudly voted the Democratic ticket, had long hair and tattoos, and had their daily devotions in mid-afternoon rather than in the morning. In each case it did not seem to detract from their passionate relationship with Christ or the effectiveness of their witness for him. One by one God began to expose what I had been taught as biblical mandates in my life as nothing more than cultural preferences.

RELATIONAL ENCOUNTERS CAN SET US FREE

It's always interesting to me how quickly cultural preferences can be exposed for what they really are by simply meeting someone who is in love with the Lord while not being captive to living up to those standards. These real life encounters seem to force us to go back to the Scriptures to see if these preferences are actually God's will, only to discover that the Bible does not present them in that manner. In meeting such individuals we discover that what we were told would be a detriment to living a life pleasing to the Lord seems to be having no such impact in these persons' lives. Thus, one of the first steps in being weaned from legalism often seems to be a relational encounter with someone who is not bound by these cultural preferences masquerading as biblical mandates.

BEING SENSITIVE TO CULTURAL PREFERENCES WITHOUT FALLING INTO LEGALISM

While we don't want to fall into a life of legalism, there can be a time to be sensitive toward cultural preferences in order to be as effective as possible in presenting the gospel in that culture. It is important we not simply challenge or reject them out of hand. Being aware of and sensitive to the standards of a particular culture can at times increase our effectiveness in mission. Thus, it is a matter of choosing which battles you really want to fight and are worth fighting.

For instance, as a youth pastor I would provide cultural training when preparing to take teams of adults and teenagers to northeast Mexico on mission outreaches. In those locations we worked alongside Mexican pastors and church members, reaching out to people in their region through acts of service and a presentation of the gospel through the use of testimonies, puppets, preaching, and worship.

As part of our training I sought to make our team sensitive to the Mexican Christians' practice of not playing cards and a desire for both males and females to dress in a conservative fashion. Is either of these cultural preferences a biblical mandate? Playing cards is definitely not clearly addressed in Scripture, and though the Bible does speak in various places about what is or is not an appropriate way to dress, Christians today in various places do disagree on what it means to dress conservatively. My point with our team was to teach them that even though they might disagree with some of the cultural standards of our Mexican brothers and sisters, the greater importance for us in going on this trip was to be as effective as possible in presenting the gospel. Therefore, we would come as humble servants for both the Mexican Christians and other people throughout their region, and manifest that humility and servant-heart by choosing to adhere to their cultural standards. Challenging their preferences was not the battle we wanted to fight. Presenting the gospel in word and deed, and inviting people into a saving relationship with Jesus Christ was.

WHAT'S WORTH SAYING YES TO?

How do we discern what cultural practices we should say yes to, while still guarding against falling into a position and attitude of legalism? Following are some examples of questions you can ask yourself that may help you discern what cultural standards are worth saying yes to in your own life:

- Is it beneficial to me personally and to the gospel generally (1 Corinthians 6:12ff)?
- Will I lose self-control and be mastered by what I participate in (1 Corinthians 6:12ff)?
- Will I be doing this in the presence of someone who I know will fall into sin as a result (1 Corinthians 8:9–10)?
- Is it a violation of the laws of my city, state, or nation (Romans 13:1–7)?
- If I fail to do this, will I lose opportunities to share the gospel (1 Corinthians 10:27–30)?
- Can I do this with a clear conscience (Acts 24:16)?
- Will this cause me to sin by feeding sinful desires (Romans 13:13–14)?
- Am I convinced that this is what God desires for me to do (Romans 13:5)?
- Does my participation proceed from my faith in Jesus Christ (Romans 14:23)?
- Am I doing this to help other people, or am I just being selfish (1 Corinthians 10:24)?
- Can I do this in a way that glorifies God (1 Corinthians 10:31–33)?

Keep in mind that a brother or sister in Christ might ask these same questions regarding the same issues you are asking about, but come up with different answers. When this happens we have the opportunity to follow the apostle Paul's counsel in Romans 14 on how to relate to one another concerning matters that are not clearly addressed in Scripture, issues that might be considered disputable matters. "Let us not pass judgment on one another," Paul wrote, "but rather decide never to put a stumbling block or hindrance in the way" of a brother or sister (Romans 14:13 ESV). His counsel provides guidance in how we can disagree with one another while manifesting hearts of love and respect for each other.

People who are seeking to be rooted in God's truth must learn to discern the difference between legalism and biblical truth. While discerning the difference between cultural preferences and biblical mandates, safe-place people will seek to create an atmosphere of love and respect for one another in which there can be an authentic dialogue concerning those issues. In the end, there may be a need to agree to disagree, all the while coming together to proclaim and demonstrate the gospel in order that souls might be saved, captives set free, and broken bodies and relationships be healed.

33

Speaking Truth from a Shared Position of Brokenness and Healing

People are not so much resistant to truth as they are to arrogance.

IN THIS POSTMODERN era, people want to be spoken *with*, not at or down to. Thus, safe-place people will make every effort to share truth with others from a shared position of brokenness and healing, not from one of arrogance or superiority. After hundreds of conversations with people over the years who are not yet Christians, and with followers of Christ who have been grievously wounded by the church, I have become convinced that people are not so much resistant to truth as they are to arrogance. They are resistant to being spoken at rather than with, and being spoken down to rather than alongside of.

There was an era when people appeared to more readily accept Christian authority figures quite literally speaking down to them from pulpits that could only be reached by climbing circular staircases. In the early 1990s I saw such a pulpit for the first time. I had traveled to Finland with my mentor Pastor Charles Miller and his wife Ann. At one point during the trip we were scheduled to be in Mikeli, a quaint, historic-looking town. Throughout the trip Charles had been doing the bulk of the teaching and preaching, so I still remember the thrill and the fear of being told I was going to preach in the 400-year-old St. Mikeli's Cathedral (an historic Lutheran cathedral) on St. Mikeli's (Saint Michael's) Day.

I clearly remember the beauty and majesty of the sanctuary and I particularly remember the pulpit because it was the first such pulpit I had ever seen. As was custom in Reformation years, it was elevated high above the floor of the sanctuary, accessible only by a narrow, circular staircase. I remember climbing that staircase and with each step I took, growing more fearful, and wondering, "who am I" to be speaking to these people—the first of whom were some seventy-five rows of pews toward the back. God was good, however, and he gave me just the right message to share with his people that day.

During the Reformation and for many years following, the congregation expected the pastor, who was often one of the most educated people in the community and the authority in all matters of Christian faith, to stand above them and speak down to them. This position was culturally acceptable then, but that is no longer the case. If people want someone to speak truth into their lives, they want a person who speaks from a position alongside them, not over them. By and large, people do not merely resist truth; they resist arrogance and superiority. John Burke writes, "The central watershed issue of postmodern thought divides over truth. Truth has gone relative!" In *No Perfect People Allowed*, he explains, "I find that most people do not have deeply thought-out convictions . . . about truths being relative; it's just an unchallenged given for most. So to talk about truth is not repulsive to them until you appear exclusive or arrogant."[108] Burke continues,

---

108   John Burke, *No Perfect People Allowed: Creating a Come-as-You-Are Culture in the Church* (Grand Rapids, MI: Zondervan, 2005), Kindle ed.

People just check out when they feel Christians are arrogant and unwilling to consider the "truth" claims of others as well. But they are very open to hearing expressions of truth and stories illustrating why God's words are true. They long to experience something firm and solid that "feels" true. They don't resist truth; they resist arrogance. . . . Generally, emerging generations do not ask, "What is true?" They are primarily asking, "Do I want to be like you?" In other words, they see truth as relational. "If I want to be like you, then I want to consider what you believe. If I don't see anything real or attractive in you or your friends as Christ-followers, I don't care how 'true' you think it is, I'm not interested."[109]

Any hint of arrogance on our part as Christians is not acceptable to a postmodern, post-Christian people. Such a position communicates a prideful, "holier-than-thou," condescending, condemning, and judging attitude. Rather, being people rooted in God's life-giving truth means speaking from the horizontal plane of our own brokenness and healing. We are not "righteous" people who are better than "sinners." Christians are people who have been wounded and broken by our own sin and the sin of others. We are people who continue to struggle with temptation and sin ourselves, while being people who praise and thank God that we have experienced his saving, freeing, and healing truth touching our sin and our brokenness. It is from that experience that we share with others who God is and who he has been for us.

Christians who are humble and in whom there is no hint of pretense are in great demand in a postmodern culture where respect for authority often flows more out of trust-based, authentic and genuinely caring relationships than from an authoritative position, office, or written source. Such Christians will be experienced as being a safe place.

---

109   Ibid.

34

RECOGNIZING THE TRUE ENEMY

*The enemy we all share wants to steal, kill, and destroy—he
wants to steal any passion for life we might have, kill any sense of
relationship between God and us, and destroy
our relationships with one another.*

BEING EXPERIENTIALLY ROOTED in God's truth requires recognizing who the true enemy is. In the years leading up to World War II, Adolph Hitler told the German people that Jews were the enemy. The Jews were not the enemy—Hitler was. It was a case of the true enemy telling the people someone else was the enemy. We cannot be a people rooted in God's truth if we think someone other than the true enemy is, in fact, the enemy.

Some Christians too often sound like they are saying the enemy is the person who is a Muslim, an abortionist, an atheist, or a homosexual. None of these people are the enemy. Each of them is someone made in the image of God and for whom Jesus gave his life. They are of great worth and to be treated with love and dignity, even while we may disagree—even strongly—with some of their beliefs or behaviors. But as persons, we are to see them and treat them as God would were he still Jesus incarnate on this earth today.

WE ALL SHARE ONE COMMON ENEMY: THE DEVIL

These people are not the enemy. We all share one common enemy—the devil. The true enemy is the devil who seeks to blind the minds of people to God's truth that would save them and set them truly free (see 2 Corinthians 4:4). In some ways every person is a victim in a war waged by the true enemy (see 1 Peter 5:18). We all have at least two things in common: a God who loves us and an enemy who hates God. Because the enemy hates God he hates all of humankind and wants to put us in harm's way. The enemy we all share wants to steal, kill, and destroy (see John 10:10). He wants to steal any passion for life we might have, kill any sense of relationship between God and us, and destroy our relationships with one another.

People who are seeking to be rooted in God's life-giving truth will acknowledge that people have value apart from their religion or lifestyle. It is not embracing the "right" religion or lifestyle that gives people value in God's eyes. God did not wait for us to adopt a specified religion or lifestyle before he chose to send Jesus to die for us. He sent Jesus while we all were still living sinful lifestyles (see Romans 5:8), and choosing to live lives our own way. This, by the way, is another thing the Bible says we all share in common— without the rebirth of a relationship with God, all humankind are like sheep who have gone astray and are doing what is right in our own eyes (see Isaiah 53:6).

While Christians may disagree with other people's choices regarding religion or lifestyles, we should be the first to defend them if they are being persecuted and made objects of senseless violence and prejudice. We should defend them because there is something of God's design in them and because we share a common enemy who is trying to put us all in harm's way through one deception or another. The enemy may tempt others to adhere to a religious system or a lifestyle we disagree with, even while he tempts us with a self-righteous, judgmental, and condemning spirit—not to mention temptations to sin a whole host of ways.

THEY ARE NOT MY ENEMY, THEY ARE GRACE GROWERS

There are times we may consider certain people who are difficult for us to be around to be our enemies. They frustrate us, challenge us, and accuse us. However, these people may actually be God's gift of grace growers in our lives. Jesus tells us in the gospels to love our enemy. People experientially rooted in God's truth will love even their enemies. How will we love our enemies? By refusing to see them as such. Being experientially rooted in God's life-giving truth requires that we recognize who the true enemy is.

Perhaps before moving on, it would be helpful for you to admit to yourself anyone you have been viewing or treating as an enemy, confess this God, telling him you want to repent (change your thinking) of this and receive his forgiveness. Then, ask the Lord to grow in you the willingness and ability to treat all people with the love and grace that God treats you with.

35

MINISTERING TO THE NEEDS
BEHIND THE BEHAVIOR

Too many Christians find their identity and sense of worth in being
right; and when we have an unhealthy need to be right we often act
in unrighteous ways. We can come across as spiritual salespersons
rather than spiritual friends.

CHRISTIANS WHO ARE experientially rooted in God's truth dare to speak to people's hunger and thirst, not just their sin. In doing so, they minister to the needs behind people's behavior. Jesus did this often. He initially looked beyond the sin and the behavior of people to the needs that lay behind and beneath. Jesus was so good at that. He still is. He does not just react to or deal with our behaviors. It's not that he ignores them or that they are unimportant. It is that he is able to discern what's going on behind or beneath them, and ministers to those needs, thereby setting people free to live differently and be truly transformed.

NOT ALWAYS THE FIRST ORDER OF CONVERSATION

Jesus did not always make a person's behavior or sin the first order of conversation with them. That was not his understanding of being the Truth. Pointing out someone's behavior or sin was not how he chose to begin conversations or relationships with people. Most often it seems he first took the time to truly care for them. Did Jesus believe in truth and sin? Of course he did! He was and is the truth. However, unlike some of us who still struggle with our own insecurities, identity, and sense of worth, Jesus did not have to prove his commitment to God by always being sure to make sin or the proclamation of some gospel truth the first topic of conversation with someone.

Too many Christians find their identity and sense of worth *in being right,* and when we have an unhealthy need to be right we often act in unrighteous ways. When we are insecure and worry about how we look to others we often feel driven to look right, act right, and talk right, thereby using other people to put notches on our spiritual belts. Or we can come across as spiritual salespersons rather than spiritual friends. This wasn't Jesus' way and it's not the way of people who want to be a safe place, not the way of a people who want to know what it really means to be rooted in God's truth.

JESUS' WAY

What was the way of Jesus? A great example is his encounter with the woman at the well in John, chapter 4. This woman was a sinner, but she was also a person who was precious in God's sight. She was so precious and worthy that Jesus literally went out of his way to encounter her at the well. He did not have to take this route to get to where he was going. He chose it intentionally just so he could meet her and speak to her. She had no idea when she woke up that morning that this would be the day she'd have a life-changing encounter with the Son of the living God. Of their encounter, John Eldredge writes,

> She has come alone in the heat of the day to draw water and they both
> know why. By coming when the sun is high, she is less likely to run

into anyone. She succeeds in avoiding the women, but runs into God instead. What does He choose to talk to her about—her immorality? No, He speaks to her about *her thirst*. "If you knew the generosity of God and who I am, you would be asking me for a drink, and I would give you fresh, living water" (John 4:10, The Message). Remarkable. He doesn't give a little sermon about purity. He doesn't even mention it, except to say that He knows what her life has been like. "You've had five husbands, and the man you're living with now isn't even your husband" (John 4:18, The Message). In other words, now that we both know it, let's talk about *your heart's real desire* since the life you've chosen obviously isn't working [emphasis mine].[110]

As we read the gospels we often find Jesus first asking people what they want, not whether they know the truth. In uncovering their heart's desires he points them to the truth. Another example of this is his encounter with the blind man beside the road to Jericho in Luke 18:34–42:

> As Jesus approached Jericho, a blind man was sitting by the roadside begging. He called out, "Jesus, Son of David, have mercy on me!" Those who led the way rebuked him and told him to be quiet, but he shouted all the more, "Son of David, have mercy on me!" Jesus stopped and ordered the man to be brought to him. When he came near, Jesus asked him, "What do you want me to do for you?" "Lord, I want to see," he replied. Jesus said to him, "Receive your sight."

It is a sad commentary that those who led the way rebuked the man. The leaders were more concerned about appearances and outward behavior than the need behind the man's behavior.

---

110 John Eldredge, *The Journey of Desire: Searching for the Life We've Only Dreamed Of* (Nashville, TN: Thomas Nelson Publishers, 2000), 36.

GETTING BEHIND THE
BEHAVIORS TO THE NEEDS

One of the most incredible qualities of Jesus Christ, a man full of both grace and truth, is that he was able to look behind people's sin and behaviors to the needs that were driving them. Jesus looked behind the blind man's acting-out behavior to his need of being healed, and his need for being born again. He looked behind the behavior of sexual immorality of the woman at the well to her need to satisfy her great thirst to be loved and cherished.

Jesus, being full of God's truth, did not water down the truth, nor did he water down the concept of sin. In fact, in the context of looking at needs behind behaviors Jesus built a relational context in which he spoke truth and set people free. The whole point of Jesus coming into the world was not to condemn the world but to save it. When we go right for the sin and the truth in someone's life, we often leave him or her feeling judged and condemned, not free. We may go away feeling good about ourselves, smug really. After all, we took a stand for the truth, didn't we? We were bold for God, weren't we? Perhaps. Or, perhaps all we really did was try to plug the holes of our own insecurity at someone else's expense.

Having the ability to look behind the behavior and the sin to the real needs of people can be a powerful dynamic in relationships. Following this example of Jesus can help us be a safe place, rather than unsafe people. David Kinnaman and Gabe Lyons share a woman's powerful story regarding this in their book *unChristian*:

I struggle with condemning. I have since I can remember.

When my husband and I were engaged, we planned our wedding in three months. One afternoon we were sorting out the next twenty tasks to complete. He hadn't called the bakery about the cake, and he still hadn't finished his guest list. With annoyance dripping out of every pore, I cut into him with all the shame and blame I could conjure up. How dare he drop the ball and ruin my afternoon. Now I would have to pick up after his incompetence!

After my verbal assault, he sat quietly with disbelief and pain in his eyes. I expected he would scold me for my tirade, but he didn't. All he said was, "Jonalyn, is that how you talk to yourself?" I was silent. I was stunned.

Then, slowly, I nodded and began to weep long and hard, realizing that this wasn't the good life, it wasn't the abundant life Jesus offered. But it was the only way I knew to be a model Christian woman planning a model wedding.

It was the first time someone took time to notice the person behind my judgmental words. He saw the state of my soul. He swallowed his own pain long enough to see that there was something self-destructive eating me. To get anything done right, to be holy, to stay pure, to walk the straight and narrow, I condemned myself into obedience [emphasis mine].[111]

When we are enabled by the Holy Spirit of God to lay down our right to defend and accuse another, and to consider what the needs behind their behavior might be, we can be someone through whom the Lord can release his healing presence to touch others' lives in their wounded places. A challenging insight for all Christians should be that the moments in Scripture where Jesus immediately begins to speak to people about sin are usually reserved for the religious, for the leaders.

Being experientially rooted in God's truth means daring to speak to people's hunger and thirst, not just to their sin. It means looking for and ministering to the needs behind their behaviors. People who do this will be a safe place, just like Jesus.

---

111   Kinnaman and Lyons, *unChristian*, 203–204.

36

REALIZING EVEN GRACE-FILLED TRUTH WILL STING

Wounds from a friend can be trusted.

— PROVERBS 27:6

BEING A PEOPLE experientially rooted in God's truth means realizing that even grace-filled truth will sting, and that though it stings for a while, it can bring healing, transformation, and freedom. What Proverbs 27:6 says is most certainly true: "Wounds from a friend can be trusted." However, even though those wounds come from a friend, and even though God uses them for great good, they still hurt.

I recall a time when that truth came to bear on my life. As the youth pastor of a large youth group with thirty or more volunteers serving on my staff each year, I always trained and encouraged those volunteers to come to me if and when they saw something in my life that gave them cause for concern. And I assured them I would do the same for them as a means for all of us to continue growing in emotional, relational, and spiritual wholeness. I have to admit, though, that I never actually expected any one of them to take me up on it.

Well, one year I brought my then ten-year-old son Andy along as the youth group was hiking in Spearfish Canyon in the Black Hills of South Dakota where we lived. It was a beautiful day and a beautiful setting for hiking. At one point, we stopped and sat down near Thunderhead Falls where I was going to teach a Bible study on how magnificent and powerful God is, with the power of the Falls crashing down behind us. As I was speaking, Andy was off to the side making some noise and drawing attention to himself, nothing really loud, but loud enough to attract attention. I tried a number of times to gently ask him to sit down and be quiet. He'd sit down for a few seconds but then jump back up and begin to draw attention to himself again. With each "gentle" encouragement to him I was becoming increasingly irritated. Irritated? Not really. I was getting angry. Then finally, I overreacted, yelled at him in anger to shut up and sit down, and embarrassed him in front of the teens and adults who were there.

A few days later, a friend of mine who was a member of the youth staff came to see me in my office. After some small talk he asked he could tell me something. I said of course, thinking that he had something hidden that was troubling him and he needed to get off his chest. I was surprised when he reminded me of the hike the previous weekend and wondered aloud if maybe I had overreacted to my son's behavior. Then he said, "Mike, as I've thought about this, I don't think Andy was only trying to misbehave or draw attention to himself. I think he was only trying to be witty and funny like his dad."

It was like an arrow had buried itself deep in my heart. As soon as my friend said it I knew it was true. Oh, how the truth hurt, oh, how it stung! I smiled and thanked my friend for sharing, but as he walked away I was angry and I was hurt. I tried for days to rationalize and justify it all away. But the truth of what my friend said just would not leave. His words were true and had been shared out of a heart of grace and love toward me. But they still hurt. They still stung.

The Lord was gracious and merciful to me in the following days, showing me how right my friend had been. A week later, in front of the youth group and my volunteer staff (since it was in front of them I had sinned against my son), I was able to confess my sin to my son and ask his forgiveness (which he graciously granted).

The truth my friend shared with me stung, but it also contributed to the healing of my relationship with my son whom I dearly cherished. It also helped me grow more in my relationship with the Lord and ended up being a good, living lesson to my youth staff and the teens of what we can do as Christians we "blow it."

There will be times when fellow Christians may not share truth as gently and lovingly as my friend did, but even when it comes "wrapped in garbage" in terms of how someone might share truth with us, may God give us the grace to sort through the garbage and see if there are any nuggets of truth that he has for us. Being a people seeking to be rooted in God's life-giving truth will mean realizing that though truth can sting for a while, it can also bring healing, transformation, maturation, and freedom.

37

WE ALL NEED GRACE-
BASED TRUTH TELLERS

*A single rebuke does more for a person of understanding than
a hundred lashes on the back of a fool.*

— PROVERBS 17:10, NLT

WE ALL NEED grace-based truth tellers, particularly if we want to be a people who are being experientially rooted in God's truth and growing in what it means to be a safe place. Grace-based truth tellers are just the kind of people you want in the band of brothers and sisters you are on mission together with. They are the ones who will lovingly help you examine your motives, and question your beliefs and behaviors when you need someone to. We all need someone to help us see our blind spots, and we all have them— blind spots, that is. This is what King David is asking God to be for him and do for him in Psalm 139:23–24 where we read, "Search me, O God, and know my heart! Try me and know my thoughts! And see if there be any grievous way in me, and lead me in the way everlasting!"

OUR CAPACITY FOR DENIAL

We all need grace-based truth tellers in our circle of friendships because our capacity as human beings to live in denial and with blind spots is astounding. I clearly recall my first encounter with people who loved me enough to risk being grace-based truth tellers for me. Stan Kellner was a short messianic Jew from Boston, Massachusetts. Billy Bob Fred Joe Chactaw Pitzer was a tall drink of water from West Virginia. They had become close friends in the Air Force while stationed at a base in Altus, Oklahoma, in the southwest corner of the state. They were Christians, and they had helped me enter into a relationship with Jesus as my Lord and Savior that absolutely set my life on a different trajectory, one for which I will be forever grateful.

Soon after becoming a Christian I began to play guitar at a local Christian coffee house in downtown Altus. I loved it. Bill played guitar there too, and Stan was always in attendance. It was fun and was always something I looked forward to. One day there was a knock on the door of my room in the dormitory on base. I opened it, and there were Stan and Billy Bob Fred Joe. "Come on in," I said. "Have a seat. What are you guys up to today?" "Well, Brad," one of them began; I don't remember if it was Stan or Bill. "We need to talk to you." "Okay, what about?" I asked. "Well, it's about the coffee house and playing on the worship team." "Yeah, what about it?" "Well, we think you need to step down and take a break."

I was stunned. I didn't know what to say or ask. Where the heck did that come from? What is this about? Finally, I asked, "What do you mean?" "Well, we can tell that you're playing guitar with us more for meeting girls than for worshipping the Lord, and we just think you need to take a break so you have some time to grow a little more in your faith." To this day I don't know why I did what I did, but I smiled and thanked them for being willing to risk sharing the truth with me face to face. "Thanks guys," I said as we all stood and they headed for the door. "We'll see you this Saturday night at the coffee house?" they asked. "You bet," I said, and then closed the door behind them.

As soon as they were gone the anger within me rose to the surface. Who the heck do they think they are? How can they tell whether I'm out to meet girls or worship the Lord? And even if I am, what's wrong with meeting girls? On and on I went, rationalizing and justifying to myself why they were all wrong and I was all right. But after a while I settled down, and I knew they were right. So I stepped off the team for a season.

After a few months I got another knock on the door. It was Stan and Billy Bob Fred Joe. They had smiles on their faces. They came in. They thanked me for being willing to step down the way I had and to focus on growing in my relationship with the Lord. They said they could see a difference in me. We think you're ready now, they told me, ready to rejoin the worship team if you'd like to. I did, and so began decades of leading worship in small groups and on worship teams, on retreats and in churches. But I had grown in my relationship with the Lord. He had helped me mature and had established more healthy motives in my heart for wanting to be a worship leader. Now, whenever I lead worship it is out of a deep desire to bring glory to him and help others connect with him in an atmosphere that is rich with a tangible sense of his presence.

Stan and Bill were truly a safe place for me that day. They were a safe place because they helped protect me from years of wasting my time living more out of my flesh than out of the Spirit of God within me. They were a safe place for me because they brought God's healing and maturing combination of grace and truth to bear on my life. Did it hurt? Yes! Did it sting? Yes! Did it embarrass me? Of course it did. And I would not go back and change it for anything in the world because it helped me experience the power of the Holy Spirit at work in my life. Because they were willing to risk me getting mad at them, I was transformed to think, speak, and act more like Jesus. What Stan and Bill did for me that day was a great gift, and they offered the gift as well as anyone can when they are offering you truth that may sting a bit. Thanks Stan and Bill, for being grace-based truth tellers in my life and helping to set me on the path I'm walking with Jesus on to this day.

TOO GREAT A RISK TO TAKE

Many of us have never invited someone else to be a truth teller in our lives. Often, it's because we're afraid of what we might find out. We don't want to face the truth. We can't handle the truth. What if the truth about me is too painful for me to bear? For others, it is a matter of sinful pride; we are too prideful to admit we have weaknesses and sin that are weighing us down and hindering us from living more fully into God's potential for our lives. Or, at other times it's because we have had graceless truth tellers wound us; people who have spoken truth to us but in legalistic and graceless ways.

However, to not have truth tellers in our lives is too great a risk to take. Dietrich Bonheoffer's words in this regard are a powerful reminder of this necessity:

> One who because of sensitivity and vanity rejects the serious words of another Christian cannot speak the truth in humility to others. Such a person is afraid of being rejected and feeling hurt by another's words. Sensitive, irritable people will always become flatterers, and very soon they will come to despise and slander other Christians in their community. . . . When another Christian falls into obvious sin, an admonition is imperative, because God's Word demands it. The practice of discipline in the community of faith *begins with friends* who are close to one another. Words of admonition and reproach *must be risked* [emphasis mine].[112]

To risk not speaking words of truth, saturated with grace and love, to one another is to risk wasting years in bondage to things we would want to be free from and would greatly benefit being free from. We all need others who will *help us live up to our best intentions and deepest values*. We have only to look at the example of Nathan in the life of David to see the value of having a truth teller in our lives. In the two of them we have a wonderful example of how both the presence of a truth teller and a willingness to humbly receive truth

---

112   Dietrich Bonheoffer, in John Ortberg, *Everybody's Normal Till You Get to Know Them* (Grand Rapids, MI: Zondervan, 2003), 172 (ellipses in the original).

can advance God's purposes in us. The presence of grace-based truth tellers will enable us to be people through whom God can carry out his purposes in the world.

> And the Lord sent Nathan to David. He came to him and said to him, "There were two men in a certain city, the one rich and the other poor. The rich man had very many flocks and herds, but the poor man had nothing but one little ewe lamb, which he had bought. And he brought it up, and it grew up with him and with his children. It used to eat of his morsel and drink from his cup and lie in his arms, and it was like a daughter to him. Now there came a traveler to the rich man, and he was unwilling to take one of his own flock or herd to prepare for the guest who had come to him, but he took the poor man's lamb and prepared it for the man who had come to him." Then David's anger was greatly kindled against the man, and he said to Nathan, "As the Lord lives, the man who has done this deserves to die, and he shall restore the lamb fourfold, because he did this thing, and because he had no pity." Nathan said to David, "You are the man! Thus says the Lord, the God of Israel, 'I anointed you king over Israel, and I delivered you out of the hand of Saul. And I gave you your master's house and your master's wives into your arms and gave you the house of Israel and of Judah. And if this were too little, I would add to you as much more. Why have you despised the word of the Lord, to do what is evil in his sight? You have struck down Uriah the Hittite with the sword and have taken his wife to be your wife and have killed him with the sword of the Ammonites. Now therefore the sword shall never depart from your house, because you have despised me and have taken the wife of Uriah the Hittite to be your wife.' Thus says the Lord, 'Behold, I will raise up evil against you out of your own house. And I will take your wives before your eyes and give them to your neighbor, and he shall lie with your wives in the sight of this sun. For you did it secretly, but I will do this thing before

all Israel and before the sun.'" David said to Nathan, "I have sinned against the Lord" (2 Samuel 12:1–13).

God gives us truth tellers that we might live up to our best intentions and values. David was blessed in having someone like Nathan who exercised courage in speaking into his life, particularly when it came to an issue of sin.

SPEAKING TO ISSUES OF SIN

We have the same need David had if we are to walk free of sin and live out our best intentions. Listen to the truth declared in the following Scriptures: "Let us strip off every weight that slows us down, especially the sin that so easily hinders our progress" (Hebrews 12:1, NLT). "Dear brothers and sisters, if another Christian is overcome by some sin, you who are godly should gently and humbly help that person back onto the right path. And be careful not to fall into the same temptation yourself" (Galatians 6:1, NLT).

Sin puts us in harm's way. Sin slows us down and hinders our progress! If this is what sin does to us, why would we want to hang onto it, continue to practice it, and run to it to self-medicate when we are stressed? Wouldn't we be better served by having a safe-place brother or sister who is able to gently and humbly, and when necessary, firmly, help us get back on the right path?

Having such grace-based truth tellers in our lives can be a great gift. What would be some characteristics you would want in a truth teller if God gave you one in your life? Write them down in the space below:

Before you read on, why not stop for a moment, pray, and ask God to send grace-based truth tellers into your life. Ask him to send someone whenever he sees that this would be a grace-gift for you. And then ask the Lord to do whatever he needs to do in you, so he can use you as a truth teller in the life of someone else in need.

Toward that end, what are things about you that God would need to change, heal, and mature to make you a grace-based truth teller for others?

Who are the truth tellers you need to go back to and apologize to for not receiving what they had to offer you at some point in your life? Dare to let God continue to do his transforming work in your life this year so that you might be a grace-based truth teller and a truth-telling receiver who can be used for God's purposes in the world today. Do this, and you will be on a trajectory toward growing in what it means to be a safe place for others.

38

STOPPING BAD REPORTS

The fear that a bad report spreads is like red meat to the enemy.

STOP THE BAD reports. I first heard that phrase as the title of a sermon preached by Pastor Fred Thoni at Wonderful Mercy Church in Gilbert, Arizona. As soon as I heard it I knew it articulated God's heart, and the cry and commitment of a safe-place people. Christians who are growing in what it means to be safe do not want to spread reports that undermine the implementation of God-given mission, vision, and values, and sow division between churches, and between brothers and sisters in Christ.

Pastor Thoni, a member of the Alliance of Renewal Churches network, based his sermon on the story of the twelve spies in Numbers 13. This Scripture passage tells us of a negative report being spread among the Israelites that sowed doubt about God's plan for them to go in and take possession of the Promised Land. The story reveals the effect that such a report, rooted in fear and a lack of trust in God, can have on us individually or corporately. In this chapter I will broaden this concept beyond the implementation of God's vision, mission, and values, and will apply it to our words about one another, as Christian individuals or churches, that sow division in our relationships with each other and damage our witness in the world.

THE IMPACT OF SPREADING A BAD REPORT

In Numbers 13:1–2 we read, "The Lord now said to Moses, 'Send out men to explore the land of Canaan, the land I am giving to the Israelites. Send one leader from each of the twelve ancestral tribes.'" Moses picks twelve men and sends them out. It's important to pause before reading on and note that God does tell Moses that he was going to give this land to the Israelites. It was a done deal. It was the Lord's will. Israel was getting the land, period, end of discussion.

You would think this word from the Lord would fill the hearts of the spies with great confidence and faith. The faithful, all-powerful God who keeps his promises tells them ahead of time what he is going to do. The end result was settled. All these spies were assigned to do was go in, check things out, and come back with a report. No matter what the opposition looked like, they would not be able to stop Israel because almighty God had already said he was going to give Israel the land.

However, confidence and faith were not the responses for ten of the twelve spies. When they returned the ten were full of doubt and fear. Evidently they forgot what God said to Moses, and thus spread a bad report. We read on in Numbers 13:25–33:

> After exploring the land for forty days, the men returned to Moses, Aaron, and the whole community of Israel at Kadesh in the wilderness of Paran. They reported to the whole community what they had seen and showed them the fruit they had taken from the land. This was their report to Moses: "We entered the land you sent us to explore, and it is indeed a bountiful country—a land flowing with milk and honey. Here is the kind of fruit it produces. But the people living there are powerful, and their towns are large and fortified. We even saw giants there, the descendants of Anak! The Amalekites live in

the Negev, and the Hittites, Jebusites, and Amorites live in the hill country. The Canaanites live along the coast of the Mediterranean Sea and along the Jordan Valley."

But Caleb tried to quiet the people as they stood before Moses. "Let's go at once to take the land," he said. "We can certainly conquer it!" But the other men who had explored the land with him disagreed. "We can't go up against them! They are stronger than we are!" So they spread this bad report about the land among the Israelites: "The land we traveled through and explored will devour anyone who goes to live there. All the people we saw were huge. We even saw giants there, the descendants of Anak. Next to them we felt like grasshoppers, and that's what they thought, too!"

What the spies encountered in the land was eye opening and heart stopping. The inhabitants were National Football League-defensive tackle big! This was the reality staring the twelve spies right in the face. There was no denying it or ignoring it. But then God never does call us to deny or ignore the situation we face, does he? To be full of faith never means denying or ignoring reality. Rather, it means understanding and believing that there is another reality greater than the one we are faced with, a reality that our great God can bring to pass.

The combination of forgetting both the word God had given Moses and that the Lord is able to create a superior reality caused ten of the spies to return spreading a bad report that threatened to undermine the mission and turn the people against their leaders. The spreading of such information can undermine and overwhelm. It can undermine God's word to his people and overwhelm them with fear. We see this happening to Israel in Numbers 14:1–4:

Then the whole community began weeping aloud, and they cried all night. Their voices rose in a great chorus of protest against Moses and Aaron. "If only we had died in Egypt, or even here in the wilderness!"

they complained. "Why is the Lord taking us to this country only to have us die in battle? Our wives and our little ones will be carried off as plunder! Wouldn't it be better for us to return to Egypt?" Then they plotted among themselves, "Let's choose a new leader and go back to Egypt!"

The bad report overwhelms the Israelites with fear. The people can't see any way God would want them to actually carry out the assigned mission and they begin to call for new leadership. This is what a report like that can do—it undermines mission and confidence in God-given leadership, and begins to sow seeds of divisiveness that turn the people against leaders, one another, and even God himself. The spreading of a bad report is most often done by a few, but does not affect just a few, it affects an entire community of faith. It is critical that we understand that a bad report spread by a vocal minority can impact an entire community and disrupt God's purposes for them and through them. Bad reports undermine and overwhelm and in the end, God's people end up settling for less than all he had in store for them.

WE DO IT TOO!

We shouldn't just pick on Israel though. We do the same thing. We spread bad reports about the mission God has given us, the tools we're using to carry it out, the leaders he's given us, and even speak badly about one another as individuals and churches. We do the same thing those ten spies did. We forget what God has said to us and we forget there can be a superior reality to the one we may be faced with. Like Israel we easily forget the word of the Lord to us regarding the mission he has called us to carry out, and we forget promises he has made to us in connection with it. When we forget, we too can be filled with fear, and our fear makes us easy targets for the enemy who is looking for every opportunity to steal, kill, and destroy any good thing God has for us. And the enemy is *always* looking for opportunities to sow seeds of division and tear apart the relationships of one Christian with another, one church with its leaders, and one church with another.

Fear distracts us from the mission. All we can see are the obstacles. All we can think of is why we shouldn't go for it. We begin to doubt, then we start to panic. We lose sight of the God for whom nothing is impossible and the word he has given us to rely on. We begin to question and doubt the direction that once seemed so clear. Our discernment becomes skewed and we're more easily confused and deceived. We begin to spread bad reports, undermine leadership, and even start accusing one another of half-truths and outright lies. Out of fear and a lack of feeling in control we sow seeds of division in our relationships with brothers and sisters in Christ and between one church and another. When that happens, it is like opening the door wide, inviting the enemy in, and providing him with just the opportunity he wants—to deceive us, and to steal, kill, and destroy what God has in store for us. The fear that a bad report spreads is like red meat to the enemy.

When we follow the example of the ten spies in Numbers, the mission God has called us to carry out is thwarted, relationships are torn apart, and we go back to living life as we had before—choosing to settle for simply maintaining the status quo. Spreading bad reports causes stagnation and ceases the advance of the people and purposes of God.

RATIONALIZING, JUSTIFYING, AND SPIRITUALIZING BAD REPORTS

When Christians spread bad reports we often rationalize and justify them with the language of concern and even with spiritual-sounding language. We question the mission that once seemed clear and was the reason we chose the leadership we did in the first place. We call a person to be our senior pastor, youth pastor, or worship leader and then suddenly pull the rug out from under them. A small but vocal minority begins to complain or withhold money from the church budget as a means of protest, but it's all done in the name of "concern." We're concerned about the very vision, mission, and values that we initially supported and even reaffirmed along the way—perhaps multiple times.

As we implement what God has called us to, something happens along the way. As we identify and begin to use the tools it takes to accomplish the task the Lord has placed before us, something changes. We begin to sense the enormity of what we've been called to. The reality of the change that's required not only in the church but also in each of us as individuals begins to be experienced. Perhaps for the first time we see the cost we will have to count, the sacrifices we will have to make, the changes we will need to embrace. We're unsettled, unsure, and we forget the word of promise the Lord spoke when we set out together. We begin to drown in fear and start grasping for anything that will help us feel safe and secure, anything, that is, but trusting in the Lord and in the leadership he has given us. We forget that being a safe-place people does not mean playing it safe.

We feel like grasshoppers at the feet of giants. Something has to be done. So we go to others and begin spreading a bad report. We may even rationalize or justify the bad report with spiritual-sounding language. Some have even gone so far as to accuse brothers and sisters in Christ, or Christian ministries and tools, as being demonized. I know. It happened to me, at a church where I once served as a member of the leadership team. In the midst of a congregational trajectory that had witnessed so much God-stuff happening that no one of us could have taken credit for it even if we had wanted to, a need for a mid-course correction became clear. Some minor but important change needed to be implemented. A small but vocal minority was unsettled and along with others I was targeted as a reason for that unsettledness. A meeting was called and I was told I had a demon and needed to repent. No demon was to be found. I'm sure I needed to repent of something but it wasn't that. The purposes of God for that church were thwarted, and to this day have not been recovered. Oh, God has certainly used all things together for good in my life and in the lives of many who were part of that amazing adventure. That's what he does, right? But I do wonder sometimes, what might have been if we, yes we, including me, had not been overwhelmed with fear and allowed the call of God on our lives as a people to be undermined.

Do we as leaders need to be willing to humble ourselves and wrestle with the counsel and questions regarding our leadership style, how we're managing the change process, or other factors that may be involved? Yes and amen. The moment we refuse to be teachable and humble we are in the danger zone.

Yet we are in just as much danger when we as the people of God allow our-selves to be deceived into thinking it is okay, even right, to spread bad reports about our leadership and one another. Stop the bad reports!

SPREADING BAD REPORTS SOWS DIVISIVENESS IN RELATIONSHIPS AND GRIEVES GOD'S HEART

Spreading bad reports also sows seeds of divisiveness in relationships between God's people. We turn on each other. We slander each other. We speak half-truths that are our version of the truth as viewed through the filters of our fear, pain, and at times, impure motives. And all the while we think we are believing and spreading the truth.

When we are overwhelmed with the fear that a bad report spreads it becomes far too easy to think the worst of one another rather than the best. It becomes far too easy to sit back and assume what others are thinking, and discern what their motives are, rather than simply going to them and asking them to interpret their thoughts, motives, and words for us so that we might get the truth straight from them.

I never cease to be amazed at how easily God's people fall into thinking the worst of one another. Is it our insecurities? Is it our jealousy of others? Is it our need to be in control and in charge? Is it our fear of change? Whatever it is, it is most certainly this—it is sad and it breaks and grieves our Heavenly Father's heart. I know that as a human father my heart breaks when my chil-dren are angry with one another and are speaking ill of or to one another. I cannot imagine how my Heavenly Father must feel when we behave like that toward one another.

It is not God's will that we spread bad reports about each other and that we settle for thinking the worst of one another or allowing our relationships to be broken and divided. When our relationships are strained or even bro-ken, it is God's will, as far as it is up to us, that we seek to reconcile with one another, not simply settle for letting the brokenness to fester and become poi-sonous to our lives and our witness. "If possible, so far as it depends on you, live peaceably with all" (Romans 12:18, ESV). "So if you are offering your gift at the altar and there remember that your brother has something against you, leave your gift there before the altar and go. First be reconciled to your brother, and then come and offer your gift" (Matthew 5:23–24, ESV).

CAN WE TALK? CAN WE CALL FOR HELP?

Is there a place for honest disagreement and the sharing of differing opinions between brothers and sisters in Christ, and in particular between leaders and the people they have been called to serve? Yes, there is. However, the tenor of those disagreements is always to be one of respect and honor. It is not God's will that we speak ill of one another, that we secretly plot to overthrow leaders, or as leaders, to force our own agenda on people rather than embrace God's agenda for them. It grieves God's heart when we treat each other in such ugly and shameful ways. But then, that is what spreading a bad report will do to us. It will cause us to treat one another in ways that even many non-Christians will not treat those they disagree with, and will give them one more reason for not wanting to hear what we have to say, let alone actually consider becoming Christians.

When our relationships with one another are being stressed and torn apart, can't we call for help? Can't we call for other brothers and sisters to sit down with us and help us communicate in more helpful ways? Can't we seek out counseling if we need to? If it's a church issue, can't we call network or denominational leaders for help before its too late? I'm tired of seeing vibrant ministries, churches, and relationships being torn apart and now existing as just shells of their former selves. Let's talk. And if we can't talk, let's call for help from others who may be able to help us talk and not miss one another in the process.

Any individual or congregation that wants to grow in what it means to be a safe place must have a desire and be committed to stopping the spread of bad reports. And toward that end we must humbly realize that without the convicting and transforming work of God in our lives, we all can far too easily fall back into patterns of thinking the worst of others and spreading slanderous lies about each other. Lord, have mercy.

Part Four

Creating an Atmosphere of
Freedom for Authentic Living

39

AN ATMOSPHERE OF FREEDOM
FOR AUTHENTIC LIVING

*Safe Place-Safe People community is a place and people where all
that is true—both the ugly and beautiful—can be faced.*

— LARRY CRABB

ONE OF THE most essential characteristics for any Christian individual,
small group, or congregation that wants to grow in being a safe place
is developing an atmosphere of freedom for authentic living. There is a great
hunger for authenticity in American culture, as reflected in the following
quote:

> We live in a culture that is starving for authenticity. We want our
> leaders, our co-workers, our family members, our friends, and ev-
> eryone else we interact with to tell us the truth and to be them-
> selves. Most important, we want to have the personal freedom and

confidence to say, do, and be who we really are, without worrying so much about how we appear to others and what they will think or say about us.[113]

The existence of this yearning for authenticity should come as no surprise, considering how much inauthentic living we have witnessed in the public arena over the past few decades. During this time we have seen:

- Government leaders, once trusted, now deceiving and misleading the public concerning the war in Vietnam, the Iran-Contra affair, as well as the yet-to-be discovered weapons of mass destruction in Iraq—and these are only to name a few
- Political leaders orchestrating break-ins and other illegal activities such as what we now know as Watergate
- Catholic and Protestant leaders publically succumbing to temptations—often the very ones they preached against so loudly from their public pulpits
- Politicians, movie stars, religious leaders, sports figures, and other figures of authority proclaiming their innocence of various accusations only to be found guilty in the end

So much inauthentic living has been manifested in the lives of public figures in our country that many of us have been left with understandably jaded, skeptical, and cynical attitudes. Isn't there at least one person we can trust to be authentically who they say they are?

We are so hungry for authenticity we don't even seem to care if a person is authentically good or authentically bad, just that they are authentic. We see this reflected in the large number of loyal followers of movies or television shows such as *Breaking Bad*. The lead character in *Breaking Bad* is a good man gone bad—albeit for reasons that are understandable. He produces and sells meth. Over time he morphs from being the good guy caught up in the

---

113   Mike Robbins, *Be Yourself, Everyone Else Is Already Taken: Transforming Your Life with the Power of Authenticity* (San Francisco, CA: Jossey-Bass, 2009), Kindle ed.

web of bad circumstances to becoming a bad guy seeking to build an empire. Through it all, however, he is authentically who he is. He does not try to pretend and this authenticity has created a huge following among viewers. We so hunger for authenticity that finding someone who is genuinely who they say they are, and gives you the freedom to authentically be who you are, is like a drink of cool, refreshing water after wandering a long time in a never-ending desert.

A GREAT NEED FOR AUTHENTICITY

Not only is there a hunger and attraction toward authenticity, there is a great need for it. The need is great because without freedom to live authentically there is no hope for authentic heart transformation. And without this kind of transformation, human beings will continue to choose ways of living that are harmful to themselves and others. Without authentic heart transformation we will continue living self-centered, self-serving, and self-promoting lives.

This reality is illustrated in the book of Judges, and is a pattern we have seen repeated time and again throughout history. The people of God choose to worship false gods and as a result engage in behaviors harmful to themselves and those around them. When they can no longer stand the consequences of their own choices they call out to God to rescue them. In his grace and mercy, God sends a leader who calls them back to the ways of the Lord. Whenever they respond in repentance, they once again experience the blessings of living life the way God designed it to be lived. However, when the leader dies, the people return to their old ways. Once again they choose to worship false gods, engage in harmful behavior, and as a result, experience painful consequences. Though they had changed their ways for a moment, there was no lasting heart transformation. This cycle continues to repeat itself to this day.

However, before we too quickly criticize the Israelites, let's be honest with ourselves. Don't we repeat this pattern in our own lives and within the lives of Christian churches today? For instance, how many times have we seen the following pattern in the life of a church? The congregation calls a new lead pastor and/or staff, and for a season the church begins to experience a healthy transformation. People are changed. They are rescued from self-centered, sin-filled ways of living. Spiritual eyes and hearts are opened. A passion for relationship with God is ignited. Joy, peace, and hope break in on lives mired in hopelessness and depression. People begin to grow in the fruit of the Spirit. They discover and become empowered to live out God's purposes for their lives. The transformation is not easy, immediate, or without challenges, but things are changing for good nonetheless. The church is experiencing a season of purpose and fruitfulness that has everyone excited.

Then, the lead pastor and perhaps some key staff members or congregational members, leave the church for one reason or another. A new lead pastor is chosen. Key staff members are replaced. New members join the church. But they don't share the same values their predecessors had, nor perhaps are they strong leaders, creating a leadership void. In this void, the people of God quickly return to old, self-centered ways of living that divide and do harm to relationships. All because too much of what had appeared to be transformation was actually based on the strong leadership they had, rather than upon authentic heart transformation. People begin parting ways with the church for a variety of reasons, leaving it just a shell of what it once had been. Enough people are left to keep the doors open and ensure the rituals continue to be practiced, but the ministry of rescuing and transforming lives is now nowhere to be found.

This repetitive cycle in the book of Judges and in our own lives illustrates the great need for authentic, lasting transformation of human hearts. When there is no genuine transformation of the heart we will always return to old patterns of harmful behavior. However, for authentic transformation of the heart to take place there must be an atmosphere of freedom for authentic living, an atmosphere in which we are given the courage to admit and face who we truly are without fear of being shamed or discarded. If we do not have this freedom we will hide who we are from others and even from ourselves. And as long as we hide, rationalize, or justify who we are, we will never experience the genuine transformation of heart required to live lives of true freedom and health.

THE DOORWAY OF AUTHENTICITY

Because the hunger and attraction for authenticity is so great in our culture, it can often be the doorway into relationship, genuine dialogue, and spiritual conversation with non-believers and fellow Christians. Where Christians seek to create an atmosphere of freedom for authentic living, they increase their potential for being experienced as a safe place by others, which in turn will increase their effectiveness in developing healthy leaders and disciples in the church, and living lives of witness in the world.

Unfortunately, the Christian Church is viewed by an increasing number of people as being inauthentic, and thus as unsafe rather than safe. Does any of the following sound familiar? "Christians just seem phony and hypocritical to me." "I wish they'd just be real. I know for a fact they struggle with the same emotions and issues the rest of us struggle with. They just don't seem to have the guts or freedom to admit it." "I can't be myself when I'm around Christians. They make me feel like I have to measure up to their standards for behavior before they're willing to accept me and enjoy my company." "There's no room to talk, really talk, with the Christians I've met. They talk at you, not with you." "Do they even know how to be real, just relax, and have fun?" Fair or not, Christians are viewed by many as being phony, hypocritical, and unable to be real, to just relax and have fun, in a word—inauthentic.

This is why Christians who are intentional in creating an atmosphere of freedom for authentic living will be better equipped for more effective witness and discipleship. And it is why creating this kind of culture is an essential characteristic in being a safe place. Before moving on, stop and ask yourself: What does an authentic person look like? How do I identify and see authenticity in a person's life? Record your answers in the space below:

Once you have done this, take time to pray and ask yourself, "Which of these marks of authenticity would I like God to help me grow in?" Then, begin to pray something like the following: "Lord, do whatever you need to do in me so I can be transformed and grow in being _____ (fill in the blank with your answer[s] to the questions above)." Then watch and listen as God begins to answer your prayer. Be attentive to what you hear and don't be surprised if he begins to connect you in relationships with others who can help you grow in that aspect of authenticity. You may be connected with God and his transforming power through a new friendship, the rebirth of an old one, or, through one of the schools of healing prayer.

Over the years I have discovered the reality of authenticity is best experienced in the context of relationships. Therefore, in the next section, let's take time to remind ourselves of the priority God places on relationships in our lives as his disciples.

40

RELATIONSHIP IS THE TASK

*Leave your gift there before the altar and go. First be reconciled to
your brother, and then come and offer your gift.*

— MATTHEW 5:24

AUTHENTICITY IS BETTER caught than taught, and it is caught best in relationships with authentic people. So much of what we learn in life is
learned in the context of our relationships with others. It should come as no
surprise then that God places a priority on the state of our relationships as
followers of Christ.

RELATIONSHIP IS THE TASK

God places a high priority on the condition of our relationships because the
message, and the mission, he has given us is for the reconciliation of relationships. The apostle Paul describes this mission in 2 Corinthians 5:17–21:

This means that anyone who belongs to Christ has become a new person. The old life is gone; a new life has begun! And all of this is a gift from God, who brought us back to himself through Christ. And *God has given us this task of reconciling people to him.* For God was in Christ, reconciling the world to himself, no longer counting people's sins against them. And he gave us this wonderful message of reconciliation. So we are Christ's ambassadors; God is making his appeal through us. We speak for Christ when we plead, "Come back to God!" For God made Christ, who never sinned, to be the offering for our sin, so that we could be made right with God through Christ [emphasis mine].

In this passage we see that relationship and task are organically connected for followers of Christ. One cannot be a Christian and focus on only one or the other. A disciple of Jesus cannot say that I am all about relationships while ignoring the task God has given us of going into all the world to make disciples (see Matthew 28:18–20). Nor can a Christian say that their focus is on the task at hand while ignoring the state of relationships in their life (see Matthew 22:37–40). Christians have been given both a Great Commission and a Great Commandment. Therefore, Christians who are growing in what it means to be a safe-place people understand that for them, relationship is the task.

"Your network of churches doesn't *do* anything," a Christian leader once told me. We were talking about the Alliance of Renewal Churches. "All you do is relationships and I don't have time for that; there's too much to be done." I have great respect for this leader and he is a friend. While I agreed with him that there is much to be done in respect to serving both the Lord and the world in which we live, I respectfully disagreed that paying attention to our relationships is doing nothing.

First of all, this leader was simply unaware of the many tasks of mission, discipleship, and leadership development our network is engaged in. It's just that all he saw—while he was busy being task-oriented—was the priority and emphasis we place on developing relationships that are emotionally, relationally, and spiritually whole. Our leaders and congregations are carrying out numerous tasks; it's just that he wasn't in close enough relationship with us to see that. However, his perception that we place a high priority on investing in the development of healthy relationships was certainly true, and this priority was nothing we were going to apologize for, because in the ARC we believe there is an organic connection between effectiveness in carrying out our missional tasks in a postmodern culture and relationships that are authentic and safe.

For Christians who are growing in what it means to be a safe place, there is no disconnect between paying attention to the state of our relationships and the tasks we are given by God. A safe-place people understand relationships to be the context in which those tasks are best carried out. And they understand that the state of those relationships can have either a positive or negative impact on how effectively those tasks are carried out.

Thus, for the safe-place Christian, relationship is the task. It is essential because it is the nature of our relationships with one another, as well as with those who are not yet Christians, that will prove to the world we are followers of Jesus Christ. Jesus himself underscored this priority when he said, "So now I am giving you a new commandment: Love each other. Just as I have loved you, you should love each other. Your love for one another will prove to the world that you are my disciples" (John 13:34–35).

Safe-place Christians understand their relationships speak loudly and accomplish much. They understand that it is how we live in relationship with one another that will say important things to others about who God is and about his impact in our lives. If we cannot learn to live in right relationship with each other, we do not have much of anything important to say or do in a culture that is to a great degree relationally distant, distrustful, and broken. For followers of Christ, relationship is the task.

RELATIONSHIPS ARE REVELATORY MIRRORS

God places a high priority on our relationships for numerous reasons. One is that it is through them that he can transform us to be more like Jesus. Proverbs

27:17 reminds us, "As iron sharpens iron, a friend sharpens a friend." It is in relationship with others that God rubs off our rough edges and uses us to help rub off the rough edges in others. Relationships can serve as a revelatory mirror in which God shows us what we really look like and how we need to be changed. And through relationships God often imparts just what we need to be truly transformed—grace and truth, love and forgiveness, and power to heal and set free.

My relationships with my wife and children have been important revelatory mirrors in my life. It is here that God has shown me where I need his work of transformation and maturation. For example, I still remember a particular day when my two oldest sons Andy and Joe were about four and three years old respectfully. I was downstairs in our family room watching the annual Nebraska vs. Oklahoma football game back when the game really counted for something on the national scene. Having grown up in Nebraska, I was a die-hard Cornhusker fan and hated Oklahoma. If there ever was a game on the annual schedule I just had to watch, this was it. I had clearly told the boys that daddy did not want to be disturbed during the game. Then I went downstairs, closed the door to the family room and settled in to watch what I hoped would be an overwhelming Nebraska victory, without being interrupted.

Sure enough, right at a particularly frustrating moment during the game (which Nebraska went on to lose) the boys burst into the family room with Andy screaming bloody murder. Joey was close on his heals, mouth wide open, trying to bite him. I lost it and yelled at them to get out of the room. "Don't you know any better than to bother me like this?" I yelled in anger at my three- and four-year-old boys. The truth of course was that, no they didn't know any better. They were only three and four.

However, even at that young age, they were God's gift to me for my own transformation and maturation. Andy and Joe were his revelatory mirrors for me because as they hung their heads and walked out of the room with tears in their eyes, God showed me what I looked like, and I hated what I saw. The man I saw was ugly and disgusting to me. How could I have done that over a stupid football game? My relationship with my boys meant the world to me.

Being a dad has always been one of my favorite things, and it still is to this day. In that moment, in the revelatory mirrors of God that my sons were for me, I saw ways I knew God longed to transform me so that I could think, speak, and act more like Jesus. That day compelled me to find the help I needed to deal with my ability to tell myself the truth, to be set free from an unhealthy self-centeredness, and to bring God's maturation to bear upon my emotional life.

But it's not only the bad stuff we see in the revelatory mirror of relationships. I just as distinctly remember holding each of my five children when they were young, holding them until they would fall asleep. As I held them I could not believe how much I loved them. It's a love that is hard to explain, one best experienced. It was in those moments that my Father in Heaven showed me how much he loves me. God places a high priority on relationships because they can be his revelatory mirrors.

A RELATIONAL ELEMENT TO COURAGE

Another reason God places such a high priority on relationships is because they can be a source of courage. In the Alliance of Renewal Churches we believe there is a relational element to courage. Relationships that are authentic and safe can provide us the courage to acknowledge and deal with issues in our lives that we might not otherwise be willing to address. The support and encouragement we receive in the context of such relationships can actually give us the courage to be intentional about cooperating with the transforming work and power of God in our lives. Without those relationships we might be content to simply go on living as we presently are, and in doing so, settle for less than all God has purposed for us. We need the relational element of courage we receive from one another if we are going to become more like Christ, rather than simply settling for knowing more information about him. But this relational element of courage will not be experienced or received unless we are intentional in developing and nurturing relationships that are authentic and safe.

God's Power Is at Work in Relationships That Are Authentic and Safe

God's power is at work accomplishing much in the context of relationships that are authentic and safe. We can experience God's healing in places where we are broken simply by being in relationship with safe-place Christians. We can receive forgiveness of sin and freedom from toxic shame by being in relationship with others who know who we truly are, yet refuse to judge, shame, or discard us. We can experience the correction and renewal of incomplete or incorrect images of what it means to be a father that we've projected onto our Heavenly Father in the context of these kinds of relationships. And we can receive the Lord's freedom from insecurity or self-doubt simply by having others who believe in us before we even believe in ourselves. God can do all this and more through his power at work in relationships that are authentic and safe.

Relationships Are the Enemy's Target

Because God can accomplish so much in our lives through our relationships with one another, it should not surprise us that this is exactly the place the enemy will attack. Our relationships with one another in our homes and our churches are the devil's number one target. As followers of Christ we must always remember we have an enemy who is real and wants to steal, kill, and destroy (see John 10:10). We have a very real enemy who intentionally schemes against us and wants to put us in harm's way. And the target of his scheming and attack is most often our relationships. So it is important to remember what author Guy Chevreau writes,

> The enemy is ever drawing us to find fault with one another. It is the essence of the distorted promise he made to Eve: "you will be like God himself, knowing both good and evil." This deception is the telling of two half-truths. One is an understatement, the other an exaggeration. Firstly, the serpent lied, for we are not like God;

we are made "in His image." Secondly, while we know both good and evil, it is an imperfect knowledge, something considerably short of God's full understanding. This partial knowledge is the source of the fault-finding and judgmentalism that tears at our relationships. Interestingly, the Greek word *daimon*—"demon"—means, "to disrupt, to rend and tear."

The enemy attacks our minds and seeks to rend our relationships through faultfinding, often with and by those closest and dearest to us.[114]

Chevreau concludes, "In all manners of ways, the enemy seeks to estrange us from one another, perpetually attempting to sow discord and division."[115]

Our enemy *will* seek to disrupt, rend, and tear our relationships with one another. We all know this. Yet, it is amazing to me how often our enemy is able to do this very thing. What's more, the seeds of division that he sows between us are the same seeds he's been using since the beginning. Even for the enemy there is nothing new under the sun. He still sows seeds of jealousy, suspicion, discouragement, and a spirit of complaint to pit us one against another, one church against another church, one denomination or network against another. Over all my years of ministry, one of the things that saddens me most is when the enemy is able to destroy the relationships between Christian brothers and sisters, doing harm to them, and to their witness to the world.

RELATIONSHIP MUST BE THE TASK

For all these reasons and more, relationship must be the task for Christians who want to develop relationships that are authentic and grow in what it means to be a safe place. God has not given us permission to simply concern ourselves with the missional task at hand while not paying attention to the

---

114   Guy Chevreau, *Spiritual Warfare Sideways: Keeping the Focus on Jesus* (Grand Rapids, MI: Baker Publishing Group, 2007), 100–101.

115   See ibid.

condition of our relationships. For followers of Christ, task and relationship are organically connected. And to ignore this is to ignore the fact that relationships that are authentic and safe are an important part of the missional task in a culture where truth is often relational before it becomes propositional. That is, people in postmodern culture will often not care what you know until they know that you care. Thus, it will be through relationships that model and provide freedom for authentic living that we will win the right to speak into peoples' lives.

41

DEFINING AUTHENTICITY AS FREEDOM FOR TRANSFORMATION

When people discover that they can reveal to a friend or pastor
those things they've kept hidden in the dark—someone, who instead
of lecturing, shaming, or even rejecting them, accepts them with
a tender and loving heart—they can begin the journey toward
believing God feels the same way toward them.

B EING AUTHENTIC IS not automatically a good thing. Any individual or organization can be authentically bad. Authenticity as it relates to being a safe
place is for the purpose of a transformation for good, a transformation that
enables us to think, speak, and act more like Jesus. This is a transformation to
be desired because the life of Jesus shows us authentic human living at its best,
authentic human living as it was designed to be experienced.

The point of creating an atmosphere of authenticity is to help us be set
free from the power of sin and toxic shame, experience God's comfort and
healing where we have been wounded and are in pain, and experience broken

relationships being reconciled, all for the purpose of being transformed to think, speak, and act more like Jesus. This is the purpose for authenticity in the lives of a safe-place people, and it will be manifested by individuals and entire congregations who are becoming more emotionally, relationally, and spiritually whole.

THE IMPORTANCE OF BEING AUTHENTIC

To be authentic means to be trustworthy, reliable, and genuine. As it relates to being a safe place, to be authentic is fundamentally about genuinely being yourself, because only when we are truly ourselves will we have the opportunity to see where God's work of transformation needs to take place. "Authenticity is about you being you—fully," Mike Robbins explains. He writes,

> It's about being yourself—understanding, owning, acknowledging, appreciating, and expressing all of who you are—both the light and the dark. Being authentic is one of the most challenging yet important aspects of our growth as human beings. It involves being totally honest about ourselves and with others. When we're authentic, we're vulnerable, aware, open, curious, and truthful above all else. We're in touch with our thoughts and our feelings, our doubts and our fears, our dreams and our passions, and so much more. When we're authentic, we're also able to own up to it when we're being phony.[116]

Not only is authenticity an essential element in our own transformation into more Christlikeness, it is also a key for increasing our effectiveness in developing healthy disciples and leaders in the church, and living lives of witness in the world. People are attracted to others who are authentically who they say they are, and offer that same freedom to others in return. Any hint of phoniness or hypocrisy will turn most people off and drive them away. Authenticity on the other hand, will draw them close.

---

116 Robbins, *Be Yourself, Everyone Else Is Already Taken*, Kindle ed.

An atmosphere of freedom for authentic living is what many people are looking for when they are considering Christianity as a spirituality to be embraced, or when they are looking for a Christian church to attend. Theology is no longer at the top of most people's lists. Acceptance, belonging, and authenticity are. It is not that theology is unimportant; it is. It's just that in our current cultural context, an atmosphere where there is a freedom for authentic living comes before believing for most on their lists of priority.

This is not to say a biblical theology is unimportant. Of course it is. Theology shapes and forms how we live, how we lead, and how we do church. Healthy leadership and church practices will reflect a solid biblical theology; unhealthy leadership and practices will reflect the lack thereof. However, the search for acceptance, belonging, and authenticity reflects the priorities and needs of many of the people in today's world.

ITS JUST NOT WHAT WE'RE KNOWN FOR

Unfortunately, Christian individuals and congregations are not generally known for fostering a relational atmosphere that provides freedom for authentic living. More often that not we are perceived, and experienced, as being more concerned with being right than being honest and authentic. This emphasis upon being right rather than honest and authentic begins innocently enough in the teaching of our children at home or in our Sunday school programs. Children are often praised and encouraged more for giving what they think the right answer is supposed to be than for being honest and authentic in the answers they give or the questions they ask. For instance, consider the following story about a children's Sunday school class shared by author-pastor Mark Herringshaw:

> "Okay class, I'm thinking of something brown and fuzzy that jumps from tree to tree. Does anyone know what I'm thinking of?" No one in the class responded, so the Sunday school teacher tried again. "Okay, it has a bushy tail, plays in your yard, and is very hard to catch. Now do you know what I am thinking of?" Again the kids remained

quiet. Exasperated, the Sunday school teacher gave it one last try. "Okay, it's a small animal that eats nuts. Does anybody know what I am talking about?" Finally, Bobby raised his hand. "Teacher, I know the right answer is Jesus, but it sure sounds like you're talking about a squirrel."[117]

Why were the students in this Sunday school class hesitant to answer the question?

Why are we hesitant when asked questions in similar settings, even though we know the answers? Could it be because we feel more pressure to make certain we are right than we do to merely be honest and authentic in who we are and what we think and what we say?

In this section we will explore what we can do to create and cultivate an atmosphere of freedom for authentic living in our relationships with one another and with non-Christians. Before moving on, let's stop and consider what an authentic person might look like to us. Think of someone you consider as being authentic. What are the characteristics about them that make them seem genuine to you? Keep these characteristics in mind as we go on to examine in more detail those things can help us create an atmosphere of freedom for authentic living for ourselves and for others.

---

117 Mark Herringhsaw and Jennifer Schuchmann, *Six Prayers God Always Answers* (Wheaton, IL: Tyndale Publishing, 2008), 2–3.

42

FINDING AN AUTHENTIC BAND

*What would you think if I sang out of tune? Would you stand up
and walk out on me?
I get by with a little help from my friends.*

—— THE BEATLES
"With a Little Help From My Friends"

I LOVE BANDS. I love authentic, good old rock 'n' roll music bands like
Credence Clearwater Revival, Grand Funk Railroad, Bob Seger and the
Silver Bullet Band, Bonnie Raitt, and the Beatles. And I love, absolutely love,
the Eagles. In fact, as I type these words I'm listening to the Eagles' "I Love To
Watch A Woman Dance." Being a child of the 1960s and 1970s, I love bands.

I also love bands of people on mission together like the Fellowship of the
Ring in *The Lord of the Rings Trilogy* and the Band of Brothers from the World
War II mini-series of the same name. The latter is particularly meaningful
for me because my dad, Darwin Bradley, was in the Navy and part of the
landing force that day at Omaha Beach. Bands like these have always given

me inspiration and a renewed sense of purpose and courage. I love authentic bands.

AN AUTHENTIC BAND

One of the great blessings God has given me is a band of brothers and sisters to be on mission with in the Alliance of Renewal Churches network. So many members in this band know what it means to create an atmosphere for authentic living because that's who they are, authentic people. They genuinely are who they say they are and give you the same freedom in return with no fear of being judged, shamed, or rejected. And this freedom for authentic living is giving us all the opportunity to be authentically transformed to think, speak, and act more like Jesus.

About the time I wrote this portion of the book I had the joy of taking a road trip with ARC band mates Danny Mullins and Graeme Sellers. We drove from Gilbert, Arizona, to the city of Orange in southern California to spend six days with another band mate, Tom Brashears. Danny, Graeme, and I spent the first day driving to Orange, listening to great music, talking about how God has been moving in our lives, and laughing a lot. Perhaps the most unique experience on the drive was being in the middle of nowhere and suddenly coming upon the General George S. Patton museum. Curiosity got the best of us so we pulled in to find out why in the world a museum dedicated to one of the greatest generals in United States history was located here in the middle of nowhere. One of the hosts inside the museum provided the explanation. The men who would be going to war in tanks in northern Africa were trained here at Camp Young because of the desert terrain. Who would have thought this stretch of desert and rock would be one of the key training bases for troops during World War II?

After our pit stop we hit the road again on the "Don't Tell Me What To Do Tour" (based on an inside joke we often shared with one another). We spent four fun-filled days in California with our friend, Tom. We golfed and went deep sea fishing, shot guns at a firing range (fired a 44 magnum—it made my day!), spent time in a Korean steam (a relaxing cultural experience), enjoyed great food

(Tom is an amazing chef), taught Tom how to play Nintendo Wii Frisbee golf (he learned faster than anyone in history), and yes, laughed a lot. And in the midst of all this fun the Lord broke in and ministered to us. As we got real with one another about life and ministry in the context of the authenticity that characterizes our relationships with one another, the Lord spoke to us, encouraged us, and renewed our hearts. What a gift to have friends who love the Lord and are real and authentic people to journey through life with.

AN AUTHENTIC BAND LEAVES YOU DIFFERENT THAN WHEN THE JOURNEY BEGAN

Having a band of brothers and sisters you can talk, laugh, cry, and make memories with can leave a person different than when the journey began, different in a good way. This kind of band allows you the freedom to be who you really are with no fear of being condemned or discarded. With a band like this you don't have to live life as a pretender. Instead you can be your most real self. And being your most real self in the present can position you to receive the healing and transformational work of God that sets you free to live as the best version of who you can be. Being a Christian who is part of an authentic band doesn't restrict you from the fullness life has to offer; it sets you free to experience it.

Furthermore, an authentic band can help you navigate the worst of what life and our enemy has to throw at us. Trust me, I know. It was an authentic band of brothers and sisters from Trinity Lutheran Church in Rapid City who helped Debi and me, and our kids, navigate the worst nightmare of any parent—the sudden death of our oldest son on his eighteenth birthday. When you are in such great pain, Christians who try to talk you out of your pain are not much help. Christians who try to theologize and provide answers as to why this has happened are not much help. And those who all too glibly throw out clichés and misapplied, misinterpreted Scriptures are of no help whatsoever.

The people who are of the most help in a time like this are those who are authentic and allow you the freedom to be the same. They know they can't talk you out of your pain and they don't try to make sure you are reacting or grieving in the "right way." They accept you right where you are, love you, and practice the powerful gift of presence just by being *with* you.

Authenticity incarnated in the lives of a band of brothers and sisters is one of the most powerful ways that God is able to impart his comfort and healing to us; one of the ways we best experience his ability to redeem even the darkest moments of our lives and bring something good out of them. Good? No, something great! Believe me, I know.

Being part of an authentic band really makes a difference in life. It makes it as full as a really great Eagles-Beach Boys-Doobie Brothers-like harmony. How can you find one? Read on.

AUTHENTICITY IS SOMETHING BEST CAUGHT

Authenticity is something one most often "catches" just by hanging out with others who themselves are genuine, not phony, superficial, or insecure. Finding an authentic band of brothers and sisters to walk with on our journey of following Jesus is one of the great joys, and unfortunately, rare privileges in life. Sharing life with this kind of band, people who are comfortable in their own skin, are truly in love with the Lord, and know how to enjoy life and not take themselves too seriously, can go a long way toward helping us become more authentic ourselves. And becoming more authentic as persons is one of the essential keys in becoming a safe place for non-Christians and Christians alike.

A RELATIONAL ELEMENT TO COURAGE IN BATTLE

Finding an authentic band of brothers and sisters is also an essential key to effectively fighting the battle of open war we experience this side of heaven. In Ephesians 6, the apostle Paul tells us we live in a world at war. He speaks of a spiritual battle going on round about us and reminds us that we really do have an enemy who schemes against us and seeks to put us in harm's way:

Finally, be strong in the Lord and in the strength of his might. Put on the whole armor of God, that you may be able to stand against the schemes of the devil. For we do not wrestle against flesh and blood, but against the rulers, against the authorities, against the cosmic powers over this present darkness, against the spiritual forces of evil in the heavenly places. Therefore take up the whole armor of God, that you may be able to withstand in the evil day, and having done all, to stand firm. Stand therefore, having fastened on the belt of truth, and having put on the breastplate of righteousness, and, as shoes for your feet, having put on the readiness given by the gospel of peace. In all circumstances take up the shield of faith, with which you can extinguish all the flaming darts of the evil one; and take the helmet of salvation, and the sword of the Spirit, which is the word of God, praying at all times in the Spirit, with all prayer and supplication. To that end keep alert with all perseverance, making supplication for all the saints (Ephesians 6:10–18, ESV).

Finding an authentic band to go to war with is essential. I've mentioned that my dad was part of the invasion force at Normandy in World War II. Whenever I watch the miniseries *Band of Brothers*, or the movie *Saving Private Ryan*, I'm reminded of my father and of what he once told me: "Son, there is a relational element to courage." The only way the men at Normandy could move up the beach after landing was through the courage they gave one another just by being together. They were all afraid, but they were not alone. They all moved forward with someone on either side of them, and being together gave them the courage they needed. Step by step, side-by-side, they were a band of brothers on a mission. Together, they were a force to be reckoned with. And that's who we can be too.

This dynamic of courage imparted through relationships is often reflected in the movies I enjoy such as the Lord of the Rings trilogy. There again is a band, the Fellowship of the Ring. They were on mission together and along the way they not only carry out the mission but share life together. They laugh together, cry together, and give one another courage to follow through on carrying out the mission they've been given—to destroy the ring!

A GIFT NOT TO BE TAKEN FOR GRANTED

A band of brothers and sisters on mission together who are authentic as persons is a great gift, never to be taken for granted. Joe Walsh of the Eagles once said, "To be part of a real band is something that not all musicians get to do in their life, and I'm real lucky to have that chapter in my book."[118] Like Walsh, I've been blessed to be in real bands made up of many authentic brothers and sisters in Christ. I was in such a band at Trinity Lutheran Church in Rapid City, and now am in just such a band once again—the ARC. So many of the brothers and sisters in this network walk in authenticity and I can see it and experience it in so many different things that characterize their lives.

Authentic band mates are not bound by legalism or striving to earn or prove their worth. Rather, they are firmly grounded in a settled sense of identity as God's beloved sons and daughters. Their worth and significance is grounded in this reality and enables them to live life trusting in the faithfulness of Jesus rather than striving to have enough of the "right kind" of faith on their own. This in turn enables them to be people who help you relax because they're relaxed. They aren't trying to prove anything to themselves or to anyone else. When they enter a room they fill the atmosphere with peace rather than tension, rest rather than weariness.

Authentic band mates in the ARC don't have a bravado that covers a multitude of hidden insecurities, nor do they feel a need to make themselves the center of attention or self-promote their churches or the latest ministry endeavor they've embarked on. People who are free to live authentically are able to rest in the mystery of hiddenness we have in Christ. They know they are already significant because of who God says they are and what he has done for them on the cross through his Son, Jesus Christ. Authentic band mates do not over-spiritualize life, nor do they feel the need to use spiritual language to rationalize or justify every decision and choice they make. They are able to

---

118 See Alison Ellwood, director, *History of the Eagles* (Showtime, 2013).

have fun and enjoy life without apologizing or feeling the need to give some spiritual justification for enjoying it.

An authentic band creates an atmosphere where it's safe to express what you are truly thinking, feeling, or wondering about with no fear of being lectured or judged. It will be made up of people who can help you ask the intimate questions, such as, "If the enemy were going to take me out, how would he do it?" They'll not only help you ask the question but help you deal with it by applying God's freeing and healing combination of grace and truth. I have grown more authentic as a person just by hanging out with the bands of brothers and sisters God has given me to journey with throughout my life as a Christian. They have been bands I've shared life with, ministered with, and simply had fun with.

How Do You Find an Authentic Band?

How do you find a band like this? First and foremost you begin by turning to the Lord and asking him to do whatever he needs to do in you, so he can make you an authentic band mate for others. Ask the Lord what he needs to transform in you, heal in you, or set you free from that is hindering you from having the freedom to be your most real self with others. Ask yourself if there is anything God wants to touch in your life that you have been hiding from others, hiding behind the shear force of your personality, position, or giftedness. Sometimes these things can blind us and others to the real needs and hurts in our lives. In short, like King David, ask God to show you if there is any grievous way in you (see Psalm 139:23–24). Then dare to seek help to address those needs through tools such as trustworthy counseling and inner healing prayer ministries.

An example of one way God may need to touch your life is in the area of expressing vulnerability. This will be addressed in more detail in a later chapter in this book. Suffice it to say at this point, without daring to make yourself vulnerable to others you will never fully experience this kind of a band of brothers and sisters. Through vulnerability you take the risk of making the real you known to another. And only in making your real self known to another can you experience the incredible gift of being part of an authentic band. We all need a band like this in our lives, but it is only in daring to open our hearts to another, and receiving their gifts of unconditional love and acceptance, that we will be able in like kind to give those gifts to another. Vulnerability is a key to finding an authentic band.

Next, pray. Ask God in prayer to give you an authentic band to be a part of. It may begin with just one other person. In fact, if you can have just one other person with whom you can truly be yourself, you will benefit greatly. This is a primary point of emphasis for us in the ARC. We want to be a network of brothers and sisters in Christ who are creating an atmosphere of freedom for authentic living in our relationships. Are we there yet? Have we arrived? Have we figured it all out? No. But it will continue to be something we are intentional about, seeking to position ourselves before God so he can do the transforming and empowering work he still needs to do in us.

Another factor involved in finding an authentic band is to carefully discern the atmosphere of any church or denomination you may be thinking of becoming a part of. Is it legalistic? Do you have to keep a lot of rules in order to feel like you belong and are accepted? Do you have to wear a mask, being someone you think others will approve of while keeping your real self hidden at all costs? It will be difficult to find freedom for authentic living in this kind of group because you will always feel you have to measure up in order to be included and belong. You'll find your thinking dominated by the "I am not enough" syndrome. When this dynamic is at work it will cause you to manufacture a false self that you present to others in order to be accepted and fit in.

On the other hand, be careful of any church or denomination that, in the name of what they perceive as authenticity, are deviating from the truth of God's Word. You will certainly be able to be yourself in such a group because they are ready to accept anyone just as they are, and leave them just as they are. Authenticity for the purpose of transformation is not one of their true values. In groups such as these you will never be challenged or helped in the areas of your life that need God's transforming power.

An authentic band does not just accept you and leave you in pain or in bondage. Jesus did not accept people and then leave them just as they were.

When he knew they were hurting or in bondage, he spoke grace-filled truth and healed them and set them free. For instance, Jesus did not simply accept the woman caught in adultery so she could "live authentically." Certainly he accepted her fully for who she was, but then he gracefully brought truth to bear upon her life so she could be set free from the consequences of sin and shame, and live more fully into the purposes of God for her life.

AUTHENTICITY IS ESSENTIAL

Finding a band of authentic brothers and sisters to be a part of is one of the essential keys for becoming more authentic in our own lives. And as we in turn are being transformed, healed, and set free to live authentic lives, God will use us to impact others. Grand Funk Railroad sang the song "We're An American Band." Maybe we could borrow their music and put some new lyrics to a theme song of our own: "We're An Authentic Band." When Christians are free to live authentically, and are being transformed to think, speak, and act more like Jesus, it is a powerful tool for mission and healing in the lives of others. Being an authentic band is one of the absolutely essential keys for any Christian individual, small group, or congregation to grow in what it means a safe place.

43

MAKING IT SAFE TO ENGAGE
IN AUTHENTIC DIALOGUE

*Because of all the baggage and lack of trust in our
post-Christian world, people need to be engaged in dialogue. Few
people are interested only in a monologue. Instead, if they listen to
a message in church, they want to process it.
They need to question it and wrestle with it. It needs to engage
them where they live life.*

— JOHN BURKE
No Perfect People Allowed

MAKING RELATIONSHIPS A safe place for authentic dialogue is one of the primary ways we can create an atmosphere of freedom for authentic living. When the emotional, relational, and spiritual atmosphere does not make space for genuine dialogue, it hinders the development of relationships that are experienced as safe and authentic. For example, consider the following story from the life of a twenty-nine-year-old mother of two toddlers who was meeting with a group of women at a church-hosted Bible study:

> We were talking about sex, intimacy, and pregnancy, stuff like that. I told them about a friend of mine who was considering an abortion. I told them her entire situation, a twenty-year-old, boyfriend left her. She's feeling really alone. I made some comment about really empathizing with my friend, that I could understand that abortion might make sense. I guess that shocked them. I know the women there are pro-life and all——I don't know what I am, pro-life or pro-choice or just myself. But the conversation shifted at that point in a really weird way. Instead of having a dialogue, I was put on the defensive. They were nice enough about it, but the ladies just kept talking *at* me, trying to fix my attitude about abortion.

> Lisa paused and softened her tone. "And here is the part that bothered me, something I never told them. What they didn't know is that *I* had an abortion——a long time ago. It was not an experience I would wish on anyone. But I can feel my friend's dilemma because I lived it. I am not sure the Christians I hung out with that morning get that.

> I guess the truth is I was hoping for some empathy myself."[119]

What does this story reveal about what makes dialogue genuine and safe? What does it demonstrate regarding the critical importance of nurturing an atmosphere where people are truly free to engage in authentic dialogue?

---

119   Kinnaman and Lyons, *unChristian*, 182 (emphasis in the original).

THE IMPORTANCE OF CREATING AN ATMOSPHERE OF FREEDOM FOR AUTHENTIC DIALOGUE

An atmosphere that is safe gives people the sense they are not only free to share what they are truly thinking, feeling, or struggling with, but that their sharing is genuinely welcomed. Such an atmosphere provides the sense that genuine vulnerability and transparency are welcome.

Where there is an atmosphere of freedom for authentic dialogue, a willingness to make oneself vulnerable and transparent is received and treated as a precious gift by those who are listening. In the case of the women in the Bible study, they did not seem concerned with creating a place that was safe for this young woman, perhaps not even for one another. They were too concerned with appearing to be right and having all the answers rather than seeking to listen, empathize, and understand. The young mother seemed to sense these women would not receive her story without lecturing, judging, shaming, and rejecting her, so she chose to remain silent.

There are too many times when this is the case among Christians. Too often we are not intentional about creating a place that is safe for people to be vulnerable and transparent. However, there are also times when the culprit is not only those who listen to a story, but the storyteller themselves. The freedom to share may actually be present, but the individual anticipates a negative response due to unresolved pain in his or her own past. This pain is still influencing them by causing them to anticipate and misinterpret how others are going to react to what they have to share. So they don't share. Not because it would not be welcomed or received. But because they have anticipated a response based on a past experience that may not be true of those whom they are with in the present.

In the case of the Bible study, the women and the young mother missed out on a powerful opportunity for life-changing ministry to take place because the emotional, relational, and spiritual atmosphere was not safe for the engagement in authentic dialogue. The young mother missed out because she remained quiet, not daring to bring into the light the wound from her past.

She did not sense there was freedom to share this painful experience and as a result was prevented from experientially knowing the full extent of God's love, forgiveness, and healing. The Bible study group missed out because they did not see the opportunity they had to be God's healing presence for this young woman. They could have experienced God using them in a very powerful way, but they missed it because they were more concerned with being right than being righteous. They were more concerned with themselves and their dogma than with what was going on in the life of the young mother, or her friend.

THE CONNECTION BETWEEN AUTHENTIC DIALOGUE AND TRANSFORMATION

Creating and nurturing an atmosphere of freedom to engage in authentic dialogue is crucial if we are to become a safe place where authentic transformation into the image of Jesus can happen in the lives of Christians and non-Christians alike. If we do not encourage and welcome genuine conversation, we will miss out on wonderful opportunities to continue the ministry of Jesus in the world today and re-present Jesus in our culture. John Burke writes,

> If the church is truly to be the Body of Christ re-presenting Jesus to the world, what should we be doing to be more like him? Notice that even though Jesus had all the answers, he still respected and valued the opinions and free will of others. He often asked questions to get people to search rather than just telling the answer. He taught in parables to pique spiritual curiosity of those truly seeking. Though he proclaimed truth with authority, he did not force his truth on others. In love, he offered what they needed and then was willing to let people disagree and walk away, even though it saddened him. Because of all the baggage and lack of trust in our post-Christian world, people need to be engaged in dialogue. Few people are interested only in a monologue. Instead, if they listen to a message in church, they want

to process it. They need to question it and wrestle with it. It needs to engage them where they live life.[120]

The freedom and opportunity to engage in authentic dialogue is important to Christians and non-Christians. What would such an atmosphere feel, look, and sound like to you? Take a few moments to reflect on that question and then write your answers down in the space below:

Following are some ways we can help create an atmosphere that welcomes genuine dialogue. You can add them to your list if you have not already.

LOVING AND VALUING PEOPLE

First and foremost, creating an atmosphere of freedom for authentic dialogue requires followers of Christ to truly love and value people no matter what some of their lifestyle choices, belief systems, or worldviews may be. To say this may seem scandalous, but it is the way of the Lord. It is his way to love and value people simply because they have been created in his image. Whether they realize it or not, he is their creator and he cares for them. God's way of loving will always seem scandalous to those who are more concerned with being right than righteous, with being religious rather Christian. To love as God loves, and to foster freedom for genuine conversation will require that we respect the thoughts and opinions of others, making sure they know we value them whether or not they ever come to agree with our beliefs about Jesus and Christianity.

Providing an atmosphere for genuine dialogue necessitates creating a place where people feel safe enough to voice what they really think and ask questions they really want to ask, rather than remaining silent. Pastor Burke writes,

---

120 Burke, *No Perfect People Allowed*, 53.

When a culture of dialogue gets created, people *far from God* who *do not typically trust Christians feel safe enough* to hang out and explore. And as we have seen time after time, a culture of dialogue allows people to put down their guard and seek, and as they truly seek just as the Lord promises, they will find him [emphasis mine].[121]

Many people believe Christians will only genuinely love them and want to spend time with them as long as they begin to behave or believe like us. In their minds, our love for them is conditional. It is predicated on the belief that they must become one of us before we'll truly care about them. In a safe-place atmosphere people experience followers of Christ who love, value, and care about them no matter what, no strings attached.

Take a moment and ask yourself the questions below. Ask the Lord to speak to you concerning them. Record your answers in the space that follows. Then seek out some mature, trustworthy Christians for insights into how you might cooperate with God in his work of transforming you in any way needed so you love others just as he does.

- What keeps me from loving people the way God loves them?
- What would God need to do in me so he could love others through me in the way he has first loved me?

TRUSTING GOD

Creating an atmosphere of freedom for authentic dialogue requires trusting God. To entrust people into the hands of the Lord requires letting go of the belief that we are the ones who need to fix, change, or control their beliefs or actions. It means truly believing God is more concerned for them than we are, and is in fact at work in their lives. It requires trusting that God's Spirit can work behind the scenes in people's hearts as we create a space where they are free to discuss, question, doubt, and explore faith at their own pace.

---

121   Ibid., 52.

This shifts the burden to change people back to where it belongs—with God alone. In turn, we can then experience the freedom to love and value people whether they agree with us or not because we realize God loves and values them whether they agree with him or not.

When Scripture tells us that God so loved the world that he sent his only begotten Son to die for the world, it was not predicated on everyone already believing in him, or agreeing with him concerning the nature of truth. Father God sent Jesus into the world, and Jesus willingly chose to come into the world, because they already loved and valued every single person. Understanding this can help us truly believe God cares so much for each person that he is going to be at work in every life. He is the one responsible to change people, not us. God is trustworthy. We can trust him with our lives and the lives of others.

PRACTICING AUTHENTIC LISTENING

Creating an atmosphere that fosters freedom for authentic dialogue requires practicing authentic listening. We are told in the Book of Proverbs, "To answer before listening—that is folly and shame" (18:13). And the Book of James encourages us, "My dear brothers and sisters, take note of this: Everyone should be quick to listen and slow to speak and slow to become angry" (1:19). Someone has said (I cannot remember the source), "The gift of being a good listener, a gift which requires constant practice, is perhaps the most healing gift anyone can possess; for it allows the other to be, enfolds them in a safe place, does not judge or advise them, and communicates support at a level deeper than words."

To practice authentic listening requires giving our full attention to the person who is speaking to us. Rather than allowing our thoughts to wander, staying focused on the person before us and on what they are telling us can communicate love. Consistent eye contact conveys our interest, and when we do speak, the tone of our voice more than what we say, can communicate the care and concern, love and acceptance that helps create a safe place for authentic dialogue. For more information on learning to practice authentic listening I highly recommend the chapter on listening in *The Marriage Book* by Nicky and Sila Lee.[122]

TURNING STATEMENTS INTO QUESTIONS

We can help create an atmosphere of freedom for authentic dialogue by turning statements of opinion into questions. Doing this can help a discussion become an invitation to engage in a true dialogue and exchange of ideas. This in turn can make our discussions a safe place where others can be honest about what they are thinking, questioning, or wrestling with. Only making statements and sharing our own opinions can make the atmosphere unsafe as the other person may feel we are lecturing or talking at them rather than with them.

To turn statements of opinion into questions requires what we were just talking about—authentic listening. As we listen to others we can become aware of more questions to ask that will help us better understand where they are coming from, and what is truly important to them. Asking questions rather than merely stating our opinions can communicate that we genuinely care about them. If we can slow ourselves down, listen, and then ask more clarifying questions rather than firing back only opinions and statements of our own, it will help us more effectively create an atmosphere of freedom for genuine dialogue. This does not mean we cannot have opinions or that we cannot state them. It may mean sharing fewer of our opinions than we normally would, as we trust that God is at work in these people's lives.

AVOID MAJORING ON THE MINORS

Creating an atmosphere that fosters freedom for authentic dialogue requires us to *not* major on the minors. How do we get off track and make the minors the majors? We can do it when our reactions demonstrate shock or offense

---

122 See Nicky and Sila Lee, *The Marriage Book: How to Build a Lasting Relationship,* (Brompton, UK: Alpha International, 2000).

when the other person uses what we consider inappropriate expressions of speech or is engaged in ways of living that do not agree with our own personal piety. I am not saying these issues are unimportant. What I am saying is there may be larger or deeper issues that we need to focus on first, trusting God will address these other issues in due time. When we center on a person's manner of speech or their lifestyle choices rather than the deeper issue they present to us or that the Lord brings to light, we are majoring on minors. There will be times that we'll be better served to hold our opinions on those issues to ourselves for the moment. Any way of speaking or living life that God considers inappropriate or harmful will be dealt with as he transforms people's hearts, meets their deeper needs, and heals their wounded pasts.

If we focus first on changing peoples' behaviors or expressions of speech that offend us or make us uncomfortable, we run the risk of quenching any desire on their part to be real and authentic with us. This in turn will ensure they remain in bondage to the deeper issues rather than being given the courage to bring them to light. Instead of opening up to us, they will continue to hide what they truly think or feel, and will run from us and from the Lord. They will feel judged, shamed, and rejected. They will turn to other sources of counsel and spirituality, rather than to Christianity and Christ to deal with their issue.

If in the moment we focus on correcting a minor issue of inappropriate speech or behavior we will have illustrated what they probably already believe—that Christians are more concerned with being right and self-righteous than in genuinely caring for someone who is in trouble or pain. Yes, we will have taken a stand for our convictions regarding issues of piety that are important to us, but we will have missed the opportunity of ministering to the real needs and deeper issues God wanted to touch and transform in that person's life. Avoiding majoring on the minors will help us create an atmosphere of freedom for authentic dialogue, an atmosphere that may just be the doorway through which others step into the healing light of God.

RECOGNIZING OUR OWN NEED FOR HEART SURGERY

Recognizing our own need for heart surgery is another important aspect in creating an atmosphere that fosters freedom for authentic dialogue. We all need heart surgery at one point or another, in the sense that things within us hinder our thinking, speaking, and acting more like Jesus. We have thoughts, fears, motives, habits, and ways of responding to others that grieve God and get in the way our transformation more fully into the image of his Son.

We need God to perform heart surgery on us. We need him to set us free from everything that prevents others from engaging in authentic dialogue with us. Like Lazarus in the book of John, we may have received the gift of new life from Jesus, but we still have old stinking grave clothes hanging on us that we need to be set free from. We have unhelpful and unrighteous ways of thinking, believing, and speaking that God wants to transform so we can more effectively continue his ministry in the world today.

As discussed earlier, such a transformation requires an atmosphere that is safe, an atmosphere in which we are given the freedom and courage to truly see and acknowledge anything in our lives that is grievous to God and harmful to us. Then as we recognize these things, to invite the Lord to do whatever he needs to do in us so we can be healed and transformed. If we will courageously acknowledge our need for God to transform and restore, and if we will be committed to encourage and support one another in this endeavor, we will find the Lord increasing our capacity to think, speak, and act more like Jesus, and to create an atmosphere that is safe for others to engage in authentic dialogue.

CHALLENGING WRONG THINKING

Finally, creating an atmosphere that fosters authentic dialogue does not mean we never challenge or confront wrong thinking or wrong behavior. Wrong thinking and behaving still need to be informed and challenged by truth. To withhold truth is an unloving thing to do because it leaves a person in bondage to the practice and consequences of their misguided thinking and behavior.

That Jesus was a safe place did not mean he withheld truth from those he encountered. For instance, he did not allow the woman caught in adultery (see John 8) to walk away having simply been loved and accepted. He also told her, "Go and sin no more." To be a safe place does not mean we withhold truth from people, but rather, we allow God's grace to inform when, where, and how we share truth.

It is important we always remind one another that Jesus valued people for who they were—beloved by Father God. Because of this, Jesus did not require people to "clean up their act" before they could hang out with him. Instead, he welcomed them as they were and as they walked in relationship with him they were either transformed or they decided it was too hard to follow him and turned and walked away. Either way, Jesus loved and valued them. This created the atmosphere for authentic dialogue we see in his exchanges with the woman at the well, Nicodemus, Zacchaeus, and many others throughout the Gospels. This in turn helped make Jesus a safe place for them. In the same way, creating an atmosphere of freedom for authentic dialogue will help us create an atmosphere that will make us a safe place for Christians and non-Christians alike.

44

MAKING ROOM FOR UNCERTAINTY AND DOUBT

*Like most Christians, I once assumed a person's faith is as strong as
that person is certain. I assumed that doubt is the enemy of faith.
It is my conviction that this certainty-seeking concept of faith is the
main reason so many of our young people abandon the Christian
faith and the main reason most nonbelievers today don't take
Christianity seriously.*

— GREGORY BOYD

CHRISTIANS CAN HELP create an atmosphere of freedom for authentic living
by making room for expressions of uncertainty and doubt. It may sound
paradoxical but in the postmodern culture in which we live, a spirituality that
demands certainty and makes no place for struggling with doubt can find it
difficult to gain an honest hearing in people's lives. In his book *Unstoppable
Force*, Erwin McManus writes,

If we seem to never struggle with the maybes, there is serious doubt whether we truly know anything at all. The traction comes when we become honest with ourselves and others—when we become cheerleaders for inquiry and seeking rather than simply knowing and finding.

Traction comes when outsiders experience the church as a place where honest questions can be asked when people journey together to discover God and find the answers in him.[123]

In a culture characterized by so much skepticism and cynicism, making room for an authentic expression of uncertainty and doubt is an essential part of making Christian individuals, small groups, and congregations a safe place. Asking questions, expressing doubts, and assuming a position of skepticism are all part of life for people in the postmodern, post-Christian culture in which we live. Having the freedom to express such things is important in our relationships with those who no longer view traditional figures and sources of authority as valid or trustworthy.

For instance, it is important Christians realize that the Bible is no longer viewed as an authoritative source for many people's lives. It does not work to respond to someone's uncertainty, doubt, or question with a glib, "Well, the Bible says." What the Bible says does not matter to them. What matters to them is whether or not we unconditionally care about them enough to make our relationships with them a place where they can freely give voice to the issues of life that they are wrestling with.

There was a time where even those who were not believers or churchgoers viewed Christian leaders, churches, and God's Word as being authoritative sources for truth. But that is no longer the case. This is why it's important that people believe their relationship with you is a safe place, a place where they can give voice to their questions and struggles with no fear of being lectured, judged, or shamed.

---

123   Erwin Raphael McManus, *An Unstoppable Force: Daring to Become the Church God Had in Mind* (Loveland, CO: Group Publishing, 2001), 134.

THE POWER OF SHARING OUR OWN UNCERTAINTY AND DOUBT

One of the most helpful elements for creating an atmosphere of freedom for authentic living is when Christians are willing to acknowledge their own wrestling with uncertainty and doubt. When we're willing to share our struggles, we make our relationships with Christians and non-Christians a safe place, and we avoid enabling others in hiding their own struggles. Author Adrian Plass writes,

> I know there are people who cannot stand the idea that Christian living can be ragged and awkward and sometimes slow. They want glorious transfiguration or nothing. That is why, when such people are allowed to lead churches, the majority of their members are deluded, very good at pretending, or puzzled and worried about their lack of progress in comparison with the "triumphant" others.[124]

Christians who are willing to be appropriately vulnerable by acknowledging and sharing their own struggles with various life issues will be more effective in helping others feel safe to acknowledge theirs. This will help create an atmosphere where people will be more likely to bring what they are wrestling with into the light, and once it's in the light, the combination of God's grace and truth, which heals and sets free, can be applied.

LETTING GO OF THE IDOL OF CERTAINTY-SEEKING FAITH

If we are to become people who are willing to be vulnerable and transparent regarding our own struggle with questions and doubts, we will need to let go of the idol of certainty-seeking faith. Too many Christians are unknowingly finding their faith in certainty rather than in the Lord. It is the certainty of all the right answers to all the right questions that gives them peace in an unsettling and tumultuous world.

---

124 Adrian Plass, *Jesus: Safe, Tender, Extreme* (Grand Rapids, MI: Zondervan, 2006), 46.

The combination of radical migration and pluralism make it much more difficult for many Christians as well as non-Christians to hold to a certainty-seeking concept of faith in an era when the world is not "over there," but lives right next door. People who hold different beliefs and ask different questions than those we are used to are no longer impersonal beings in another country, but people we know and work with and who live in our neighborhoods. As Greg Boyd writes, "It's much easier to remain certain of your beliefs when you are not in personal contact with people who believe differently. But when you encounter people with different beliefs, and when those people's sincerity and devotion possibly put yours to shame, things become quite a bit different."[125]

Over the decades of living as a disciple of Jesus who has remained committed to following him through some extremely painful and horrific times, I have come to believe that the certainty-seeking concept of faith is not a biblical model. This re-examination of the concept of faith in my life is based on my best attempt at an objective reflection on scripture, my life experiences, and the writings of authors such as Gregory Boyd. Boyd himself has gone through a time of re-examination concerning this concept of faith. He writes,

> My re-examination of the biblical concept of faith led me to the conclusion that the concept of faith that equates strength with certainty and that views doubt as an enemy is in fact, significantly different from the biblical model. . . . While the certainty-seeking model of faith is psychological in nature, the biblical concept is covenantal. . . . This model of faith allows us to embrace a rationally anchored faith that is nevertheless compatible with whatever level of doubt, and however many unresolved questions, a person may have. Unlike the house-of-cards approach to faith, this model of faith does not incline one toward an all-or-nothing mindset, and thus isn't shaken if a person feels compelled by evidence to accept that one, or any number of biblical narratives, are not rooted in history.[126]

---

125   Gregory A. Boyd, *Benefit of the Doubt: Breaking the Idol of Certainty* (Grand Rapids, MI: Baker Books, 2013), Kindle ed.

126   Ibid.

The certainty-seeking model of faith demands that we have it all figured out and are unwavering in our beliefs. The Christian who buys into this, feels the pressure to have all the answers. They are unable to live at peace in the midst of unanswered and unresolved issues and questions. The moment something they've been certain of is brought into question because it's been snatched out of the realm of ideology or theology and becomes real and personal for them, their faith may waiver, wilt, and for some, even fade away.

The certainty-seeking model of faith is an idol that does not serve us well in living Christian lives in a postmodern world. Nor does it help us in living out our desire to develop loving, caring relationships with people who do not share our theological positions. It becomes an idol because it is certainty that we base our trust in rather than in God himself.

One of the most helpful things we can learn is that it's possible to be a person of strong faith who does not have all the answers and does in fact struggle with questions and doubts. This kind of Christian is certain of the truly important and non-negotiable things in their relationship with God, things such as his unconditional, unshakable and extravagant love for them, and their salvation by grace through faith in Jesus Christ. When these kinds of foundational issues of faith have become that which we are certain of and the only ones that we feel we must be certain of, we are able to live in peace and love with others even while we all struggle with different questions and doubts about life and faith.

DOUBT HAS GOTTEN A BAD RAP

Doubt, by the way, is not the dirty word many Christians make it out to be. It's gotten a bad rap in many Christian circles. Doubt is not the same as unbelief. In the Bible, unbelief refers to a willful refusal to believe or a deliberate decision to disobey God. But doubt is something different. When we doubt, we're being indecisive or ambivalent over an issue. "Doubt does not mean denial or negation," wrote theologian Karl Barth. "Doubt only means swaying and staggering between yes and no."[127] In *The Importance of Doubting Our Doubts,* the renowned preacher Henry Emerson Fosdick declared,

> The capacity to doubt is one of man's noblest powers. Look at our world today and see the innumerable beliefs and practices, from communism up and down, which ought to be doubted! The great servants of our race have been distinguished by the fact that in the face of universally accepted falsehoods they dared stand up and cry: I doubt that! Without the capacity to doubt, there would be no progress.

In this sermon Fosdick preached,

> Think of the scientific realm! The earth is flat, the sun circles round it—when such ideas were everywhere accepted, a few bravely dared to disbelieve them. Every scientific advance has started with skepticism. . . . Galileo was right when he called doubt the father of discovery. . . . Anyone who thinks he can achieve great faith without exercising his God-given capacity to doubt is oversimplifying the problem.[128]

A freedom to express genuine doubt and uncertainty can be an essential key in our journey of faith. Doubt can play a positive role in our emotional, relational, and spiritual growth. For example, a growing number of people in western culture doubt the assumptions and promises of the Enlightenment, Rationalism, and the subsequent de-mythologizing of the Bible. Today they are beginning to doubt the assertion that stories in the New Testament about Jesus healing people and setting them free from demonic spirits are simply myths as many Christian theologians and pastors are trying to tell people today. As a result of this positive function of doubt, more and more people

---

127 Karl Barth, *Evangelical Theology: An Introduction* (Grand Rapids, MI: William B. Eerdmans Publishing, 1979, Karl Barth, 1963), 125.

128 Henry Emerson Fosdick, quoted in Thomas G. Long and Cornelius Plantinga, *A Chorus Of Witnesses: Model Sermons for Today's Preacher* (Grand Rapids, MI: William B. Eerdmans Publishing Company, 1994), 111–113.

are beginning to effectively pray for the sick, and we are hearing an increasing number of verified accounts of people being physically, emotionally, and relationally healed, and being set free from the effects of demonic spirits upon their lives.

THE POSITIVE IMPACT OF DOUBT AND UNCERTAINTY IN MY OWN LIFE

I have personally experienced the positive role that wrestling with doubt and uncertainty can play in a person's life. A willingness to ask questions and express doubts was an essential part of the process of the Lord blowing up a God-box I had constructed in my early years as a Christian. A God-box is the box in which we put everything we think we know about who God is. It is our understanding of how he thinks and how he acts in the world today. It includes the limits we place upon God based on that understanding. As you can imagine, our understanding of who God is and how he acts in the world is often flawed and incomplete, as is our God-box. Unfortunately, we do not often see this. God, however, is so good that he will graciously blow up our God-box when he sees the one we have constructed is too small, even when blowing up our box sends us into a spiral of unsettledness and frustration.

Early on in my journey with the Lord, he graciously blew up the box I had constructed regarding his willingness and ability to work in and through historical mainline churches, and in regards to reality of who the Holy Spirit is today. I became a Christian in January of 1974 at the age of twenty-one while serving in the United States Air Force. I became part of a wonderful discipleship group led by a retired Air Force master sergeant and his wife who lived near Altus, Oklahoma, where I was stationed. Fourteen of us from the base were involved in this group and we were given a strong foundation in our relationship with Christ. For this I will forever be grateful. One of the things we were taught was that, "The Bible says it, I believe it, and that settles it." We were given a rock-solid foundation that the Bible is in fact the word of God, a foundation that has never wavered and has always served me well in my forty-one years as a Christian.

Unfortunately, we were taught a couple of interpretations of what Scripture says that were not quite as helpful. For instance, we were encouraged to avoid mainline, historical Christian churches because they would most likely be dead, dry, and of no use to God. We were also taught that anything charismatic was from the devil. So believing in healing, deliverance, and other miracles was no longer needed because this kind of work by Holy Spirit ended with the age of the apostles. This was what I believed as I left the Air Force after four years and headed home to Omaha, Nebraska.

It was still my position when a couple of years later a pastor walked into the Christian bookstore I was managing. I remember he looked like Friar Tuck to me. He introduced himself as Pastor Al Asper, a Lutheran pastor. As we visited he asked a favor. He asked if I would begin to stock some books by authors such as Kenneth Copeland, Kenneth Hagin, Derek Prince, Bob Mumford, and others. I knew these were authors who were "charismatic," that is, they believed the power of the Holy Spirit was still at work in the world today. I asked Pastor Al, "Just out of curiosity, why would you as a Lutheran pastor be interested in books like these?" "Well, I'm a charismatic Lutheran-Christian," he said. Before the filter in my brain could stop me, I blurted out, "You can't be that. You can be Lutheran. You can be charismatic. But you can't be both." Pastor Al simply smiled at me and said, "Of course you can. How about I buy you a cup of coffee and we talk about that?"

So began many meetings over coffee with Pastor Al Asper. He listened so patiently and lovingly to all my questions. He gave me the freedom to wrestle with my uncertainty and doubt regarding the possibility that the power of the Holy Spirit was still active in the world today, a freedom I was not given in the particular brand of Christianity I was involved in at that point in my life. He took me back to God's Word and helped me re-examine some of the unhelpful teaching and interpretations I had been given. One thing led to another until a time came when I experienced the baptism of the Holy Spirit.

I have lived the last thirty-seven years experientially knowing the power of the Holy Spirit in my life, and through me, in the lives of others. I have witnessed people being physically, emotionally, and relationally healed, and set free from the harassment and oppression of demonic spirits. All this was made possible because a Christian pastor made our relationship a safe place for me to express my uncertainty and doubt. My life was forever changed. By the way, this safe-place pastor went on to become my father-in-law. I will forever be grateful to Pastor Al Asper who became one of the first safe-place people in my life.

EXPRESSING UNCERTAINTY, DOUBT, AND QUESTIONS IS PART OF SPIRITUAL SEARCHING

If I had not been given the freedom to doubt, my life would not have been changed for the good, changed to more fully live into God's purposes for me. Without this freedom my God-box would still be much too small. This same freedom is especially important today in a culture such as ours that is one of spiritual searching for so many. To a great degree, Americans are a spiritual people. It is just that they do not always or automatically turn to the Christian church to quench their spiritual thirst. In a spiritual culture such as the one in which we live, any faith or religion that cannot make a place for an honest expression of doubts, questions, and struggles will be suspect in the eyes of searchers.

To not allow people to express what they're wrestling with will hinder rather than foster true spiritual growth. And there is as much need in the lives of Christ-followers to express these things as there is in the lives of non-Christians. Most of us go through many different phases in the course of our Christian lives. We go through seasons of great faith and trust in the Lord, and we go through seasons of questioning, doubting, and even despair. Without the freedom to express these things, our growth in faith will be stunted. When we too quickly stifle any expression of uncertainty and doubt we can cause people to withdraw from relationship with us. This breaking off of relationship can then hinder them from coming to embrace truth that is new to them, and experience a fuller relationship with the Lord as a result.

Just as much as non-Christians, followers of Jesus need the freedom to express what they are struggling with or questioning without being lectured, judged, or shamed. Have you ever found yourself editing some of your true thoughts, questions, and doubts before you share them in the presence of other Christians? If so, why? It's because we are afraid they will not be received. We are afraid we will just be lectured or put down. So we remain quiet, not giving voice to what we are really wondering about, really wrestling with.

People who are quick to criticize or condemn those who doubt would do well to recall admonitions in Scripture such, "Have mercy on those who doubt" (Jude 22) and "Be merciful, even as your Father is merciful" (Jesus in Luke 6:36). On being merciful to those who may struggle with doubts, author Adrian Plass writes,

> Be merciful to others when you are floating along on a cloud, feeling like Billy Graham cubed, and they are trudging their way miserably over the grey surface of the earth, wondering why they ever believed in God in the first place. It will be your turn to need encouragement next week or month or year. . . . Be merciful to yourself when doubt creeps in, and you don't want it to, but it does anyway.[129]

Our ability to be of real help to others, as well as to ourselves, is based to a great degree upon our willingness to create an atmosphere in which honest doubts and searching are welcome, an atmosphere in which they are viewed as part of the normal process of Christian living.

BE ON GUARD FOR INAUTHENTIC DOUBTING

Making room for uncertainty and doubt is an essential part of creating an atmosphere of freedom for authentic living and genuine dialogue. At the same time, however, we must guard against what we might call inauthentic doubting. Inauthentic doubting occurs when people are proud that they are known as the skeptics and doubters without genuinely wanting to seek after truth. If

129 Plass, *Jesus*, 43–44.

we are to allow room for authentic doubt, we must at times be willing to challenge the inauthentic doubters to be willing to be *honest doubters*. Inauthentic doubters are like the man in this story:

> Once upon a time a man announced to his family, neighbors and co-workers that he was dead. When his wife took him to the local psychiatrist he was given the task of researching the medical school journals until he had a firm conviction on the question, "Do dead people bleed?" After weeks of reading he returned with the verdict that the evidence was overwhelming—dead people do not bleed. The psychiatrist smiled and grabbed a pin he had set aside for this very moment. He poked the man's finger and waited for the man's response as several drops of blood dropped from his finger. The man turned ashen white and cried, "Amazing! Dead people do bleed after all!"[130]

Some people like to doubt and appear to be skeptical or cynical just because of the reaction they get from other people. This expression of uncertainty, doubt, and questioning is not healthy because this person is not really open to seeking truth; they've already made up their mind what truth is and they simply like to argue for the sake of arguing. Thus, not every expression then of uncertainty and doubt should be accepted without any challenge at all. We do well to try to discern the authenticity in those who are seeking in order to know how best to respond to them and pray for them.

Making room for uncertainty and doubt is an important part of the journey of spiritual searching for Christians and non-Christians alike. Any individual, small group, or church who makes room for their free expression will do a better job of truly loving and caring for people than those who do not. The former will be a safe place, the latter will not.

---

130 Don Bierle, *Surprised by Faith* (Lynwood, WA: Emerald Books, 1992), 24.

45

MAKING ROOM FOR DISAPPOINTMENT WITH GOD

Honest lament can express a vibrant faith; one that has learned to embrace life's hardships as well as its joy and to lift everything— everything—to the Father in prayer.

— PETE GREIG

Get up, God! Are you going to sleep all day? Wake up! Don't you care what happens to us? Why do you bury your face in the pillow? Why pretend things are just fine with us? And here we are—flat on our faces in the dirt, held down with a boot on our necks. Get up and come to our rescue. If you love us so much, help us!

— PSALM 44:23–26, THE MESSAGE

I F YOU LOVE us so much, help us! So the psalmist cries out to God. He and others have been crying out to the Lord but have not heard him respond. They're disappointed. Frustrated. And they don't mince words in letting him know it. Expressing disappointment, frustration, and even anger with God is quite common in the Bible. Providing freedom for the expression of such emotions is one of the ways we can help create an atmosphere of freedom for authentic living today.

This thought is foreign to many Christians, and is rarely taught or modeled in seminary training for pastors. However, one of my favorite professors in seminary—Dr. Ray Anderson—actually was very intentional in helping his students see the freedom God gives us to express our frustrations with him. He once told me this story that he shared with a group of pastors-to-be in a class he was teaching:

> I was in my office one day when a woman came in and sat down across from me. She began crying and sharing that her baby had recently died. She had prayed, her church had prayed, and they all felt sure God was going to heal her baby, but in the end God had still allowed her baby to die. She was brokenhearted and disappointed with God. She then stood up and began shaking her fist at God and blaming him.
>
> Ray asked the class, "So, what would you future pastors do for this woman?" One student had a thought that he would turn to the Scriptures and show her why she should not be disappointed with God, why she shouldn't be feeling this way and why she should have a stronger position of faith. In the end the student decided not to share these thoughts and was happy he didn't when Ray told the class that he got up from behind his desk, walked around and stood by the woman and joined her in shaking his fist at God because he knew God had "big shoulders."[131]

---

131   Ray Anderson as told to Mike Bradley, Fall 2002.

What do you think of this story? What is there about what the professor said or did in the story that you appreciated? What was there that you might do differently, or that even offended you as you read his account?

LIFE IN THIS WORLD CAN DISAPPOINT AND FRUSTRATE US

Life in this fallen and broken world can knock the stuffing out of us. I say this as one who has had his share of blows in life, particularly the sudden death of my oldest son on his eighteenth birthday. Life is not fair and it is not without trials and tribulations. It can knock the air out of us and leave us disappointed with God, and sometimes downright angry and disappointed with his people too. Such emotions are understandable when one considers how much pain and suffering there is in the world today. The images abound on network and cable news shows, and on the Internet. J. P. Moreland and Tim Muehlhoff recount just a few in their book *The God Conversations*:

> The sight of thick black smoke pouring out of twin skyscrapers on September 11th. A massive wave in Asia that pummels eleven countries, leaving tens of thousands dead. A roadside bomb exploding while American soldiers hand out toys to Iraqi children on Christmas day. Thirty-three students killed by a deranged shooter on Virginia Tech's campus. A family member or friend who suffers through a long illness, or, like my son, dies unexpectedly, suddenly, and tragically.[132]

With such images come questions. Questions such as: Is God immune to our suffering? Why did he ever allow evil to enter the world in the first place? Where was he on 9/11? Why didn't he intervene and save or heal my loved one? Why doesn't he just put an end to pain and suffering? These are difficult questions for Christians to hear, even more difficult for us to give ourselves

---

132   J. P. Moreland and Tim Muehlhoff, *The God Conversation: Using Stories and Illustrations to Explain Your Faith* (Downers Grove, IL: IVP Books, 2007), 19.

freedom to ask. But where followers of Jesus will give themselves and others freedom to ask these questions, and struggle and wrestle with them, they will already be on the way toward creating an atmosphere that is a safe place, an atmosphere filled with the freedom to live authentic lives.

Only those who have not yet experienced any real pain or suffering in life are obnoxious enough to suggest there is no reason we should ever be disappointed with God. Only they would deny a person permission to feel angry with the Lord, or to express their disappointment in him. A safe-place people on the other hand will not deny people the freedom to feel whatever it is they are feeling in the midst of their pain and suffering.

Rather than trying to defend God, the first priority of Christians who are safe is to be fully present, listen carefully, and acknowledge the emotions, thoughts, and questions a hurting person is struggling with. They understand that anyone might want to scream in the face of tragedy and unfairness. Christians are not immune to this, if they are honest. For instance, as described by Moreland and Muehlhoff, one of Christianity's great defenders, C. S. Lewis, writes of his devastation when his wife, Joy, died from cancer:

> In *A Grief Observed*, Lewis lets us in on the anger and confusion he experience after his loss. "Where is God? . . . Go to him when your need is desperate, when all other help is in vain, and what do you find? A door slammed in your face, and a sound of bolting and double bolting on the inside. After that, silence. You may as well turn away."
>
> Lewis is candid in saying that he could have used a screaming room of his own. In fact, after Joy's much-prayed-for remission ends, he did yell at God. "Time after time," Lewis wrote, "when he seemed most gracious, he was preparing the next torture. . . . I wrote that last night. It was a yell rather than a thought."[133]

---

133 Ibid., 20–21 (ellipses in the original).

OUR GOD HAS BIG SHOULDERS

A people who are safe and authentic give others the freedom to shake their fist at God when they feel the need, without fear of being lectured, judged, or shamed. Why? Because a safe-place people know that our God is a God of broad shoulders. They know that the Lord is big enough to handle our being real.

Years ago there was a movie called *Islands in the Stream* based on the life of Ernest Hemingway, starring George C. Scott as Hemmingway. The movie depicts the time in Hemmingway's life when he is living on a Caribbean island, having been separated from his wife and three sons. The sons come to visit their father for the summer. The oldest son was in his late teens, the second in his mid-teens, and the youngest son was ten or eleven.

In a scene I still clearly remember decades later, the boys are on a screened-in porch that runs completely around the house. It's evening and they are beginning to fall asleep on cots Hemmingway had set up for them. A gentle summer breeze blows across the veranda as the boys lie in their beds, talking with one another. At one point the discussion suddenly breaks into a pillow fight. In walks Hemmingway and for just a moment the boys cease hitting each other, frozen in time with their pillows in launch position, and staring in trepidation at their father; but then, as if shot from a cannon, they attack him in unison. The boys hammer him with their pillows. They're striking their dad with such vigor that feathers begin to fly everywhere.

All three boys and their father are laughing as they continue to pummel one another with their fluffy weapons. With the pillows loosing all their feathers, the two oldest boys stop hitting their father and back away, but the youngest son stands right in front of Hemmingway and continues to strike. Soon all the feathers in his pillow are gone too. He drops the now empty pillowcase but continues to beat his father on the chest with his fists. He's laughing, laughing hard, but then suddenly his laughter turns into tears, his smiling face suddenly contorted in anger. Finally, the young boy's arms grow weary. He lowers them and slowly stops hitting his father and leans into him. In a scene I will never forget, rather than respond with anger, Hemmingway looks lovingly down at his son, enfolds him in his arms, and says ever so gently, "It's okay, Davey, it's okay. I understand."

So it is with our Abba Father and us. He knows we are in pain, confused, disappointed, and frustrated. He knows the world, the flesh, and the devil have had their way with us. Our Heavenly Father knows that along with the pain and the brokenness there are emotions, so many emotions, that we feel, and need to express and work through. Like Hemmingway's character in the movie, our Father understands. He is not afraid of our being real with him. He is not afraid of our disappointment, our frustration, and our anger. He loves us. He understands.

A great example of God's welcoming a real and authentic exchange is found in Numbers 11:1–17. Here we witness an encounter between Moses and God:

> And the people complained in the hearing of the Lord about their misfortunes, and when the Lord heard it, his anger was kindled and the fire of the Lord burned among them and consumed some outlying parts of the camp. Then the people cried out to Moses, and Moses prayed to the Lord, and the fire died down. So the name of that place was called Taberah, because the fire of the Lord burned among them. Now the rabble that was among them had a strong craving. And the people of Israel also wept again and said, "Oh that we had meat to eat! We remember the fish we ate in Egypt that cost nothing, the cucumbers, the melons, the leeks, the onions, and the garlic. But now our strength is dried up, and there is nothing at all but this manna to look at." Now the manna was like coriander seed, and its appearance like that of bdellium. The people went about and gathered it and ground it in hand mills or beat it in mortars and boiled it in pots and made cakes of it. And the taste of it was like the taste of cakes baked with oil. When the dew fell upon the camp in the night, the manna fell with it. Moses heard the people weeping throughout their clans, everyone at the door of his tent. And the anger of the Lord blazed

hotly, and Moses was displeased. Moses said to the Lord, "Why have you dealt ill with your servant? And why have I not found favor in your sight, that you lay the burden of all this people on me? Did I conceive all this people? Did I give them birth, that you should say to me, 'Carry them in your bosom, as a nurse carries a nursing child,' to the land that you swore to give their fathers? Where am I to get meat to give to all this people? For they weep before me and say, 'Give us meat, that we may eat.' I am not able to carry all this people alone; the burden is too heavy for me. If you will treat me like this, kill me at once, if I find favor in your sight, that I may not see my wretchedness." Then the Lord said to Moses, "Gather for me seventy men of the elders of Israel, whom you know to be the elders of the people and officers over them, and bring them to the tent of meeting, and let them take their stand there with you. And I will come down and talk with you there. And I will take some of the Spirit that is on you and put it on them, and they shall bear the burden of the people with you, so that you may not bear it yourself alone."

In this passage we witness Moses expressing his frustration and questions to God in an unfiltered manner. He doesn't hold back. He doesn't stop to clean it up so it sounded nice to God. He just shared from his heart, and God met him there. In these verses we don't hear God lecturing Moses, nor does the Lord judge or shame him. He listens. He understands. And then he responds. Our God has big shoulders.

GOD WELCOMES OUR WRESTLING WITH HIM

It's not only Moses who gets real with God in Scripture. The Psalms are full of unfettered exchanges between the psalmist and the Lord, full of the psalmist authentically putting words to his emotions, and asking the questions he needs to ask in response to what's going on in his life. Job gets real with God too. Even Jesus himself tells the Heavenly Father what he's really thinking and feeling. They all knew that God's shoulders are big enough to handle authentic expressions of disappointment and frustration in the full range of emotions he built into us. This does not scare God away. Instead, he actually welcomes it, takes advantage of it, and uses it as an opportunity to speak to us and transform us. A great example of this is the wrestling match between Jacob and the Lord. We read of it in the book of Genesis:

> But during the night he got up and took his two wives, his two maidservants, and his eleven children and crossed the ford of the Jabbok. He got them safely across the brook along with all his possessions. But Jacob stayed behind by himself, and a man wrestled with him until daybreak. When the man saw that he couldn't get the best of Jacob as they wrestled, he deliberately threw Jacob's hip out of joint. The man said, "Let me go; it's daybreak." Jacob said, "I'm not letting you go 'til you bless me." The man said, "What's your name?" He answered, "Jacob." The man said, "But no longer. Your name is no longer Jacob. From now on it's Israel (God-Wrestler); you've wrestled with God and you've come through" (Genesis 32:22–28, The Message).

Instead of resisting Jacob's challenge, the Lord welcomes it. So much so, that in the end God changes Jacob's name to mirror the new trajectory of his life, a trajectory that sets Jacob on a path to live more fully into the purposes of God than ever before. Jacob becomes Israel—one who wrestles and prevails with God.

The Bible is full of stories about those who are willing to wrestle and prevail with God. In fact, as Greg Boyd writes, "There is a strong motif running throughout Scripture that suggests that being willing to honestly struggle with God and with his word lies at the heart of true faith. God encourages his followers to raise questions and to struggle with him!"[134] God encourages a relationship such as this to the point that he renames not only Jacob, but also an entire nation, Israel—people who struggle, wrestle, and prevail with

---

134   Boyd, *The Crucifixion of the Warrior God*, 10.

God. Jacob's encounter with God was not a singular event in the Bible. Boyd reminds us,

> Many of the heroes of the faith throughout the Old Testament lived up to this name. Like Jacob, they had the courage and the integrity to challenge God when his behavior seemed "strange" and "alien" (Isaiah 28:21). Abraham, for example, was forthright in pushing back on the Almighty when he shared with him his plan to annihilate Sodom and Gomorrah (Genesis 18:23–33). Moses had enough faith to protest God's plan to annihilate his covenant people (Exodus 32:10–14). He then challenged Yahweh's expressed plan to send the Israelites into the Promised Land without him (Exodus 33:12–16). Significantly enough, far from being offended at the audacity of these challenges, God responded positively to all three, with the later two resulting in a merciful alteration of the divine plan. When God's people wrestle with him, it seems, it affects God as well as humans![135]

A safe-place people will give themselves and others freedom to wrestle with God. They will seek to create an atmosphere in which a person can question God or authentically express to him what they are really thinking and feeling, with no hint of lecturing, judgment, or shame from him. A safe-place people will understand that it is actually in wrestling with God that we can be set free and transformed, much like the scene in the movie *Forrest Gump* where an angry and hurting Lt. Dan struggles with God in the midst of a hurricane. Do you remember that scene? Lt. Dan and God go toe-to-toe in the midst of the storm. And it is only after going through the storm and engaging in an angry shouting match that Lt. Dan is able to find peace with God, with himself, and get on with the life that lays ahead of him.

God welcomes our willingness to honestly struggle and wrestle with him because in doing so, we are running to him, not away from him. It can be in the place of authentic struggle that we, like Jacob, are transformed and set upon a new path for our lives. It can be in those moments and seasons of

---

135 Ibid., 11.

great pain, disappointment, and frustration that we find ourselves standing at a crossroads. When Jacob stood at his own crossroads that night, he refused to go back. Instead he pushed through and he prevailed with God. The Lord would rather we do that than settle for a life of suppressed thoughts and feelings that looks tidy but is a life lived settling for less than what he had in store for us. He welcomes our willingness to wrestle because in the struggle we can be transformed and empowered to live lives that kick at the darkness until it bleeds daylight.

The Bible Is Full of Lament

People who create an atmosphere for authentic living make room for the role of lament. Too many Christians try to rush people to Easter while leapfrogging Holy Saturday. That is, we do not give people permission and freedom to lament and complain, and to be sad, frustrated, or angry. In his excellent book *God on Mute,* Pete Greig writes,

> How very fragile our faith must be if we can't just remain sad, scared, confused and doubting for a while. In our fear of unknowing, we leapfrog Holy Saturday and rush to the resurrection. We race disconcerted to make meaning and find beauty where there simply is none. Yet.[136]

A safe-place people realize that God himself gives this kind of freedom to people. For instance, we have the example of Job:

> I cannot keep from speaking. I must express my anguish. I must complain in my bitterness. Am I a sea monster that you place a guard on me? If I think, "My bed will comfort me, and I will try to forget my misery with sleep," you shatter me with dreams. You terrify me with visions. I would rather die of strangulation than go on and on like

---

136   Greig, *God on Mute,* 202.

this. I hate my life. I do not want to go on living. Oh, leave me alone for these few remaining days (Job 7:11–16).

God does not step in and correct Job for freely expressing his anguish. The Lord allows him to give voice to how he is really thinking and feeling. Then there is the psalmist who authentically expresses his feelings and gives voice to very real questions as part of his journey back to a position of trust in the Lord:

I cry out to God *without holding back*. Oh that God would listen to me! When I was in deep trouble, I searched for the Lord. All night long I pray, with hands lifted toward heaven, pleading. There can be no joy for me until he acts. I think of God, and I *moan, overwhelmed with longing* for his help. You don't let me sleep. I am *too distressed even to pray!* I think of the good old days, long since ended, when my nights were filled with joyful songs. I search my soul and think about the difference now. Has the Lord *rejected me* forever? Have his promises permanently failed? Has God forgotten to be kind? Has he slammed the door on his compassion? And I said, "This is my fate, that the blessings of the most high have changed to hatred." I recall all you have done, O Lord; I remember your wonderful deeds of long ago. They are constantly in my thoughts. I cannot stop thinking about them. O God, your ways are holy. Is there any God as mighty as you? You are the God of miracles and wonders [Psalm 77:1–10, emphasis mine]!

And again in Psalm 88:1–9 and 13–18:

Oh Lord, God of my salvation, I have cried out to you day and night. Now hear my prayer; listen to *my cry*. For *my life is full of troubles,* and death draws near. I have been dismissed as one who is dead, like a strong man with no strength left. They have abandoned me to death, and I am as good as dead. I am forgotten, cut off from your care. You have thrust me down to the lowest pit into the darkest depths. Your anger lies heavy on me; wave after wave engulfs me. You have caused my friends to loathe me; you have sent them all away. I am in a trap with no escape. My eyes are blinded by my tears. Each day I beg for your help, O Lord; I lift my pleading hands to you for mercy. . . . O Lord, I cry out to you. I will keep on pleading day by day. O Lord, why do you reject me? Why do you turn your face away from me? I have been sickly and close to death since my youth. I stand helpless and desperate before your terrors. Your fierce anger has overwhelmed me. Your terrors have cut me off. They swirl around me like floodwaters all day long. They have encircled me completely. You have taken away my companions and loved ones; only darkness remains [emphasis mine].

Even Jesus himself freely and authentically expressed his anguish and distress to Father God:

He took Peter and Zebedee's two sons, James and John, and he began to be filled with anguish and deep distress. He told them, "My soul is crushed with grief to the point of death. Stay here and watch with me." He went on a little farther and fell face down on the ground, praying, "My Father! If it is possible, let this cup of suffering be taken away from me. Yet I want your will, not mine" (Matthew 26:37–39).

Jesus called out with a loud voice, "Eli, Eli, lema sabacthani?" which means, "My God, my God, why have you forsaken me?" (Matthew 27:46).

In *God on Mute* Greig points out,

It is important that we learn to lament. Jesus himself was overwhelmed with sorrow, wrestled and cried out to God, begged for another plan, and allowed his friends to see that this was how he felt. Five days earlier, his shoulders had slumped, his eyes had filled with tears, and he had mourned for Jerusalem while the crowds around him partied and praised.

Lamenting is more than a technique for venting emotion. It is one of the fruits of a deepening spiritual life that has learned to stand naked before God without shame or pretense. Honest lament can express a vibrant faith; one that has learned to embrace life's hardships as well as its joy and to lift everything—everything—to the Father in prayer. As the author Richard Foster says of the lament psalms, "They give us permission to shake our fist at God one moment, and break into doxology the next."[137]

God invites us to lament to him in 1 Peter 5:7, where we read, "Cast all your cares on him for he cares for you." "But," ask some, "How do I express my lament before God? What should I say?" Pastor John Niewald shares helpful counsel in forming our laments, using the acronym CARE.[138] First, Niewald counsels us to Complain. He sites examples such as David in Psalm 13:1–5 and Heman in Psalm 88. Next, he tells us to Appeal to God's nature as he sites the example of Jehoshaphat in 2 Chronicles 20. God's is a nature of unconditional love, long suffering, and faithfulness toward us. Third, he encourages us to Remind God of what he, the Lord, has said, and he points to Jacob's prayer in Genesis 32:9–12:

> Then Jacob prayed, "O God of my grandfather Abraham and my father, Isaac—you told me to return to my land and to my relatives, and you promised to treat me kindly. I am not worthy of all the faithfulness and unfailing love, but O Lord, please rescue me from my brother, Esau. I am afraid that he is coming to kill me. But you promised to treat me kindly and to multiply my descendants."

Finally, John encourages us to Express our total trust in God, which may or may not come with the feeling that we trust him, but in faith we do. He points us to

---

137 Ibid., 84–85.

138 Used with permission from John Niewald.

Job as our example when Job declares, "Though he slay me, yet I will trust him" (Job 13:15). Each of these individuals in Scripture, as well as others, lamented before God as part of their process in dealing with the challenges and tribulations in life, and ultimately, returning to a place of faith and trust in the Lord.

PART OF A HEALTHY RELATIONSHIP

Jesus, the psalmist, and Job are among many people in Scripture who model for us the freedom to be real and authentic with what we are thinking, feeling, and experiencing. This freedom to be genuine is part of a healthy relationship with the Lord and part of the process that ultimately leads people back to a position of trust in him. To put up a false front of faith, joy, and peace when something else is really going on inside of us is to communicate to people that Christianity is a religion of hypocrisy—you cannot really be you.

A real and authentic people will not try to fix one another when we are disappointed with God. Rather, we will give one another freedom to give voice to our disappointment, and we will stand beside one another, daring to believe and trust in the Lord for those who cannot believe and trust because of what they are going through. A safe-place people will not feel the need to have all the answers or try to solve the mystery of what those who are battling disappointment with God are going through. They will know that much of the power of God is resident in his name, Emmanuel, God with us. People who are safe will know the power of presence. As Henri Nouwen has written, "The friend who can be silent with us in a moment of grief and bereavement, who can tolerate not knowing, not curing, not healing and face with us the reality of our powerlessness, that is the friend who cares."[139]

A people who can make room and give freedom for expressing our disappointment, our frustration, and our anger with God will be viewed, and experienced, as authentic. They will be the safe-place people those who are in pain run to in times of need.

---

139 See Henri Nouwen, *Out of Solitude: Three Meditations on the Christian Life* (Notre Dame, IN: Ave Maria Press, 1974) 73.

46

LIVING AN AUTHENTIC
EMOTIONAL LIFE

The gospel portrait of Jesus is that of a man exquisitely
attuned to his emotions
and uninhibited in expressing them.

— BRENNAN MANNING
A Glimpse of Jesus

Emotions are the language of the soul. They are the cry
that gives the heart a voice.

— DAN ALLENDER AND TREMPER LONGMAN
The Cry of the Soul

M AKING ROOM FOR the expression of emotion is an essential element in
creating an atmosphere of freedom for authentic living. Emotions

are central to what it means to be human. There appears to be no prohibition to their expression in the Bible, in fact, quite the contrary. In the Old Testament, and particularly in the Psalms, we see every human emotion on display: unbridled joy, peace, hope, jealousy, anger, sadness, grieving, depression, and more. The psalmist is intricately aware of what he is feeling and freely expresses his emotions in a very genuine manner. And in the Gospels, Jesus does too.

Creating an environment that gives permission to listen to our emotions and express them in a healthy manner is an important key in being a safe place. Safe-place people are able to identify and articulate their own emotions, and are able to help others grow in identifying and expressing theirs. Too often, however, Christians can knowingly or unknowingly make people feel they must fake or hide what they're truly feeling in order to belong and be accepted. When this happens it creates an atmosphere that is unsafe.

I clearly recall a time when I was made to feel this way. I was part of a church staff that included both ordained pastors and laypersons. We met weekly for devotions, personal sharing, and prayer. I still remember one such staff meeting, over twenty years later. As we sat in a circle the senior pastor asked us to share how our week had been, based on a scale of one to ten with one being terrible and ten being great. As we went around the circle people shared that their weeks had been anywhere from a seven to a nine. Evidently, we all thought that only Jesus could have a ten. When they got to me I was struggling with what to share because the days preceding our meeting had been anything but a seven-to-nine kind of week for me. The dishwasher had broken down, the computer was acting up, one of our cars had required major repairs, and to top it off, I had had a bad argument with Debi (which had been my fault). Finally I decided to just say it the way it was and told everyone, "My week has been a four at best."

Immediately from the opposite side of the circle one of our pastors spoke up with more than a hint of passion in his voice and said, "Mike, I bind that negative confession in the name of Jesus, and remind you that the apostle Paul calls us to rejoice, and again I say rejoice." Everyone was caught off guard, most of all me. I looked at him and said, "Actually pastor, my week really has been a four at best," and went on to explain why. Raising his voice with even more passion than before he exhorted me, "Don't do that. Brother, rejoice, and again I say rejoice!" "But I don't really feel like rejoicing right now," I responded, "Right or wrong, that's where I'm at today." Then, he told me, "Mike, you need to just step out in faith and declare the truth of God's Word with a rejoicing heart."

I didn't know what to say at that point. Finally, after what seemed like a long and awkward period of silence I looked at him and asked, "Pastor, do you love me?" "Of course," he replied immediately (and I believe he really did). "Okay then," I said, "If you really love me, you're going to need to just accept where I'm at this morning. If you don't, I will never dare to share what I'm really thinking or feeling with you ever again."

The silence in the room was deafening. The proverbial pin could have dropped and sounded like a clanging cymbal. Finally, the senior pastor spoke up. "You know what," he said, "I think we need to start over and go around the group again." As we did, some people still had weeks that were a seven, eight, or nine, but a few lowered their numbers. The senior pastor looked at me and said, "Thanks Mike. Thanks for giving us the gift of being real and honest with us. I want us to be like that as a staff and I want us to learn how to accept and love one another where we're really at so we can get back to a place of rejoicing."

The other pastor who had lectured me in front of the others later apologized and asked for forgiveness. Not only that, he also told me he appreciated my courage in sharing because he too had weeks that were a four at best but always felt he had to put on a fake front for the sake of others. His gifts of repentance, vulnerability, and transparency were a wonderful model for me, and because he shared with me in that way I asked him to pray for me. Wow! His ministry to me in prayer was off the charts good, so good that I remember it to this day. This was one of my first encounters in learning how important it is to have the freedom to express our feelings in a genuine manner, and how that freedom positions us to experience the transforming work of God. Christians who encourage and model that kind of freedom will be viewed and experienced as a safe place. In their presence, people will sense that they have permission to authentically be who they are, and will be more apt to genuinely acknowledge their true feelings.

THE BAD RAP ON EMOTIONS

Emotions have been given a bad rap by many Christians. Too many times we ignore what our emotions are trying to tell us and suppress them because we don't want to be known as emotional people. We've been told that's something to be avoided at all cost because emotions are dangerous and not to be trusted. And that can be true when emotions, rather than Jesus, are allowed to control our lives and rule our decision-making.

But when we're helped to find the proper place and role for emotions under the Lordship of Jesus, we discover that they are gifts from God, designed us to help us celebrate life, grieve loss, and warn us when something is not right. Emotions are messengers, and it's to our detriment if we don't learn to listen to them and express them in healthy ways. Brennan Manning writes, "Whether positive or negative, feelings put us in touch with our true selves. They are neither good nor bad; they are simply the truth of what is going on within us. What we do with them determines whether we live lives of honesty or deceit."[140] Dan Allender and Tremper Longman put it this way, "Ignoring our emotions is turning our back on reality; listening to our emotions ushers us into reality. And reality is where we meet God." In *The Cry of the Soul* they write:

> Emotions are the language of the soul. They are the cry that *gives the heart a voice*. However, we often turn a deaf ear—through emotional denial, distortion, or disengagement. We strain out anything disturbing in order to gain tenuous control of our inner world. We are frightened and ashamed of what leaks into our consciousness. In neglecting our intense emotions, we are false to ourselves and lose a wonderful opportunity to know God. We forget that change comes

---

140 Brennan Manning, *A Glimpse of Jesus: The Stranger to Self-Hatred* (San Francisco, CA: HarperSanFrancisco, 2003), Kindle ed.

through brutal honesty and vulnerability before God [emphasis mine].[141]

Learning to listen to our emotions can enable us to more accurately identify and discern reality in our lives. That in turn can then open our hearts to invite and allow God to do whatever he needs to do in us so that he can do whatever he wants to do through us.

JESUS AND EMOTIONS

Jesus is our model in all things. In his life we see humanity defined and lived at its best. Manning reminds us that humanity defined at its best in Jesus includes living an authentic emotional life. Christ clearly listened to and genuinely expressed his emotions:

> To ignore, repress, or be inattentive to our feelings is to fail to listen to the stirrings of the Spirit within our emotional structure calling us to creative response.

> Jesus listened. In John's gospel we are told that, "he was moved with the deepest emotions" (11:33). Grief, frustration, and sadness all spontaneously broke through when "he drew near and came in sight [of the city], he shed tears for it and said, if you in your turn had only understood the message of peace" (Luke 19:41). There was no trace of emotional restraint when Jesus roared, "You liars! The devil is your father and you prefer to do what your father wants" (John 8:44). When dining at Simon's house in Bethany, there was more than a hint of irritation, as he said of the woman who anointed him with costly nard, "Leave her alone. Why are you upsetting her?" (Mark 14:6). We hear utter frustration in the words, "How much longer must I put with you?" (Matthew 15:17), unmitigated rage in "Get behind me,

---

141 Dan B. Allender and Tremper Longman, III, *The Cry of the Soul: How Our Emotions Reveal Our Deepest Questions about God* (Colorado Springs, CO: NavPress, 1994), Kindle ed.

Satan! You are an obstacle in my path" (Matthew 16:23), extraordinary sensitivity in "Who touched me? I felt that power had gone out from me" (Luke 8:47), and blazing wrath in "Get them out of here! Stop turning my Father's house into a marketplace" (John 2:16).

The gospel portrait of Jesus is that of *a man exquisitely attuned to his emotions and uninhibited in expressing them.* One finds in Christ no attitude of scorn, contempt, fear, ridicule, or rejection of feelings as being fickle, flaky, and unreliable. They were sensitive emotional antennae to which He listened carefully and through which He perceived the will of His Father for congruent speech and action" [emphasis mine].[142]

As Manning wrote, Jesus was "a man exquisitely attuned to his emotions and uninhibited in expressing them." Jesus, in fact, expressed a wide-range of emotions such as the following:

- He was greatly disturbed in spirit and deeply moved and felt distress (John 11:33; Mark 3:5; Luke 12:50)
- He shed tears (John 11:33–36; Luke 19:41)
- He was angry (Mark 10:14; Mark 3:5)
- He was furious at the crass commercialism in the temple (John 2:13–17)
- He showed astonishment (Matthew 8:10; Mark 6:6; Luke 7:9)
- He had an emotional longing to be with the twelve apostles (Luke 22:15)
- He has compassion for widows, lepers, and blind men (Matthew 20:34; Mark 1:41; Luke 7:13)[143]

---

142 Manning, *A Glimpse of Jesus*, Kindle ed. (bracketed phrase in the original).
143 Ibid.

God himself models an authentic expression of emotions for us, and his example gives us permission and freedom to do the same. Peter Scazzero reminds us,

- God saw that it was very good (Genesis 1:25, 31). In other words, God delighted, relished, beamed with delight over us
- The Lord was grieved that He had made man on the earth, and His heart was filled with pain (Genesis 6:6)
- I, the Lord your God, am a jealous God (Exodus 20:5)
- For a long time I have kept silent, I have been quiet and held myself back. But now, like a woman in childbirth, I cry out, I gasp and pant (Isaiah 42:14)
- The fierce anger of the Lord will not turn back until he fully accomplishes the purposes of His heart (Jeremiah 30:24)
- I have loved you with an everlasting love; I have drawn you with loving-kindness (Jeremiah 31:3)
- How can I hand you over, Israel? My heart is changed within me; all my compassion is aroused (Hosea 11:8)
- He began to be sorrowful and troubled. Then he said to them, "My soul is overwhelmed with sorrow to the point of death" (Matthew 26:37–38)
- He looked around them in anger and, deeply distressed at their stubborn hearts, said to the man, "Stretch out your hand" (Mark 3:5)
- At that time Jesus, full of joy through the Holy Spirit (Luke 10:21)[144]

Scriptures such as these, and others, teach us that living an authentic emotional life is modeled for us by God himself, and is one of the primary characteristics of the *imago dei* in our lives. Thus, it is something to be embraced, not denied or suppressed.

---

144 Peter Scazzero, *The Emotionally Spirituality: Unleash a Revolution in Your Life in Christ* (Nashville, TN: Thomas Nelson, 2006), 70–71.

PLAYING ALL EIGHTY-EIGHT KEYS

When we mistakenly suppress our feelings and influence others to do the same, we are forced into living lives of stunted emotional growth, which in turn will hinder us from having an ability to express the full range of emotions God has built into us. When that happens, it not only has a negative impact on the individual, but also on those around him or her. We will be unable to be in touch with what we're really feeling and will be limited in the number of emotions we're able to access. This creates a combination that manifests itself in unstable and unhealthy expressions of emotion.

That certainly was the case for far too many years in my life, until that is, one of my mentors told me, "Mike, there are eighty-eight keys on a piano's keyboard. Our emotions are like that, but you only know how to play one key on your emotional keyboard. No matter what you're feeling, it only comes out one way. If you're sad, it comes out angry. If you're afraid, it comes out angry. If you're discouraged or depressed, it comes out sideways in anger. We need to help you learn how to have the freedom to play the other eighty-seven keys on your keyboard when you need to."

My mentor was right, and with his help and the help of others I began to learn to play other keys. I also learned that it's important that we allow for all eighty-eight keys to be played when needed. Not forty-four or fifty-five, but all eighty-eight. Too many Christians believe we're only allowed the freedom to play a handful of keys rather than having permission to access and play all eighty-eight. For instance, many, if not most, Christians encourage the playing of emotional keys such as love, joy, and peace while withholding permission to play others. They mistakenly discourage the expression of keys such as anger, frustration, depression, disappointment, and sadness.

However, this is not a biblical perspective, nor is it healthy. When those emotions are present they are trying to tell us something or alert us to some danger. We need to listen to them and to hear what they are trying to communicate. When we suppress them we're robbed of a gift from God and are experienced as people who are living in denial and are inauthentic as persons. It gives life to the stereotype that followers of Jesus are superficial and even phony, rather than real and authentic.

A safe-place people will allow the freedom to express a full range of keys on our emotional piano—even when we don't always express them in healthy ways. We're safe when we remain committed to loving one another, even while we are expressing our feelings in unhealthy and unrighteous ways. We're safe when we're committed to not rejecting or discarding one another even while our emotions are coming out sideways, that is, when we are taking our feelings out on those around us rather than with the person or persons who we're really struggling with. However, we also make it a safe place for each other when we set healthy boundaries so we do not allow an unhealthy expression of emotions to become an ongoing pattern in our lives. Not calling one another to account when we are habitually unhealthy in our expression of feelings is actually an unloving thing to do because it robs us of the opportunity to be of real help to one another, and leaves the person who is struggling stuck in patterns of living that put them and others in harm's way. It makes us unsafe rather than safe.

A person, small group, or congregation who are growing in being a safe place will make room for a healthy expression of the full range of emotions. This is modeled for us in Scripture, particularly in the book of Psalms. Growing more healthy and mature in our awareness and expression of what we are feeling will play a role not only in our transformation into a greater degree of Christ likeness, but in equipping us for the kingdom assignments God has for us to carry out. Ask the Lord how he wants to help you become more healthy and whole in this aspect of your life.

We all need help along our journey in following Jesus. Seek out a mature Christian friend, a trustworthy counselor, or a gifted inner healing prayer minister, or all of the above. Seek them out, examine where you are presently in your awareness and expression of emotions. Process with them where you are and how you would like to grow and mature. Then go after it. If you do, it will increase your capacity to create an atmosphere of freedom for authentic living and enable you to be experienced by others as someone, who, like Jesus, can be a safe place.

47

AUTHENTIC AND APPROPRIATE
VULNERABILITY

Without the willingness to be vulnerable we will not be able to live
as authentic persons. And without the freedom to be who we really
are we will never experience a transformation that empowers us to
think, speak, and act more like Jesus.

A WILLINGNESS TO be appropriately vulnerable is an essential key in creating an atmosphere of freedom for authentic living. Nationally recognized author and researcher Brene Brown identified this characteristic while researching the impact of shame on people's lives. While conducting her research Brown noticed that people who were living emotionally healthy lives all modeled an appropriate vulnerability. She refers to such people as the "Wholehearted" in her book *Daring Greatly*. She writes,

> Wholehearted living is about engaging in our lives from a place of
> worthiness. . . . The Wholehearted identify vulnerability as the

catalyst for courage, compassion, and connection. In fact, the willingness to be vulnerable emerged as the single clearest value shared by all of the women and men whom I would describe as Wholehearted. They attribute everything—from their professional success to their marriages to their proudest parenting moments—to their ability to be vulnerable.[145]

What Brown recognized in the lives of the Wholehearted is true for Christians who want to be healthy followers of Jesus, because without the willingness to be vulnerable we will not be able to live as authentic persons. And without the freedom to be who we really are we will never experience a transformation that empowers us to think, speak, and act more like Jesus. Furthermore, not only will we be incapable of living authentic lives ourselves, we will not be able to give others the freedom to be genuinely who they are either. Thus, appropriate vulnerability is a critical component for creating an atmosphere of freedom for authentic living and transformation.

To be vulnerable is to be capable of being wounded, and open to attack or assault. Being vulnerable in an authentic manner involves a willingness to expose the reality of who we are in order to help others, even at the risk of people assaulting and wounding us with our own information. However, it's a risk we must take if we're to experience living as fully as possible into God's purposes for our lives.

A COST TO BE COUNTED

There is a cost to be counted in becoming someone who has the ability and willingness to be appropriately vulnerable. That cost is to accept God's work of brokenness in our lives. We all must be broken in order to live authentically vulnerable lives. We are sinful and broken human beings who live in a fallen—and in many ways corrupt—world. Living in such a world teaches us at an early age how to protect ourselves from the hurt others can inflict upon

---

145 Brene Brown, *Daring Greatly: How the Courage to Be Vulnerable Transforms the Way We Live, Love, Parent, and Lead* (New York: Penguin Group US, 2012), 10–12.

us. Unfortunately, adopting various defense mechanisms to keep ourselves from feeling pain also keeps us from experiencing emotions such as love, joy, and peace, blessings that living an appropriately vulnerable life can bring.

Defense mechanisms serve like the hard shell of a coconut. In order to get to the sweet fruit within, the shell must be broken open. It is the same way in our lives. In this sense, while uncomfortable and even painful, brokenness is a good thing and the cost is worth being counted. Pastor-author Graeme Sellers reminds us that, "the real work of brokenness as understood in Scripture is to bring us into deeper union with God so he can work through us regardless of our situation."[146] It is only in a deeper, more intimate relationship with the Lord that God can help us build the granite-strong foundation of love and a settled sense of identity that enables us to dare making ourselves vulnerable and transparent with others.

JESUS WAS APPROPRIATELY VULNERABLE

Jesus was appropriately vulnerable. He modeled this in many passages of Scripture. For instance, we read in Matthew 26:37–38, "He took Peter and the two sons of Zebedee along with him, and he began to be sorrowful and troubled. Then he said to them, 'my soul is overwhelmed with sorrow to the point of death. Stay here and keep watch with me.'" Jesus did not hide the sorrow he was feeling behind some false sense of bravado and faith. He didn't put on a mask and try to reflect a false sense of strength and confidence. Instead, he openly expressed his emotional turmoil in front of his friends. Jesus, in a word, made himself vulnerable to Peter and the sons of Zebedee.

Could Peter and the others have run to the rest of the disciples and exposed Jesus' vulnerability? Could they have told the others about Jesus struggling with what God was calling him to, and even use this information against him to sow seeds of discord and try to sabotage his leadership? Yes, they could have, but they didn't. Instead, they were good stewards of his gift of

---

146 Graeme Sellers, *You Never Know*, a sermon shared at Wonderful Mercy Church, (Gilbert, AZ, July 2014).

transparency. This in turn gave them a model and permission to be appropriately vulnerable in their own lives.

Examples of transparency from the life of Jesus, and from the lives of others, can be a source of encouragement and inspiration for us to follow their lead. For instance, this story from author John Ortberg had just such an impact on me:

> When I look in on my children as they sleep at night, I think of the kind of father I want to be. . . . I look in on them as they sleep and I remember how the day really went: I remember how they were trapped in a fight over checkers and I walked out of the room because I didn't want to spend the energy needed to teach them how to resolve conflict. I remember how my daughter spilled cherry punch at dinner and I yelled at her about being careful. . . . I yelled at her—to tell the truth—simply because I'm big and she's little and I can get away with it. And then I saw that look of hurt and confusion in her eyes, and I knew there was a tiny wound on her heart that I had put there, and I wished I could have taken those sixty seconds back."[147]

As I read this story I found myself wanting to be strong enough to admit when I've failed, as Ortberg did, and when appropriate, to be willing to share my failings as a means of teaching and encouraging others. This is just one example of the impact that a willingness to be appropriately vulnerable when God calls us to can have in the lives of others.

POTENTIAL FOR DANGER

While it's good and right that we affirm the important role vulnerability has in creating an atmosphere of freedom for authentic living, it's also important we note the potential for danger. When we humbly share the reality of who we are with others, there is the potential for them to misinterpret what we

---

147 John Ortberg, *The Life You've Always Wanted* (Grand Rapids, MI: Zondervan, 1997), Kindle ed.

share, or even use it against us. Therefore, it's important we seek to be wise and follow the leading of the Holy Spirit in deciding when and to whom we dare to make ourselves vulnerable. It is also essential that we grow in discerning how much of our stories we choose to share.

There is potential for danger because not everyone is a good steward of our gift of vulnerability. When someone is in bondage to legalism, generally insecure, and jealous, or has never seen a healthy transparency modeled, they can be poor stewards of what we have shared with them. They may use the information to feed their own egos or even sabotage us. It is important therefore that we learn to not be too quick in sharing openly with some people, while on the other hand daring to make ourselves vulnerable when we sense it is the right person, time, and place to do so.

Growing in this wisdom is a process. There may be times you choose to share with someone and they hurt you by responding in a judgmental and condemning way, or by using the information against you. Take the time to reflect on those experiences and learn from them what you can. Also, be sure to ask God for the grace to forgive those who were not good stewards of your gift. You do not want to be stuck in unforgiveness. That's not healthy for you. Also, ask yourself if there is something more you can learn about hearing the guidance of the Holy Spirit in your decision-making. Seek out mature Christians who have a proven track record in hearing and following the leading of Holy Spirit and process your thoughts and questions with them.

GREAT POTENTIAL AND POWER

While there is certainly potential for danger, there is also blessing and power in learning when, where, and how to be appropriately vulnerable and transparent. You can be the vessel through which God imparts courage and hope to those who are drowning in a sea of discouragement and hopelessness. When this is a person's present reality and they encounter someone who can not only relate to where they are but are willing to make themselves vulnerable by sharing their own story, it can be just the thing they need to stay afloat.

Your transparency can be the way God brings his healing, sustaining, and transforming power to bear on their lives.

This ability of God to redeem our stories and use them for good in the lives of others has certainly been the case in my life in multiple instances. One of those is when the Lord calls me to share the story of my journey through the worst nightmare of a parent's life—the sudden and tragic death of our oldest son, Andrew Michael, on his eighteenth birthday. I do not easily or often share the story. I try to listen for the prompting of Holy Spirit before I choose to share it. However, whenever I have, God imparts renewed hope to those I share it with as they hear of God's goodness and faithfulness, and his ability to redeem and restore in the wake of even the most horrific moments of our lives. It reminds them the Lord is present with them, and is for them, in those very moments when it feels like he is absent at best, or abusive at worst.

God has greatly comforted my family and me through the presence of authentically vulnerable people in our lives. It is a privilege to now share with others the comfort with which we've been comforted. As we learn to choose wisely when to be authentically vulnerable before others, we can impart hope, courage, and freedom. As we do, we help create an atmosphere of freedom for others to live authentically vulnerable lives too.

VULNERABILITY IN THE LIVES OF LEADERS

This can be especially true when leaders choose to exercise appropriate vulnerability and transparency. One such example comes from the life of a member of the national leadership team for the Alliance of Renewal Churches. One Sunday he was preaching on the topic of debilitating fear. However, he chose to not just preach it, he intentionally chose to share how he had been gripped by an irrational fear the previous week. Members of his congregation, or even other Christians in the community where he lives and listen via podcast, could have easily used his testimony against him. They could have accused him of not having enough faith, and of being weak and ineffective as a leader.

However, after daring to share his story, he was approached by many of the church's members who told him he had put words to their experience, and for this they were grateful. His choice to make himself vulnerable that Sunday created an atmosphere of freedom for his congregation and others in the community to believe it would be okay for them to follow suit. In this particular instance what he modeled for them gave many people a renewed sense of hope. And in addition, a number of them felt led to pray with one another to be set free from the bondage of fear that had enveloped them. They did pray for each other that day and many were set free. That is the power of appropriate vulnerability and transparency at work in and through the life of a leader when he or she models these things for others.

A LIVING EXPRESSION OF BIBLICAL TRUTH

The reason such openness can be powerful in people's lives is that it is an expression of the biblical truth that when we are weak, God can be strong. The apostle Paul articulates this well when he writes, "'My grace is sufficient for you, for my power is made perfect in weakness.' Therefore I will boast all the more gladly of my weaknesses, so that the power of Christ may rest upon me" (2 Corinthians 12:9, ESV). Scripture passages such as this help establish a much needed theology of weakness for our lives, which is a very important part of the foundation for cultivating an atmosphere of freedom for authentic living.

Paul wrote almost half the books of the New Testament and expanded Christianity in the first century in a way that remains unsurpassed to this day. Even so, his authority and position as an apostle were seriously challenged on more than one occasion. One such instance took place in the city and church of Corinth. "Super-apostles" had come there with a ministry of signs and wonders. They also spoke of revelations and experiences with God. Claiming a special, unique authority from God, they gradually drew the congregation's loyalty to themselves and away from Paul.

In 2 Corinthians 12, Paul argued for the authenticity of his leadership not by appealing to his own visions and revelations from God, nor to his successes and gifts in ministry, but instead he pointed to his weaknesses. Why? Because Paul believed that being weak and not trusting in our own abilities and strengths gave God freedom to be powerful in and through us. Making his appeal in such a manner was a powerful example of a leader choosing to be vulnerable and transparent rather than dig in and protect himself.

In other places, Paul chose to make himself vulnerable as he established a foundation for his authority and leadership by identifying all he had suffered for the Lord (see 2 Corinthians 11:16–33), not by listing all of his great victories. He was openly transparent about his feelings (2 Corinthians 2:4, 6:11–12), frustrations (2 Corinthians 2:12, 5:3–4), failures (2 Corinthians 4:7–9), fears (2 Corinthians 7:5), fights (2 Corinthians 7:5), and frailty (2 Corinthians 1:8, 12:7–10). Paul also made his heart vulnerable to others in passages such as Acts 20:22–24; Romans 7:7–25; 1 Corinthians 4:11–13; 2 Corinthians 1:8–11, 6:3–10, 11:5–12, 11:21–33, 12:1–10; and Philippians 3:4–10, 3:13–14, 4:10–20.

In sharing his weaknesses and sufferings, Paul knowingly opened himself up to attack from others, and some did attack. But his vulnerability also imparted courage, freedom, and hope to many people in Corinth, and his example continues to do the same for us today.

THE BLESSING OF CRACKED POTS

Like Paul, we all have weaknesses, and have experienced some form of hardship and suffering. We are not perfect. We are, as it were, vessels that are sometimes cracked and leaking. However, cracked pots can be a source of great power and blessing, as illustrated in the following story:

There once lived a water carrier in India. He used two large pots for his task. He suspended a pole across his neck and attached a pot at each end of the pole. One of the pots had a big crack in it while the other pot was perfect. The perfect pot always delivered a full portion of water from the stream to the master's house, while the cracked pot arrived only half full each day.

For two years this water carrier made the same journey. The perfect pot became proud of its accomplishments. The cracked pot was ashamed of its imperfection and miserable that it was able to accomplish only half of what it had been made to do. Finally, one day by the stream, the cracked pot spoke to his owner about his bitter failure, "I am ashamed of myself, and I want to apologize that I have only been able to deliver half my water to your house. There is a crack in my side that causes water to leak out. Because of my flaws, you don't get full value from your efforts.

Then the water carrier replied, smiling, "As we return to the master's house, I want you to notice the beautiful flowers along the path." On that trip from the stream, the cracked pot looked around.

"Did you notice there are flowers only on your side of the path, but not on the other pot's side?" the master commented. "That's because I have always known about your flaw, and I took advantage of it. I planted seeds on your side of the path, and every day while we passed these spots, you watered them. Now for two years I have been able to pick those beautiful flowers to decorate my master's table. Without you being just the way you are, I would not have this beauty to grace his house."[148]

God has always used cracked pots. In 2 Corinthians 4:7 Paul says,

But we have this treasure in jars of clay, to show that the surpassing power belongs to God and not to us. We are afflicted in every way, but not crushed; perplexed, but not driven to despair; persecuted, but not forsaken; struck down, but not destroyed; always carrying in the body the death of Jesus so that the life of Jesus may also be manifested in our bodies.

Scripture shows us time and time again how God works in the world through those who are imperfect and do not have it all together. These are people such as Moses who stuttered, had a short fuse, and was a murderer. David's armor didn't fit, he was too young, and he had an affair, murdered, and abused power. Hosea's

---

148 Sacinanda Swami, *Wisdom Stories*, "The Cracked Pot," http://www.sacinandanaswami.com/en/s1a38/wisdom-stories/the-cracked-water-pot.html (accessed December 2, 2014).

wife was a prostitute. Amos's only training was farming (no prophetic training or degree at all). Jacob was a habitual liar and cheat. Jonah ran away from God's will for his life. Gideon and Thomas both wrestled with doubt. Jeremiah battled depression and Elijah suffered from burnout. And Martha was beset by worry. All these people had weaknesses and imperfections, yet the power of God was strong through them. All these people were cracked pots. So are you and I.

Authentic Christian living is not about having it all together, always living in victory, always being full of faith and joy. It can include all those things, but authentic Christian living also includes our ongoing struggles with sin, doubts, questions, and most especially our failings and weaknesses. Authentic Christian living is about having people who we can be honest with about such things. This requires an atmosphere in which we can be appropriately vulnerable and transparent with at least a few trusted, mature friends and authority figures.

BE CAREFUL WHO YOU ARE VULNERABLE WITH

Many of us are afraid of being vulnerable, and rightly so at times. We're afraid others will ostracize us or use our vulnerability against us. Some people will. There are some who say you should always let it all hang out and never have an unexpressed thought or feeling. This is neither wise, nor biblical. There is a time to be deliberately selective about what we reveal and to whom we reveal it. It's important to know we have the responsibility and freedom to make that choice, and for good reason.

There will be people with whom you should always remain guarded. Proverbs 20:19 says, "A gossip can never keep a secret; be careful around people who talk too much." There is a time and place for selective communication. People who consistently make judgmental statements, give premature advice, or violate confidences are definitely people to beware of.

On the other hand, there are those with whom it is not only appropriate, but a blessing to be open with because such openness is an important and necessary key to developing more intimate relationships. Vulnerability and transparency are essential elements in the deeper relationships we hunger for. John Ortberg tells us, "One of the great writers on friendship, a twelfth-century English abbot named Aelred of Rievaulx, wrote that we owe love to all people, but only to a proven friend are we to entrust 'the secrets of the heart.'"[149] In relationships that are safe we can dare to entrust others with the secrets of the heart, and as we do, we will experience God's work of encouragement, healing, and transformation.

We all need such relationships because each one of us is, as Brennan Manning writes, a bundle of paradoxes and it is only in the context of relationships where it is safe to be vulnerable that we can be helped to process and work through the paradoxical puzzle that is us. Manning captures this sense that is true of every one of us when he writes,

> When I get honest, I admit I am a bundle of paradoxes. I believe and I doubt, I hope and get discouraged, I love and I hate, I feel bad about feeling good, I feel guilty about not feeling guilty. I am trusting and suspicious. I am honest and I still play games. . . . [However,] to live by grace means to acknowledge my whole life story, the light side and the dark. In admitting my shadow side I learn who I am and what God's grace means. As Thomas Merton put it, "A saint is not someone who is good but who experiences the goodness of God.[150]

We need a family and community of safe-place people to whom we can talk out loud, just as Manning has done here. We need people with whom we can be real about the bundle of paradoxes that make us who we are.

VULNERABLE AND TRANSPARENT ABOUT THE GOOD STUFF TOO

Being vulnerable and transparent does not only involve being real about our pain and our weaknesses. It also includes having people in our lives with

---

149 Ortberg, *Everybody's Normal Till You Get To Know Them*, Kindle ed.

150 Brennan Manning, *The Ragamuffin Gospel: Good News for the Bedraggled, Beat-Up, and Burnt Out* (Sisters, OR: Multnomah Books, 1990), 23.

whom we can be real and authentic about our joys and our successes. In fact, one characteristic of a person who is emotionally whole and healthy is that they are genuinely able to celebrate with someone else even while they themselves may not have much to celebrate.

One of the memorable gifts I've been given in life was a friend's joy for Debi and me when we moved from Minneapolis to Gilbert, Arizona (a suburb of Phoenix). It was a season of improbable provision from the Lord in our lives. My friend genuinely rejoiced and celebrated with me during this season even though he was in a long season of waiting for the very provision God was showering upon us. He is still waiting as I write this. However, that did not stop him from making my joy complete. I have no doubt he too is going to experience that improbable provision from God one day, and when he does, I'll get to celebrate with him. But in the meantime, he did not wait until he had his provision to be truly happy for me. A friend like that is a friend worth having.

SOME HELPFUL BOUNDARIES

If we want to create an atmosphere of freedom for an expression of healthy and authentic vulnerability we would be wise to recognize and set some boundaries, such as the following:

1. There are situations in which caution makes sense, such as times when your confession of vulnerability and transparency may cause young believers to be tempted in their faith. Don't misunderstand: young people want—and need—to experience transparency in their leaders, but this is not synonymous with graphic detail. Do not be quick to make yourself vulnerable with young people, and when you feel you must, be wise in the amount and content of the material you share with them.
2. The motivation of vulnerability and transparency is important: Our culture teaches people to be candid and blunt. Entire television shows are built around people being this way with one another. But this motivation usually revolves around self-centeredness—you have a right to express

your true feelings and your rage, and in doing so to exact revenge on those who have hurt you. Instead, the Christian way to approach vulnerability and transparency is to realize our candidness should be motivated by a desire to have a pure heart before God and others. So slow down, and ask God to help you examine your heart and motivations for wanting to express yourself in vulnerable and transparent ways. One of the ways he may help you is by leading you to share some of your story with a trusted, mature Christian friend or leader. However, if you choose to do this, do not go with your mind already made up as to what you are going to do, or you will simply find yourself rationalizing and spiritualizing why you are not going to heed their counsel.

3. Don't encourage expressions of vulnerability to feed a person's insecurity or unhealthy need to be needed: It is not healthy when a person makes themselves vulnerable to each person they come in contact with, or are constantly making themselves vulnerable. This can be a signal of legitimate, unmet needs for affirmation and significance that they are trying to have met in an illegitimate manner.

4. Don't allow the freedom to be vulnerable to be used as a way to justify or spiritualize misbehavior: Another form of inauthentic vulnerability is attacking another person personally and then justifying it by saying, "well I'm just being authentic." We are not given permission to attack one another verbally and emotionally in this way. If it happens and the other person is very understanding and quick to forgive that will be helpful, but it still does not give us permission to do this.

An atmosphere of freedom for authentic vulnerability can be like a fresh breath of air in a world in which so many people have only experienced inauthentic expressions of vulnerability, or no vulnerability at all. Christians who are able to be authentically and appropriately vulnerable will be a safe-place people who can help create and nurture an atmosphere of freedom for authentic living for themselves and others.

48

CREATING A SAFE PLACE TO FAIL

Far better it is to dare mighty things, to win glorious triumphs even though checkered by failure, than to rank with those poor spirits who neither enjoy nor suffer much because they live in the gray twilight that knows neither victory nor defeat.

— PRESIDENT THEODORE ROOSEVELT

AN ATMOSPHERE OF freedom for authentic living must include the freedom to fail. A safe-place people are intentional in developing an environment in which it is safe to fail, an environment in which a person can fail but is not identified as a failure. Creating this kind of atmosphere can give people the courage to take Holy Spirit-led risks. And taking those kinds of risks is critical in the process of developing healthy disciples and leaders who are able to live as fully as possible into God's purposes for their lives.

How often have you heard the following question used as a means to encourage people to embrace challenge and risk failing: "If money was no issue, and the possibility of failure was erased, what would you attempt to achieve?"

I've been asked that question many times over my thirty-plus years in ministry. However, I've begun to wonder if better questions might be: "If your perception and response to failure were changed what would you attempt to achieve? Or, what dreams that you've had would you dare to go after if you felt differently about failure?" Just imagine what we might attempt and how we might live if our view of failing was changed. What impact might it have on our lives if our minds were renewed concerning failure in general, and how we believe God views it in particular? I believe it just might inspire us to take the Holy Spirit-led risks that the Lord calls us to take.

My First Attempt in Risking Failure

In 1979 I was given the Regional Manager of the Year award in the Zondervan Family Bookstore group, a nationwide chain of Christian bookstores. I was so successful that year that I completely paid off my wife's college loans with my bonus check. Business was good and I was rising quickly in the ranks.

However, while this was happening God was at work birthing a passion in me to help connect teenagers with Jesus. I had been serving as a volunteer in the youth ministry at church, and my joy in that ministry was growing. Even as my success in business was on the rise, Debi and I were sensing what we thought might be a call from God to take the position of youth pastor at our small church, a congregation of 125 members and only four teens.

Debi's father had been the pastor of this church and we had dreamed of working together. Then suddenly, he died from a heart attack in 1980. After a time of grieving and going through a search process, the church had called and hired a new pastor, a returning missionary from Bangladesh. The new pastor told the call committee and the elders of the church that he believed God wanted to raise up a strong youth ministry in this small church, but that this was not an area of gifting or passion for him. So, if they were going to hire him they needed to hire a youth minister also. After much prayer and discussion, this small congregation decided to take a risk and issue a call to someone for this position, believing that God would provide finances that were not presently available. This meant the person they called would also need to have faith in God's provision for that which was not yet visible. The person they chose to make this offer to was me.

Of course the salary they were able to offer was a small fraction of what I had made that last year I worked for the Zondervan Corporation. However, God is good. He was so good that he made it very clear in a number of different ways to my wife and me that this was a Holy Spirit-led risk he wanted us to take. The Lord spoke to us so many times in so many different ways that leaving the bookstore business and becoming a youth pastor became the thing we could not, not do.

One of the ways I heard God speak during this time was through a thought I had while praying one day. It was a thought that carried a certain weight to it, so much so that I felt compelled to share it with Debi. The thought was this: *I would rather you risk failing than fail to take the risk*. Now, looking back over thirty-six years of God's provision and blessing, it's easy to see that was in fact God speaking to us. At the time however, it stirred up a whole range of emotions for both Debi and me. It was exciting and scary at the same time. In the end, we became so convinced this was God's call upon our lives that we said yes to the invitation from the little church outside of Omaha to become their first-ever youth pastor. By the way, in that little church God grew the youth group from four to over forty kids in a year, while also adding an additional number of young adults who served as volunteer youth staff members alongside of me. Many of those teens and young adults are serving the Lord in churches and ministries in the United States and around the world today.

Making a move like that felt like a risk at the time, and on the surface may have appeared to be unreasonable. After all, who leaves a salary and job trajectory like the one I was on with Zondervan? Many people overly spiritualize something like this and say it was really no risk at all because God was in control. Yes, he was. However, when you are the one leaving behind an almost six-figure salary for a fraction of that amount, it feels risky. In the end, of course, God made it clear that it was a risk he wanted us to take, and looking back we are glad that we did. We have never regretted saying yes to God's call.

In our minds God had called us to move on from the bookstore to the youth ministry in that little church. We became convinced that moving on with God when he calls us was the best thing to do, even though it may involve a risk of failing in some way, shape, or form. Moving on with God even in the face of potential failure and even though it may seem unreasonable to some has always been characteristic of people who follow God. As Brennan Manning writes, "The reality of a Christian is that of men or women who leave what is nailed down, obvious, and secure and who walk into the desert without rational explanations to justify their decisions or to guarantee their future. Why? Solely and simply because God signals this movement and offers it His promise."[151] A distinctive characteristic of those who follow God's call on their lives has always been a willingness to risk failing rather than failing to take the risk.

TO NOT RISK FAILING IS TO CHOOSE TO REMAIN BARREN

If we choose to not risk failing when we think God is calling us to take that risk, we are making a choice to remain barren. This was the choice set before Abram and Sarai. There came a time when they were called to move on with God. He called them to leave the place they knew and in which others knew them, and to move on with no clear destination or reasonable sense of purpose in mind.

The call is recorded in Genesis 12:1–3: "The Lord had said to Abram, 'Leave your native country, your relatives, and your father's family, and go to the land that I will show you. I will make you into a great nation. I will bless you and make you famous, and you will be a blessing to others.'" Walter Brueggemann writes, "The speech of God to this barren family, then, is a call to abandonment, renunciation, and relinquishment. It is a call for a dangerous departure from the presumed world of norms and security. . . . But notice, the summons is not law or discipline, but promise. The narrative knows that such departure from securities is the only way out of

---

151 Manning, *A Glimpse of Jesus*, 16.

barrenness. . . . *To stay in safety is to remain barren; to leave in risk is to have hope*" (emphasis mine).[152]

Genesis 11:30 seems like a "throw away" line in that chapter's long litany but it provides a powerful context for this call of God on Abram and Sarai's lives in chapter twelve. Sarai was "unable to become pregnant and had no children" (NLT). Sarai was barren. If Abram and Sarai had chosen safety and had refused to risk failing, as Brueggemann wrote, they would have remained barren.

How many of us make that very choice yet today? Oh, we've made the choice to say yes to Jesus as Savior and Lord, receiving gratefully his gift of eternal life. Often however, we then settle into a comfortable, even complacent way of living Christian lives. We live comfortably, never knowing what else Jesus may have had in store for us, things that we would not allow ourselves to believe or to dare to take a risk for. What Brueggemann says of Abram can be true for the community of God's people today—to stay in safety when God is calling us to take a risk is to remain barren! And it is not God's heart for us as a church that we remain barren, but rather that we be fruitful and multiply (see John 15:1–8).

God would rather we risk failing than fail to take the risk when he calls us, so that we will not remain barren but instead experience the work he wants to do in us and through us so we are a source of blessing to others. Creating a place where it is safe to fail can provide the relational element of courage we all need in order to take the Holy Spirit-led risks God wants us to take.

Being a safe place does not mean we will be safe from danger or disappointment. Jesus said, "In this world you will have trouble" (see John 16:33). Jesus himself willingly walked into danger on our behalf, and at the time it appeared that he had failed. It may have seemed that way, but God is so powerful and so good that he can cause something incredible to rise from the ashes of what looks like failure in our lives.

---

152 Walter Brueggemann, *Genesis* (Louisville, KY: Westminster John Knox Press, 1982), 118.

Being a safe place does not mean we will be safe from failure, adversity, and harm. It does mean that when we encounter these situations, we are surrounded by a band of brothers and sisters who will still be for us and against anything that harms us. It does mean God, whose love is unshakable, unconditional, and extravagant, still and always loves us. And it does mean he loves us with a love that appears scandalous to many when he chooses to stay with us, and use us for his good purposes even though the failures we have experienced are due to our own poor decisions.

DON'T SIMPLY BE FOOLISH

While we do want to create a place where it is safe to take Holy Spirit-led risks, we need to realize there is a difference between taking a Holy Spirit-led risk and simply being foolish.

> A man appeared before St. Peter at the Pearly Gates. "Have you ever done anything of particular merit?" St. Peter asked. "Well, I can think of one thing," the man offered. "Once, on a trip to the Black Hills out in South Dakota, I came upon a gang of bikers, who were threatening a young woman. I directed them to leave her alone, but they wouldn't listen. So, I approached the largest and most heavily tattooed biker and smacked him on the head, kicked his bike over, ripped out his nose ring, and threw it on the ground. I yelled, 'Now, back off!! Or you'll answer to me!'" St. Peter was impressed, "When did this happen?" "Just a couple minutes ago."[153]

Jesus had the wisdom to discern between the two and at times chose to avoid taking certain risks. John 10:39 and 11:53–54 tell us of times Jesus chooses not to walk through a crowd rather than risk taking them on. In the book of

---

153   Found at Zen of My Cat, http://zenofmycat.blogspot.com/2006/10/man-appeared-before-st-peter-at-pearly.html. See also John Ortberg, *If You Want to Walk on Water You Have to Get Out of the Boat* (Grand Rapids, MI: Zondervan, 2001).

Acts we read of the apostle Paul choosing to leave a city when his life is in harm's way rather than foolishly standing his ground (see Acts 17:10).

There are times when God's wisdom is to take unnecessary risks and place others or us in the path of adversity and in harm's way. The key is discerning between a risk that is truly being led by the Holy Spirit and one that is of our own design. This is why we need a band of brothers and sisters to journey with, men and women who can help us discern between the two. This is why Proverbs 15:22 tells us, "Without counsel plans fail, but with many advisers they succeed" (ESV). And in Proverbs 20:18 we read, "Plans succeed through good counsel; don't go to war without wise advice" (NLT). Learn to discern the type of risk by cultivating your relationship with the Lord, learning to hear his voice, and surrounding yourself with wise truth-tellers.

REDEFINING FAILURE

A people who are growing in what it means to be a safe place will help one another develop an ability and willingness to take Holy Spirit-led risks by helping each other distinguish between being a failure and failing; the two are not automatically the same. For a people who are safe, failing is not the worst thing that can happen to a Christian. Failing to learn from failure however can be. Furthermore, failing does not make one a failure; this is not an issue of identity for safe-place people.

To learn from failing requires redefining what we perceive it to be. This involves understanding the difference between "failing backward" as John Maxwell puts it, or "failing forward." Failing forward is part of the process of succeeding and is viewed as a positive, not a negative, a sign of strength not weakness. Maxwell contrasts the two in the following manner:

Failing Backward	Failing Forward
Blaming Others	Taking Responsibility
Repeating the Same Mistakes	Learning from Each Mistake
Expecting Never to Fail Again	Knowing Failure Is a Part of Progress

Expecting to Continually Fail	Maintaining a Positive Attitude
Accepting Tradition Blindly	Challenging Outdated Assumptions
Being Limited by Past Mistakes	Taking New Risks
Thinking *I am a Failure*	Believing Something Didn't Work
Quitting	Persevering[154]

The apostle Peter was one who "failed forward." Ortberg points this out in *If You Want to Walk on Water You Have to Get Out of the Boat:*

Did Peter fail?

Well, I suppose in a way he did. His faith wasn't strong enough. His doubts were stronger. "He saw the wind." He took his eyes off of where they should have been. He sank. He failed.

But here is what I think. I think there were eleven bigger failures sitting in the boat. They failed quietly. They failed privately. Their failure went unnoticed, unobserved, criticized. Only Peter knew the shame of public failure.

But only Peter knew two other things as well. Only Peter knew the glory of walking on the water. He alone knew what it was to *attempt to do what he was not capable of doing on his own.* . . . .And only Peter knew the glory of being lifted up by Jesus in a moment of desperate need. Peter knew, in a way the others could not, that when he sank, Jesus would be wholly adequate to save him. . . . The worst failure is not to sink in the waves. The worst failure is to never get out of the boat [emphasis mine].[155]

---

154 John Maxwell, *Failing Forward: Turning Mistakes into the Stepping Stone of Success* (Nashville, TN: Thomas Nelson Publishers, 2000), 8.

155 Ortberg, *If You Want to Walk on Water*, 23.

A people who are safe will applaud when we, like Peter, get out of the boat, even if we fail in the process. A people who are safe will help us redefine what it means to fail and will still be there to help us process and learn from our failures. They will help us truly believe that failing does not mean we are a failure.

FAILING DOES NOT MEAN WE ARE FAILURES

Failing does not mean we are failures. Thomas Edison once said, "Many of life's failures are people who did not realize how close they were to success."[156] Succumbing to failure may simply be, as Edison's points out, giving up without realizing how close we are to success. Maxwell writes,

> Every successful person is someone who failed, yet never regarded himself as a failure. For example, Wolfgang Mozart, one of the geniuses of musical composition, was told by Emperor Ferdinand that his opera *The Marriage of Figaro* was "far too noisy" and contained "far too many notes." Artist Vincent van Gogh, whose paintings now set records for the sums they bring at auction, sold only one painting in his lifetime. Thomas Edison, the most prolific inventor in history, was considered unteachable as a youngster. And Albert Einstein, the greatest thinker of our time, was told by a Munich schoolmaster that he would "never amount to much."[157]

History is filled with men and women who failed but were not failures. Abraham Lincoln was such a person:

- He lost his job in 1832
- He was defeated for the legislature in 1832
- He failed in business in 1833
- He was elected to the legislature in 1834

---

156 Thomas Edison, quoted in Maxwell, *Failing Forward*, 21.
157 Maxwell, 21.

- He suffered the loss of his sweetheart, who died in 1835
- He suffered a nervous breakdown in 1836
- He was defeated for speaker of the state legislature in 1838
- He was defeated for nomination for Congress in 1843
- He was elected to Congress in 1846
- He lost his re-nomination for Congress in 1848
- He was rejected for the position of land officer in 1849
- He was defeated for the Senate in 1854
- He was defeated for the nomination for Vice President of the U. S. in 1856
- He was defeated again for the Senate in 1858
- He was elected President of the United States in 1860[158]

A people who are safe will help us redefine what it means to fail and will still be there to help us process and learn from our failures. This in turn, will help create and sustain an atmosphere of freedom to live authentically, and to take Holy Spirit-led risks.

FAILURE CAN BE ONE OF OUR BEST TEACHERS

In a safe place, failure can be one of our best teachers. Failure can either crush us or build us up and instruct us, depending on the view of failure that we, or our supervisors and mentors, have. For example, as a teacher one of my first encounters with failure happened because of the view a senior pastor I worked for had of failure, and because he intentionally sought to make our staff and our church a safe place for taking Holy Spirit-led risks.

I was a young, headstrong youth pastor who had been called to serve a large church in Rapid City with only four teens (there's that number again) active in the senior high youth group when my wife and I arrived. I was full of energy and vision. What I did not have was a lot of patience or an understanding of how to work out that vision and channel that energy while working with a church council and membership who were not necessarily ready to

---

158   Ibid., 26.

jump on board with the vision I had for the youth ministry—at least not as quickly as I thought they should.

One evening at the monthly church council meeting I proposed we place a pop machine in the fellowship hall for the teens, their friends, and members of the church. The immediate response of many of the council members was negative. They pointed out the sugar rush this might give the kids, and the potential for pop stains on the carpet. I, in turn, pointed out we were in as much danger of stains and sugar rushes from the coffee, cream, and sugar that the adults drank every Wednesday night and every Sunday morning. I even pointed out the coffee stains that were already in the carpet. The discussion went back and forth, but when it was apparent that getting the pop machine was not going to happen I slammed my notebook shut and stormed out of the meeting.

When I got home I vented to my wife. After venting for a while, however, I began to realize what I had done and my anger was replaced with fear. So I sat there waiting for what I was sure would be a phone call from the senior pastor to lecture me on my outburst and perhaps even fire me. Well, he did call. Here it comes, I thought. I'm toast. I'm fired. But all he asked was "Are you okay?" All he wanted to know was how I was feeling. We talked for a while, he told me to get a good night's sleep, and we agreed to get together the next day.

The next day we spoke face to face about the council meeting and he helped me begin processing my feelings, and asked questions to help me un-cover why I had such an overreaction to the meeting. He also began to help me learn how to work with people in bringing about the changes that need to be made in order to carry out God's purposes and not merely our own in a church, or in this particular case, in a youth ministry. He helped me learn how to identify and discern which battles are worth fighting.

Over the years this senior pastor made it a safe place for me, and for the rest of the staff, to take Holy-Spirit led risks, even to risk failing. Because of his view of failure, we were all enabled to learn and grow. Failure in the hands of God and leaders and people who are a safe place can be a wonderful teacher.

A place where it is safe to fail is an essential element in creating an atmosphere of freedom for authentic living. In this kind of atmosphere where there is freedom for authentic living and where failure is not the worst thing that can happen to someone, our effectiveness for developing healthy leaders and disciples in the church and living lives of witness in the world will be increased. There is more to be said on this topic and for further reading on it I would recommend John Maxwell's book *Failing Forward*.

49

IN CLOSING

The greatest need of our time is for the church to become what it has seldom been: the body of Christ with its face to the world, loving others regardless of religion or culture, pouring itself out in a life of service, offering hope to a frightened world.

— BRENNAN MANNING

BEING A SAFE place for the dangerous kind is a metaphor designed to inspire and spur us on to becoming more like Jesus; nothing more, nothing less, and nothing else. It is a word picture intended to help us consider more intentionally how we can think, speak, and act more like him in the world today so we can impact others with God's power and love.

BEING A SAFE PLACE AND THE HOLY SPIRIT

If being a safe place for the dangerous kind is nothing more than a metaphor for wanting to think, speak, and act more like Jesus, then it is imperative we ask this question—What was it that enabled Jesus to live life the way he did? The answer to that question is not an *it* but a *who*. It was his fellowship with God the Father and his relationship with the person of the Holy Spirit that enabled Jesus to live the life he lived. Further, it was the power of the Spirit at work in and through him that enabled Jesus to impact people with God's power and love. If this was true for Jesus, how much more must it be true for us?

It is crucial that we understand we can only grow in becoming a safe place for the dangerous kind through the transforming power of the Holy Spirit. This is not something that can be accomplished in our own strengths or abilities. Thus, continuing to be filled with the Holy Spirit and experiencing his power at work in us and through us is essential if we are to grow in thinking, speaking, and acting more like Jesus; so much so that this is exactly what the apostle Paul exhorts us to experience in Ephesians 5:18—to keep on being filled the Spirit.

Sharing in more detail about how we can create a safe place for experiencing the fillings of the Holy Spirit is beyond the scope of this work. It is a topic I intend to address in a subsequent book. For now, however, I would recommend *Surprised by the Power of the Spirit* by Jack Deere or *The Holy Spirit is Not For Sale* by Lee Grady for anyone who is interested in doing more reading on this subject.

TWO FINAL THOUGHTS

In closing there are two final thoughts I want to leave with you about growing to be a safe-place people. First, don't be surprised if all kinds of acting out behavior begins to be manifested when you become more intentional about being a safe place. When this behavior happens, it can frustrate you and leave you wondering why things seem to be going so badly after you just committed yourself or your group to living out the safe-place principles. Actually, acting-out behaviors that appear so suddenly can be evidence that there is now freedom to live more authentically. The issues that people are now verbalizing or demonstrating were there all along, but the freedom to acknowledge them and deal with them was not. Now you, or your group, have become safer. People, in turn, begin to believe that they can authentically be who they are with no fear of judgment, shame, or rejection. Therefore, the acting out seems to appear suddenly and out of nowhere. Take heart, this may be a sign that you are in fact growing in becoming a safe-place people.

At the same time, however, don't allow interpreting this as a positive sign lull you into thinking you can just allow acting out behavior to be expressed without setting healthy boundaries. As followers of Christ we are not given the freedom to remain stuck in the stuff of our lives, or act like jerks to each other, all the while rationalizing or justifying it by saying we are just "being authentic." While we do want to accept, listen, and empathize with one another, there comes a time when it is necessary to take steps to deal with whatever is causing us to act out. If we do not, we will be like the man in John, chapter five, who sat around the pool in Bethesda for thirty-eight years without so much as dipping a big toe in the water. Sometimes we get stuck in our stuff to the point we even begin to find our identity in it, and get attention from others for it. We become the guy or gal who has issues and are content to live with that as our identity. Remember, the purpose of being a safe place is never meant to be an end in itself, but rather to create an atmosphere for transformation, an atmosphere in which we can be healed and set free to become more like Jesus.

Second, as you grow in being a safe place, don't be surprised when you get push back from people. You can misinterpret this as meaning you are still in an unhealthy place, but it may not be you but those around you who are unhealthy. The fact that you are becoming more emotionally, relationally, and spiritually whole will upset unhealthy people and systems. They were okay with you as long as you were in that unhealthy place with them. But now that you are being set free from that place and those issues, it upsets their status quo and they will push back in some way, shape, or form. They will criticize you, judge you, and may even reject you. But stay the course. Do not settle for less by going back to that place or those relationships just because they are comfortable and known. Continue to surround yourselves with a new band of brothers and sisters who are committed to walking out a journey to greater wholeness by your side.

Thank you for reading this book and for your interest in embracing the safe-place vision. I pray you will grow in it as an individual, as a leader, and as a church or para-church ministry. The world needs you to. Our culture needs you to. The world and our culture need more safe-place Christians. As Brennan Manning writes,

> The greatest need for our time is for the church to become what it has seldom been: the body of Christ *with its face to the world, loving others regardless of religion or culture, pouring itself out in a life of service, offering hope to a frightened world,* and presenting itself as a real alternative to the existing arrangement. . . . I want neither a blood-'n'-guts religion that would make Clint Eastwood, not Jesus, our hero, nor a speculative religion that would imprison the gospel in the halls of academia, nor a noisy, feel-good religion that is a naked appeal to emotion. I long for passion, intelligence, and compassion in a church without ostentation, gently beckoning to the world to come and to enjoy the peace and unity we possess because of the Spirit in our midst [emphasis mine].[159]

As individuals, churches, and entire networks or denominations, let's grow in what it means to be a safe place that we might become Christians who have our faces to the world, are not turned away from them, and are impacting others with the love and power of God, regardless of religion or culture, belief or lifestyle. This is the church at her best. This is the church living as a safe place for the dangerous kind.

---

159 Brennan Manning, *The Signature of Jesus* (Sisters, OR: Multnomah Books, 1988), 7.

BIBLIOGRAPHY

Allen, Woody. *Getting Even*. New York: Random House, 1971, 1978; audiobook, 2010.

Allender, Dan B. *To Be Told: Know Your Story, Shape Your Future*. Colorado Springs, CO: Waterbrook Press, 2005.

Allender, Dan B. and Tremper Longman, III. *The Cry of the Soul: How Our Emotions Reveal Our Deepest Questions about God*. Colorado Springs, CO: NavPress, 1994.

Anderson, Neil T. *Victory over Darkness: Realizing the Power of Your Identity in Christ*. Ventura, CA: Regal Books, 1999.

Anderson, Neil T., Mike Quarles, and Julia Quarles. *Freedom from Addiction: Breaking the Bondage of Addiction and Finding Freedom in Christ*. Ventura, CA: Regal Books, 1996.

Anderson, Paul. "Are You a Balanced Leader?" In *Especially for Pastors* 105 (May 2004). St. Paul, MN: Lutheran Renewal, 2004.

————. *Breaking the Strongholds*. Paul Anderson, 2007.

————. *The Father's Gift: The Empowering Presence of the Holy Spirit*. St. Paul, MN: Master's Institute Press, 2001.

Anderson, Ray S. *Dancing with Wolves while Feeding the Sheep: The Musings of a Maverick Theologian*. Huntington Beach, CA: 2001.

————. *The Gospel According to Judas*. N. P.: Helmers & Howard, 1991.

————. *The Shape of Practical Theology: Empowering Ministry with Theological Praxis*. Downers Grove, IL: InterVarsity Press, 2001.

————. *An Emergent Theology for the Emerging Church*. Grand Rapids, MI: Zondervan, 2005.

Arnott, John. *The Importance of Forgiveness*. Tonbridge, Kent, England: Sovereign World Limited, 1997.

Arterburn, Stephen and Jack Felton. *Faith That Hurts, Faith That Heals*. Nashville, TN: Thomas Nelson Publishers, 1991.

————. *More Jesus, Less Religion: Moving from Rules to Relationship*. Colorado Springs, CO: Waterbrook Press, 2000.

Arterburn, Stephen, Frank Minirth, and Paul Meier. *Safe Places*. Nashville, TN: Thomas Nelson Publishers, 1997.

Bailey, Kenneth. E. *Finding the Lost: Culture Keys to Luke 15*. St. Louis, MO: Concordia Publishing House, 1992.

Barna, George. *The Second Coming of the Church*. Nashville, TN: Word Publishing, 1998.

Barth, Karl. *Evangelical Theology: An Introduction*. Grand Rapids, MI: William B. Eerdmans Publishing, 1979; Karl Barth, 1963.

Batterson, Mark. *Wild Goose Chase: Reclaim the Adventure of Pursuing God*. Colorado Springs, CO: Multnomah Books, 2008.

Belcher, Jim. *Deep Church: A Third Way Beyond Emerging and Traditional*. Downers Grove, IL: InterVarsity Press, 2009.

Bell, Rob. *Love Wins: A Book about Heaven, Hell, and the Fate of Every Person Who Ever Lived.* New York: HarperCollins, 2011.

Bellah, Robert N. *Habits of the Heart: Individualism and Commitment in American Life.* Berkeley: University of California Press, 1985, 2008.

Benne, Robert. *Reasonable Ethics: A Christian Approach to Social, Economic and Political Concerns.* St. Louis, MO: Concordia Publishing House, 2005.

Bierle, Don. *Surprised by Faith.* Lynwood, WA: Emerald Books, 1992.

Blue, Ken. *Healing Spiritual Abuse: How to Break Free from Bad Church Experiences.* Downers Grove, IL: InterVarsity Press, 1993.

Bonhoeffer, Dietrich. *Discipleship.* Minneapolis, MN: Fortress Press, 2003.

Bosch, David. *Believing in the Future: Toward a Missiology of Western Culture.* Harrisburg, PA: Trinity Press International, 1995.

Boyd, Gregory A. *Benefit of the Doubt: Breaking the Idol of Certainty.* Grand Rapids, MI: Baker Books, 2013.

————. *The Crucifixion of the Warrior God: Re-Interpreting Old Testament Violence in Light of the Cross.* Downers Grove, IL: InterVarsity Press, 2015.

————. *God at War: The Bible and Spiritual Conflict.* Downers Grove, IL: InterVarsity Press, 1997.

————. *God of the Possible: A Biblical Introduction to the Open View of God.* Grand Rapids, MI: Baker Books, 2000.

————. *Is God to Blame?: Beyond Pat Answers to the Problem of Suffering.* Downers Grove, IL: InterVarsity Press, 2003.

————. *Repenting of Religion: Turning from Judgment to the Love of God*. Grand Rapids, MI: Baker Books, 2004.

————. *Satan and the Problem of Evil: Constructing a Trinitarian Theodicy*. Downers Grove, IL: InterVarsity Press, 2001.

Breen, Michael and Walt Kallestad. *The Passionate Church: The Art of Life-Changing Discipleship*. Colorado Springs, CO: Cook Communications Ministries, 2005.

Bromiley, Geoffrey W., gen. ed. *The International Standard Bible Encyclopedia*, Vol. 2. Grand Rapids, MI: William B. Eerdmans Publishing Company, 1982.

Brown, Brene. *Daring Greatly: How the Courage to Be Vulnerable Transforms the Way We Live, Love, Parent, and Lead*. New York: Penguin Group US, 2012.

Brueggemann, Walter. *Cadences of Home: Preaching Among Exiles*. Louisville, KY: Westminster John Knox Press, 1997.

————. *Genesis*. Louisville, KY: Westminster John Knox Press, 1982.

Buchanan, Mark. *Your Church Is Too Safe: Why Following Christ Turns the World Upside Down*. Grand Rapids, MI: Zondervan, 2012.

————. *Your God Is Too Safe: Rediscovering the Wonder of a God You Can't Control*. Grand Rapids, MI: Multnomah Publishers, 2001.

Bultmann, Rudolf. *Kerygma and Myth*. London: Society for Promoting Christian Knowledge (SPCK), 1953.

Burke, John. *No Perfect People Allowed: Creating a Come-As-You-Are Culture in the Church*. Grand Rapids, MI: Zondervan, 2005.

———. *Mud and the Masterpiece: Seeing Yourself and Others through the Eyes of Jesus.* Grand Rapids, MI: Baker Books, 2013.

Callahan, Kennon. *Effective Church Leadership.* San Francisco, CA: Jossey-Bass, 1990.

Carson, D. A. *The Intolerance of Tolerance.* Grand Rapids, MI: William B. Eerdmans Publishing Company, 2012.

Chapman, Mike. *Authentic Living in an Artificial World.* Chattanooga, TN: Turning Point Ministries, 2004.

Chevreau, Guy. *Share the Fire: The Toronto Blessing and Grace-Based Evangelism.* Shippensburg, PA: Revival Press, 1997.

———. *Spiritual Warfare Sideways: Keeping the Focus on Jesus.* Grand Rapids, MI: Baker Publishing Group, 2007.

Claiborne, Shane. *The Irresistible Revolution: Living as an Ordinary Radical.* Grand Rapids, MI, 2006.

Cloud, Henry and John Townsend. *How People Grow: What the Bible Reveals about Personal Growth.* Grand Rapids, MI: Zondervan, 2001.

———. *Safe People.* Grand Rapids, MI: Zondervan, 1995.

Cole, Neil and Phil Helfer. *Church Transfusion: Changing Your Church Organically—From the Inside Out.* Jossey-Bass Leadership Network Series, August 2012.

Cook, Jerry. *Love, Acceptance and Forgiveness: Being Christian in a Non-Christian World.* Ventura, CA: Regal Books, 1979.

Cooke, Graham. *Approaching the Heart of Prophecy: A Journey into Encouragement, Blessing, and Prophetic Gifting.* Winston-Salem, NC: Punch Press, 2006.

———. *A Divine Confrontation.* Shippensburg, PA: Destiny Image Publications, 1999.

———. *Qualities of a Spiritual Warrior.* Vacaville, CA: Brilliant Book House, 2008.

Cornwall, Judson. *Let Us See Jesus.* South Plainfield, NJ: Bridge Publishing Inc., 1981.

Crabb, Larry. *Becoming a True Spiritual Community: A Profound Vision of What the Church Can Be.* Nashville, TN: Thomas Nelson Inc., 2007.

———. *The Safest Place On Earth.* Nashville TN: Word Publishing, 1999.

———. *Shattered Dreams: God's Unexpected Pathway to Joy.* Colorado Springs, CO: Waterbrook Press, 2001.

———. *Soul Talk: The Language God Longs for Us to Speak.* Nashville, TN: Integrity Publishing, 2003.

Craik, Dinah. *A Life for a Life.* Goucestershire, United Kingdom: Dodo Press, 2008.

Curtis, Brent and John Eldredge. *The Sacred Romance: Drawing Closer to the Heart of God.* Nashville, TN: Thomas Nelson Publishers, 1997.

Dalbey, Gordon. *Broken by Religion, Healed by God.* Folsom, CA: Civitas Press, 2011.

Dean, Kenda Creasy, Chap Clark, and Dave Rahn, *Starting Right: Thinking Theologically about Youth Ministry.* Grand Rapids, MI: Zondervan, 2001.

Deere, Jack. *Surprised by the Power of the Spirit*. Grand Rapids, MI: Zondervan, 1993.

Dirks, Morris. *Forming the Leader's Soul: An Invitation to Spiritual Direction*. SoulFormation, 2013.

Dodson, James. *Ben Hogan: An American Life*. New York: Broadway Books, 2004.

Driscoll, Mark. *Radical Reformission: Reaching Out without Selling Out*. Grand Rapids, MI: Zondervan, 2005.

Drum, Dave. *Jesus' Surprising Strategy: A Mandate and a Means for City Transformation*. Tucson, AZ: Adam Colwell's WriteWorks Publishing, 2013.

Ebner, Gwen. *Wholeness for Spiritual Leaders: Physical, Spiritual, and Emotional Health Care*. Create Space, 2009.

Eldredge, John. *The Journey of Desire: Searching for the Life We've Only Dreamed Of*. Nashville, TN: Thomas Nelson Publishers, 2000.

————. *Waking the Dead: The Glory of a Heart Fully Alive*. Nashville, TN: Thomas Nelson Publishers, 2003.

————. *The Way of the Wild Heart: A Map for the Masculine Journey*. Nashville, TN: Nelson Books, 2006.

————. *Wild At Heart: Discovering the Secret of a Man's Soul*. Nashville, TN: Thomas Nelson Publishers, 2001.

Eldredge, John and Stasi. *Love and War: Finding the Marriage You've Dreamed Of*. New York: Doubleday Religion, 2010.

Ellul, Jacques. *The Subversion of Christianity*. Grand Rapids, MI: Eerdmans Publishing Company, 1986.

Fee, Gordon. *Paul, the Spirit and the People of God*. Peabody, MA: Hendrickson Publishers, 1996.

Ferguson, Sinclair B. *The Grace of Repentance*. Wheaton, IL: Crossway Books, 2010.

Fretheim, Terence E. *The Suffering of God: An Old Testament Perspective*. Philadelphia, PA: Fortress Press, 1984.

Friesen, James G., E. James Wilder, Anne M. Bierling, Rick Koepcke, and Maribeth Poole. *Living from the Heart Jesus Gave You*. Pasadena, CA: Shepherd's House, Inc., 1999.

Frost, Michael. *Seeing God in the Ordinary: A Theology of the Everyday*. Peabody, MA: Hendrickson Publishers, 2000.

Frost, Michael and Alan Hirsch. *ReJesus: A Wild Messiah for a Missional Church*. Peabody, MA: Hendrickson Publishers, Inc, 2009.

————. *The Shaping of Things to Come: Innovation and Mission for the 21st Century Church*. Peabody, MA: Hendrickson Publishers, 2003.

Gibbs, Eddie. *Way to Go: Thirty Readings on a Journey with Jesus*. Downers Grove, IL: InterVarsity Press, 2003.

Goldingay, John. *Walk On: Life, Lost, Trust, and Other Realities*. Grand Rapids, MI: Baker Academic, 2002.

Grady, J. Lee. *The Holy Spirit Is Not For Sale: Rekindling the Power of God in an Age of Compromise*. Grand Rapids, MI: Chosen, 2010.

Graham, Ruth Bell. *Prodigals and Those Who Love Them: Words of Encouragement for Those Who Wait.* Grand Rapids, MI: Baker Books, 1991.

Grieg, Pete. *God on Mute: Engaging the Silence of Unanswered Prayer.* Bloomington, MN: Bethany House Publishers, 2007.

Greig, Pete and Dave Roberts. *Red Moon Rising: How 24-7 Prayer Is Awakening a Generation.* Lake Mary, FL: Revelation Books, 2006.

Groothuis, Douglas. *Truth Decay: Defending Christianity against the Challenges of Postmodernism.* Downers Grove, IL: InterVarsity Press, 2000.

Grudem, Wayne. *Bible Doctrine: Essential Teachings of the Christian Faith.* Grand Rapids, MI: Zondervan, 1999.

Guder, Darrell L. *Missional Church: A Vision for the Sending of the Church in North America.* Grand Rapids, MI: William B. Eerdmans Publishing Company, 1998.

Gumbel, Nicky. *Questions Of Life.* Colorado Springs, CO: Cook Ministry Resources, 1993.

Halter, Hugh and Matt Smay. *The Tangible Kingdom: Creating Incarnational Community.* San Francisco, CA: Jossey-Bass, 2008.

Herringhsaw, Mark and Jennifer Schuchmann. *Six Prayers God Always Answers.* Wheaton, IL: Tyndale Publishing, 2008.

Hession, Roy. *Be Filled Now.* Fort Washington, PA: Christian Literature Crusade, 1967.

Hunsberger, George R. and Craig Van Gelder. *The Church between Gospel and Culture.* Grand Rapids, MI: William B. Eerdmans Publishing Company, 1996.

Hunter, George. *The Celtic Way of Evangelism: How Christianity Can Reach the West . . . Again.* Nashville, TN: Abingdon Press, 2000.

————. *Church for the Unchurched.* Nashville, TN: Abingdon Press, 1996.

Hunter, Todd. *Christianity Beyond Belief: Following Jesus for the Sake of Others.* Downer Grove, IL: InterVarsity Press, 2009.

Hybels, Bill. *Courageous Leadership.* Grand Rapids, MI: Zondervan, 2002.

Jackson, Bill. *The Quest for the Radical Middle: A History of the Vineyard.* Cape Town, South Africa: Vineyard International Publishing, 1999.

Janz, Denis R. *A Reformation Reader: Primary Texts with Introductions.* Minneapolis, MN: Fortress Press, 1999.

Jenkins, Richard. *The Next Christendom: The Coming of Global Christianity.* New York: Oxford University Press, 2011.

Johnson, David and Jeff VanVonderen. *The Subtle Power of Spiritual Abuse: Recognizing and Escaping Spiritual Manipulation and False Spiritual Authority within the Church.* Minneapolis, MN: Bethany House Publishers, 1991.

Johnston, Graham and Haddon W. Robinson. *Preaching in a Postmodern World: A Guide to Reaching Twenty-first Century Listeners.* Grand Rapids, MI: Baker Books, 2001.

Jones, E. Stanley. *The Unshakable Kingdom and the Unchanging Person.* Nashville, TN: Abingdon Press, 1972.

Jones, Tony. *The New Christians: Dispatches from the Emergent Frontier.* San Francisco, CA: Jossey-Bass, 2008.

Kallenberg, Brad J. *Live to Tell: Evangelism for a Postmodern Age*. Grand Rapids, MI: Brazos Press, 2002.

Keller, Timothy. *The Prodigal God: Recovering the Heart of the Christian Faith*. New York: Dutton, 2008.

Kendall, R. T. *Total Forgiveness*. Lake Mary, FL: Charisma House, 2007.

Kenyon, E. W. *Two Kinds of Faith*. Kenyon's Gospel Publishing Company, 1998.

Kimball, Dan. *The Emerging Church: Vintage Christianity for New Generations*. Grand Rapids, MI: Zondervan, 2003.

Kinnaman, David and Gabe Lyons. *unChristian: What a New Generation Thinks about Christianity . . . and Why It Matters*. Grand Rapids, MI: Baker Books, 2008.

Kittelson, James M. *Luther the Reformer: The Story of the Man and His Career*. Minneapolis, MN: Augsburg Publishing House, 1986.

Koehler, Edward W. A. *A Summary of Christian Doctrine*. St. Louis, MO: Concordia Publishing House, 1939.

Koivisto, Rex A. *One Lord, One Faith: A Theology for Cross-Denominational Renewal*. Eugene, OR: Wipf and Stock Publishers, 1989.

Kraft, Charles H. *Christianity with Power*. Ann Arbor, MI: Servant Publications, 1989.

————. *Deep Wounds, Deep Healing: Discovering the Vital Link Between Spiritual Warfare and Inner Healing*. Ann Arbor, MI: Servant Publications, 1993.

————. *Defeating Dark Angels: Breaking Demonic Oppression in the Believer's Life.* Ann Arbor, MI: Servant Publications, 1992.

Krzyzewski, Mike. *Leading With the Heart: Coach K's Successful Strategies for Basketball, Business, and Life.* New York: Warner Books, 2000.

Ladd, George Eldon. *The Gospel of the Kingdom: Scriptural Studies in the Kingdom of God.* Grand Rapids, MI: William B. Eerdmans Publishing Company, 1959.

Lamott, Anne. *Bird by Bird: Some Instructions on Writing and Life.* New York: Anchor Books, 1994.

————. *Small Victories: Spotting Improbable Moments of Grace.* New York: Riverhead Books, 2014.

Larson, Bruce. *The Preacher's Commentary Volume 26: Luke.* Nashville, TN: Thomas Nelson Publishers, 1983.

Lencioni, Patrick. *The Advantage: Why Organizational Health Trumps Everything Else in Business.* San Francisco, CA: Jossey Bass, 2012.

Lee, Nicky and Sila Lee. *The Marriage Book: How to Build a Lasting Relationship.* Brompton, UK: Alpha International, 2000.

Lewis, C. S. *Mere Christianity.* New York: HarperCollins, 1952.

Lloyd-Jones, D. M. *Life in the Spirit.* Grand Rapids, MI: Baker Book House, 1973.

Long, Thomas G. and Cornelius Plantinga. *A Chorus Of Witnesses: Model Sermons for Today's Preacher.* Grand Rapids, MI: William B. Eerdmans Publishing Company, 1994.

BIBLIOGRAPHY

Lose, David J. *Confessing Jesus Christ: Preaching in a Postmodern World.* Grand Rapids, MI: William B. Eerdmans Publishing Company, 2003.

Love, Rick. *Peace Catalysts: Resolving Conflict in Our Families, Organizations, and Communities.* Downer's Grove, IL: InterVarsity Press, 2014.

Lucado, Max. *A Grip on Grace.* Dallas, TX: Word Publishing, 1996.

Luther, Martin. *Preface to the Acts of the Apostles.* Grand Rapids, MI: Kregel Publications, 1976.

————. *The Table Talk of Martin Luther.* Mineola, NY: Dover Publications, 2005.

Lyons, Gabe. *The Next Christians: Seven Ways You Can Live the Gospel and Restore the World.* New York: Doubleday, 2010.

Machen, J. Gresham. *Christianity and Liberalism.* Grand Rapids, MI: William B. Eerdmans Publishing Company, 1923.

Manning, Brennan. *Abba's Child: The Cry of the Heart for Intimate Belonging.* Colorado Springs, CO: Nav Press, 1994.

————. *A Glimpse of Jesus: The Stranger to Self-Hatred.* San Francisco, CA: HarperSanFrancisco, 2003.

————. *The Ragamuffin Gospel: Good News for the Bedraggled, Beat-Up, and Burnt Out.* Sisters, OR: Multnomah Books, 1990.

————. *Ruthless Trust: The Ragamuffin's Path to God.* San Francisco, CA: HarperSanFrancisco, 2000.

————. *The Signature of Jesus.* Sisters, OR: Multnomah Books, 1988.

Maxwell, John. *Failing Forward: Turning Mistakes into the Stepping Stone of Success.* Nashville, TN: Thomas Nelson Publishers, 2000.

McIntosh, Gary L. and Samuel D. Rima. *Overcoming the Dark Side of Leadership: How to Become an Effective Leader by Confronting Potential Failures.* Grand Rapids, MI: Baker Books, 2007.

McLaren, Brian D. *The Church on the Other Side.* Grand Rapids: Zondervan, 2000.

————. *Everything Must Change.* Nashville, TN: Thomas Nelson Publishing, 2007.

————. *A Generous Orthodoxy.* Grand Rapids, MI: Zondervan, 2004.

————. *More Ready Than You Realize: Evangelism as Dance in the Postmodern Matrix.* Grand Rapids, MI: Zondervan, 2002.

————. *A New Kind of Christian: A Tale of Two Friends on a Spiritual Journey.* San Francisco, CA: Jossey-Bass, 2001.

————. *The Secret Message of Jesus: Uncovering the Truth That Could Change Everything.* Nashville, TN: W Publishing Group, 2006.

McManus, Erwin Raphael. *The Barbarian Way: Unleash the Untamed Faith Within.* Nashville, TN: Nelson Books, 2005.

————. *Seizing Your Divine Moment: Dare to Live a Life of Adventure.* Nashville, TN: Thomas Nelson Publishers, 2002.

————. *Soul Cravings.* Nashville, TN: Nelson Books, 2006.

————. *An Unstoppable Force: Daring to Become the Church God Had in Mind.* Loveland, CO: Group Publishing, 2001.

McNeil, Reggie. *The Present Future: Six Tough Questions for the Church.* San Francisco, CA: Jossey-Bass, 2003.

McVey, Steve. *Grace Walk.* Eugene, OR: Harvest House Publishers, 1995.

McVey, Steve and Mike Quarles. *Helping Others Overcome Addictions: How God's Grace Brings Lasting Freedom.* Eugene, OR: Harvest House Publishers, 2012.

Merrill, Dean. *Sinners in the Hands of an Angry Church.* Grand Rapids, MI: Zondervan, 1997.

Merton, Thomas. *Seeds of Contemplation.* New York: Panthea Books, 1956.

Middleton, J. Richard and Brian J. Walsh. *Truth Is Stranger Than It Used to Be: Biblical Faith in a Postmodern Age.* Downers Grove, IL: InterVarsity Press, 1995.

Miller, Donald. *Blue Like Jazz: Nonreligious Thoughts on Christian Spirituality.* Nashville, TN: Thomas Nelson Publishers, 2003.

————. *Searching for God Knows What.* Nashville, TN: Thomas Nelson Publishers, 2004.

Moody, D. L. *Secret Power.* Ventura, CA: Regal Books, 1987.

Moreland, J. P. *Kingdom Triangle: Recover the Christian Mind, Renovate the Soul, Restore the Spirit's Power.* Grand Rapids, MI: Zondervan 2007.

Moreland, J. P. and Tim Muehlhoff. *The God Conversation: Using Stories and Illustrations to Explain Your Faith.* Downers Grove, IL: InterVarsity Press, 2007.

Mounce, William D. *Basics of Biblical Greek.* Grand Rapids, MI: Zondervan, 1993.

Mueller, John. *Christian Dogmatics*. St. Louis, MO: Concordia Publishing House, 1934.

Mullholland, M. Robert. *Invitation to a Journey: A Road Map for Spiritual Formation*. Downers Grove: IL, InterVarsity, 1993.

Murray, Andrew. *Experiencing the Holy Spirit*. New Kensington, PA: Whitaker House, 2000.

Murray, Stuart. *Post-Christendom: Church and Mission in a Strange New World*. Carlisle, PA: Paternoster, 2004.

Nathan, Rich and Ken Wilson. *Empowered Evangelicals: Bringing Together the Best of the Evangelical and Charismatic Worlds*. Ann Arbor, MI: Servant Publications, 1995.

Nee, Watchman. *The Release of the Spirit*. New York: Christian Fellowship Publishers, Inc., 2010.

Newbigin, Lesslie. *The Gospel in a Pluralistic Society*. Grand Rapids, MI: William B. Eerdmans Publishing Company, 1989.

Nouwen, Henri. *Out of Solitude: Three Meditations on the Christian Life*. Notre Dame, IN: Ave Maria Press, 1974.

———. *The Return of the Prodigal Son: A Story of Homecoming*. New York: Doubleday Dell Publishing Co., 1994.

Ortberg, John. *Everybody's Normal Till You Get to Know Them*. Grand Rapids, MI: Zondervan, 2003.

———. *If You Want to Walk on Water You Have to Get Out of the Boat*. Grand Rapids, MI: Zondervan, 2001.

BIBLIOGRAPHY

————. *The Life You've Always Wanted: Spiritual Disciplines for Ordinary People.* Grand Rapids, MI: Zondervan, 1997.

————. *Soul Keeping: Caring For the Most Important Part of You.* Grand Rapids, MI: Zondervan, 2014.

Osborne, Grant R. *The Hermeneutical Spiral: A Comprehensive Introduction to Biblical Interpretation.* Downers Grove, IL: InterVarsity Press, 1991.

Palmer, J. Parker. *Let Your Life Speak: Listening for the Voice of Vocation.* San Francisco, CA: Jossey-Bass, 2000.

Park, Charles. "Biblical Authority in a Postmodern World." *Cutting Edge Magazine* 15, no. 2 (Fall 2011).

Payne, Leanne. *The Broken Image: Restoring Personal Wholeness through Healing Prayer.* Grand Rapids, MI: Baker Books, 1981.

————. *Real Presence: The Christian Worldview of C. S. Lewis as Incarnational Reality.* Grand Rapids, MI: Baker Books, 1995.

Peterson, Jim. *Church Without Walls: Moving Beyond Traditional Boundaries.* Colorado Springs, CO: NavPress, 1992.

Pinnock, Clark. *Flame of Love: A Theology of the Holy Spirit.* Downers Grove, IL: InterVarsity Press, 1996.

Plass, Adrian. *Jesus: Safe, Tender, Extreme.* Grand Rapids, MI: Zondervan, 2006.

————. *The Sacred Diary of Adrian Plass Aged 37 ¾.* Grand Rapids, MI: Zondervan, 1987.

Powers, Isaias. *Healing Words from Jesus.* New London, CT: Twenty-third Publications, 1996.

Riddell, Michael. *Threshold of the Future: Reforming the Church in the Post-Christian West.* London, England: Society for Promoting Christian Knowledge (SPCK), 1998.

Riddell, Michael, Mark Pierson, and Cathy Kirkpatrick. *Prodigal Project: Journey into the Emerging Church.* London, England: Society for Promoting Christian Knowledge (SPCK), 2000.

Robbins, Mike. *Be Yourself, Everyone Else Is Already Taken: Transforming Your Life with the Power of Authenticity.* San Francisco, CA: Jossey-Bass, 2009.

Roberts, Richard Owen. *Repentance: The First Word of the Gospel.* Wheaton, IL: Crossway Books, 2002.

Roxburgh, Alan J. *The Missional Leader: Equipping Your Church to Reach a Changing World.* San Francisco, CA: Jossey-Bass, 2006.

———. *The Missionary Congregation, Leadership, and Liminality.* Harrisburg, PA: Trinity Press International, 1997.

Sayers, Dorothy L. *Creed or Chaos?* New York: Harcourt Brace, 1949.

Scazzero, Peter. *The Emotionally Healthy Church: A Strategy for Discipleship That Actually Changes Lives.* Grand Rapids, MI: Zondervan, 2003.

———. *Emotionally Healthy Spirituality.* Nashville, TN: Thomas Nelson, 2006.

Schaeffer, Francis. *Mark of the Christian.* Downers Grove, IL: InterVarsity Press, 1970.

Schlink, M. Basilea. *Repentance—The Joy-Filled Life*. Minneapolis, MN: Bethany House Publishers, 1968.

Sellers, Graeme. *The Dangerous Kind*. Graeme Sellers, 2012.

Silvoso, Ed. *Prayer Evangelism: How to Change the Spiritual Climate Over Your Home, Neighborhood and City*. Ventura, CA: Regal Books, 2000.

Smedes, Lewis B. *Forgive And Forget: Healing the Hurts We Don't Deserve*. New York: Pocket Books, 1984.

————. *Shame and Grace: Healing the Shame We Don't Deserve*. San Francisco: Harper, 1993.

Steinke, Peter L. *How Your Church Works: Understanding Congregations as Emotional Systems*. Herndon, VA: Alban Institute, 1993.

Stetzer, Ed. *Planting New Churches in a Postmodern Age*. Nashville, TN: Broadman & Holman Publishers, 2003.

Stroebel, Lee. *The Case For Faith: A Journalist Investigates the Toughest Objections to Christianity*. Grand Rapids, MI: Zondervan Publishing House, 2000.

Sweet, Leonard. *11: Indispensable Relationships You Can't Be Without*. Colorado Springs, CO: David C. Cook, 2008.

————. *Aqua Church: Essential Leadership Arts for Piloting Your Church in Today's Fluid Culture*. Loveland, CO: Group Publishing, 1999.

————. *The Church in Emerging Culture: Five Perspectives*. Grand Rapids, MI: Zondervan, 2003.

————. *Postmodern Pilgrims: First Century Passion for the 21ˢᵗ Century World.* Nashville, TN: Broadman & Holman Publishers, 2000.

————. *Soul Salsa: 17 Surprising Steps for Godly Living in the 21ˢᵗ Century.* Grand Rapids, MI: Zondervan, 2000.

————. *The Well-Played Life: Why Pleasing God Doesn't Have to Be Such Hard Work.* Tyndale House Publishers, 2014.

Swindoll, Charles R. *Grace Awakening.* Dallas, TX: Word Publishing, 1990.

Tan, Siang-Yang and Douglas H. Gregg. *Disciplines of the Holy Spirit.* Grand Rapids, MI: Zondervan, 1997.

Taylor, Daniel. *In Search of Sacred Places: Looking for Wisdom on Celtic Holy Islands.* Saint Paul, MN: Bog Walk Press, 2005.

Torrance, James B. *Worship, Community and the Triune God of Grace.* Downers Grove, IL:
InterVarsity Press, 1996.

Tozer, A. W. *How to Be Filled with the Holy Spirit.* Eastford, CT: Martino Fine Books, 2014.

Turner, Steve. *Imagine: A Vision for Christians in the Arts.* Downers Grove, IL: InterVarsity Press, 2001.

VanVonderen, Jeff and David Johnson. *The Subtle Power of Spiritual Abuse: Recognizing and Escaping Spiritual Manipulation and False Spiritual Authority within the Church.* Minneapolis, MN: Bethany House Publishers, 1991.

Walter, Robert. *If I Have Been Forgiven, Why Do I Still Feel So Bad?* Robert Walter, 2014.

Walton, John H. *The NIV Application Commentary: Genesis.* Grand Rapids, MI: Zondervan, 2001.

Wangerin, Walt. *Reliving the Passion: Meditations on the Suffering, Death, and Resurrection of Jesus as Recorded in Mark.* Grand Rapids, MI: Zondervan, 1992.

White, Thomas B. *The Believer's Guide to Spiritual Warfare.* Ventura, CA: 2011.

Willard, Dallas. *Renovation of the Heart: Putting on the Character of Christ.* Colorado Springs, CO: Nav Press, 2002.

Williams, Don. *Jesus and Addiction: A Prescription to Transform the Dysfunctional Church and Recover Authentic Christianity.* San Diego, CA: Recovery Publications Inc., 1993.

Wimber, John. *The Way In Is the Way On.* Boise, ID: Ampelon Publishing, 2006.

Wright, N. T. *Simply Christian: Why Christianity Makes Sense.* San Francisco, CA: HarperSanFrancisco, 2006.

Yancey, Philip. *Prayer: Does It Make Any Difference?* Grand Rapids, MI: Zondervan, 2006.

————. *Soul Survivor: How Thirteen Unlikely Mentors Helped My Faith Survive the Church.* New York: Doubleday, 2001.

————. *What's So Amazing About Grace?* Grand Rapids, MI: Zondervan, 1997.

Yanconelli, Michael. *Messy Spirituality.* Grand Rapids, MI: Zondervan, 2002.

Young, Chad H. *Authenticity: Real Faith in a Phony, Superficial World.* Downer's Grove, IL: InterVarsity Press, 2012.